ACCIDENTAL FEMINISM

Accidental Feminism

GENDER PARITY AND SELECTIVE MOBILITY AMONG INDIA'S PROFESSIONAL ELITE

Swethaa S. Ballakrishnen

PRINCETON UNIVERSITY PRESS

PRINCETON & OXFORD

Requests for permission to reproduce material from this work
should be sent to permissions@press.princeton.edu

Published by Princeton University Press
41 William Street, Princeton, New Jersey 08540
6 Oxford Street, Woodstock, Oxfordshire OX20 1TR

press.princeton.edu

ISBN 9780691213606
ISBN (pbk.) 9780691182537
ISBN (e-book) 9780691199993
LCCN 2020942527

British Library Cataloging-in-Publication Data is available

Editorial: Meagan Levinson and Jacqueline Delaney
Production Editorial: Debbie Tegarden
Jacket/Cover Design: Karl Spurzem
Production: Erin Suydam
Publicity: Kate Hensley
Copyeditor: Karen Verde

Cover Art: *Ascent* (2014), Zarina Hashmi, courtesy of the artist's estate and
Luhring Augustine, New York

This book has been composed in Miller

Printed on acid-free paper. ∞

Printed in the United States of America

10 9 8 7 6 5 4 3 2 1

For
Valambal, Thangamma, Parvati, Pattammal, Akila, Lakshminarayani,
Jechi

A line of fierce women who, sans rhetoric, first schooled
me in feminism through story, example, and love

Krupabai's education had been unlike most girls of her own race or of ours. . . . So that when asked by her teachers to "parse" a word she had no idea what was required of her, though her knowledge of grammar made her quite equal to the task when the term, new to her, was explained.

—INTRODUCTORY MEMOIR BY MRS. H. B. GRIGG,
TO KRUPPABAI S. SATTHIANDHAN,
KAMALA: A STORY OF HINDU LIFE, MADRAS:
SRINAVASA VARADACHARI AND CO., 1894, P. XXII

Blame not the poor Indian woman for her love of jewelry . . . She knows well that they are the only things that will not be taken away from her at her husband's death, or when any trouble or calamity overtakes the family. She sees her future independence in them.

—SATTHIANDHAN 1894, P. 142

My sister discovered this out-of-focus, faceless, family photograph while cleaning our parents' attic a few Madras summers ago. Amma's explanation was relentless: "This is what happens when you give a four-year-old a camera—*korangin kaiyile poomalai*."[1] Appa, no longer four years old, looked sheepish: "It was an accident."

I am lucky to have many dear memories of my grandparents. But this accidental photograph of them, taken by our four-year-old father, is one of my favorites. Even though I cannot see her face, I know my *Thathi* is shy-smiling in it because my grandfather is holding her too close in public. I know from years of being trained with his design aesthetic that my *Thatha* is kneeling down to my grandmother's height so that my young father can frame the picture right. I know that *Thathi* is pregnant with my favorite uncle, that the tripod my father was asked to be careful with slipped after this photo was taken, ruining the camera, that Appa's mischief will recursively become cemented as family folklore.

This picture has been constant philosophical company during this book writing process. It has made me grateful for surprise findings, nudged me to *see* rather than look. It has taught me the value of the non-apparent, the power of imagination, the usefulness in pursuing the accidental. But it has also laid out limitations. *Once we make sense of the accidental, what then?*

This picture gives me a lot and I am grateful. But what I wouldn't do to see their faces again.

1. An old Tamizh proverb implying "what else could you expect?" It translates to "[It is like] giving a monkey a flower garland."

CONTENTS

Can Feminism Be Accidental?

DRAWING FROM OBSERVATION and interview data with 130 profession-als over four years, this book illuminates new ways in which professionally educated middle-class women and men experience social mobility in post-liberalization India. In tracing their stories and career paths, I show how meanings of self and hierarchy infiltrate all workplaces but at the same time diverge in their specific attributes from what we might normally expect. In particular, the book demonstrates that when the experiences of women in elite law firms are juxtaposed with those of their peers in other similarly elite pro-fessional sites, the law firms show unexpected levels of gender parity. What is more, this surprising outcome is not so much the result of the firms' thought-ful commitment to creating feminist organizations, but rather of a combina-tion of structural conditions that come together to *do* gender differently. The central consideration within this book is of these firms that might offer pro-gressive possibility without caring about the cause or even believing it to be an important organizational value. What can we do, it asks, with the acciden-tal, the unintentional, when it produces seemingly "good" or visibly egalitar-ian outcomes? But, first, *what does parity or even equality have to do with "feminism"*?[1]

In a book that I have returned to with deep ritualistic reverence these past few years, Sara Ahmed (2016:32) recalls how Audre Lorde taught her to turn toward what is difficult because that is what allows us to do what is politi-cally necessary, even when it is personally complicated. I don't think Lorde or Ahmed were thinking about lending feminist credentials to oblivious corpo-rate law firms when offering that wisdom.[2] But I invoke their inherited lega-cies to help frame my disquiet with choosing to frame this project, these out-comes, this phenomenon I write about, as feminist. During the past decade, as I have tried to make sense of this project, I have simultaneously also strug-gled with my relationship to the range of meanings that have been attributed to this term. Like—and with[3]—others, I've raged at the commercialization of feminist politics, the liberal hegemony that has occupied its geography, the implications of its intended consequences, and the limits of association.[4] As a global south queer[5] with a tremendous range of local north advantages,[6] I've remained conflicted about the texture of my political stakes and solidarity within these movements.[7] At the same time, over the same years, I've also, to paraphrase a friend with whom I was recently discussing identity at middle age, started to wear the weight of my identities more lightly.[8] Perhaps as a result, I find myself conflicted more than ever about the work that goes into claiming categories,[9] the context within which they can offer support and expansiveness rather than anxiety, and in some contexts, the inherent privilege in being able to speak of them as identity in the first place.[10]

At a recent meeting of a gender and legal theory class I teach (aptly perhaps for this context, called GUILT![11]), a student asked me why Sarah Palin was not a feminist. Although the question itself was meant to be provocative, I felt it to hold in its core—perhaps because I want to see it—a kernel of critical inquiry about membership within movements and the politics of those who cannot—or will not be—seen as part of it. Notwithstanding any views I may have about Palin, the query raised pertinent questions about movement actors, their process, and vocal membership.

The limits of feminism—just as for all social movements—have been historically predicated on the viability of lines of membership and the apparent invisibility of those people excluded by the act of inclusion. The common thread across traditionally conceived "micro" feminist movements—e.g., second wave, intersectional, global, Islamic, queer[12]—has been a certain kind of fragmentation by peripheral actors, predicated on the lack of identification with what is seen as a more mainstream movement. Such bifurcations along the lines of naming and claiming have long dissected all social movement politics, but illuminating them is especially central for our time, in which speaking across factions has become more essential than ever:[13] Where do movements draw their perimeters of included actors and how do we account for fractures? If an actor opens up access and representation to disenfranchised women and models a new possibility of gendered success (as, one could argue, Palin *has*), does it, by such expansion, regardless of their rhetoric, become a feminist act or process? Leaving the governance implications aside, how do we think of this subset of included others? Are all exclusions similar? Whose exclusion is legitimate? And whose framing of legitimation has value? Speaking of value, is there value in analytically lumping disparate categories under the umbrella of feminism? What purchase does that category synthesis—or even the very notion of categories—offer us? Shining this light also illuminates a set of questions that have plagued other social movement actors—who gets to speak and on behalf of whom? Alongside those who feel movements do not speak for them are others who strategically resist the logics of a movement:[14] how do we think of their agency and voice?[15] And given these new associations and cleavages, when do we take, as Halley (2008) would urge us to, breaks from feminism, and on whose account?

These questions have offered me new tools to think about agency and praxis, and they have forced me to consider the weight of intention as a frame of analysis. All of these deliberations of people in and opposed to movement, diverse as they may be, are still encased within the logic of an intentional inquiry. Actors within the movement use its structures a certain way, and those who resist it use those very structures to diminish their significance (again, as one could argue, Palin has). In contrast, the distinction that emerges from the narratives in this book is the lack of *claiming* or engagement by the actors and institutions in any direction. Which urges us to consider a new set of questions about motive—has intention always been relevant? How do we understand processes where intentions have been agnostic, absent? When a set of actors produce new inclusion by performance that has the potential to infuse its environments with movement possibility, is it less of a movement for not claiming that nomenclature? It is this distinction that is central to this theorizing. This becomes especially relevant when thinking about the perverse advantages of such *non-naming*—since the act of *not* categorizing a process may save it from the backlash that its institutionalized naming might have otherwise attracted. How, then, do we consider the possibilities of *not* calling a movement or mechanism by its name, *without* intention?[16]

I hope it is clear that I ask these questions and offer the possibility of category amalgamation from a place of deep vacillation. I recognize sorely how including under the feminist identity umbrella a set of actors who not only undo in many ways their gains, but also actively choose to disassociate with their identity politics, is a complicated decision. I do not inherently think there is value in expanding categories *ad idem* and I am deeply indebted to the agentic, hard-won movement actors who have allowed us the gains of feminism as we know it.[17] It would be remiss to read this book as one that questions the work and worth of intention in these movements. As someone trained in the language and theory of feminism, especially in the contexts of the souths, I owe my elders a tremendous debt. As I argue in other work (Kannabiran and Ballakrishnen 2021), thinking about truly feminist ways forward, especially for law and legal institutions, demands that we recall and be led by the sight, criticality, and largesse of the rich, intentional history of these very movements.

But alongside my discomfort in this paradoxical category clubbing is a sense of trust in meaningful intellectual expansion that might lie beyond the comfort zones of known categorization. Alongside the dithering is a faith that the pursuit of theory can demand befuddlement and a muddling of one's personal stakes and politics. A claim, perhaps, that a thing need not be one thing or another: that it can exist in multiplicity, be from many sources. The women in my study might not actively think of themselves as feminists, they certainly are not visibly organizing for collective (or even their own) benefit, and the organizations they are housed in are not governed by feminist politics, principles, or policies. I also recognize that as an analytical project, the lack of intention might not always serve us: there might, for example, be no gain in reading a parity outcome within an elite capitalist enterprise alongside the story of, say, powerful everyday solidarity displayed by the Muslim women on the streets of Delhi's *Shaheeh Bagh*. Although neither set of women is likely to actively claim feminist labels, their respective disassociation from those labels is predicated on different logics. There are clearly differences in accidental claimings that are predicated on the peculiarities of a specific process. But in offering this juxtaposition of women who are incidentally part of movements they did not seek to be part of against their more agentic peers, I hope to implicate the analytical work that intention can do more crucially.

Even so, beyond frameworks, to return to the original question—is parity feminism? Beyond not being sufficient, seemingly feminist optics (like a focus on parity) can be dangerous, as governance feminism (Halley et al. 2018) warns us. Part of the book's task is to heed that warning and analyze all organizational wins with caution. Another is to explore the possibility of locating the feminist actor in these narratives and to try and reframe what we consider to be feminist anew. A third part is to cull an exception to that warning: yes, institutional response that performs governance agendas by co-opting feminist optics is specifically cunning: but if the optics themselves were not intentionally sought, perhaps they deserve different kinds of categorization?[18] Of course, even such a proposition is not without ethical complication: for example, even if the institutional co-opting was not strategic at the start, it might well be employed in the future. Besides, to the extent we can reframe what we consider to be feminist, is such a reframing useful or capable of integrity? And if such reframing and focus on gendered representation does the work of transforming an institution, how do we think of such access and transformation in the context of professionals and diversity work more generally? Would it, for instance, just produce more "bleached out" professionalism (Wilkins 1998) where there is more gendered representation but it is not substantively diverse in its cultural production, or a "no-problem problem" (Rhode 1991) where firms feel like they have "done enough" even as "second generation biases" (Sturm 2001; Ely, Ibarra, and Kolb 2011) and inequalities persist within them? Will these actors and institutions now and in the future suffer from not having a clear "architecture for inclusion" (Sturm 2006; Dobbin and Kalev 2007) because it does not have clear leadership and responsibility (Ahmed 2012) that have been time-proven to be the best markers for gains in diversity? *Nothing in this book is meant to suggest that happenstance equality and inclusion can or should replace intentional, thoughtful creation of organizational cultures.* It is only meant to—in theorizing about a site condition— persuade the intellectual possibility that there is work being done by incidental actors too, work that can change the ways in which other, non-incidental actors may choose to engage with these sites over time. Paying attention to accidental forces that could have started a process might also help us consider the things that we can do more agentically now that it is in motion: it could reveal ways to directionally alter these processes with intention, along a path dependency that is now set with a certain kind of momentum.

I recognize the slippery slope inherent in this argument's turn—if we speak from a position of personal privilege on behalf of those who don't want to be included and/or those who do not think inclusion is useful, we run the risk of polluting the intentions of the movement in the same way we might by including those who don't need saving, those whose inclusion in such emancipation is problematic. And then there is the politics of knowledge production and who someone's theory speaks to and who it can work for. Still, perhaps framing narratives as "accidental" allows us new tools to be critical of them. As Ratna Kapur (2018) cautions us, the work of radical theorists cannot be to shy away from that which does not feel naturally radical or aligned in our politics. The worry of being co-opted or falling down slippery slopes cannot, in itself, be our excuse for not accessing these tools and being critical about their life in this world we inhabit—a world we share with others very different from us but who nonetheless are soldiering toward similar ends. We especially cannot let the fear of slippery slopes keep us further entrenched in our own intellectual boundaries.

So, the question framing this book, beyond its empirics, beyond its argument, at its essence, is this: even if identities need intention to be claimed, is intentional identity—or vocal membership—exhaustive? Or can lack of intention still do some work worth paying attention to, even if the work is not about emboldening such movements or identity? I don't claim to have definitive answers to any of these questions. As I've mentioned, I ask these questions with a lot of vulnerability about my own political commitments to the idea of intentionality. But I think affording research the chance to expand our intellectual navigations beyond safe acceptance is integral to this process. And it in this vein that I offer the possibility of accident as a theoretical positioning to understand progress.

I have lived what I know now to be a life of alterity, *a queer life*, long before I knew *queer* was a word or a performed politic.[19] When I started to identify with it more over the years, and meaning-make with(in) it in ways that called for visibility and vocal membership, I remember my mother writing down *k-v-e-e-r* on a sticky note to remember its pronunciation. My mother is an accidental adoptee of my lived praxis: a woman who still does not understand or care for the word's institutional weight, someone who certainly does not know its language and rhetoric, and an apolitical bystander that might have just as easily never imagined anything beyond the heteronorm if I had lived any number of the other lives that just as easily could have been mine. Yet, with a life of reframing and recommitting without intending to, she is still better queer community to me than those who are capable of performing the language of solidarity much better than she can. Does her origin story and agnostic political commitment make her any less of an ally? Does it get watered down by the fact that her position is conditional on her beloved child luring her into happenstance allyship? How much more diluted is it by my certainty that she would have never considered her position otherwise, just as she does not consider any number of other intersectional identities critically? That she would have remained embedded in her preconceived fears about alterity? Can the dilution be salvaged by the fact that her fears of queer alterity were first modeled by horror stories of predatory harassment? That these stories were from her childhood in a Malayalam-medium government school where organic queer language and meaning-making were even more out of reach than they were to me twenty years later, receiving an elite education that allowed me to experience what Ahmed calls the "continuous clicks" of acknowledgment for queer identity and theory? What do we do with these layered inconsistencies? If what we are seeking when we say community is others who have our and *only our* contexts of journeying—and goddesses know I say this as someone buoyed by this precious community over and over *and over* again—how many people might we eventually have left to share kin with? And can we continue to avoid the obvious: that even if not kin, clan (or, at least, meaning) -making across difference is increasingly important for our times?

These organizations I write about and the women within them who have attained professional mobility in a single generation have very little concretely in common with my mother.[20] My *Amma*'s day job as an office manager was work that would serve to put her children through school (and was not always enough to send them to college); it was never a profession,[21] let alone an elite one. She certainly did not imagine the kind of leisure in her life that would include the possibility of a solo vacation in Barcelona or any of the other luxuries my respondents describe. Yet, there are synergies between these firms I study, the women in these firms, and my mother. They are connected with their relative indifference. And it is the fecundity inherent in their blasé attitudes that the theoretical bedrock of this book rests on.

ACCIDENTAL FEMINISM

The Accidental Emergence of India's Elite Women Lawyers

ON A LATE SUMMER evening in 2013, I was walking on Tulsi Pipe Road toward the Lower Parel train station, grateful for the relief from the indoor air-conditioning and not yet far enough in my walk to start hating Mumbai's humidity. I had just finished an interview with a young female law firm partner that had gone far longer than the time I had allocated for it. This meant rescheduling my next interview, but I recall having a skip in my step because of how hopeful Sitara Kumar's account seemed at the time. The oldest girl of three siblings, Sitara had graduated from one of the country's top national law schools at age twenty-two and made partner before her thirty-third birthday. She dated, but told me she had no plans to marry any time soon.[1] She was widely regarded in her field, had a dedicated client base, and within her first few years with the firm was earning more than her father made in his long tenure as a local bank manager in a small South Indian town. She was close to her parents, but lived alone in one of Mumbai's high-rise apartments, a short-for-the-city cab ride away from work. As we spoke about her next big trans-action, her clients, whom she shared a love-hate relationship with, and her next international solo vacation, it was becoming clear to me that Sitara was portraying a particular strain of class attainment whose texture was distinct from other accounts of "elite workers,"[2] especially within the region, and that it was an especially striking gendered account of high-status professional work.

This interview took place early in my fieldwork, focusing on the chang-ing nature of the legal profession in India. At the time, while there was some mounting evidence that gender was playing out differently in the small oases of elite law firms, I did not yet know how common or substantively divergent Sitara's story would be from the vast literature on gender and professional work. In the year preceding this interview, women made up about 70 percent of the partnership cohort of elite law firms like Sitara's, but I was embedded in enough empirical evidence from other sites to know that such demographic shifts were hardly constitutive of formal equality or progress. At the same time, the increasing presence of women partners in these firms offered a tension. The elite transactional law that Sitara and her peers practiced was neither feminized labor, nor was it low paying—the two most common explanations for feminization of work.[3] Given that India was still home to one of the least feminized legal professions in the world, what could explain this gender shift in its most prestigious and well-paying organizations?

Still, it was not just the representation of women in these firms that was an empirical anomaly. Recent studies on the global south[4]—and in India in particular—had started to stress the mobility implications of neoliberalism,[5] especially the rise of a certain kind of middle-class urbanity and class possibility (e.g., Deshpande 2003; Fernandes 2006; Lukose 2009; Nadeem 2009; Patel 2010; Radhakrishnan 2011; Fuller and Narasimhan 2014; Subramanian 2015; Upadhya 2016). Yet, the accounts of the lawyers I met diverged in important ways from this model, not just in terms of the economic rewards they reaped,[6] but also in terms of their praxis when compared to other accounts of professional mobility in the region. Over the next several months, I would hear more stories from women and men in glass offices who would tell me about their modest beginnings and their current lifestyles with the same comfort and confidence: the single-generation jump to a certain kind of modernity, the impossibility of predicting that jump before it happened, the relative ease of adapting to it once it had taken place. For many of these *first-generation professional elites*, their accounts of their journeys sounded akin to those of meritocratic victors describing their status—legitimate, hard won, almost natural. Over the course of my research, Sitara's story of mobility would have some parallels to other kinds of elite professionals, but the ways in which she and her peers in elite law experienced professional parity would remain in stark contrast both with their peers in India and to the mainstream experience of gendered professional work globally. And, upon additional examination, it would stop giving me as much comfort. Instead, over the course of my fieldwork and the years that would follow it, the fractures in these success stories would become even more apparent than they had been on that sweltering walk in August 2013.

This book, in some ways, is a consolidation of that journey from hopefulness to cautious discomfort about the state of India's legal profession. It unpacks the skip in my step about an optimistic finding—of women lawyers achieving new kinds of professional success within Indian "big law"—first with celebration for the extension of mobility that success affords, and then, more critically, to reveal its layered underpinnings. In approaching these rewards with circumscribed celebration, this book reveals a set of structural conditions that fortuitously have come together to create environments of emancipation for these women lawyers: including organizational novelty and the imagined forces of globalization, a particularly receptive interactional audience, and the specific contingencies of a particular cultural moment in India's neoliberal history.

This unpacking is also at the core of my argument about what I term *accidentally feminist* organizations: I find that, despite being agnostic to the cause of feminism, and using the governance language of meritocracy and modernity, many elite law firms in India have managed to produce the kinds of environments that more agentic organizations with committed interests in diversity have failed to produce in other sites. Not only are women well represented at entry and more senior levels in these law firms, they also experience their environments rather differently from their peers in similar kinds of organizations globally and locally. In doing so, these firms have not only managed to create historically unimaginable spaces of possibility for women, they have also managed to set path dependencies for organizations to have more (possible intentionally) feminist futures.

The hesitation in taking such "success"[7] at face value is justified. Reflective of its committed critical tradition, law and society research is predicated on the assumptions of the systemic reproductions of hierarchy, especially by and within institutions producing lawyers (e.g., Garth and Sterling 2009; Garth 2015, 2020; Basheer et al. 2017) and those shaping their careers (e.g., Dezalay and Garth 1996, 2002; Wilkins and Gulati 1996; Tomlinson et al. 2019), especially in emerging country contexts (e.g., Liu 2008; Wilkins, Khanna, and Trubek 2017). From that broad perspective, one could argue that the "success" that women in elite law firms are enjoying is a straightforward reflection of their intersectional caste and class advantages that dilute the disadvantage that gender might pose.[8] Still, successful women in my sample were not just upper-class women; rather, they were a cohort of "first-generation professional elites" whose financial independency from (and often, benefaction toward) their parents was central to their ability to access individual agency. Further, while caste certainly remains a fundamental framework of all analyses, rewards for high-caste women typically have not been found in the labor market. In fact, as feminist scholars have argued, caste advantage in India has been traditionally enacted by women *not* entering the market (Caplan 1985). And while high-class women were more likely to be better educated, to the extent they undertook paid employment outside the home, it was likely to be non–labor intensive (Ray and Qayum 2009) and essentialized sector-specific (e.g., teachers, clerical workers; Caplan 1985). Just as with other transnational sites of gendered labor (e.g., Freeman 2000), with the advent of liberalization, there has emerged a rising body of work on India suggesting a more layered process of capital and cultural flows that mark these processes. Not only do data reveal that there is a steady decline in women's labor force participation,[9] but research has also generally taken the approach that while liberalization has changed the nature of outcomes slightly for high-caste women (e.g.,

Fuller and Narasimhan 2014), women's entry into the labor market continues to include an onus that they do so in respectable, status-retaining ways (e.g., Radhakrishnan 2011). Particularly, under the nationalist construction of the "global," the boons of global work (i.e., monetary rewards, independence) have been intertwined with signifiers of moral doom. To access the boons without penalty and achieve success in the global labor market, research suggests that most women have had to actively perform the embedded expectations of their middle-class identity by committing to sexual nonpromiscuity (Nadeem 2009), family responsibility (Patel 2010), and austerity (Lukose 2009; Radhakrishnan 2009).

As I illustrate in this book, the women in my sample—a demographic of urban, middle-class women who attended competitive law schools and joined high-paying firms—were less likely to perform within these confines of middle-class consumption and praxis. For many of the women in my study, class background was relevant for the performance of a cosmopolitan professional culture, but that performance did not always require them to uphold the standard expectations of their class. At the same time, their class advantage had its own circumscriptions, and women with similar class backgrounds were subject to different forms of pushback depending on the organizations they were in. As a result, even with similar caste and class advantages, women lawyers in new and elite law firms had very different lived professional lives from their peers who worked in more traditional legal practices or in modern consulting firms. Together, these similarities and differences in their lived experiences, especially against the backdrop of other professionals in the country, offers new insights into processes of global mobility.

In particular, by using the comparative case of women in management consulting—a site that is similar in professional prestige and organizational demands to these law firms—this book illuminates the ways in which caste and class alone do not explain the unique position this subset of women lawyers enjoy. Although women in all kinds of elite firms were buttressed by positional advantages, women in consulting firms continued to experience their environments as stiflingly gendered despite organizational commitments to change the culture, but they deemed this "understandable" given the Indian context. None of which is to suggest that the law firms that are at the core focus of this book are nongendered—in fact, over the course of this book, I'll argue just how very gendered they still are. But in offering spaces of relative parity and posture-able nondiscrimination to their inhabitants, this book suggests that they have produced a set of interrelated, if compromised, feminist path dependencies. Shielded from the need to defend their actions as gendered (which might have attracted backlash, or seemed polarizing), certain law firms instead have managed to offer spaces where, despite not meaning to do gender differently, there exist early institutional blueprints for sustainable demographic parity.

This book describes the range of conditions—each, as I will argue, incidentally conceived—that came together, in this case, without intention, to nevertheless produce these demographic parities for elite women lawyers. From schools that were set up to produce elite social justice lawyers, and then happened to emerge alongside market liberalization and the conception of new transactional legal practice; to frameworks of essentialism and familial responsibility that incidentally get queered to offer different kinds of relational rewards, this book reveals a set of cascading reasons that came together to produce unexpected parities and offer unintended agencies to a certain cohort of women but not others. Of course, in revealing these conditions, this work hopes to start a conversation about a set of bigger questions: If gender parity is produced without an agentic movement or institutional sanction, is it still (or was it ever) feminist? And should the steep costs of "good" outcomes keep us from celebrating them? When a set of unintended conditions results in seeming equality, is it desirable or is it dangerous?

Gendered Mobility and High-Status Work: Locating the Surprise of Parity

In 2012, more than half the lawyers elevated to partnership at two of the largest law firms in Mumbai were women. Not only were women entering these firms at the same rate as men, they were being retained and advancing at similar rates to their male peers. This finding was an empirical anomaly within the predominantly male Indian legal profession. But it was also a pattern in utter contrast with accounts of gender in professional work more generally.

The legal profession in India has traditionally been male. Although the country enacted legislation as early as 1923 to admit women to the bar, the number of women has remained low.[10] And despite some optimistic predictions that a gender-equal profession was imminent, women represent less than 10 percent of all lawyers by most predominant accounts.[11] Ethan Michelson's comparative demography of the legal profession (2013) suggested that the number of women who self-identify as lawyers in census data is about 5 percent of all lawyers—which is about half the number of women recorded in bar council admission records for a similar time period (table 1). This might be explained by the number of lawyers technically enrolled in the bar who do not practice law—a demographic slip that is common in these data.[12] Nevertheless, even the most optimistic of these numbers reflect the relative lack of gender parity in the Indian legal profession more generally.

To the extent studies on gender in the legal profession exist in the country, case studies in smaller courts (e.g., Sethi 1987; Nagla 2001; Sharma 2002) confirm expectations from the broader literature on women and work in India. Most women in these studies were young, unmarried, and from forward caste[13] communities (Nagla 2001) and continued to encounter strong gendered

Table 1. Male and female advocates enrolled with state bar councils (March 31, 2007)

State Bar Council	Men	Women	Total	% Women
Andhra Pradesh	58,147	9,605	67,752	14
Assam, Nagaland, etc.**	9,703	2,022	11,725	17
Bihar**	89,594	3,043	92,637	3
Chhatisgarh	10,000	4,949	14,949	33
Delhi	30,000	8,549	38,549	18
Gujrat	38,586	9,208	47,794	19
Himachal Pradesh	4,680	741	5,421	14
Jammu and Kashmir	2,832	597	3,429	17
Jharkhand	5,407	485	5,892	8
Karntaka**	37,861	6,756	44,617	15
Kerlala	30,000	6,437	36,437	18
Madhya Pradesh	60,000	9,208	69,208	13
Maharashtra and Goa	78,522	5,636	84,158	7
Orissa	31,000	6,993	37,993	18
Punjab and Haryana	42,411	4,265	46,676	9
Rajasthan	35,000	5,823	40,823	14
Tamil Nadu	46,575	5,902	52,477	11
Uttarakhand***	359	76	435	17
Uttar Pradesh*	195,780	6,000	201,780	3
West Bengal	50,000	2,261	52,261	4
Totals	**856,457**	**98,556**	**955,013**	**10**

Source: Bar Council of India (no longer publicly available on website, last accessed 2009).
* March 31, 2006.
** December 31, 2006.
*** March 31, 2007.

expectations as they navigated the profession (Sethi 1987:46). Mishra's 2015 study offered a slight nuance with respect to the Lucknow High Court—there were still fairly few women at the bar, but they were enrolling in larger numbers than ever before (3 percent of all registered advocates between the years 1962–1997, compared to 12.3 percent in 1998–2005).

These gendered barriers to litigation practice are confirmed by more recent accounts as well. They are—unsurprisingly—steeper in higher levels of practice. Women are sparsely represented as judges (tables 2a, 2b), senior counsel (figure 2), or bar council office bearers (figure 3). For example, only five of the 397 senior advocates in the Supreme Court of India between 1962 and 2011 were women (Makhija and Raha 2012). And for the few women

Table 2a. Men and women judges by court (2018, historic)

Court	Current (2018)			Historic*		
	Total	Men	Women	Total	Men	Women
Supreme Court of India	24	22	2	205	200	5
Delhi High Court	35	27	8°	162	147	15
Calcutta High Court	37	31	6	41**	39**	2**
Madras High Court	62	50	12°	38**	37**	1**
Bombay High Court	69	59	10°	398	391	7

Source: Court websites of the Supreme Court and High Courts.
* Note that all historic totals include judges appointed in a given court (who were not sitting judges in 2018). The historic timelines of appointment vary by court and start at the year the first judge was appointed: i.e., Supreme Court (1950), Delhi High Court (1966), Bombay High Court (1862), Calcutta High Court (1862), Madras High Court (1862). Note that Bombay, Calcutta, and Madras High Courts were pre-independence courts, whereas the Delhi High Courts and Supreme Court were post-independence courts formed after 1947. Housed in presidency towns, the Bombay, Calcutta, and Madras High Courts were established by Queen Victoria's letters patent under the Indian High Courts Act 1861.

Until late 2018, the current sitting chief justices in Bombay (Acting Chief Justice Tahilramani), Delhi (Acting Chief Justice Mittal), and Madras (Chief Justice Banerjee) High Courts were all women. They have since been replaced by male justices.
** Official court websites give data only about past Chief Justices.

Table 2b. Historic Gendered Representation of Professionals (2002)

Category	1961		1971		1981		1991	
	Male	Female	Male	Female	Male	Female	Male	Female
Judges and Magistrates	98.4	1.6	98.9	1.1	97.8	2.2	97.1	2.9
Legal Practitioners and Advisers	99.3	0.7	99.0	1.0	95.4	4.6	93.2	6.8
Legal Assistants	99.2	0.8	99.9	0.04	98.8	1.2	98.9	1.1
Jurists and Legal Technicians	99.0	1.0	99.9	1.0	98.9	1.1	98.3	1.7

Sources: Nagla (2001: 77); Sharma (2002: 96).

in these positions, systems remain deeply problematic. Indira Jaisingh, the first woman to be designated as a senior advocate by the Bombay High Court (which has bestowed this distinction on only five women in the last three decades), has gone on public record describing a culture of deep sexism in the courtrooms[14] and is currently leading a challenge against sex discrimination before the Supreme Court. Further, despite their growing representation in law faculties, women still occupy few positions of power in academia,

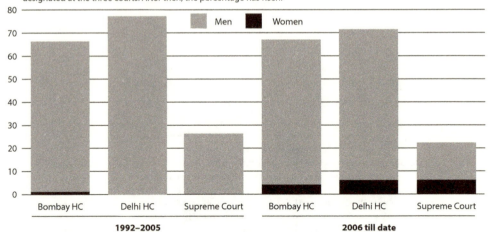

UNEQUAL DISTRIBUTION
Men/women designated senior from 1992–2005/after 2005 at three top courts. Until 2005, only one woman was designated at the three courts. After then, the percentage has risen.

FIGURE 2. Gendered Representation of Senior Advocates.
Source: Kian Ganz, Legally India, July 15, 2015.

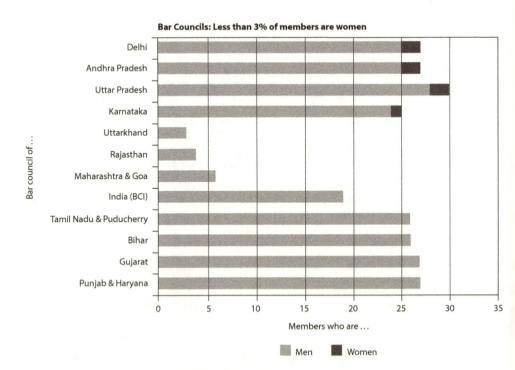

FIGURE 3. Gendered Representation of Bar Council Officers.
Source: Legally India, July 12, 2016.

even (indeed especially) in new elite law schools (Ballakrishnen and Samuel 2020).[15]

Yet the fortunes of the elite lawyers I studied were not just in utter contrast with India's legal profession. They also stood in contrast to broader accounts of gender and professional work in India and globally. Broadly, the feminization of any workforce—that is, the increasing number of women in any line of work—can be explained in two broad ways. The first is a purely functionalist efficiency argument grounded in micro-essentialism (for a review, see Charles and Bradley 2009): women are thought to be better at different tasks; the skill sets needed for certain jobs are coded as female even in otherwise male workspaces (for example, secretaries in traditionally male, hierarchical companies); and as a result of this gendered call for specific skills, women are advantaged to a limited extent within these occupational spheres (Reskin 1993). The second explanation for feminization is that an occupational field or subfield becomes disregarded or devalued because it is low-prestige or no longer professionally "pure" (Sandefur 2001). In other words, women (and other minorities) have better access to lower-prestige jobs that high-status actors—i.e., men—do not want because they have access to higher-prestige work (England 1992). In addition to the gendered pipelines getting people *into* jobs, it is also important to consider what happens once women are *in* these jobs. And here too, women are disadvantaged. Women are less likely to have access to high-status work and, simultaneously, work that gets more feminized is more likely to be deemed less prestigious. Of course, not all work is predetermined to be feminized across all contexts, and in professional industries like IT (in India), a kind of "gender neutrality" offers women the opportunity to enter and be empowered if they so choose (Mukherjee 2008). Still, as Upadhya has illustrated in her work on IT professionals, these measures of neutrality are often performative: although software companies try to have "women-friendly policies" like flexible work arrangements and special mentoring, they nonetheless halt women in their careers because much of women's lives outside of work remain unchanged (2016:156). It is not just that the work of managing children and family pressures continues to demand women's time, it is the constantly recurring demand (both within and outside of work) that women make choices that reprioritize work which in turn shapes their careers. Upadhya's account tracks with my own general findings in the consulting industry, another similarly set up MNC model of work: the discrimination, even when covert, is not coded as such because of the range of overt structural conditions that are established to recruit and retain women. Nonetheless, women's success is not guaranteed because it is expected that they will eventually and inevitably choose to leave, which results in their not being seen as "long term investments" (2016:158). This habitus, Upadhya argued, pushes women to the bottom of their professional ladder.

As a result, most accounts of women and work revolve around work that is either seen as "female work" (e.g., in "care work" industries) or otherwise low prestige and underpaid. And this is even more true in sites outside the global north. Unlike traditional class analysis, which was notorious for not paying attention to gender (e.g., Goldthorpe 1983), recent research on global economic mobility has been much more conscientious (Sassen 2000; Torche 2015; Donner and Santos 2016). But it is not surprising that in these nuanced accounts of women and work, especially in the context of international development and progress in the global south, the focus remains (if not more concentrated) on these sectors. In India, for example, the studies on women and work outside of agriculture have been primarily concerned with informal and low-wage employment (e.g., Raju and Bagchi 1993; Paul 2009; Swaminathan 2012; Agarwala 2013). This book does not seek to take away from the important work that has unpacked the layered relationship between globalization, work, and gender. But studying these elite sites through the same lenses of labor and development does not do justice to the myriad ways in which these spaces can be interrogated.

With the advent of liberalization, there have been some studies examining the different types of work becoming available to women, but these too have been largely confined to routine, segregated, and task-intensive labor (Mukherjee 2008) within sectors such as IT (e.g., Jhabvala and Sinha 2002), outsourcing (Patel 2010), foreign export (Jeyaranjan and Swaminathan 1999), and telemarketing (Gothoskar 2000). The limited research on professional workforces tends to confirm an essentialist prejudice behind feminization in select family-friendly subfields like OB-GYN for female doctors (Sood and Chadda 2010), "customer relations" human resource positions for female managers (Gupta et al. 1998), or communication-related managerial posts for female engineers (Patel and Parmentier 2005). For instance, Patel and Parmentier (2005) show that female engineers in India from elite engineering schools (Indian Institutes of Technology or IITs) continue to be relegated to the periphery of organizations and that they lag significantly behind their male peers in earning power. The number of women matches and sometimes surpasses the number of men in entry-level managerial positions, but women advance much more slowly than their male peers who started with them (Kumar 2001). Further, women face strong entry constraints (Desai 1977), fewer opportunities for intra-organization training and education (Buddhapriya 1999), a resistance to women in positions of power (Nath 2000; Naqvi 2011), and an overall male bias (Gulhati 1990), even among managers who think of their organizations as meritocratic (Gupta et al. 1998; Gupta and Sharma 2003). In addition, the women who do enter these professional tracks are subject to persistent gender role expectations and penalties for deviance, forcing them to perform, a form of "neoliberal respectable" femininity" (Radhakrishnan 2009; Freeman 2015). I review this literature and its implications, especially as it applies to patterns in lawyers' professional mobility, in other parts of this book, but I highlight these broad narratives here because it is against this backdrop of relative impossibility that my findings about success-ful women professionals in prestigious legal firms take shape. This is not a book that focuses on gender and globalization from a top-down emancipation narrative.[16] In interrogating professional elites, rather than laborers or even middle-class, white-collared, salaried employees, this account offers a differ-ent view of the relationship between gender, globalization, and mobility. Key to this difference is that these women, as I show in the next chapter, are not confined to many of the relationships between modernity and mobility that have plagued their predecessors and even peers.

Of course, there is no way to understand these findings as emergence from impossibility without taking into account the embedded intersections that produce such possibility. It is self-evident that no writing about gen-der is complete without acknowledging its intersections with other sorts of inequality. And it is here that the comparative case of management consul-tants, as I explain below, offers a chance to unpack the relative limits of these mechanisms and to further highlight the particular workings of class for elite women lawyers, and the complications it presents to our understandings of mobility. As other stratification theorists following the tradition of Bour-dieuian social topography have argued, class is never just economic. Access to social capital and the ability to display it impacted outcomes for the women in my sample, especially in terms of the assumptions of cultural fit (chapter 2), interactions with like-minded peers (chapter 4), and the kinds of embedded structural advantages they had to buttress their professional experiences (e.g., access to domestic help and urban family networks who could help with family care, chapter 5). But their mobility experience and cultural praxis, I suggest, were simultaneously also impacted by interactional performance and orga-nizational possibility that was predicated on a range of regulatory processes incidental to these individual level outcomes. And it is to these macro factors that were central to this project's emergence that I turn to next.

Framing the Accidental: The Advantage of India's Legal Profession as a Research Site

In the glass-lined office where we had our interview, Sitara seemed native to her environment—her suit tailored to fit, her matte black pumps revealing that she was not going to walk on a cramped Mumbai road to catch the train. Yet, when I asked her if this had been the future she imagined as a little girl, she reminded me that corporate lawyers were "just not a 'thing'" when she was young. The fact that being a corporate lawyer was not a "thing" for young Sitara is the same fact that motivated the research in this book. Over a two-decade period follow-ing India's liberalization reforms in 1991, the country's professional landscape completely changed, offering a useful theoretical lens through which to observe larger sociological questions about change and persistence.[17] Unlike kids who dreamed of becoming cardiologists and mechanical engineers (doctor and engineer were common, almost obligatory choices for ambitious students in India), young Sitara couldn't have known she wanted to be a corporate lawyer (to the extent that any child knows they want to be a corporate lawyer, that is) because that career trajectory did not exist before the turn of the new century. Law firms like the ones where I conducted interviews—locale-agnostic spaces featuring expensive art, cellophane-covered swirly mints in conference rooms, and foreign and local clients alike in dark business suits—did not exist at all before the mid-twentieth century, much less take the form of lockstep partnerships located in multi-floor, multi-city law firms in "business districts."

Market dynamics have been central to our understanding of microprocesses like professionalism and organizational change (Evetts 2003). Market globalization, in particular, has offered new research incentives to scholars interested in the transnational ramifications of the legal profession (e.g., Faulconbridge and Muzio 2008, 2012; Liu 2008; Dezalay and Garth 2010; Wilkins et al. 2017; Abel et al. 2020). A similar theoretical purchase motivated the research in this book. In 1991, the Indian government, in response to a payment crisis, initiated a process of economic liberalization and market deregulation (Nayar 1998). These reforms had important financial and currency implications, and they were central to shaping the scope of India's professional service sectors because they introduced the gradual privatization of predominantly state-run sectors and the liberalization of foreign direct investments and trade. Following these reforms, India witnessed the entry of multinational professional firms and the emergence of new professional services (e.g., management consulting) alongside older professions like law, accounting, and banking. But even among existing professions, liberalization brought about organizational changes, and new kinds of firms began to emerge alongside individual and small-group practice. This new way of organizing professional work was crucial to the design of this research because it offered insights into the emergence of new kinds of work and, particularly, a cohort of what other scholars have termed "elite workers" (Portes 2010:106). To the extent that it exists, research on professionals in the emerging world either focuses on these workers as new, unsure inhabitants of a global market economy or sets them up as predetermined heirs of this new status because of their own inherited capital. In contrast, the professionals in this book were early incarnations of a new sort of cosmopolitan actor. As I detail in chapter 1, they were not an ascription-driven superclass of global elites (Khan 2012), but neither were they conflicted and unsure new entrants to these spaces. Instead, they were a cohort of domestically educated, middle-class bred, first-generation professional elites who were becoming consumers of elite spaces, networks, and markers as a function *not* of their origin, but rather of their relationship to global capital and networks. This is perhaps not the first example of neoliberal mobility following a macro regulatory change in an emerging country context,[18] and this is certainly not India's first class of intellectual elite who have been able to access new mobility in a single generation.[19] But to the extent it is gendered and related to modernity and middle-class morality in this particular way, this case is unique.

As I elaborate in chapter 1, two specific consequences of liberalization reforms were central to this project's research design because they offered purchase for analytical sampling across cases (Yin 2003). First, while some professional practices like litigation remained unaffected by liberalization measures (Galanter and Robinson 2014), others, like international transactional law and management consulting, only emerged as a consequence of the foreign direct investment that liberalization permitted (Galanter and Rekhi 1996). Liberalization brought a considerable influx of foreign investment and capital which in turn sparked a need for new kinds of transactional professionals to service this influx. Second, in addition to new kinds of work, market liberalization also introduced new kinds of work *and* workplaces. India had no local offices of multinational consulting firms before 1991. To the extent they existed, ad hoc local independent consultants worked across a range of industries essentially as freelancers before liberalization with no formal connections to global firms. But the main industry players following 1991 were global professional services whose emerging economies practice included offices—and therefore, a new workforce—in India. In contrast, although many elite Indian law firms had been founded in some form (usually as family businesses or practices) before market liberalization, they emerged into their current form—as sophisticated, full-service, "big law" firms with "open" partnerships that included actors beyond closed circles—following these 1991 reforms (Gupta et al. 2017).

And here too, other regulatory conditions offered case variation. While most elite professional service sectors such as banking and management consulting are organized like standard MNCs, with international investment and firm organization, the Advocates Act (1961) restricts international investment into the Indian legal profession and forbids the "practice of law" by non-Indians.[20] This produced a unique organizational and service circumstance: the significant influx of foreign capital and the absence of local competition meant that large domestic law firms had a fertile opportunity to evolve as a "one-stop shop" for commercial matters (Galanter and Rekhi 1996; Krishnan 2013). As Gupta et al. (2017:49) argued, this "milieu provided the space, opportunity, and demand for law firms to emerge as indispensable service providers to the major domestic and foreign players in the Indian economy."

Despite such crucial regulatory differences, these various new kinds of professional service firms also shared important similarities: elite law and management consulting firms were both similarly exclusive when it came to staffing, they paid high salaries, were considered highly prestigious, and recruited incoming cohorts of successful candidates from elite national law and business schools. At the same time, they varied in many ways—they were differently managed, they valorized different tasks as crucial to their professional identity, and they serviced different kinds of clients. And, as I detail below, each of these variations revealed itself to be significant in the creation of differential contexts for the professionals who worked there.

[ACCIDENTAL] DESIGN AND CASE SELECTION

This research benefited from its multi-year design, which allowed an iterative analytical process not just between data and existing research but also between data collection and analysis before subsequent rounds of comparative sampling (Yin 2003). When I began this project in 2011, I planned to do a qualitative study about the experience of lawyers in neoliberal professional service firms.[21] Like other researchers (Pratt 2000) inclined to inductive organizational research, I was interested in elite Indian law firms because they were an extreme case ideally situated for building theory through qualitative research. As firms structurally cut off from direct Western influence but still responding to the large market for international legal services, I saw these firms as prime sites to investigate firm emergence and experience during a transitional market, especially as juxtaposed against more traditional kinds of legal practice. From this initial data, an emergent theme was that of gender "not being an issue" among professionals in newer law firms. Subsequent interviews (2012–2013) specifically probed ideologies around gender and paid attention to the experience of gender in the workplace. In both these stages of the project (2011, 2012–2013), I used variations in emergence before and after the 1991 liberalization to make sense of the ways in which novelty enabled professionals in the Indian case to navigate their environments. As I described earlier, this focus on novelty was initially guided by the variations in organizational emergence that the 1991 reforms offered. However, upon analyzing the relevance of the gender finding, I found it was also useful to test the proposition that new kinds of work environments could offer the potential to renegotiate rigidly set background assumptions about gender (Ridgeway and Correll 2004; Ridgeway 2011). Extending beyond the empirics of Western organizations and career outcomes that grounded this theory (e.g., Smith-Doerr 2004), this research was broadly refocused to ask: What kinds of negotiations are possible at the individual level following drastic labor market changes?

Following these theoretical and empirical motivations (Eisenhardt 1989), I chose to focus on two sites that showed this variation in organizational structure and the nature of work across firms. The *first* was the case of traditional litigation practice that was still organized in pre-1991 fashion around individual practitioners or small partnerships. The *second* was the case of transactional law firms created after the 1991 liberalization that worked on new kinds of transactional work (e.g., mergers and acquisitions, capital markets, and international banking). In addition to doing different sorts of work (i.e., kinds of practice), the two types of firm centered on different tasks as well. Traditional litigation practice in India involved drafting and appearing on behalf of predominantly domestic clients in local and state courts as well as limited advisory work on specialized areas. In contrast, the post-1991 corporate law firm model was set up to respond to a need for Indian lawyers in commercial transactions. Although many of these corporate firms also worked with litigators, their predominant practice was to advise, consult, and negotiate on behalf of sophisticated corporate clients who often brought repeat business. I also interviewed lawyers in elite but traditionally organized litigation practice in order to evaluate the advantage of new sites (Ridgeway 2011). From my interviews and observations in the field, it became clear that newer firms were indeed impacted by globalization and that women in particular experienced their careers very differently in these new firms.[22]

In 2013, when it became clear from the first two waves of analysis that novelty of work and organizational structure alone could not explain the variations observed in different organizations, I decided to add a *third* site to the project, allowing me to focus on relationships between the local and the global via clients and organizational structure. This was not to change the focus of the research project—which remained very much centered on legal professionals across sites. The impetus for this addition of a third site was not motivated with the intention to offer a comprehensive account of another field, nor was the attempt to make the comparison comprehensive in all aspects. Rather, it was motivated by a particular strategy of research design rooted in empirical variation to offer explanations for underlying mechanisms. While the comparisons in the early part of the project were useful for teasing out mechanisms of novelty, they were all cases within the legal profession that were necessarily domestically owned and managed. I theorized that if novelty was indeed what was behind the difference between women in older litigating practice versus those in new kinds of transactional law firms, then other kinds of new firms ought also to expose their inhabitants to similar surroundings. However, a scan of the management consulting sector—an equally prestigious professional field that was also "new"—revealed that women did not enjoy the same kinds of representation there as in the new law firms. This offered the extension for the preliminary hypothesis that novelty was the only mechanism at play, and that varying some of the other site characteristics could offer analytical purchase. My theoretical impetus for choosing a third case was to introduce variations in organizational factors like ownership, management, and external audience (i.e., clients). I was particularly interested in the differences between external-facing domestic firms and internal-facing international firms (table 3). Pursuing this line of sampling offered useful analytical variation since transactional law firms were, as I describe above, domestically man-

Table 3. Indian professional service firms: Management and clients

	External-facing clients or transactions	Internal-facing clients or transactions
Externally owned or managed	Process outsourcing	Consulting, banking, accounting services
Internally owned or managed	Elite law firm	Domestic law firm, litigation

aged while servicing international clients. In contrast, the *third case* of management consulting firms was set up in a classic MNC model—i.e., as local firms of global conglomerates that dealt with local clients and transactions. To explore this intuition of theory following method further, I conducted these interviews in 2014–2015. The three sites, as I explain in the previous section, were similar enough to warrant comparison in that they were all highly prestigious work sites with professional entry requirements (table 4). But their structural variation (in organization, nature of work, and external audience/clients) offered a triangulated research design for understanding the ways in which these variations impacted cultural understandings about work and workers.

I deal with the differences in these global and local synergies across sites in the next chapter, but it is worth mentioning that although it is not the focus of this research, the IT sector offers an important juxtaposition against which to consider the globalization of the sectors I focus on in this book. Even for the casual observer, the explosion of the IT sector has been the capstone of globalization in the local professional landscape.[23] While professions like law, accounting, and consulting have been influenced by global forces to varying degrees, none of them have been to the same extent as in the IT industry, just in terms of scope.[24] Altogether, IT has been central to the cultural revolutionizing of the idea of global "work" in the Indian context[25] and for young graduates especially, global IT firms and career paths have become prominent sites to invest their aspirational capital. The impact of globalization on emerging country elites, especially in terms of understanding the systemic reproduction of internal hierarchies, has been well documented (for examples across different international adaptive contexts, See Dezalay and Garth 2002). However, the case of IT work in India has offered pertinent nuance to this reading: as a movement not restricted to just the elites, it has meant a reorientation of India's newly mobile middle class (Singh 2009; Nadeem 2013). Recent global attitudes research (Milanovik 2013) has shown that the main "winners of globalization" have been middle classes of emerging market economies. And as a fiscally profitable sector not riddled with traditional bureaucratic practices, India's IT sector has become the core destination for middle-class college aspirants keen on collecting on these rewards. But this kind of "mainstream work

Table 4. Comparison of Cases

Case Dimensions	Traditional Litigation	Consulting	Elite Transactional Law
Commonalities			
Type of professional	Professional degree	Professional degree (predominantly elite)	Professional degree (predominantly elite)
Status of profession	Varied	High	High
Differences			
Organizational structure	Old	New	New
	Individual practice, partnerships	Global MNC firms, local Indian offices	Domestically managed firms, lockstep partnerships
Predominant nature of work / transactions	Old	New	New
	Court appearances	Advisory, transactional	Advisory, transactional, negotiation
Clients	Old	Old	New
	Domestic clients, traditional	Domestic clients, traditional	International clients, large domestic conglomerates

globalization" (Ballakrishnen 2016) is distinct from the more niche professional service industries like management consulting and law, the two main professional fields I deal with in this book.

MAKING SENSE OF THE SURPRISE FINDINGS: ACCIDENTAL FEMINISM

In unpacking this finding of elite lawyers in India navigating their new, seemingly egalitarian workplaces, this book pays homage to the exception represented by these women's success while simultaneously assessing the incidental costs of that success. As I argue, many factors came together to offer the lived possibilities that the women in my sample were able to experience. At the most abstract level, some part of the divergence in lived experience might be explained by the novelty of their environments, as I detail in chapter 2. Not that novelty in and of itself could produce "good" gendered outcomes (to the extent parity is a "good" outcome, yes), but the new kinds of work in this context allowed a fresh possibility for renegotiating the imagined ideal workers who could perform this work. And, unlike most of the legal profession, which was steeped in gendered scripts about the actors who were best positioned to do this work, elite transactional firms offered a new exit from old frameworks. As I argue throughout this book, these firms were not set up to curate progressive possibility for the lawyers they recruited, and within them there certainly was not an active culture that offered an articulated set of advantages to women. But as professional spaces with a *lack* of the explicit *dis*advantage rampant in the rest of the profession, these firms afforded a new chance at professional possibility, especially to graduates from new elite schools. This in turn allowed the actors within the space a shot at a special kind of circumstance negotiation that went beyond the context of mere emancipation to actual class negotiation and consciousness. Much of the research in the lineage of unpacking unintended consequences (Merton 1936) focuses on well-intentioned policies that ultimately result in divergence that goes against the spirit of the initial intention. In research on women and diversity in STEM fields, for example, Erin Cech and colleagues (Cech et al. 2011; Cech 2015; Cech and Blair Loy 2019) unpack a range of cultural mechanisms of inequality production, to show how innocuous or even good cultural practices and beliefs can produce bad outcomes for minority actors. These set beliefs of what "good workers" can do help frame our understandings of accessible equality, especially within well-intentioned narratives. But what about the reverse—what about innocuous or even bad cultural practices that inadvertently allow institutionally fertile spaces to nurture good outcomes? What do we do with those outcomes and what do we do with the possibilities of such equality?

The particular impacts of globalization on professional work is a theme that frames much of this research. But the actual mechanisms at play in producing the lived experiences of the actors I study are more nuanced and interconnected, even as they work within the ambit of macro-processes. This book makes a recursive, layered argument over the course of four empirical chapters that illuminate a range of structural conditions at play in creating this unexpected parity in elite law firms but not in other similar sites. It is this exceptionalism that grounds the empirical core of this book. In the first empirical chapter (chapter 2), I explore the role of institutional novelty in moderating the experience of gender. I show how the emergence of the Indian elite law firm has been uniquely shaped by the newness of the work and the organizational structure—as well as a new, neoliberal workforce not found in other professional firms of similar status. Gender theorists and social psychologists (e.g., Ridgeway 2011) have theorized about the disadvantage preexisting frameworks pose for those attempting to negotiate entrenched hierarchies, and the limited advantages offered by newness. I find that as new firms doing new work, these elite law firms are indeed advantaged by being able to escape strong preconceived notions of work and identity. In addition, the newness of the law *schools* that socialize these firms' workers contribute to the firms' multi-layered advantage, an advantage not enjoyed by other firms that are similarly structured by globalization (i.e., management consulting) but that draw their workforce from more long-established educational institutions (like older engineering and business schools). Ultimately, I show how globalization and class come together to renegotiate traditional assumptions of gender and the framework of an ideal worker. I argue that the gender outcomes in these firms result not from a movement for gender equality, but instead from the emergence of the Indian law firm as a new site of high-prestige global labor.

The second empirical chapter (chapter 3) explores a set of organizational conditions that have helped establish gender-egalitarian outcomes in these professional firms—particularly, in that these firms are new *domestic* firms struggling for legitimacy in a global market for legal services. Indian law firms, unlike other neoliberal industries in the country, are domestically founded and managed. I show that this unique structural premise forces them to use two distinct logics of emergence. First, firms use a *differentiation logic* to distinguish themselves from traditional firms that foreign clients are likely to see as "traditional" and kinship based—and therefore not modern and sophisticated enough. Second, they use a *mimicking logic* that mirrors global processes to aggressively signal compatibility and likeness with their global peers.

I argue that emerging in a context of questionable legitimacy leads these internally managed (but externally facing) firms to signal their modernity in various ways. One way they suggest that they are "just like global firms" is by not overtly discriminating on the basis of gender. Their emphasis on nondiscrimination is particularly intentional; while banking and consulting firms may be similarly committed to gender equality, at least on the surface, as local offices of large multinational conglomerates these firms are already globally legitimate. Law firms, on the other hand, see their nondiscrimination as an explicit function of being modern and meritocratic. Meritocracy is notorious for seeming fair while resulting in inegalitarian outcomes. But in the Indian case, this lack of discrimination constructs an oasis of egalitarianism in an otherwise hostile legal profession, leading the women who join these firms to stay there. I posit that the reason for these seemingly feminist workspaces is not so much a function of agentic effort on the part of the firms, but instead, an emergence riddled with *speculative* isomorphism, where firms, in order to aggressively signal competence and modernity, mimic and replicate what they believe to be global ideal types of egalitarian order.

These imagined workings of globalization are premised on very particular interactional conditions. In chapter 4, I tease out the ways in which relationships between female professionals and their clients, peers, and mentors help create and reinforce interactional hierarchies in these spaces. Certainly, professionals in these firms have been socialized to be comfortable in mixed-gender settings. But although supportive peer interactions are necessary to create an environment of gender parity, women in elite law firms also are especially backed by an important external audience that does not actively discriminate on the basis of gender—their *clients*. Elite law firms in India, unlike their traditional counterparts, retain a "sophisticated" client base of international and high-end domestic clients. This setup affords a comparatively advantageous position—especially for women lawyers—for a range of reasons. First, many clients are comfortable with women in their workplace and as allies in transactions. Whereas my respondents described clients from small domestic businesses as often being uncomfortable with women associates, they reported that gender was less likely to be a factor for clients of elite law firms. Second, the nature of the legal work handled by these firms (business, transactional) does not prime gender frames in lawyer-client interactions. Talking about transaction terms around a large merger, for example, is less personal than discussing the terms and conditions for a small family business. Women lawyers in smaller firms repeatedly described male clients who were hesitant to trust female lawyers with personal or familial transactions. In contrast, women in large elite law firms had the advantage of not priming intimate and personal conversations because they were working on more formal transactions. Third, the closed market for legal services offers another interactional advantage—retained and repeating clients. As retained counsel for most large transactions happening in the country, these firms do not need to explicitly recruit clients (which is often a gendered task). Together, these structural conditions—none of which has been put in place to consciously "do" gender differently—distinguish elite law firm interactions from those found in other elite professional spaces.

In the last empirical chapter (chapter 5), I trace the role of families and life course in determining the unlikely gender outcomes found in these large law firms. I show that, as one would expect, the origin families that most professionals come from are deeply homogenous (middle-class, high-caste, urban) but that similar class and caste advantages don't translate into gender advantages in other elite professional careers. I argue that the particular advantage of the legal profession is that the career trajectory allows for a more progressive work-family balance. In particular, women in elite law firms typically start their careers in their early twenties and are in a position to become partner in their early thirties—this timeline for promotion allows women to be in positions of power while they negotiate childcare and maternity leave, whereas women in other elite professions tend to be junior colleagues when they make agentic life course choices and are penalized accordingly. Yet, the fact remains that the structural career trajectory in these law firms was not introduced to make women more competitive candidates for partnership, but instead, emerged as a response to a concentrated, high-growth legal services market. In addition to this final condition of accidental feminism, I also highlight the ways in which this unprecedented success for Indian middle-class women in the workforce depends on two existing inequalities in the grander Indian system: a ready, caste-dependent labor force that supplies affordable housework support and childcare; and a penultimate generation of close female family members (mothers and female in-laws, mostly) who are not in the workforce and are available to provide free and ready household support systems.

Over the course of these four empirical chapters, I show that these four structural conditions have converged to create gender parity in ways that other, more targeted endeavors have failed to achieve. I argue from the perspective of each of these four different conditions that the creation of egalitarian gender outcomes in select firms is not straightforward or intentional but, instead, *accidental*, coming at the cost of other underlying inequalities. In particular, I suggest that gender parity in this system, while a welcome oasis, is not the result of a successful intervention to create egalitarian spaces. Instead, it is a function of several structural conditions that confound external factors of globalization and endogenous factors of class and gender inequalities. The overarching finding in this book, then, is that gender egalitarian outcomes can be created and supported without intention and that these forms of unintended parity are often buttressed by other inequalities and mechanisms of stratification. The unlikely case of the elite Indian law firm shows us how gender-egalitarian change is not just accidental or unintended but can also flow out of a conjuncture of seemingly minor and inconsequential institutional characteristics. Paying attention to these individual conditions as well as their unique overlay is at the core of this book's endeavor.

⟨⟩

In many ways, that walk home on August 2013 after the interview with Sitara was nothing out of the ordinary. I would walk on that road many times before and after, resisting the smells from roadside pakora vendors, wedged between an overflowing street and a packed line of general stores that sold everything from newspapers and tobacco to the casual evening full-service shave and haircut. That particular evening though, I was full of the kind of research euphoria[26] that one can only feel for the briefest (but purest) moments in fieldwork such as this, and I was eager to get back to my computer in Matunga. I remember thinking it would be so much better if I just took a cab instead of waiting for the train that would take me four stops to my station and then walking another thirty minutes to get home. If I had not given in to that impulse, I would have been at the Lower Parel station, only a few meters away from the spot where, that same evening, a twenty-two-year-old photojournalist was violently abused by five men in the abandoned Shakti Mills compound.

The Shakti Mills gang rape, as it would come to be known, would loom large on Mumbai's collective conscience for the remainder of my fieldwork. It would poke holes in the city's proud identity of being a "liberal and safe" place for women, especially when compared to the capital Delhi, which in recent years had been the site of notorious gender-related atrocities and strong activist movements generated in their wake. At the time of the harrowing event, only a few blocks away, corporate "midtown" Mumbai was business as usual—negotiating, drafting, and closing transactions and brokering multimillion-dollar deals in apparent oblivion. This is not especially remarkable. Such ironic juxtapositions take place across the world and they are hardly cause for documentation. What *is* of note, though, are the ways in which this event was dissected as an aberration in the days that followed and how women and men I spoke to acknowledged the tragedy but remained ambivalent about its impact on their own lives or assumptions about personal safety. "This *just* does not happen in [Mumbai]," one lawyer told me as we spoke in the back seat of their chauffeur-driven luxury sedan commuting between two meetings. What was perhaps closer to the truth was that this just did not happen to people *this lawyer knew* in Mumbai.

In writing this book, I remain willfully self-aware of the limits of its reach. This is a small section of women against the backdrop of a country still deeply imbued with difficult cultural understandings about women's lives and worth. And it deals with a cohort of women who, despite being a small segment of the population, do not see themselves as such. At the same time, in offering an in-depth portrayal of the mechanisms that allow for this sliver of the population to flourish, this book challenges many of the dominant narratives around women, modernity, and mobility in a part of the world that has traditionally been introspected under very different conditions. Studying these emerging elites offers us an opportunity to engage with a different strand of this complex discourse.

ONE

FOCI

Market Liberalization
and the Changing Nature
of Professional Work

GLOBAL PROFESSIONAL OPPORTUNITY following India's liberalization in 1991 has been an important lens through which to study new kinds of economic opportunity (Singh 2000; Dossani 2008; Evans 1995; Fuller and Narasimhan 2014; Subramanian 2015) and theorize about its implications for stratification and possibilities for mobility (Deshpande 2003; Fernandes and Heller 2006; Jodhka and Newman 2007; Jodhka 2012; Jodhka and Prakash 2016; Jodhka and Naudet 2017). But whereas the mainstay of that research has been the Information Technology (IT) sector, as I mention in the previous chapter, this book tracks a slightly different sort of mobility. The legal and consulting professionals in my study were similar to IT professionals in that they were products of a neoliberal country, employed in organizations and sectors that did not exist in the same vein before liberalization. But they varied distinctly in that they were a much smaller cohort of selectively recruited professionals who, upon graduation, entered a very different class bracket from their counterparts in IT. This difference in cohort size and scope means that the narratives of the professionals in this book are not as pervasive as those of IT professionals when it comes to "ushering global ideologies in public imagination" (Deshpande 2003, 2006; Upadhya 2016). At the same time, this smaller cohort affords a portrait of a different sort of mobility because it consisted of professionals with access to newly elite firms with high—and, importantly, "merit-based"—barriers to entry. Many of my informants insisted that their new status was a function of individual merit rather than inherited privilege. But accounts of Indian mobility processes,[1] especially for women, have traditionally also emphasized women's need to—despite visible and more widespread success—additionally navigate codes of appropriateness and "respectable" middle-class morality (e.g., Radhakrishnan 2011; Freeman 2015). Particularly, even (and, perhaps especially) high-caste women have traditionally had to manage this precarious balance. Here too, the stories in my data offered variation. Professionals in my sample were relatively homogenous in that they were urban, middle-class, and English-speaking. But they felt entitled to their new class position especially *because* they did not inherit it in obvious ways. Because they had graduated from a specific kind of school that was valorized in a specific sort of market, their success felt "earned." Many of the people I spoke to were quick to justify their lifestyles on exactly this kind of basis—their dads did not get them their jobs, their dads did not even know of these jobs. How could access to these spaces be tainted?

Merit-based justifications of mobility like "earned" and "just" are not unique to the Indian case. And the idea that cultural "fit" and cultural capital can skew what we otherwise think of as merit is not new. That cultural capital can signal different kinds of class beyond economic wealth has been a long instituted theoretical core of the literature on social reproduction (Bourdieu 1972). More recent studies on elite professional work (e.g., Rivera 2012, 2016; Friedman and Laurison 2019) and elite education (e.g., Armstrong and Hamilton 2013; Khan 2012, 2013) have rebuked the myth that meritocracy is truly committed to "fair" access. Instead, this line of research has shown how inequality occurs anew within the guise of merit (Armstrong and Hamilton 2013; Khan 2013), by offering what looks like truly equal opportunity but in fact is based on a range of cultural "fits" and activities (Rivera 2016) that reinforce the "class ceiling" protecting those with preexisting advantage (Friedman and Laurison 2019).[2] Indian accounts of social reproduction (e.g., Fuller and Narasimhan 2014; Subramanian 2015) have reinforced these arguments about merit, cultural capital, and access, especially when considering the role of caste privilege in determining new kinds of sociocultural capital that look like merit while still doing the work of innate social reproduction and elite hierarchies.[3]

Yet, even graduates from similar class positions experienced their environments across different elite organizations in different ways. Neela, for instance, who made more in her first year as a mid-tier consultant at a global firm than her parents likely made at retirement, was part of a first generation of elites who lived and spoke in the rhetoric of the elite without having emerged from it. Neela wasn't the daughter of a wealthy businessman who maintained his class position by not working in industry. She was, instead, the daughter of a bank officer and a schoolteacher who, with their middle-class upbringing, never could have imagined living the life she did as an adult. Neela's middle-class roots no doubt socialized her into thinking of education as the ultimate mobility "teleporter"; and her private-school, English-speaking upbringing— classic signposts of the urban, upper-caste family—were crucial in schooling her about what was "cool" and a "cultural fit."

Globalization and its effect on institutions has been viewed mainly as an economic or political project. The case of emerging Indian law firms, however, suggests that it is also a social and cultural project, often maneuvered by invisible scripts and cues that have implications for how these environments are navigated. Institutionalization of global norms is not usually observed at this level because data like these are often unavailable—a micro-perspective gives us fresh insight and complicates our understanding of the mimetic isomorphism of global firms. By focusing on activity and meaning-making processes across different organizational sites, this research draws from micro- and meso-level data that institutional scholarship acknowledges as critical (Powell and DiMaggio 1991:16) but rarely employs in its macro-level inquiry. Doing so gives us unique empirical access to observe how potent concepts like legitimacy and decoupling actually play out in these international organizations. Additionally, by investigating at this micro-level with a multi-site case study, this research not only joins a growing effort to observe institutionalism playing out in organizations (see Thornton 2004; Hallett 2010; Greenwood et al. 2017 for review), it adds rigor to this reorientation by situating it in a comparative case-study context.[4]

This chapter outlines the macro market reforms that framed the context within which personal career trajectories like Neela's took shape, highlighting the exceptional case—and incidental factors—that framed the emergence of India's corporate legal elite. I begin by describing the exceptional mobility of these particular global professionals, highlighting the ways that their case differs from the kinds of mobility and praxis widely associated with other Indian professionals, both historically and in the present day. Then I use the variations between the different kinds of global work in India to describe how the novel forms of institutional emergence within the legal profession were especially crucial in establishing the unique—and accidental—circumstances that allowed for the emergence of these women lawyers in elite transactional firms.

Leisure, Membership, and Agency: Praxis of Elite Professionals

Nita was a partner at an elite law firm in Mumbai. Sipping herbal iced tea in one of Mumbai's "Midtown"[5] bistros, she was relatively blasé as she told me about her marital status: "If I find a guy and it works out, great—but I am not looking. I don't know if I want to be married or have kids—and without it, I know I am not unhappy. Doing something for the sake of doing it makes no sense." Nita was one of several women in their mid-thirties I interviewed for whom marriage and children were not a foregone conclusion. She had just bought her first apartment in Mumbai, minutes from where her parents lived, so she lived "near but not *with*" her family. Her commute downtown in her chauffeur-driven car (that she had bought with her own money a few years ago and was looking to upgrade) was, following new construction in Mumbai, only one new super-fast expressway drive away but comfortable enough so she could take calls on her commute. She described her family as "middle-class and traditional in many ways" but also said that they understood that she was happy and didn't push her to do the "traditional marriage thing." When we finally managed to meet for lunch after weeks of trying to schedule it, she apologized for her crowded calendar. In fact, she said, she was leaving that night for a vacation with her girlfriends (all of whom were her age and two of whom were also unmarried), heading to Barcelona for the long bank-holiday weekend when work was, as she described it, "light." When I asked her if there was a special reason for the trip, her explanation revealed that the trip itself was the event: as she put it, "What is the point of all this if you don't travel?" For Nita, "all this"—her long hours at work and the stress involved in her job—made her feel she deserved time away for leisure.

This book is not original in suggesting we focus on leisure and consumption as a way of understanding the ways class and caste are "done" (Veblen 1899; Deshpande 2003; Currid-Halkett 2016). Yet, Nita's choices demand particular attention beyond the classic social consumption patterns that determine category constituencies of elite, non-elite, and middle class. Nita's class status was not just a matter of ownership and location—professionals and elites alike had iPhones and went to malls—or even just about using these things to intermingle with an imagined world community. What distinguished Nita's class access was that she did not automatically need to worry about how her life choices would be read in her actual, immediate communities or her community of origin. Vacationing in Barcelona with other professional women her age was exactly the sort of expenditure—and life choice—that stood sharply against the chaste relationship to consumption that forms a foundation for Indian middle-class legitimacy (e.g., Donner and Santos 2016; Kesavan 2016). Nita identified her family as "middle class," but her life was marked by kinds of praxis not available to the average middle-class woman in India.[6] Instead, in a single generation, Nita had ridden on her own mobility from a family with "traditional values" to a position from which she was able to disassociate herself from the pressures of her class morality. It is this transition that this book examines.

Nita's "bank-holiday" trip to Barcelona with her friends suggests another currency at the disposal of this new elite professional class—discretionary time. While accounts of their middle-class peers observed the ways in which women felt they owed explanations to their families and communities for how they used their time, many of the professional elites in my research did not feel that their schedules needed to be vetted by others, especially when it came to their personal leisure. Aditi, a young law firm partner in her early thirties who lived by herself in her Bandra apartment, explained the hard, but in her mind fair, way she balanced home and work:

I still manage on most days to [get to] sleep at 10 pm, get up at 6 am, play squash every day, have my breakfast and read my paper with my morning tea. I work solid hours, yes—but I have not had to compromise on anything.

Similarly, Aarushi, another senior partner—married and in her forties—who took her personal time seriously commented on how she worked around the long hours in the firm by waking up early and making the mornings her personal time. "No one gets here [to the firm] till about 10:30 or 11:00," she said, "and I am an early riser—so I just make the mornings mine. I play golf, I catch up with my friends, I get some *nariyal pani* [tender coconut water]—and then I am ready to start the day and put in all the long hours." For many of these women, personal time had to be carved out of the long hours that their professional lives demanded. But, unlike most traditional middle-class women, they seldom explained their use of time in the context of those they shared their lives with. At the same time, playing squash and golf as the balance for working long hours did not fit the traditional Indian model of upper-class leisure activities for women. Instead, respondents demonstrated the more hybrid cultural praxis that sets this class apart—one that overturns both old notions of leisure as well as the constructed demands of middle-class domesticity.

As members of this new elite professional class, these women were also part of a cosmopolitan clique. On a sultry Saturday in the summer of 2013, I met Kumar, an up-and-coming lawyer in his mid-thirties, in one of Mumbai's newer country clubs where he and his wife Ira—who worked in another, similarly prestigious firm—had just secured a membership. In the welcome air-conditioning of the club's "members only" coffee shop, they told me over cool fresh lime sodas and masala peanuts how they were the first in their respective families to have this sort of membership because these clubs, unlike the "old Bombay clubs," did not require existing family referrals. The conversation was rhythmically interrupted by their respective cell phones—a melody I'd come to expect in these interviews—but when they apologized for it, they explained that it was not work, but the weekend that they were planning for. Each of them had been traveling so much the past weeks that they had not had a chance for proper downtime with their friends in the city, so all the coordination was for a party at their house later that day—a "night of debauchery" as Kumar described it. In this conversation about leisure and socializing, in which it was obvious Kumar and Ira were both equal partners and purveyors, Kumar recalled how he was called out early in his career about gendered assumptions that unfairly excluded his female colleagues:

And I remember once all the guys got together and have a night out and we were drinking away. So a friend of mine, a female counsel, she calls me the next day and she says, "What is wrong with you guys? Why can't you call us and now make us a part of your network. So we drink with you, we party with you. And you start referring work to us." And I was stunned, hearing that. And I said okay, I should make it a point. It's not fair at all. We should make it more inclusive. Get over this stupid childish concept of "boys' night."

These were not men and women, then, who had conventional moral scruples about "smoking and drinking": two classic harbingers of universal modernity (and the doom of globalization) according to the Indian middle class (e.g., Nadeem 2009). In particular, these were not women who were averse to gender-blind socializing after work hours with their colleagues. In fact, there was a certain sense that being excluded from these spaces was offensive. Within these class coordinates, a new kind of professional elite was emerging—one that upended the typical balance between nation, morality, and modernity.

What made this transgression of middle-class norms possible was the promise of membership within a more cosmopolitan, nation-agnostic cohort of global professionals, a "fit" among like-minded community members that was conceived and valorized as early as when these professionals applied for these positions. Neela, a mid-tier consultant introduced earlier in this chapter, who was in her late twenties who worked for a global consulting firm, explained that it was exactly this "cultural fit" that had her excited to be part of this "cool" crew. She recalled the "Day Zero" placement event at her business school, and how the recruiting team from the consulting firm she eventually joined stood out against the vast number of other kinds of employers:

> If I think about all the events I attended, the reason consultants stand out is that, by nature of what they do, they are a lot more—do not know what the word is—*presentable*. They are incredibly smart people, they know how to talk about anything, they have a wide range of experience, and the best part of meeting them in a [recruitment] event is that it's not like an interview . . . they are there and they are like "Hey, we just want to speak to you as a person, we want to see if you fit culturally." . . . I had a great conversation with a partner about travel experiences. . . . We both spoke about disastrous flight experiences . . . and it was great. They do not seem as single-dimensional as others in industry.

Neela revealed that she had since realized that all this casual posturing by partners of "pulling up their sleeves" or saying "what's up?" or "let's just talk" was just standard strategy to seem "cool" to students. At the same time, she admitted that the personal connection forged by this familiarity had been paramount in her decision to join this firm, and that that informal spirit continued to convince her that the firm was the right "fit" for her.

Professional spaces have undergone a sea change since 1991, but this transformation has been largely limited to enlarging and stabilizing the middle class (Fernandes and Heller 2006; Radhakrishnan 2009; Fuller and Narasim-han 2010; Patel 2010; Nadeem 2013; Vijayakumar 2013). In contrast, the kinds of pathways and praxes employed by people like Nita, Neela, or Kumar were not about entering or maintaining middle-class positions, but instead about inhabiting new elite class spaces that were nonetheless familiar. And although their elite class status afforded them access to vacations in Europe and country club memberships, that status was not a function of their financial indepen-dence alone. Origins mattered in dictating what "cultural fits" people were attracted to, but their understanding of that "fit" did not necessarily pertain to how much wealth someone came from. Neela's conversation with the partner that recruited her about "disastrous flight experiences" speaks of a particularly nuanced—and novel—neoliberal understanding of class. Many of my respon-dents drew attention to the significance of what they saw as their own merit as a key to success and were keen to differentiate themselves from those that were born into "rich" families or, worse, those whose professional access was determined by their parents' class or connections. Neither Neela nor the part-ner who recruited her came from upper-class families, but in graduating from the schools they did at the time they did, they were creating an interactional cohort of elites that had similar experiences and the language to speak about them in "cool" ways. And this was a recognizable class in itself; as one lawyer explained it, "most of the people who come here would never be mistaken for anything but a lawyer because we come from a certain strata of society."

Yet, although this class-sanctioned homophily was likely to make young female consultants like Neela feel more at ease in their firms, it didn't ensure that they were treated on a par with their male peers when it came to exter-nal interactions. As I detail in chapter 4, when it came to important external audiences such as clients, women like Neela went back to being caricatures of their obvious identities—young women who had gone to elite graduate schools but who still, at the heart of it, reminded older men of their granddaughters. They were women who were treated well but weren't always trusted to handle a transaction on their own. Class advantages could help them get through the door, but once in, other kinds of recurring patriarchal scripts kept them bound.

Most women in elite law firms, however, were differently placed with regard to the middle-class morality paradigm (with regard to respectable femininity and morality in the case of professional workers). As the story of Kumar's col-leagues shows, women lawyers in elite firms saw socializing with clients as a strategy for advancement. And (as we will see in chapter 4), their reasons for not engaging with it (or their frustration with it) were much more about not having the time or inclination than about concerns of moral stigma. These exas-perations resemble those given by professional elites, say, in the US, but it is a framework that subverts our assumptions of the kinds of gendered negotiations Indian women might make. Instead, these comparisons suggest that it is not just Indian exceptionalism—i.e., the often underlying justification employed (as discussed in chapter 4) that "in India it is hard to be a woman"—that explains the nexus between globalization and work for some women. In part, these particular constructions of morality have to do with the fact that modernity as constructed within the context of elite professional work makes morality a function of class, not gender. At least some of the story is simply that these are women who make a great deal of money, who are not living with and/ or dependent on their parents, are not subject to the same kind of scrutiny around their moral choices as they might have been if they did. Freed from family and social expectations, they are capable of transcending the kind of morality crutches that would have otherwise trapped them (especially in terms of who they marry, how early they marry, when they come home, etc.). Part of this freedom is also attributed to the fact that they were doing "good work" or important work that was globally visible as prestigious (i.e., they worked in "big law") and locally coded as important (i.e., many of these lawyers would talk about the ways in which their deals made the headlines, and how that always was a source of excitement for them and their parents/friends in terms of what they were doing and how relevant it was).

But again, this is not a streamlined or linear class argument of the kind we might expect. Those who enjoyed this type of expansion of the morality construct were both richer than and financially independent from (or even financially responsible for) their middle-class parents. They necessarily came from a middle-class context in which the new inflow of their salaries often put them in a new class bracket that was beyond that of their parents *and* transformed these young professional into their parents' safety net or support system. The result was a subverted familial hierarchy where the kinds of gendered performance that adult children might be called to perform elsewhere changed in ways that allowed those children to have more negotiating power with their families. So whereas a rich woman, despite her wealth access, might still be constrained by models of morality that keep her dependent on—and subject to scrutiny by—her parents, these middle-class women had greater access to mobility and to independence as a function of their specific mobility.

At the same time, highlighting this modernity and morality frame allows for a clearer appraisal of the ways in which work necessarily offers distinctly different experiences for different actors.[7] Cultural capital, as I offer over the course of this book, is always important and never goes away. But the same class or fit advantage that allows women in elite law firms to navigate modernity and morality (e.g., by asking explicitly to be included in a happy hour hangout with male colleagues) does not extend to women within more traditional fields because of the structure of work. Women who were in more traditional kinds of firms and legal practice were, as I show in the next chapter, differently situated because of the ways in which litigation involved a more traditional client base and operational construct of what women could do. This preexisting framework of an ideal worker implicated new kinds of barriers.

As a result, even though networking was as important in litigation as in elite firms (indeed, arguably more so, as solo or small firm litigators did not have the organizational structure of a large law firm to provide clients on retainer, especially at initial stages of their careers), women in litigation who were seen as being *too* modern could have their opportunities backfire or require them to constantly code shift depending on context. As we will see over and over again, these interplays between morality and modernity remained deeply site-specific, reinforcing the importance of comparative sites and contexts in research such as this.

India's Market Liberalization and the Varyingly "Global" Nature of Work

Laying out the foundations of research on the sociology of professions, Macdonald (1995) explains how the professions are fertile ground for investigating the sociological heartlands of culture, monopoly, closure, and stratification. While Macdonald's "professional project" was fundamentally interested in Western economies and hierarchy, over the last three decades sociologists have applied his theoretical premise to more global patterns of occupational and organizational change (Cooper and Robson 2006; Faulconbridge and Muzio 2012). The impetus for this is obvious: with the expansion of international business over the last three decades, new kinds of organizational forms, processes, and phenomena have emerged as necessary solutions to sustain and supplement different models of global production. And as a response to the demand for efficient and territory-agnostic services, we have seen a rise in complex "transnational" (Bartlett and Ghoshal 1989) or "globally integrated" (Palmisano 2006) organizations across the world that purport to blur the boundaries between the local and the global (Prahalad and Doz 1999).

For emerging economies like India, the novelty of this organizational emergence has been doubly pertinent. First, research focusing on the subcontinent's new identity as a service provider has been quick to highlight the ways in which these new businesses and organizations have influenced India's economic and political contexts (Evans 1995; Dossani 2008). Second, these new kinds of global organizations and workspaces have allowed Indian professional workforces to be employed in unprecedented ways both in terms of structure and culture. Research on Indian elite professional workforces reveals that these new global organizations have been pivotal in creating new cultures of professionalism (Khadria 2001; Mirchandani 2004; D'Mello and Sahay 2007) and are seen as avenues to new forms of legitimacy and social capital (Mirchandani 2004; Ballakrishnen 2011; Radhakrishnan 2011; Nadeem 2013). Thus, together, these organizations have helped create and sustain new professional spaces and, with them, new kinds of professionals. Yet, this emergence has not historically been good for women's outcomes in the labor market, and demographic research suggests that women—despite having equal or higher educational outcomes[8]—continue to enter the labor force in significantly lower proportions than men.[9] In fact, over time, market liberalization, has, at the aggregate, resulted in worse outcomes for Indian women's labor force participation overall,[10] bringing to bear the uniqueness of the professional sites at the center of this book's analysis.

At the same time, given India's market liberalization, there has been a natural variance in the structural conditions that set up these different professions. And, as this book lays out, these different conditions have offered different kinds of embedded realities for their inhabitants. By the end of the twentieth century, the professional landscape for law in India had begun to change dramatically following a range of financial reforms in 1991 that opened the markets to foreign investment. As I start to argue in the previous chapter, these reforms shifted the government's economic policy to include a greater investment in the private sector as well as a more codified pathway for foreign direct investment. Still, not all industries were exposed to foreign intervention and attention the same way, and this staggered liberalization set in place different emergence trajectories for different sectors and professionals alike.

The 1991 reforms, for example, conceived brand new professional spaces that had never before existed, like Information Technology (which has received a lot of attention in popular and scholarly press alike) and, to a more peripheral extent, professional service firms like management consulting (which has received relatively little attention). But even in sites where globalization did not result in a complete overhaul of preexisting professional norms—like the legal profession—the reforms introduced novelty and organizational change to existing professional spaces. As a result, in professions like law, the reforms propagated new actors and clients that demanded professionals who could cater to new kinds of transactional work such as international mergers and acquisitions and global public offerings.

But these professional spaces were also varied in another significant way: their manner of relating to their global counterparts. While consulting and IT followed a traditional multinational corporation (MNC) model, in which control and ownership often rest with a global organization, organization in law has been less in touch with Western organizational scripts. As I elaborate in chapter 4, this organizational variation was crucial to the creation of unexpectedly gender-equal outcomes in these new law firms. Independent of those outcomes, however, the variation in kinds of work was central to the frameworks of these professions—and, therefore, the professionals in them. For instance, there is no doubt globalization changed the types of work that came under the purview of lawyers. But while new organizational entrants joined India's professional legal system, a strong domestic political movement resisted the entry of global lawyers and practice firms. Law remained, as I elaborate below, internally regulated and outside the professional purview of international firms—adding yet another layer of specificity to this emergence story. Thus, while globalization of markets produced neoliberal sectors like IT that were intrinsically dependent on international value chains and organizations, sectors like law continued to be deeply nationally regulated, leaving foreign firms as distant frameworks of inspiration.

Management Consulting—Globally Organized Local Work

Although human resource consultants and company managers existed prior to liberalization reforms in 1991, it was only following liberalization that global management consulting firms brought their practices to India. And to the extent we limit our analysis to novelty alone, the emergence of this professional field was not all that different from IT. But unlike IT, which took the service industry by storm and reshaped the public consciousness of "international work," the professionalization of India's management consultants happened on a considerably different scale. For instance, despite having been introduced to the Indian market at around the same time, consulting is, at best, a US$1-1.5 billion market as compared to the estimated upward totals of US$48 billion domestic revenues market that is the IT service industry.[11] Similarly, while IT employs somewhere in the orbit of three million workers, most management consulting firms have 50-400 client-facing consultants depending on the firm and office location—thereby working at an entirely different order of magnitude when it comes to operation and infiltration.

But despite these differences, both these sectors professionalized under the influence of globalization, albeit through different mechanisms. Like the IT sector, management consulting firms are privately owned and managed with predominantly bureaucratic scripts focusing on industry best practices and attention to global comparisons. But the triggers for these formations are slightly different—while IT companies were organizing their professional spaces in response to global clients, practices, and ideology (Radhakrishnan 2011; Aaftaab 2012; Nadeem 2013), consulting firms have had more limited (yet more direct) access to these global scripts as Indian offices of foreign firms. As firms set up by global entities interested in exploring Indian markets, these firms may encounter local resistance to organizational standardization, but they predominantly operate in standard multinational corporate fashion, following structural cues from their original global blueprints. In contrast, IT professionals are situated in new (and often domestic) organizations set up to respond to foreign clients, workflows, and practices. Finally, these sectors attract and retain a very different type of professional worker. The scale of IT operations in India allows for a range of professionals to be recruited—thereby widening the opportunity window for more and more Indians to partake in the mobility project. In contrast, the smaller management consulting sector maintains a more restrictive recruitment process that limits itself to elite graduates from the country's top business and engineering schools.

Management consulting firms are, however, important sites for understanding the ways in which professional identities and margins have been shaped by globalization in emerging economies. In particular, even though they comprise only a small portion of the population, these elite professional sectors play a crucial role in shaping India's new professional elite class. Nowhere is this more obvious than in the comparison of median professional salaries in these two sectors. While the median starting salary for a systems engineer in Mumbai, India is INR 546,302 annually (about US$9,000 per year), starting consultant salaries are almost four times that, at INR 2 million (about US$32,552 per year) *and* include a performance-based variable bonus of up to INR 600,000 (about US$9,766). By offering entry-level salaries that were unthinkable for senior partners even a few decades ago, these new firms offer a new (if very small) cohort of young Indians a chance at speedy mobility that is not feasible in the much larger IT sector. Thus, these outposts of global professional service firms advance dramatically higher rewards to a very limited pool of talented, upwardly mobile Indian graduates.

India's Legal Profession: Accidental Counter-Emergence of Elite Law Schools and New Kinds of Elite Law Firms

To the extent we think of professional transformation as an outcome of "specific historical, political or professional conditions" (Cotterell 1998:177), India's liberalization reforms were a critical market impetus for the reshaping of its legal professional order. While India boasts having one of the largest legal professions in the world,[12] its professional landscape was materially altered, at least in some marked ways, with market liberalization in 1991. In particular, the dramatic expansion of international trade and transactions required new laws and regulations and, consequently, lawyers to implement them (Flood 2017; Wilkins et al. 2017). Over the last three decades, India began to see the burgeoning of both new kinds of legal practice (e.g., cross-border mergers and acquisitions) (Varottil 2017) and new kinds of lawyers who could perform such transactions (Krishnan 2010; Papa and Wilkins 2011; Gingerich and Robinson 2017).

These reforms were accompanied by the emergence of two coincidentally allied institutional innovations within the profession: legal organizations that emerged in direct response to them, and a new brand of elite law schools whose emergence synergistically—and without direct intention—coincided with these liberalization processes. In turn, the path dependency that ensued between these schools and firms was crucial to this cultural production of a specific kind of legal professional as well as to the specific gendering of women lawyers in elite transactional firms. I will later detail the ways in which this socialization was crucial for making the ideal lawyer legitimate as an actor across a range of settings and interactions, but here I offer an emergence history that outlines how these interrelated mechanisms were set in motion.

NEW DOMESTIC CREDENTIALING FOR AN OLD PROFESSION: NATIONAL LAW SCHOOLS

Although there is deep stratification within the legal profession, the bar to entry remains relatively low. Lawyers are governed by the Advocate Act, 1961, which stipulates that lawyers must have a law degree, be at least twenty-one years old, and pay a stamp duty and a modest fee to enroll in a bar council. Admission to one bar allows lawyers to practice in every court. An estimated 50,000–80,000 students graduate annually from over 900 law schools, but efforts of the Bar Council of India (BCI) to require a national qualifying examination have generated controversy and legal challenges (Venkatesan 2011).[13] A national qualifying exam is urgently needed, given India's long-standing problem with "phantom lawyers" (not all lawyers on the record are in fact verified or even qualified to practice law) who have distorted any accurate or predictable portrait of the profession.[14] Further complicating these demographics are the highly localized and specific natures of legal practice in different parts of the country, where lawyers in Uttar Pradesh (with the most lawyers) or Punjab and Haryana and Delhi (with high lawyer densities) are fundamentally different from those in states like Jharkhand or Jammu and Kashmir (which have small but faster-growing legal professions).[15]

Amidst this hyper-variation in the general legal profession, the emergence of the National Law Schools gains significance. Save for a few "islands of excellence,"[16] the state of Indian legal education continues to be not that different from the "indifferent to deplorable" condition Gandhi described in the 1980s (1989:375). A law degree is still considered easy to obtain, especially since many talented students choose other subjects (Dhru 2010). Nonetheless, as in other countries, a law degree in India confers status, regardless of whether the holder practices (Rosalio 1970), and this is especially important for those seeking political office (Arora 1972). But the benefits may be diminishing. For example, while fifteen members of Narendra Modi's forty-four-member cabinet hold law degrees (the most common professional degree), only 7 percent of current Lok Sabha members are lawyers (compared with 36 percent of the first Lok Sabha in 1952 and 31.8 and 29.1 percent respectively of the Seventh and Eighth Lok Sabhas).[17]

The country remains glutted with law schools—1,390 of them as of 2013 (Gingerich and Robinson 2017)—only a small fraction of which are "elite."

Yet these elite schools (and their several hundred annual graduates), while not representative of the country's estimated 60,000 annual graduates, offer insight into an institutional shift that is reshaping the Indian legal profession. Historical accounts of legal education in India (e.g., Krishnan 2004; Gupta 2006; Ballakrishnen 2009; Menon 2009) agree that the National Law Schools were created in the late 1980s in response to the need for a "model" law school—a "Harvard of the East"—which could provide quality legal education (Menon 2009:40). India had similar specialized schools in engineering (Indian Institutes of Technology) and business (Indian Institutes of Management), which were highly selective and seen as globally competitive. The goal was to create an equally rigorous and competitive domestic law school, or National Law University (NLU). The first such school—National Law School of India University (NLSIU)—was established in Bangalore in 1986 after years of deliberation (Mathur 2017), with tangible and symbolic investments from the BCI, the judiciary, local government, and external actors like the Ford Foundation (Krishnan 2004). Madhava Menon, widely regarded as the godfather of this innovation, was committed to creating an institutional model distinct from traditional Indian law schools. Still, Menon was never alone in the process—while he certainly deserves all credit for realizing the vision, momentum had already been generated by Upendra Baxi (a prominent jurist enlisted by the BCI for this task) and Justice Mohammad Hidayatullah (Mathur 2017). Baxi, in fact, described himself as having been "heavily pregnant for 13 years," only to "allow a caesarian surgery, after all, by Madhava Menon" (Baxi 2007:19 n.39).

Paternity battles surrounding genesis aside, following the recommendation of the Ahmadi Committee at the Chief Justices' Conference in 1993, a consortium of government and judicial stakeholders established four more schools based on the NLSIU model within the decade: in Hyderabad (National Academy of Legal Studies and Research, or NALSAR), Bhopal (National Law Institute University, or NLIU), Kolkata (National University of Juridical Sciences, or NUJS), and Jodhpur (National Law University Jodhpur, or NLUJ). In 2017, there were seventeen schools based on the model, with more planned in each state. The quality and reputation of these schools vary, but based on independent law school rankings (e.g., India Today, IMS India), student preferences (Gingerich and Robinson 2017), and employer mentions (Gingerich, Khanna, and Singh 2017), NLSIU and NALSAR occupy the highest tier (often joined by NUJS; see Ganz 2010). These schools provide five-year multi-disciplinary undergraduate programs rather than the traditional three-year graduate program. Entry to these top-tier schools is awarded through a highly competitive exam (no similar barriers exist for other law schools). And students are evaluated on a range of criteria, including research papers, class participation, and internships (whereas rote memorization and lectures are the norm in traditional law colleges). In addition, there are elite private law schools like the

Jindal Global Law School, which use a modified LSAT for admissions and have international institutional collaborators and a young, globally trained faculty. In contrast, older "legacy schools" (e.g., Delhi Law Faculty) pride themselves on their low cost (about US$100 a year compared to about US$2,000 at the national law schools and about US$8,500 at Jindal Global Law School) and commitment to the litigating bar (Gingerich and Robinson 2017:534).

There have been other changes in access to international legal education. Foreign legal training, especially in England, was a status symbol for India's old legal elite, but some of their successors have preferred US LL.M. programs (Ballakrishnen 2011). Although students agree that the latter enhance their professional toolkit and offer "exposure and multicultural diversity" (Ganz 2012), the impact on the profession has varied (Ballakrishnen 2011). While those seeking an LL.M. degree are increasingly strategic about preparing for successful admission into these programs (e.g., by investing in judicial clerkships, Chandrachud 2014), the degree's value on the domestic and international job markets remains uncertain (Legally India 2012).

Pedagogic innovations were crucial in shaping these new law schools (Schukoske 2009; Gingerich and Robinson 2017) whose success was ensured by their competitive entry requirements. While exams previously were administered by individual schools, all national law schools now use the Common Law Admission Test (CLAT). In 2017, about 45,000 students took this test (compared to about 11,000 in 2008, when it was first administered). These numbers are significant because each school admits only 80–120 students annually. Entry barriers at elite schools have also engendered other new institutional actors: prep schools like the Law School Tutorials (started by three NLSIU alumni) prepare students for the increasingly competitive entrance exams;[18] and online platforms like MyLaw.net (again, spearheaded by an NLSIU alumnus) seek to democratize legal education through online course videos and learning apps.[19] Elite schools' selective recruitment has aided graduates in signaling their competitiveness in the emerging corporate legal market (Gingerich et al. 2017; Nanda et al. 2017). Although these schools did not initially intend to be feeders for new elite law firms (Gingerich and Robinson 2017:528), a majority of their graduates populate organizations that did not exist three decades ago: global-style corporate law firms, legal departments of large multinational corporations, banks, and legal process outsourcing firms.

Some of this symbiosis reflects disenchantment with the possibilities available in litigation. Only 12 percent of senior lawyers and judges believed that "bright youngsters" with law degrees were becoming litigators; a mere 6.5 percent of students wanted to practice in the Supreme Court, and just 4.92 percent in the High Courts (Dhru 2010). Instead they gravitated toward new organizations that did not rely on the informal networks (Galanter and Robinson 2014) and industry "godfathers" (Dhru 2010) that characterized litigation recruitment. These new organizations spoke the language of meritocracy, which students from elite schools found appealing. As Gingerich and colleagues (2017) have shown, the structure of the new recruitment system—a formal recruitment committee, faculty advisers, official recruitment days—dovetailed well with that of the law firms. The difference between these schools and the failing traditional system persuaded their students that the market would perceive and reward their value accurately. What students could not demand from a stable, entrenched litigation system, they had a better chance of finding within these new firms, which were sensitive to global ideals of meritocracy. For those unwilling or unable to strive for the brass rings of litigation victories, or uninterested in doing so, emerging firms offered financially rewarding careers and a sense of being valued.

Furthermore, these schools have not passively accepted a symbiotic relationship with the emerging market. Many current commentators point to the decline in political commitment among lawyers, given the profession's history. It is true that Indian lawyers played significant political roles, both during and after the independence struggle and in social movements of the 1970s and 1980s. But, though lawyers' engagement might seem less obvious now, it would be misleading to call them apolitical. A new intellectual and political legal elite—largely trained in the national law schools—has played crucial roles in setting up law-related NGOs (e.g., the Alternative Law Forum, the Centre for Law and Policy Research, the Centre for Social Justice, the Indian Institute of Paralegal Studies) and legal education initiatives (e.g., the Increasing Diversity by Increasing Access "*IDIA*" project by Shamnad Basheer, online legal training and strategy think tanks like Rainmaker, MyLaw.net, and, more recently, Agami). Legal scholars trained in these schools are also active in research think tanks focused on the intersections between law and public policy. Legal activists have similarly been key players in and commentators on sociolegal political movements concerning sexual harassment, queer rights, the death penalty, pro bono legal services, Internet governance, and intellectual property. Still others are part of a new wave of legal academics in India (Ballakrishnen and Samuel 2018) and abroad (Sharafi 2015). Yet, despite this small and growing cohort of intellectual legal elite who are graduates from these schools, these schools have mostly jettisoned the original ideal of the "moral law school" (Dezalay and Garth 2010:235). Rather than adhering to the original blueprint of producing primarily liberal and socially relevant lawyers (Krishnan 2004; Ballakrishnen 2009; Menon 2009),[20] these schools have instead evolved to include an institutional apparatus that makes their students attractive to India's simultaneously emerging elite corporate law sector. Recent research on law school innovation and pedagogy confirms that this is not incidental: law schools are making committed choices to introduce curriculum changes, elective choices, and extracurricular activities that might help students access law firm careers (Gingerich and Robinson 2017). These organizational decisions have reinforced students' own preferences for "secure placement in a corporate desk job." Altogether, this represents the biggest structural change within the post-liberalization legal profession: the rise of a corporate legal elite whose members are chosen not by ascription but on the basis of achievement and merit—a distinction that, as I show in the following chapters, was central to making these particular law students feel "at home" in the new law firms that employed them.

INDIA'S BIG LAW:
LOCALLY ORGANIZED GLOBAL WORK

In addition to new kinds of lawyers being produced in new law schools, new legal organizations also emerged as India took part in the global political economy following the 1991 market reforms. Although not entirely "new" in actual terms, Indian corporate law firms arrived on the scene in conjunction with what has generally been accepted as a marked market shift in India's professional space from national to "global" (Papa and Wilkins 2011; Wilkins et al. 2017). Specifically, before 1991, private investment in domestic industries was not allowed and trade was heavily regulated. This meant that domestic lawyers were involved mainly in domestic transactions. However, with liberalization, domestic law firms had to reinvent themselves to deal with a range of international cross-border transactional work (e.g., mergers and acquisition, private equity, and international finance transactions). While lawyers with successful pre-liberalization practices started many of these firms, it was only post-1991 that the organization of elite law firm practice began to mimic the institutional prototype of the Anglo-American corporate mega-law firm (Galanter and Rekhi 1996; Krishnan 2013; Gupta et al. 2017). The context in which these firms emerged was important for a number of reasons, including the fact that it put them in a uniquely vulnerable position, vis-à-vis their peers within the profession as well as with their global audiences (see chapters 3 and 4).

But this innovation in organizational forms was not the only way in which post-liberalization legal markets were special. The increased foreign direct investment and transactional work for lawyers (Nanda et al. 2017; Varottil 2017; Wilkins and Fong 2017) co-existed with a protectionist legal profession prohibiting the entry of foreign lawyers and law firms. The Advocates Act 1961 §§ 24, 37 restricts the practice of law to Indian citizens and practitioners from countries offering reciprocity.[21] And while the BCI has allowed a few individual foreign lawyers (all of Indian origin) from recognized universities[22] to practice in Indian courts,[23] foreign law firms are still excluded. The meaning of "practice of law" in the Advocates Act 1961 has been hotly debated since the first foreign law firms attempted to establish liaison offices in India in the early 1990s (Singh 2017:371). The Bombay High Court ruled in *Lawyers Collective v. Bar Council of India Chadbourne, Ashurst, White & Case, and Others* (2009) that the "practice of law" is limited to Indian citizens. But in 2012 the

Madras High Court held that nothing in the Advocates Act prohibited foreign lawyers from visiting India on a "fly-in/fly-out" basis or subcontracting legal work to outsourcing firms. In March 2018, the Supreme Court ruled that foreign lawyers could visit on a "casual basis" and advise on foreign laws and international commercial arbitration, so long as such visiting and advising was within the rules of the BCI.

These decisions confirm a well-established practice. Many foreign law firms have dedicated India desks either in London or elsewhere in Asia, usually Singapore or Hong Kong (Singh 2017:384). At various times starting from the early 2000s, Clifford Chance, Linklaters, and Allen & Overy have had "best friend" agreements with Indian law firms (AZB & Partners, Talwar Thakore & Associates, and Trilegal, respectively). Similarly, Indian legal process outsourcing firms (LPOs), which do everything from document support and back office work to drafting and negotiating contacts for global firms and corporations, have not been found to have contravened the "unauthorized practice" restrictions of either the United States or India.[24] (India does not have an institutionalized paralegal system.) Data on the LPO industry is hard to collect, but it appears that they often employ non-lawyers, technically, their work does not constitute the "unauthorized practice of law" (Khanna 2017). Thus, although the broad provisions of the Advocates Act prohibit entry, India continues to offer a range of hybrid professional spaces that circumvent this blanket barrier.

Yet, as Krishnan argues (2009:4), the situation is neither unambiguous nor easily explained by monolithic logics like "large firms want a monopoly" or "real lawyers don't care." Corporate law firms have fiercely guarded their monopoly against possible inroads of foreign firms, claiming they are underprepared for global competition while simultaneously preparing for and hedging against a future that might include these foreign firms (Singh 2017). Smaller law firms and litigators have been ideologically opposed to foreign firms for "nationalist" reasons (Krishnan 2010; Singh 2017). Competitive threats come not just from foreign firms that have found ways around regulatory barriers but also from a new generation of "peel off" law firms that have grown tired of restrictive practices (Krishnan 2013). By contrast, the "cream of the crop" litigators who should be unconcerned about the entry of foreign firms (which will still need them to appear in court) nevertheless have strong views about liberalization, which fluctuate with the political climate (Ganz 2015). Although the future of liberalization is uncertain, there is consensus that a further opening will yield healthier market conditions for many actors (Krishnan 2013; Galanter and Robinson 2014; Khanna 2017; Singh 2017). Furthermore, despite what may seem like a transformation, this layer of professionals in question is still only a small segment of the population: Krishnan (2013:25–31) suggests there are only two hundred corporate law firms in the country. And although commentary on legal blogs and websites remains focused on these elite law schools and firms, most Indian lawyers are still trained in local colleges and practice in environments shaped by communal networks. Thus, despite changes for a tiny sliver of the total, the bulk of the legal profession has remained relatively unaltered over the last thirty years. From this perspective, ascription continues to shape entry and success for most lawyers. Nevertheless, the new organizations emerging after liberalization in the early 1990s have valorized, and even demanded, entrants whose claims are based on merit. Together, this emergence certainly introduced new kinds of lawyers to new kinds of professional practice, and this new cohort of law graduates, and the parallel elite of commercial lawyers, feel empowered to assert themselves in a profession historically hostile to them. But in the process, this emergence has created a new kind of elite professional space and class that is distinctly different from the conditions it emerged from, causing an intra-professional stratification which is more complicated than just the mapping of a tale of linear mobility.

⟨⚊⚊⚊⟩W⟨⚊⚊⚊⟩

The most important change within the legal profession over the last thirty years has been the impact of globalization, which has created new kinds of workspaces and professionals. It has also had another, less predictable, consequences for the middle-class law graduate without contacts: a chance to renegotiate gender hierarchies. Yet this is hardly an uncomplicated success. While women partners in elite firms perceive less discrimination, their reference points are the experiences of other kinds of professionals, and indeed women litigators, who confront major obstacles and more blatantly hostile work environments.[25] And although they are not always traditionally elite (i.e., from "legal families"), successful women professionals also enjoy the intersectional advantage of other kinds of cosmopolitan cultural capital: their parents are often professionals themselves, and they are socialized in urban city schools and proficient in English. Simply put, these are women whose presence in the profession, while novel, does not threaten other entrenched inequalities of caste and class. Furthermore, this might be a short-lived advantage given the institutional youth of these organizations. In light of what we know about persistent gender inequality (Ridgeway 2011) and the fact that women in similar sites often qualify their understandings of success over time (Hunter 2002), the future of this advantage is uncertain.

At the same time, in many ways, not much has changed since early portraits of the Indian legal profession. And it is important to keep in mind that this book focuses on a very small, albeit important, slice of the larger profession. A majority of the country still practices law in ways that are unperturbed by globalization and its implications. Prestige and networks are still central: litigation, in particular, still depends on relationships with government, and many "grand advocates" are closely and publicly linked to political parties (Galanter and Robinson 2014).

Despite these qualifications, when juxtaposed against the nepotistic patterns of reproduction in the rest of the profession, elite law firms appear to offer young lawyers greater ease of entry and upward mobility. However, a handful of elite firms dominate most transactional work. And given their process of recruitment (i.e., mostly from elite law schools), these firms still breed an unequal—albeit novel—homophily. Different accounts confirm this meritocratic inequality. Data from IDIA (an organization committed to increasing diversity in law schools) reveal that most law schools are predominantly Hindu and forward-caste,[26] and recent empirical research on students in these law schools confirms long-standing suspicions that caste and socioeconomic status significantly influence success in these schools (Jain et al. 2016:150–153; Sharma et al. 2020). English remains the dominant language (Jain et al. 2016: 37). Few students come from rural areas like the northeast and Kashmir (Basheer et al. 2017:578), and these students' educational experiences are significantly different from those of the majority. Although there are not yet enough longitudinal data to confirm this, one could hypothesize that these variations affect careers. Even when networks are not directly useful to obtaining permanent jobs in new law firms, they can help students land the internships that can lead to jobs (Gingerich et al. 2017:558). As Basheer and his colleagues have argued (2017:578), the new national law schools have been good at teaching "lofty ideals of social justice and equality, but have a serious issue of manifest injustice in their face."

Altogether, despite the relative advantage of newness—a mechanism I explore in fuller detail in the following chapters—none of this analytical reasoning about novelty suggests that new firms *suo moto* got all the things right. Or even that this novelty was instantly correlated to being "modern." In offering novelty as a possible explanation, I am suggesting only that newness in regulation was one part of a larger set of moving puzzles, each of which was differently relevant and advantageous to different groups of students and professionals, at different points in time.

Newness, for example, did little to feminize legal academia in these elite law schools. As we show in other work studying gendered legal academics around the world (Ballakrishnen and Samuel 2020), Indian law schools continue to be male-dominated. Men are more likely than women to be academic deans and vice chancellors (the notable exceptions, interestingly, are in more traditional law schools rather than in new schools). Men are more likely to have tenure and be represented on academic councils. They are more likely to be cited and referenced in the classroom, and their scholarship is more likely to be referenced and cited and prescribed in pedagogy.[27] In contrast, feminist scholarship and scholarship by women must constantly face the double bind of both carving a niche for itself and simultaneously recalibrating that niche to have more breadth. And the few feminist scholars who have tried to make the spaces their own have had to deal with backlash.[28]

Such a characterization falls in line with earlier elaborations of these law school spaces as new but not necessarily progressive. For instance, almost twenty-five years ago, Ann Stewart critiqued Indian law school spaces, noting that "in India, feminism has yet to establish itself firmly within the legal academy" (Stewart 1995:254). This is not unlike a more recent recollection by Ratna Kapur about her time in NLSIU during its early years, when the law school, despite its overtly progressive agenda, "hardly had any feminist spaces" and only "some marginal engagement in a couple of courses in jurisprudence" (Sircar 2016:149). Of course, this was not just about pedagogy and culture. Despite enrolling an equal number of men and women through the years, the NLUs have been unable to match these gender-equal demographics within their faculty. Even after thirty years, NLSIU, the first of these NLUs, has only one (of seven) full-time faculty members who is a woman (and she is a professor of history rather than of law). The NLIU and the NUJS have no female full professors. Among the more junior faculty positions, the share of women is rising, although men continue to predominate, and very few women hold senior positions within these institutions (see Ballakrishnen and Samuel 2020 for the notable exceptions).

In spite of these caveats, however, novelty was an important factor in determining the gendered outcomes this book presents. And the alignment of these mechanisms that led to the outcomes I examine in subsequent chapters was not a matter of specific intention. Yet, even though the mechanisms leading to this co-dependent and symbiotic emergence were accidental, they set in motion new kinds of renegotiations—both in terms of the nature of work lawyers could do and the kinds of lawyers who could be socialized to do it. In the next chapter, I deal with the specificities of this socialization and the frameworks for gender and work that it helped mold.

TWO

FRAMES

Women Can't Match Up

THE STICKY ASSUMPTIONS OF
GENDER AND WORK

A PERSUASIVE THEORETICAL explanation for entrenched inequality is that most spheres of professional work have historical ideas about the kind of candidate most qualified to do a particular job (Acker 1990; Kanter 1993; Ridgeway and Correll 2004; Ridgeway 2011) and that these frameworks result in organizational cultures and biases that are hostile to new entrants like minorities and women (Sommerlad 2011, 2015; Pearce, Wald, and Ballakrishnen 2015; Rhode 2016). These cultural biases are particularly problematic because they often result in an unequal valuation of gender-typed traits in favor of men (England et al. 2002; Levanon, England, and Allison 2009; England 2010), where women are seen as non-ideal workers, especially in highly prestigious work contexts (Acker 1990; Epstein 1993; Kanter 1993; Pierce 1996; Williams 2001). Social psychologists, in particular, have argued that one such way in which gender is "done" is by the construction and attachment of a persistent *gender frame* (Ridgeway and Correll 2004) or a background identity that offers repetitive salience to gender across interactions by relying on "common" cultural scripts of gendered stereotypes. Ridgeway (2011) further extends this conceptualization of a background identity and an ideal worker to what she refers to as a "primary gender frame" for coordinating social relationships. By infusing gendered meanings into the structures and practices by which work interactions are organized, she argues that gender becomes an all-pervasive and inescapable frame of reference with embedded beliefs about status and difference. As a result, not only are all social interactions fraught with background identity and assumptions, but they are also feeder mechanisms into creating an inescapable construct of identity and difference which makes gender-based inequality persistent even in seemingly more egalitarian workplaces (Ridgeway 2011). This line of research argues that even within new kinds of organizations or "sites of innovation," there are pessimistic outcomes for gender because change in cultural beliefs about gender *lags* behind changes in material circumstances between men and women, and all new institutions are organized based on the existing gender-unequal blueprints of their predecessors. But not all sites of innovation are riddled with the same obstacles, and in particular sites of economic and social innovation, Ridgeway offers a theoretical exception. In other words, under some limited circumstances, these sites offer an opportunity for gender constructs to be renegotiated and problematic gender-unequal frames to be revised. When the organization is a site of innovation *and* the basic framework of the job is not particularly gender typed, she theorizes that the background gender frame is only diffusely relevant. This categorization of new sites of innovation is useful because it gives us some hope for breakthroughs in existing hierarchies.

In this chapter, I suggest that newly emergent law firms in India are one example of these innovative sites and that this reconstruction extends professional advantages to young Indian female lawyers who have traditionally been excluded from the rewards of the Indian legal profession. While not an active mechanism in itself, this framework of gender (or, as I will argue, the diffuse form of it) sets the base for this unlikely and unintended advantage that women in Indian law firms are positioned to access. In line with a substantial body of research on women in elite workplaces (e.g., Epstein 1993; Pierce 1996), women lawyers in established firms had to contend with a male "ideal type" and mostly came up short against this imagined ideal. For instance, unlike women in elite transactional firms, women in litigation consistently came up against a harsh double-bind: they were not aggressive enough to be effective lawyers or they were too aggressive for women. Further, they felt that they had to work "twice as hard" and "not get emotional" lest they get dismissed by their peers and clients for being "too girly." Women in traditional firms were also bereft of relatable role models at more senior levels. Rupa, an older, unmarried senior litigator in the Bombay High Court (one of the few) told me she was fortunate because she "did not face problems because of gender" and attributed it to her ability to communicate in English and to her late father's "good will in the profession." These inherited advantages of language and networks were not available to all and, when available, rarely transferable to lawyer daughters. And even for this well-connected lawyer, navigating an established male system was critical—in addition to the advantage of her connections, Rupa admitted that she still made sure to "never leave the court with anybody frowning." Even for the few successful women, then, the cost to "not feel gender" in their everyday lives was steep and often included a likeability paradox that was intrinsically feminized.

In contrast, connections were of little help to lawyers in elite corporate law firms and women were not called upon to be "just like men." In particular, this chapter reveals how a combination of three novel emergence conditions created a framework of novel re-stratification. First, because there was no "ideal type" of a global corporate lawyer, women were not wedded to preexisting frameworks of identity and propriety. As a result, unlike their peers in litigation, they were not constantly working against the assumption that they were "bad fits." This is not to argue that stereotypes or gendered assumptions about work did not affect women in newer firms—as I show in chapters 3 and 4, essentializing logics of what men and women were meant to do continued to plague women in newer law firms, but the diffuse understandings of the nature of the work advantaged women in these firms in ways that women in traditional professional practice with more set logics of the ideal worker could not access. Second, as organizations deeply committed to the ideology of global meritocracy, these firms recruited from National Law Schools that were—much like themselves—products of liberalization. These new, highly selective law schools, as I elaborate in the previous chapter, graduated equal numbers of men and women from their programs, and it was preposterous for these modern firms to demarcate these "meritorious" graduates based on gender. Finally, in addition to the structural novelty of these schools and firms, the relative newness of work (e.g., international banking, mergers and acquisition) created yet another novel space that allowed women to renegotiate existing gendered hierarchies. In tracing this difference between old and new firms of similar professional repute, this chapter offers empirical weight and extensions to the insight by gender theorists that novelty of new institutions could offer new advantages for women. And in doing so, it unpacks the first structural condition responsible for accidental feminism—the new gendered frameworks afforded by the simultaneous institutional emergence of new "modern" firms and schools that could supply them "meritocratic" professionals.

Persistent Background Frameworks of Gender

Researchers of organizational stratification have made a serious case for thinking of the repetitive salience extended to gender, across various levels of analysis, as a "background identity" (Ridgeway and Correll 2004) that creates both gender-unfriendly "ideal workers" and organizations (Acker 1990). But while presumptive gender stereotypes are omnipresent, not all sites are equally gendered. Ridgeway and Correll (2004), for example, argue that gendered background identities become particularly relevant in situations that prime gender—i.e., in sites where actors of different sex categories interact in contexts where their common goals are linked to preexisting gender stereotypes. This, naturally, is problematic in the workplace because not only is it a site where men and women interact constantly, but it is also where the "common knowledge" about what they are each good at is predetermined. Together, these prescriptive assumptions have been detrimental to women in the workplace because it leaves them stuck between frustrating double binds and multiple identities—for instance, women are both victim blamed for "not asking" for their share of career rewards (Babcock and Laschever 2003) and levied a steep "social cost" of negotiation when they do (Bowles, Babcock, and Lai 2007). And, in turn, by setting roles and assumptions about gender and work, they set in motion ways in which organizations get gendered (Acker 1990).

This conception of persisting gender frames offers a multilevel theory not only for current institutional arrangements but also for future institutions that emerge out of existing blueprints. Since the modern world demands constant reconstruction of social institutions that reflect the ongoing social, political, and economic changes in society, workplaces are constantly changing, to evolve themselves and to give way to new kinds of innovative work cultures. At the same time, because cultural beliefs are hard to change, changes in material outcomes are not always in sync with these framing beliefs. Thus, where people come together at sites of innovation that are tied to existing gendered cultural beliefs, the background frame of gender continues to operate in more traditional ways than the new circumstances and will activate itself in gender-conforming ways. Based on this buffering process, the most prescriptive elements of gender stereotypes (hierarchy and deference, for example) will be the last to change (and therefore, the most likely to be continually adopted, even in new sites of innovation). On the other hand, more individual perceptions about gendered traits may be easier to change—but either way, changes in gender beliefs will necessarily lag behind men's and women's material circumstances. As a result, even in *sites of innovation*, there remains a threat of persisting gender inequality because these new institutions are organized based on existing gender-unequal blueprints of their predecessors.

But not all sites of innovation are riddled with the same obstacles, and, in particular, Ridgeway's theory offers theoretical exception in sites of economic and social innovation. When the organization is a site of innovation *and* the basic framework of the job is not particularly gender typed, she theorizes that the background gender frame is only diffusely relevant. For example, she uses the example of research on life sciences startups (Smith-Doerr 2004; Whittington and Smith-Doerr 2005, 2008; Whittington 2007), which consistently show very positive gender outcomes in the workplace. Since these are new kinds of organizations (startups) *and* the substantive nature of their work (life sciences) is not strongly gender-typed, Ridgeway argues that these sites of innovation do not have a persistent blueprint that enforces strong gender stereotypes. In turn, they create only modest disadvantages for the women who are employed within them. On the other hand, more male-typed jobs (e.g., IT work), even in sites of innovation (e.g., in IT startups) are restricted by the constraints of the background gender frame they operate within because, even though the site (i.e., the startup) is technically a new form of work organization, the work done is deeply gendered. Thus, women employed in sites of innovation with a diffuse gender stereotype (*bio startups*) have relative advantages over both women in traditional workplaces (*IT companies*) as well as women in other sites of innovation where the gender frame is less diffuse (*IT startups*). In other words, under some limited circumstances, these sites offer an opportunity for gender constructs to be renegotiated and problematic gender-unequal frames to be revised. This potential for escape from the otherwise monotonous reconstruction of gendered hierarchies is imperative not only because it affects the particular institution but also for the broader implications for gender inequality it offers.

Together, this categorization of new sites of innovation is useful because it gives us some hope for breakthroughs in existing hierarchies. And nowhere is this possibility for renegotiation more useful than in global workspaces, which are brimming with innovation and organizational emergence. From Mountain View to Mumbai, there are new kinds of organizations and types of professional practice that didn't exist even a few decades ago. In some cases, it is innovation in types of work and practice, while in others it is the introduction of an entirely new kind of work. Although not empirically concerned with the effects of global capital and workflow, Ridgeway's constructs of evolution and change offer valuable tools to analyze these new changes in the global economy.

Gendered Pathways and Educational Socialization

The wealth of empirical research on women in high-status organizations reflects strong evidence for the theoretical positioning that background frameworks disadvantage new entrants. Studies on elite women professionals show that women are disadvantaged at entry (Gorman 2005), have less helpful career referents (Gibson and Lawrence 2010), form fewer meaningful networks (Ibarra 1997), have barriers to promotion (Dencker 2008), and are overall structurally set up against advancing within the firm (Kanter 1993; Williams et al. 2012). And, globally, the legal profession has been a prime site for the creation and reproduction of these gendered workspaces (Epstein 1993, 2000; Pierce 1996; Schultz and Shaw 2003; Kay and Gorman 2008). Particularly in large law firms, we know that women have encountered significant obstacles because of a range of institutional factors, including lack of formal structures of inclusion (Kay and Gorman 2012), limited mentorship (Mobley et al. 1994; Ramaswamy et al. 2010), stereotype-ridden professional ideology (Wald 2009), male-friendly partner composition (Chambliss and Uggen 2000), and a general preference for male law-firm capital (Kay and Hagan 1998). Research also shows that these factors have resulted in wage disparities (Hagan and Kay 1995; Dinovitzer, Reichman, and Sterling 2009), missed partnership opportunities (Walsh 2012), and a host of other kinds of inequalities (Sterling and Reichman 2012, 2016). Research has also begun to reveal ways in which women may adopt "coping strategies" for inclusion and validation (e.g., Hatmaker 2013), but the predominant narrative is of women responding to a biased system that is likely to reproduce unfavorable hierarchies (Sommerlad 1994, 2002; Davies 1996; Adams 2005; Witz 2013).

To explain these entry and advancement patterns, scholars have begun to pay special attention to the role of education and socialization in reproducing gender inequality, in particular, the importance of socialization[1] in acculturating a sense of identity "fit" between the individual and an organization (Cech et al. 2011; Hatmaker 2013; Cech 2015). For instance, while Cech and colleagues (2011) suggest that the relative lack of women's "professional role confidence" within the "culture of engineering" contributes to their attrition from the field, Seron and colleagues (2016) go further, stating that professional socialization has important implications for the cultivation of this confidence. It is a similar exposition of professional socialization advantages that this chapter seeks to present.

Global contexts offer new ways to reflect on the implications of these studies. For example, the growing research from sites outside the global north—especially in sites that are not typically thought of as "gender-friendly," like the Middle East (Zahidi 2018)—reveals how women are not "left out" of STEM pipelines in the same ways, calling for different kinds of measures to retain gendered talent.[2] In the Indian context too, gender differences exist in professional participation, but they are not always determined by the same kinds of supply-side factors as in the West (Mukhopadhyay 2004; Kumar 2012). Despite optimistic projections of the region's future and the possibilities for parity,[3] labor force participation rates for women have been in steady decline since liberalization[4] and relay high levels of inequality, even if there is some variation in kinds of participation and location of work.[5] Simultaneously, organizational inequalities persist and women, to the extent they enter the formal workforce,[6], continue to face stiff barriers to success and advancement (e.g., Vinze 1987; Nath 2000; Budhwar et al. 2005; Terjesen et al. 2009). For instance, recent data on the "future of work" (Chapman et al. 2018) reveals, in addition to India's low female labor participation (about 27 percent), a wide average gender wage gap (almost 40 percent) and a strong tendency of *not* choosing women to occupy positions that are seen as having the most growth within companies.[7] Further, as the last chapter reveals, the legal profession in particular has been generally hostile to feminization. As Michelson (2013) strikingly suggests, while most of the world's professions have feminized over the last half century, India still remains predominantly male, with only about 5 percent women in the legal profession (compared to an average of about 30 percent globally). Unsurprisingly, as the last chapter explains, this representation becomes even starker at senior positions. For instance, at the time of data collection, among the more than two hundred senior counsels in the Mumbai High Court, only one active senior counsel was a woman. In contrast, as this book unpacks, women in leading law firms have a very different experience. What is at the core of this difference?

Ridgeway's theory might suggest that this is a function of temporality—older organizations are more set in their ways than newer organizations and, consequently, more likely to be wary of new entrants. However, even among similarly new and elite professional firms, differences are stark. In particular, my research suggests that while women in new law firms experience work environments that are relatively gender-agnostic, women in consulting firms do not enjoy a similar privilege. Contrasting these two cases of novel field emergence against gendered accounts of the traditional litigation system in India (e.g., Sorabji 2010) that has stayed relatively unchanged following globalization (e.g., Mishra 2016; Rajkotia 2017), this chapter focuses on the relationship between institutional novelty and socialization to shed light on its implications for theorizing about professional stratification more generally.

These data reveal two kinds of significant comparisons within these professional spaces. The first is between older and newer kinds of professional practice. In line with the other evidence, older firms were more rigid in their expectation of an ideal worker, and the exclusion of women within these firms was legitimated by these constructs. Still, novelty alone was not sufficient explanation. The second set of comparisons—between different kinds of newer professional practice—revealed the importance of pre-entry socialization in dictating the nature of inclusion that newer firms offered. Together these findings have implications for extending other research on feminization that suggests that the gendering of organizations needs to be understood not just by blatant exclusion of women, but also by their kinds of specific inclusion (Davies 1996).

The Advantage of New Frames: Traditional Litigation versus New Kinds of Professional Work

High-status workplaces are organic environments for the application of this background framework of gender because they have historically been male-dominated (Charles and Grusky 2004). One reason this is problematic for new entrants such as women and minorities is that when the parameters of an ideal worker are already set, any and all deviations from this construct suffer a penalty (Acker 1990). Viewed from this perspective, the stark findings of gender disadvantage flow naturally. If the ideal worker is a man without family responsibilities (Williams 2000; Jacobs and Gerson 2004) then it follows that women who are seen as natural caretakers are levied a motherhood penalty (Correll et al. 2007; Blair-Loy 2009) and stigmatized for being "flexible" workers (Allen and Russell 1999; Epstein et al. 1999; Judiesch and Lyness 1999; Blair-Loy and Wharton 2002; Wayne and Cordeiro 2003; Albiston 2007; William et al. 2012; Padavic, Ely, and Reid 2019).

The roots of this gendered framework are starkly obvious in the legal profession worldwide but also particularly discernable from the historical context of the Indian legal profession.[8] Although demarcation of subclasses within the professions is a global phenomenon, the magnitude of stratification within the Indian legal profession is a more extreme representation of a "winner-takes-all" style process.[9] While a few successful lawyers have high prestige in the community and flourishing legal practices, most of India's (approximately) one million law graduates work for meager wages and variable prestige.

Historically, this stratification was a simple case of access to resources. With few domestic education institutions to train students, law in colonial India was reserved for the elites. But equally relevant was that elite legal education, especially since it involved the foreign education of unmarried daughters, was restricted to elite *men*. With independence in 1947, these male foreign-educated lawyers continued to take prime positions in government and polity, but the severance of colonial ties meant restricted access to foreign education for all. With British education no longer accessible even with resources, the country was forced to rely on a domestic legal education system that had no recourse to meet the demand. In turn, this substandard credentialing alternative helped put in place a strong intergenerational advantage transfer system. Since schools could not be trusted to train lawyers, practice-based training was the only alternative. And since the prominent lawyers at that point were already elite men from prominently networked families, only those who had access to them had access to the profession. This substandard education played another systemic role in strengthening this demarcation. With few quality institutions and a low entrance threshold (high acceptance rate, minimal tuition), law began to be perceived as a non-challenging career prospect. Branded as an "easy" choice, legal education continued to be a last resort for students who, upon graduation from high school, were unable to pursue more prestigious professional careers (engineering, medicine). Since supply (substandard educational institutions) and demand (unmotivated students) factors both devalued the merit of this legal credentialing, the only people who could control and access these professional rewards were those born into them.

With the professional rewards out of reach and the steep time commitment that conflicted with traditional life course choices (law in India was traditionally a graduate degree, which conflicted with what was considered an appropriate marriage age for women), few women went to law school and even fewer joined the profession following graduation (Gandhi 1987). And as we know from recent demographic data (Michelson 2013), this trend has not changed over the last three decades. While legal professions in other countries have become more feminized, India remains consistently male with a meager representation of women—less than 10 percent of all advocates admitted to the Bar are female.[10]

One extension of this segregation is that Indian litigation practice, like other accounts in the global legal profession (e.g., Pierce 1996), is a professional site where gender impacts everyday interactions and experiences through hegemonic practices, stereotypes, and unequal interactions. Mohan, a male litigator in his thirties who was in charge of a practice that, in his own words, could as easily have been his sister's, elaborates on this gendered distinction:

> The chances of a future life are at stake when you are a rude, abrasive lawyer and a woman—you are setting up a foundation, at least that is the perception, of how you are going to be judged. My sister had the same opportunities as me, and she would have been a much better lawyer than me, but she chose not to because of this perception— she didn't want to be judged . . . And clients have other perceptions too—women are unique because of this reputation that can be tainted. You think of women as people you want to keep safe and take care of—you don't want them mistreated, not overburdened and while you give them their respective dues and there is no inequality, it's still a perception.

The comment that female "rude, abrasive lawyers" are susceptible to judgment is interesting because Mohan mentions later in the interview that it is exactly these qualities of aggression that make male lawyers successful in courts. The differences in the pathways between Mohan and his sister highlight the importance of gendered frameworks in defining professional identities in litigation. Even as he attests that there is "no inequality" and women are treated well without being "mistreated or overburdened," Mohan's account suggests that such treatment does not guarantee professional rewards and that women are simultaneously likely to be judged harshly when they act in ways that might challenge that identity.

It is not surprising then that courthouses and litigation practice—where the majority of these lawyers are employed—were (and continue to be) strongly male-typed workplaces. And as a result of this strong sex segregation, traditional litigation practice in India was—and continues to be—a core site where gender is done. Historically, women, to the extent that they worked in these litigation offices, were secretaries or stenographers, and most of these traditional firms displayed (and continue to display) similar hegemonic practices, unequal interactions, and gender stereotypes as other ethnographers (Pierce 1996) of the legal profession have recorded. In a similar description of these gendered expectations, Priya, a young litigator, revealed that judges were prone to "testing boundaries" with women, often expecting them to have emotional reactions and evaluating their seriousness in the courtroom accordingly:

> most judges won't yell at a woman who is making these mistakes, you know? [Someone] who is being an idiot—they wont yell in the way they might have yelled [to teach] a man: they don't give any woman their time. They are always afraid that the girl is going to break into tears.

Similarly, a senior litigator—a successful older man who was a second-generation practitioner—once asked me when I was speaking to him about his practice why I was surprised about the lack of women in the profession. In his words, "They all come and join, but then they have to leave when they get married and it becomes difficult to be in Court. . . . Also, you have to shout and scream in the Courts, and why do they want that headache."

His comment was not telling of a unique position—many litigating lawyers referenced the ways in which legal work was essentialized by gender; especially in courts where this identity of work was closely tied to the ability to be assertive and loud. This line of explanation for the lack of senior women in the profession was evidence of two basic and persistent framework assumptions—one, that women were not on track to join professional practice because their traditional gender-typed roles of marriage and care-giving were to take priority. And two, that women were considered less likely to "shout and scream in the courts" and therefore were unlikely candidates for this line of work. In their book on strategies for what works for women at work, researchers Williams and Dempsey highlight the descriptive *"Prove It Again"* bias as an important obstacle against creating gender agnostic workplaces. They show how women, even when not blatantly discriminated against, are set up to meet different standards because they are constantly required to demonstrate their competence, even if they have proven to be on par with their male peers (Williams and Dempsey 2014). Seen together with the persistence of the background frame, this notion of "being on par" becomes even more problematic because it requires a standard for what is expected, an assumption about who is best assumed to meet it, and a constant appraisal of others who don't seem like natural fits.

Alongside demographics of the field more generally, these indicative accounts from Mohan and Priya confirm that in an established professional field like litigation, the assumptive standard of an ideal worker is better met by men (for example, men had the ability to "shout and scream in court") and women, even when they did meet it, were under constant appraisal and subject to backlash. As a result, Priya and other women like her had to navigate a professional environment where women who were seen as not being strong enough for the tasks at hand (e.g., "they are always afraid the girl is going to break into tears") and their careers as too futile for seniors to invest in (e.g., "they don't give any woman their time"). This exclusionary setup that elite professional practice creates for women is not novel in itself. But it establishes an important comparison point for appreciating newer workplaces without similar embedded expectations. In particular, if high-status work was necessarily riddled with gendered assumptions of the ideal worker, what was it about new and elite law firms that made them especially fertile for progressive gender outcomes? I deal with the exception new firms could employ to renegotiate these set preexisting hierarchies in the next part of this chapter.

Unlike fixed notions of what it meant to be a litigating lawyer, professionals in newer fields like transactional law and consulting felt differently restricted by this imagined notion of the ideal worker. In contrast to the gendered assumptions that plagued women in fields where ideas of work were more steeply set, women in large Indian law firms—and, indeed, the men who worked with them—felt that gender overall was "not an issue" and that it was not a main determinant of their career trajectory and success. Lata, a senior associate at an elite law firm, describes this comparative ambivalence while describing her identity and work experience:

> People don't think of it as an issue—I get the perspective would have been different if I had been a litigating lawyer. For example, when I was interning [in a litigating office], my senior was a woman and I know that judges looked at a case differently when a male lawyer was arguing instead of a female lawyer. So if I had been in litigation, it would have been different. But not here, not at all.

Similarly, newness of work and organization helped women professionals in new kinds of consulting firms as well. As new firms with new kinds of professionals, there was similar mobility regarding the constructed identity of a "good consultant," and although this identity was negotiated along other lines of difference, gender was not an immediately discriminating factor as it was in more traditional practice. Saraswati, a fourth-year management consultant, suggested that although there was not a "single senior consultant with a child and a client-facing role," her environment was "pretty egalitarian" and that there were "very few actual situations" where gender distinctions mattered in her work. In Saraswati's words, "per se, there is no difference in our ability to do the work or in consulting . . . the only difference, however, comes in getting to the higher levels."

Her account suggests that gender was still relevant to Saraswati's professional identity but, unlike for Priya, there were no defined differences in the "ability to do the work" because she was a woman. This contrast between Priya and Saraswati is useful to highlight the distinctions between older and newer sites. All work is gendered, but unlike old sites, where expectations about the perfect worker were set and women had to constantly prove they were either "just like men" or "not too much like women," the notion of the ideal worker in newer sites felt a bit more diffuse. They had to contend with gendered hurdles ("isn't a single senior consultant with a client-facing role who has a child") but these were not because they were inherently believed to be unfit for the job by clients and peers ("per se, there is no difference").

The Limitations of Novelty: New Law versus New Consulting

To the extent they did not have to continuously prove that they were the right "fit" for the job, the accounts of Lata and Saraswati seem similar. However, while Lata and Saraswati both had the advantage of not having to compete against a fixed ideal type of a "good litigator" or "good consultant," their work environments varied drastically in gender composition. Saraswati's professional life was not as blatantly sexist as Priya's, but despite feeling like there were no "technical" differences, her caveat about more senior consultants is pertinent because it reveals the underlying inequalities in environments that look and feel egalitarian in other ways.

In contrast, Lata worked for a corporate law firm, within a team with a female partner, and was herself a mid-level associate on what she felt was a clear track to partnership. In speaking about her progress and success within the firm, Lata, like many of her within-firm peers, reported gender as not being a consideration and highlighted how her advancement across different levels of the firm (i.e., at both associate and partner levels) was "on track" and on par with male colleagues of similar standing. By her account, she had the same opportunities as her male peers in terms of "promotions, bonuses, or getting clients." For Lata, and other women in her firm, gender was not an explicit issue that threatened their career prospects. Research on successful professional women has offered notes of caution in interpreting overly optimistic accounts by women who downplay the role of gender (Demaiter and Adams 2009; Britton 2017). And it would be naïve to assume equal representation of women meant that new elite law firms were not gendered in their own ways. But in creating environments where women felt like they were not actively disadvantaged against, new law—and not *all* new—firms offered a site of aberration.

One reason gender was "not an issue" for Lata and her peers was the blasé way in which their male peers accepted—and even expected—their successes. As lawyers trained predominantly in new domestic law schools that were gender-egalitarian at intake and graduation, men and women alike were still negotiating the frameworks of what it meant to be an elite law firm lawyer. Take this explanation provided by Nitin, a new partner at one of the elite law firms, about why the gender difference seemed redundant to him:

> I went to law school with these [women]—many of them beat the S*** out of me in class—why would they be different in a meeting or inter-action here? Just because they are a woman? I'm going to say there is no difference—and it is not just because I can't think of anything. Be it competence, client facing ability, you name it—there is no difference. Does a team of 4 boys differ from a team with 2 boys and 2 girls or 4 girls? Maybe banter—(*laughs*)—but that too depending on how close they are. But for [the] most part—No!

In contrast, professionals in consulting firms were typically graduates of older engineering and business schools, where gendered frameworks and meanings were more strongly embedded and the demographics themselves were less gender-balanced. Most consultants—male and female alike—agreed that the "70/30 ratio" (of men and women respectively) was ideal but not exactly possible in more senior levels for a range of attrition reasons, including incoming cohort demographics in business schools, women's "choices," and the inevitable strains of cultural assumptions about gender *in India* that made it hard for women to stay. Vihaan, a senior consultant, justified, like many of his peers, his firm's gender composition as a direct result of similar business school demographics:

> There are no women at the top, but in the mid-manager level, there is probably 70/30 . . . yes, favoring men, but maybe I am being optimistic. But you cannot do anything about this. You also have to look at the supply side and the selection pool that feeds into this sector, both from engineering and business schools. [Name Of Firm] tries very hard to pick women—I mean, not that they get preferential treatment or anything, but if you see, the number of women in the firm is a higher representation than the number of women in business school—it's hard to do. Besides, not all business schools have the same male-female mix—cities like Bangalore have more women than business schools in cities like Calcutta or worse, other B-cities . . . so making that representation filter up is difficult.

Vihaan's reasoning is grounded in his experience. Elite business schools and engineering programs, as main feeder schools into consulting firms, were central to socializing professionals. And their gender composition impacted the choices firms made at recruitment. Elite business schools—from which consultants in these firms typically are hired—have between 16 percent and 38 percent women (class of 2018) in an average group of about four hundred students a year. This gender ratio is even further skewed among schools in smaller cities and in smaller schools (less than 300 students), which have closer to 6–10 percent compared to schools in Mumbai (about 35 percent female). This is a jump from even a few years ago (class of 2015), when one hundred women acceptances (in each school) were seen as a "race that had gone too far" and "at the cost of merit."[11] But alongside the skewed numbers, being socialized in environments where women were a minority had other implications for the ways in which gender played out in interactions. Farhan, another mid-level consultant who had gone through what he called a "typical consultant" track of an elite engineering and business school education, described it as follows:

> Women have it really tough in [Consulting Firm Name]. They are still a minority and have very high rates of attrition. It's inevitable—with family and children, they just can't keep up with the highly competitive environment. So women typically exit after a child, because then they have to take six months off to have the child and when you are on a tenure system, six months means you are no longer in your cohort, so you have to necessarily compete with your juniors. And when that happens, women get emotional and leave.

Farhan's description that women's attrition is "inevitable" is similar to accounts that other consultants shared about these trajectories. But his explanation informs the underlying gendered constructs of this "inevitability." Women colleagues, by this description, were unlikely to be successful within a "highly competitive environment," both because of their competing personal concerns and their obvious emotional response to this call for balance—attrition. Similarly, Mihir is another consultant who makes this connection between the elite schools he graduated from and his current work environment:

> There were 414 students in [Engineering School], but only 30 or even 22 girls. . . . With a percentage like that, there are not that many interactions with women or that much training on how to be around women. . . . What you learn from just being in an environment like [Consulting Firm] you don't in [Engineering School] because it is not available to you. I think I got that training from [Business School], which had more women and also teams where you had to work with women in. I know it is a bad word, but this exposure to the opposite sex, to girls, only happened in business school, where 25, or sometimes as high as 35 percent were female.

Unlike Nitin, who was used to women colleagues in his own competitive environment because many of them "beat the s*** out of him" in law school, for consultants like Farhaan and Mihir, women were new and unlikely entrants into a competitive system for whom entry was an exception and attrition was "inevitable." Instead, the general consensus among consultants was that while firms were "male heavy," they were not "as bad as" the schools that they had most recently graduated from. This, as Mihir suggests below, made consulting firms much better in comparison to the schools from which they recruited. And as a consequence, any lack of gender equality was seen as an individual— rather than an organizational or institutional—problem:

> [Business School] had 30% vertical reservation for women and [Consulting Firm] doesn't. So even though women are recruited in equal proportion or numbers [of the 17 in his cohort, 3 were women], there is no policy that forces them to stay. This is in spite of [Consulting Firm] not caring if women take time off, putting their clock on pause, etc.

The Importance of Framing in the Indian Law Firm Context

In any organizational emergence story, building truly innovative workspaces is difficult because old frameworks of operation and management always attach themselves to new forms (Padgett and Powell 2012). In this case, conventional logic would assume that any new firm typically would have adopted the same hierarchies that reflect the rest of the environment it is embedded within. If anything, these new law firms should have been as steeply gendered as the professional framework they sprouted from. Yet, *how have these law firms managed to differentiate themselves from the larger gender-bound profession?* One explanation is that, as new organizations with mild preexisting frameworks of reference, the structural positioning of these firms is particularly conducive to the construction of new gendered hierarchies. A key factor in moderating the experience of gender was the advantage of being situated in new organizations. Some of this variation depended on the element of novelty—women in newer types of firms had different associations of what it meant to be a female professional—but novelty alone was not enough to explain their experience. I allude to this mechanism of novelty in the previous chapter, but this chapter clarifies it further by specifically contrasting the experiences of women in new and "modern" firms with their colleagues in older, more traditional firms. The legal profession extended itself well to this comparison because, unlike in entirely novel industries like IT or management consulting, new, post-1991 legal firms were organizations that emerged within an established professional ecosystem. To highlight the role of institutional novelty, and to allow for a richer appreciation of the relative oasis that these firms offer, in this chapter, I contrast the experience of women in new elite law firms to those who navigate their organizational predecessors—more traditional firms engaged in litigation practice. As I laid out in chapter 1, this contrast was rooted in analytical variation.

Following from the previous chapter, by the end of the twentieth century, the professional landscape for law in India had begun to change dramatically following a range of financial reforms in 1991 that opened the markets to foreign investment.[12] And two broader changes in the legal profession were particularly relevant in this transformation—liberalization measures brought about new kinds of law schools that trained incoming cohorts of elite lawyers and, simultaneously, new kinds of organizations that employed these lawyers—law firms.

First, the 1990s witnessed an increase in the quality of domestic recruits who could be employed by these law firms. During the 1990s, the Supreme Court of India and the Ministry of Education set up a range of highly selective law schools (the National Law Schools) to produce well-trained domestic lawyers. Unlike the domestic schools before them, these schools had high standards of entry, a rigorous curriculum, and an invested applicant pool. Seen as a prestigious education, these schools began to attract highly motivated high school seniors who, until then, both because of the lack of prestige and their own networks, had not considered law as a career choice. Most important, these schools admitted and graduated an equal number of men and women—and not just because they had a dedicated commitment to increasing the number of women in the profession.[13]

While the number of women enrolled in law schools had increased in the decades following independence, women role models in the profession were still few and far between. The handful of women in senior positions within the profession were either spouses or daughters of famous male lawyers. The courts had an increasing number of women advocates but they continued to face strong gender-typed hurdles. In time, however, the success of these National Law Schools (which offered women a five-year undergraduate degree in law) ushered in new and ambitious female talent into the legal profession that was responding, in part, to an increasingly international marketplace. These women lawyers began gaining access into law firms and legal practices that, until then, were off-limits to them.

Second, this wave of educational reform was well timed with broader changes in the Indian economy. The open markets also resulted in the first spate of global investors, and thus, clients. This spearheaded a decade of institutional reform and readjustment that resulted in new organizations that structurally resembled their Western counterparts' law firms. Traditionally, legal practice was organized around small, family-run practices whose recruitment was basically through word of mouth or known networks. Non-family members rarely were promoted to partner track positions and equity was never shared to "outsiders." Modeled after the normative egalitarian prototype of the Western law firm, the new firms, in contrast, had egalitarian recruitment, promotion opportunities, and equity-sharing compensation. While part of this restructuring was in response to a sudden increase in transactional work (and, potentially, the dearth of family members or networked "others" who could efficiently respond to this spate of international sophisticated work), some of it was also the need to fit the global standard of an achievement-based system.[14]

New Firms for New Work: Elite Law Firms as Sites of Innovation

The emergence of these new law firms following the market liberalization in 1991 provides an ideal background for testing the impact of preexisting frames. While traditional legal practice was rife with gendered role expectations that female lawyers felt consistently measured against, women in elite law firms felt that gender was not a main determinant of their career trajectory and success. In addition, most women in these law firms reported strong organizational and interactional advantages within the firm, especially in contrast with women in other legal workspaces. For example, women felt that they were much better advantaged in their large law firms when compared to litigation practices, where hierarchical settings were strong. When Lata, the senior associate at an elite law firm, was asked about her salience as a woman lawyer, she responded that people just did not think of it as an "issue." And this testament to equal treatment in the firm also included more specific remarks about how women fared in relation to their male peers once within the same firm. In speaking about their progress and success within the firm, women across firms reported gender as not being a consideration and highlighted how their advancement across different levels of the firm (i.e., both at associate and partner levels) was "on track" and on par with male colleagues of similar standing. Consider Lata's response to whether her gender interfered with her work, for instance:

> I don't think so—I have never felt that way. I don't know about other firms, I won't be able to tell you but this firm is very egalitarian. I don't think you are ever looked at differently because you are a woman when it comes to promotions, bonuses, or getting clients. I joined with two other guys at the same time in the same firm and I have never had different opportunities—we were on the same track.

And Lata's position didn't emerge from just an idealized assumption about the firm she worked for. Her firm recruited more women than men the year that she was recruited—two, as she highlights above, in the same "track" who started at the same level at the firm as herself—and a little over half the lawyers who had been promoted to partnership that year were women. From where Lata was positioned, gender was not an explicit issue that threatened her career prospects. And, in contrast to women like Priya who constantly had to respond to the weight of their predetermined expectations, women like Lata in elite law firms were spared this ordeal of proving repeatedly that they were the right fit for the job. While there certainly were assumptions about women that were primed in interactions, lawyers in these firms were hard pressed to describe the ways in which gender substantively (especially negatively) mattered. Instead, lawyers and clients alike described not just a tolerance for women lawyers, but a preference for women in the interests of the "work being done well" or the "matter being taken care of." Clients of senior lawyers in large, elite law firms preferred female lawyers and partners because they were more confident about women in these firms being careful and dedicated to ensuring quality. As I discuss in chapter 4, these essentialized logics of how men and women did work and the positive reinforcement of their capabilities had its own set of limitations. But essentialized logics of women's work could only serve as an advantage because background frameworks of what it meant to be an ideal worker doing this job were not yet specifically set in the case of the Indian transactional lawyer.

Again, the crucial difference in these experiences is the base expectation of what these professional spaces saw as an ideal worker. Unlike Lata, Priya, the litigator who painted a picture of an emotional minefield as she described the courtroom, started from a place of difference—where the construct of an ideal worker (a man who can withstand criticism) was already set and where her seniors in the environment (judges) were "testing" her against that ideal to either accept or reject her. She had to contend with a workforce that was already biased against her favor for not being a man and likely to penalize her for being too emotional as a woman. In contrast, lawyers in these elite law firms started in an environment that was, in being new, not circumscribed by the same expectations. Instead, they were operating in new spaces where the work demanded skills that were not predominantly framed by preexisting gendered expectations: in other words, there was not a set logic of who would be most ideally suited to do this work. If anything, they were operating in environments where qualities that typically would be penalized for being feminized were valued. When the nature of the work demanded attention to detail and the ability to negotiate with what lawyers often referred to as a "cool head," the aggressive, male lawyer who was "careless and overconfident" was not so much of a natural choice. Take this illustration by Yamuna, a colleague of Lata's who was also a senior associate, explaining the advantage of transactions with a female partner:

> for example, I have worked with a male partner and a female partner. One negotiation, I went with a male partner and at the end of the negotiation, everyone was really angry and it ended on a bad note. The next time, I went with a female partner [with the same team, clients] and the experience was much different—it was not as charged. They realized they were negotiating with two women and they were much more polite than they were when they were dealing with a man and a woman. So I do think it happens that being a woman helps in a transaction like this.

As I further elaborate in chapter 4, the fact that being helpful or "not charged" would "help" in a transaction is, in itself, not something that would typically advantage professional women. In fact, research on women in the workplace suggests that lack of aggression is usually detrimental to success within high-prestige organizations (Babcock and Laschever 2003). Yet, this did not disadvantage law firm associates in the Indian setting. Women partners in elite law firms agreed that they had different styles of lawyering and negotiating—but this socialized difference did not necessarily disadvantage them. Divya, a female partner at an elite law firm, spoke about her trajectory compared to her male peers:

> I would never kick up a fuss about a raise or demand to be put on a certain matter. And because I am not pushy like that, it is more likely to be given to me, the [managing partner] is more likely to work with me, more likely to give me the matter, than he is with X [the male partner peer], who is "being an ass" by asking for these things.

This feminization of work in itself is not uncommon. And there are several accounts of female labor being preferred for reasons of care and precision (e.g., comparable narratives of feminization factory workers in comparable countries like Mexico, (Salzinger 2003) and Malaysia [Ong 2010]). However, this preference in a high-pressure work environment where you would imagine aggression and competitiveness (traditional male-typed values) rather than good behavior and commitment to detail (female-typed values) is rather novel. Women across sites did work differently and interacted with their peers, superiors, and clients in ways that were in line with traditional accounts of socialization and gender typing. Yet, in these different situations, this labor and attitude was received differently.

The advantage of these new law firms is especially relevant in light of their comparative context. For elite law firms, their innovative organizational structures alongside new kinds of work meant that neither the work nor the context in which it was done was predeterminately gendered like litigation practice was. But this was not the only point of comparison. Women in elite law firms also felt the gender bind less than their contemporaries from in-house legal departments. This is interesting because globally, this site is relatively gender-friendly. For example, in their internationally represented case studies on women lawyers, Schultz and Shaw (2003) show that across countries women have trouble advancing in larger, more established firms, but fare better in in-house positions as legal advisers. In the Indian case, women lawyers who worked "in-house" fared better than their peers in traditional litigation, but still felt the background frame of their hierarchical organizational structure influence interactions and experiences. As old organizations that traditionally employed men, they retained strong gendered assumptions about the ideal worker, which, as other scholars have warned, offers important scripts for the new organizations that come in their wake (e.g., Sommerlad 1994, 2002; Davies 1996; Adams 2005; Bolton and Muzio 2008). As a result, even though the nature of the work that they were doing had been significantly altered by globalization post-1991, their innovative work alone could not offer them the same advantage of an ambiguous gender frame as it did women in elite law firms. Take for example this account by Mona, an in-house lawyer in her late twenties who has been working for the same in-house department since she graduated from law school five years ago:

> I have done well—but I know that sometimes it hurts to not be a man. When we travel on transactions, for example. It is such a man-friendly company that I feel like I come in the way of people doing what they would otherwise do. They would never tell anyone that, of course. But I know if they could choose between me and a man, they would—in an instant.

Mona's work, by her own admission, is different from what an earlier generation of lawyers would have done in the company. Liberalization has meant that the company has more dealings with foreign collaborators and associates and that transactions are more international. However, within the context of the company, the ideal worker is still male ("*it is such a man-friendly company*") and most interactions are still fraught with this tension ("*I know if they could choose between me and a man, they would—in an instant*").

New Workers for New Work—The Advantage of the Elite Law School

Tracing the evolution of these firms from an organizational perspective is useful because it helps in understanding one set of structural factors that have resulted in new kinds of professional workspaces. But while speaking about the evolution and history of these firms, most senior lawyers involved in recruiting spoke about the changes in legal education and the subsequent quality of recruits available. In turn, this "new era" of legal work was produced by new kinds of legal labor within these firms because as chapter 1 notes, most lawyers in elite firms were graduates of new and elite National Law Schools.

The structural salience of this National Law School supply dynamic is significant while trying to understand the production of gender hierarchies within these firms for a few reasons. First, unlike other elite professional degree-granting schools in the country, the National Law Schools were set up to recruit a gender-balanced sample of students. As a result, they offered a new entry point for women—even if it self-selected a certain kind of class advantage—to unprecedented professional workspaces. Further, because these elite, highly selective schools were pitted against the clique-friendly litigation practice, students (men and women both) felt it offered them a meritocratic chance at legal practice, especially in light of the firms that were emerging temporally alongside these firms. Senior women lawyers in large, elite firms commonly spoke about how getting into one of these law schools meant[15] new access to the profession. For example, a partner who was an early National Law School alumnus told me how refreshing it was that she did not "have to *know* someone" to secure her career, especially since the lack of such connections in her family would have otherwise deemed her an outsider to the traditional profession. This feeling of democratized access was common and new schools were seen as special in offering an alternative to traditional hostile environments of legal practice that were mostly connected by kinship (Dezalay and Garth 2010)—a distinction that was more salient for its women graduates than its male graduates. But it was not just that these schools offered paths to careers that were not available to women before. They also offered a socialization that most alumni spoke of as distinct from the traditional Indian higher education model—a professional education that was not just gender-balanced in the classroom, but also pushed them to think critically about social issues. Jasveen, a twenty-nine-year-old senior associate in an elite law firm describes her legal education as "unlike regular colleges" in the country and different from the "mainstream" because it exposed her and her peers to progressive themes:

> NLS made me the person I was. Unlike in regular colleges, I got in NLS the kind of exposure that was life shaping . . . there is no doubt that the person I am is a response to that exposure. Regular colleges have mainstream thinking—but NLS was all about the alternative: an exposure to queer culture, violence against women, discrimination. And once you go there, you start noticing it everywhere around you—that is what that kind of full exposure does to you.

Queer culture and discrimination might not seem like ultra-progressive exposure in college campuses in the West, but keep in mind that this is in an Indian context where most professional schools did not have any type of socialization or coursework in these subjects. And Jasveen's use of these examples highlights particularly feminist themes and patterns in this elite legal education that peers in other elite professional schools in the country were not regularly exposed to. This sort of gender socialization and awareness and the ways in which that shaped their experiences was common among graduates in these National Law Schools (NLS)—men and women alike. And in migrating from one closed network (law schools) to another (elite law firms), these cohorts of lawyers were trained by their preexisting frameworks to be accepting of (even *expecting*) gender-egalitarian workspaces when they joined these firms. As Nitin reminds us, he attended law school with the women he now works with—*why would this gender composition suddenly be an issue here?*

Other New Sites Still "Framed": The Case of Management Consultants

Management consultants are a good comparison to these elite law firm lawyers because they worked in neoliberal firms within professional silos concentrated around new kinds of advisory work that Indian professionals didn't concern themselves with in the same way before 1991. Yet, while similarly employed by new workspaces and doing new work, management consultants found the gender divide much more apparent in their everyday work. And while there were a handful of senior women in Mumbai's consulting firms, Mumbai's two most prestigious law firms are equally staffed with women and male lawyers at entry and at senior partnership. Significantly, as I mention above, large consulting firms were usually split 70/30 in favor of men, and that divide was even more stark in the case of senior client-facing positions.

The comparative socialization of students that I discuss in the previous section is useful to shed light on how novelty of firms alone doesn't account for the advantage certain legal professionals enjoy. Of course, it would not do this comparison justice to paint a picture where professionals in elite law firms thought gender made *no* difference and men and women in consulting reported a workplace reminiscent of a *Mad Men* episode. In these new scenarios where work and the worker were being negotiated, women and men alike across different kinds of firms felt the impact of these innovative frames. But while there was a chance to negotiate some things, others remained firmly set. Saraswati's explanation that there were "very few actual situations where it feels like a man v. woman" reminds us of the power that daily interactions hold in crafting narratives about representation of work. If women in fact felt that there were few circumstances where their gender was primed, the failure to advance in their careers—which was obvious to most women, given how few women were in senior, client-facing positions—feels like a personal rather than institutional mechanism. This cognitive dissonance between egalitarianism assumptions and actual outcomes reeks of the persistence Ridgeway speaks about when she describes these frames of gender. It also dovetails necessarily with why women don't advance in most workplaces.

Preexisting frames have been critical in dictating the experience of professionals—both within the legal profession and outside of it. In more traditional firms, women felt the double bind sharply between what was expected from a male lawyer (an ideal worker) and the ways in which women deviated from that expected norm. Newer firms were advantaged in that there was no preexisting expectation and idealization of a typical worker since the work that was done was novel. As new sites that are performing new types of work, elite law firms were well positioned to structurally renegotiate existing hierarchies for a range of reasons. First, as I explained above, organizing a legal practice around firms and partnerships was in itself a stark structural contrast to the existing forms of practice within the legal profession. Unlike their earlier lawyer's offices and litigation chamber counterparts that were closely tied by "old boys'" networks, these new post-liberalization firms were organized much more like their global counterparts in that they were firms with partners and associates, a fixed salary, transparent promotions and bonuses, and institutionalized recruitment. This sort of organizational setup might not be innovative per se—but it was very novel in the context of the historical Indian legal workforce that had previously organized around private practitioners, with little consideration for firm formation, salary structures, or nonfamilial recruitment.

Second, at the time of their incorporation, not only were these firms structurally novel, they were also dealing with global transactional work that was new and needed novel expertise. Unlike litigation, which was an entrenched practice and had sticky stereotypes associated with "good" and "bad" lawyers, transactional work was essentially a neoliberal work product that demanded skills whose gender type had not yet been set in stone. While senior litigating lawyers could differentiate against female attorneys in the court for not being "assertive enough" or on a par with their male role models, transactional work in comfortable environments was such a new form of work that it had no attachment to a predominant gender frame. This lack of association was key to setting in place a diffuse framework of expectation and role formation where gender was not primed in the construction of the ideal worker. Since there was no preconceived notion of what a *mergers and acquisition* or *international banking* or *capital markets* lawyer ought to be, look, and act like, there was no "preference" for a male transactional lawyer. This lack of expectation allowed for a more interactive negotiation of the hierarchy, and, over time, the creation of a new one.

Finally, if it was just innovative work and structure that made the difference, all firms that were set up post-1991 should be bastions of gender equality. And while firms are certainly more hospitable to their female lawyers than traditional litigation practice, not all firms are gender-egalitarian in the same way. In contrasting elite firms doing global work with their domestic counterparts, it is possible that the work itself was so intimately associated with being prestigious "global" work that the association to the West helped diminish what might otherwise have been a stronger gender frame.

But organizational novelty at the point of entry alone couldn't win the battle—gender outcomes in elite law firms were also advantaged by the novelty of its supply pool that was socialized to accept gender-neutral outcomes *before* entering these firms. And this is where, in terms of gender socialization, consulting firms, which shared many firm characteristics with elite law firms, couldn't leverage the advantage of newly a-gendered frameworks. Together, it is this simultaneous novelty of law schools and law firms that truly did give them a chance to experience their work in new, egalitarian ways. As a result, even though they populated new firms doing new work, women in management consulting felt the sticky disadvantage of their gendered frameworks attach, while lawyers in elite law firms felt more flexibility to push their gender-prescribed boundaries.

Hostile work environments where women are vocally discriminated against are no longer the descriptive posters of gender inequality in modern organizations (although in my years of fieldwork there were many examples of these blatant environments too). As other researchers of organizational stratification warn us, inequality in organizations no longer needs to *look* starkly unfair or unequal. Instead, these organizations host and perpetuate an equally dangerous strain of inequality that stems from invisible background frameworks (Ridegway 2008) and second-generation biases (e.g., Sturm 2001; Ibarra, Ely, and Kolb 2011, 2013; Wynn and Correll 2018) that speak of the war as already having been won while continuing to cement structural differences. As a result, Vihaan's claim that there was nothing to be done because it was just the nature of the supply-side dynamic, epitomizes the dangerous ways in which legitimate reasons allow for inequality to persist. This is similar to other consultants (e.g., Bhavesh in chapter 3) who felt that the organizations themselves were invested in their employees, which is why the environments were mostly equal, with some exceptions in advancement that could be explained by personal choices at the individual actors' level. The idea that the organization is equal and fair and that inequality in leadership is a function of supply-side choices and restrictions (in this case, women who don't make the promotions they might have otherwise made because they don't have the same owner-ship over their time as their male peers) is troubling because it gives organ-izations a clean slate. Even though Bhavesh's firm had few senior women, he still thought about his surroundings as egalitarian and meritocratic—where women were ill represented because they weren't able to do what their male peers did for whatever "understandable" reason. In contrast, women in elite law firms—domestic firms facing what they classified as "sophisticated clients" who would not prime gender—seemed to be best positioned to leverage these middle-class advantages both within and outside the firms.

But what makes Nita (from the previous chapter) and Nitin think about gender and status a certain way that didn't extend to Vihaan's version? I've tried to suggest here that it is a function of the institutions they are embedded in and who they interact with in those institutions that allow for these variant strains of neoliberal realities. That is, over and above being part of an educated middle-class cohort of men and women accessing professional opportunities in the age of liberalization, two additional structural factors worked in their favor. First, unlike male peers such as Vihaan, women such as Nita in elite law firms had colleagues like Nitin who were socialized *prior to joining the firm* to deal with mixed gendered settings where women yielded power. Sec-ond, as the chapters that follow suggest, they interacted with actors outside these firms who were less likely to obliquely prime gender in their interactions, thereby forming an environment where they could ride on the advantages of their class-based capital.

At the core of this comparative experience is that even when keeping class constant, environments can change experience. While most—if not all—of these elite professionals are second-generation middle class, their relative compatibility and fit within these elite life chances came from a conjuncture of going to the graduate schools they did, at the particular time in history that they did, and the ways in which these two things were valorized by the insti-tutions they joined upon graduation. And that it is a variation in these three factors that afforded very different kinds of experiences even within this seem-ingly tight class of the first generational elite professional.

Sticky Assumptions of Gender and Work

Building truly innovative workspaces is difficult because, no matter how radi-cal, old frameworks of operation and management still attach themselves to new organizational forms (Padgett and Powell 2012). But while organizational genesis certainly "does not mean virgin birth" (5), this research reminds us that new kinds of work environments have some leeway in introducing new kinds of workers who are seen as good fits for the tasks at hand. Unlike women in litigation who constantly had to counter—and fall short of—the benchmark of an ideal male professional, women in newer work environments like transactional law and management consulting felt less constrained by a predetermined idea of the perfect professional. As newly emerging professional fields, the cultural meanings of what constituted a "good corporate lawyer" or a "good consultant" were still in flux, and as fields not predisposed to being gender-typed, both transactional lawyers and consultants alike shared this structural advantage.

In addition, women in these new organizations were also advantaged by the idea of a global, cosmopolitan professional. As graduates from some of the country's best schools, hiring these professionals was a matter of pride for many modern organizations and reflected their ideological commitment to "meritocracy," a mechanism that I unpack in greater detail in the next chapter. Further, as urban professionals from English-medium schools, "fit" within organizations was equally buttressed by the advantages of class. But holding the advantage of class constant across elite workspaces, women in law firms still were able to navigate their environments with less sticky constructs than their peers in consulting.

To explain this variation, firm and work novelty, in themselves, were not enough. As new organizations with mild preexisting frameworks of reference, the structural positioning of new firms was conducive to the construction of novel gendered hierarchies. But what additionally advantaged lawyers in new transactional firms was the exposure to gender-egalitarian constructs *before* entering these workspaces. Elite lawyers who were trained in law schools with gender-balanced entry were better equipped to unlock the advantages of "innovative" gender frameworks than elite consultants who, despite working for new organizations, remained circumscribed by the sticky frameworks of gender that their male-dominated schools of engineering and business advanced.

Although this contrast between professions offers one way in which elite law firms framed the experience of their inhabitants, it is certainly not meant to suggest that elite law firms were devoid of gendered meanings altogether. In chapter 4, I show that although differently valorized, there were deeply pervasive gendered meanings that permeated each of these sites. Similarly, neither is this to suggest that lawyers were advantaged because law schools were created with the intention to establish egalitarian workspaces. As I suggest earlier in this book, the new national law schools were hardly designed as feeder schools for law firms, and these schools remain gender-imbalanced and unequal in other important ways (e.g., Ballakrishnen and Samuel 2020, regarding recruiting female faculty and creating feminist spaces; see Basheer et al. 2017 for caste and class inequality). Instead, the gender-equal entry into these schools—and subsequent reinforcement in these firms—was predicated on other factors, among them a high threshold for entry that attracted the most competitive students (regardless of gender), and new kinds of testing (which were not yet gender-typed). It remains relevant to note that although some schools have vertical reservation for women, they've historically never needed to be enforced because women have always been overrepresented in the general category. Further still, it is also possible that the initial gender balance was predicated on the fact that law was not always seen as a uniformly high-status professional field and therefore attracted fewer entrants of high status (i.e., men). But more than anything, the symbiotic co-establishment of new law schools alongside new elite law firms was happenstance. And the reinforcing pattern for gender equality that it offered between students and professionals was, even if fortuitous, accidental. At the same time, while this way of meaning-making was an overarching mechanism, it still offers only a part of the explanation. In the following chapters, I show the factors at play in creating this unique parity—and the ways in which their reliance on this background framework buffered the effectiveness of their possible advantages.

THREE

FIRMS

Just Like an
International Firm

THE ADVANTAGE OF NOT BEING GLOBAL

THE NEWNESS OF these modern firms, as I suggest in the previous two chapters, was central to framing the ways in which individual professionals experienced their environments. Believed to be "bad fits" or "not ideal" for their jobs because they were not like their male ideal types, women in traditional professional practice were constantly being sized up against a range of gendered expectations. At the same time, for firms that emerged following market liberalization in 1991, notions of what it meant to be a "good corporate lawyer" or a "good management consultant" were still in flux, and the ambiguity allowed women some leeway in renegotiating their status. Still, while newer firms certainly created less prejudicial environments for women, this achievement could not be chalked up to organizational novelty alone. If, after all, a firm could achieve equality simply by being new, that equality would be found far beyond the rather unlikely environs of post-liberalization India. And yet it was in India, not in Silicon Valley, where women were telling me "gender did not matter."[1]

This chapter extends the analysis of novelty from the individual level to a more organizational perspective. No doubt the advantage of newness played a big part in scripting how individuals were viewed and treated. But equally important were the ways in which novelty moderated how *organizations* identified and wanted to be seen. In exploring the ways in which this organizational identity was presented and negotiated, this chapter reveals the building blocks for another counter-intuitive finding—i.e., that it was *domestic* law firms, rather than local offices of international firms, where women professionals seemed to flourish.

As I suggested in chapter 1, the design of this project arose out of the natural variation in organizational novelty and professional emergence generated by Indian liberalization. The 1991 reforms created a landscape where professionals and organizations across fields were similar in many ways but crucially different in others. In particular, new transactional law firms and new management consulting firms offered a useful contrast because, although all were organizationally "new," they varied in other important factors, beginning with the fact that India's liberalization policy prohibited foreign investment in the legal profession. As a result, consultants worked in classic multinational organizations, whereas similarly elite transactional lawyers worked in elite *domestic* firms. Further, consulting firms were local branches of global firms that were set up to service domestic clients; whereas elite law firms were domestic firms that were retained by a range of sophisticated national, and, importantly, international clients. Thus, in addition to being new, these new corporate law firms were organized as domestic firms facing an increasingly international market for professional services. This natural variation in organizational structure and audience between similarly elite professional firms was, as I show in this chapter, crucial to these differential experiences. Specifically, unlike Indian banking and consulting firms that were local offices of elite global conglomerates, transactional law firms struggled with issues of organizational legitimacy and felt the need to differentiate themselves aggressively from their more traditional peers (i.e., domestic litigation firms). Chapter 2 describes how this played out at the individual level, whereby employees from new, highly selective domestic law schools were highly prized by these new firms. This chapter considers the way in which these firms signaled meritocracy and modernity by being "just like global firms" in a range of ways to claim legitimate membership and identity. It focuses particularly on one way in which such identity claiming was done by not focusing on gender as a disadvantaged identity. Partners would talk about how merit and progress were of the utmost importance, to get the "best person in" rather than to stay stuck with archaic notions of a gendered ideal worker. At the same time, neither was the project a strategic governance one: women were not being recruited *to* signal meritocracy. They simply were not actively disadvantaged as they might have been in other, more traditional organizational contexts because, as I describe in the previous chapter, there was no set framework of an ideal worker they were working against, and the most egalitarian outcome in this case happened to be the recruitment of students from the most elite schools, which graduated students at gender-equal rates.[2] In turn, by creating conditions where women were not actively discriminated against, these firms offered an oasis of parity where, in the name of modernity and egalitarian merit, outcomes for women would result in ways that were less fruitful in other organizational contexts.

Needing to be "just like global firms" is not in itself an unusual motivation for a new firm's organizational choices. There is a long line of global
institutions research showing that modern organizations around the world
model themselves to look similar to their global counterparts because convergence is a low-risk legitimacy strategy.[3] Especially in environments that are
not yet stable—and emerging economies seemingly offer a plethora of these
environments—looking "global" offers organizations a way to distinguish
themselves from peers in profitable ways. In their groundbreaking 1983 piece
on isomorphism,[4] Paul DiMaggio and Walter Powell suggest that one way
this convergence happens is through a process of institutional mimicking, in
which organizations mimic cues from their peers and ideal types to signal and
enhance their institutional membership and standing within a given environment.[5] In the resultant isomorphism, schools, banks, and hospitals around
the world develop increasing levels of similarity. Yet, alongside this convergence is a parallel series of failures in which ideal types fail to transfer to the
new environment: despite the desire to look and seem global, there is often
"decoupling" between what organizations are and what they seem to be.[6] As a
result, schools, banks, and hospitals across the world might all *look* the same,
but they have very disparate levels of efficiency in their different local contexts.

This slippage between the ideal and the actual can be seen in the Indian
consulting firm case. As local organizations reorganized the global, they
encountered a running conundrum—how to adhere in spirit to what is easy
to mimic in form. On the face of it, as global organizations, these firms had
a range of built-in mechanisms for creating gender-friendly environments,
ranging from informal peer events like women's-only seminars to more structural protections like maternity leave policies and flexible work times. However, women in consulting believed that only some of these modern, global
measures could "stick" in their own personal contexts because "it was, after all,
India." This disillusionment is telling for two reasons—first, it confirms a pit-
fall of global isomorphism: global organizations can (and increasingly do) look
the same, but the "same" in different places necessarily takes into account local
flavors and readjustments. And second, it reveals that when organizations
internalize this line of reasoning, the burden of blame shifts from the organization to the environment.

In the case of global management consulting firms, consultants working
in the India office perceived their organizations to be "doing all they could"
but constrained by a local environment that would not let such innovation
flourish. For example, Bhavesh, a rising senior consultant, told me that organizations like his firm were committed to worldwide gender equality, but that
"in India" it did not always work, because women had a range of other constraints that interfered with them being successful consultants. Bhavesh's
explanation for the scant representation of women in his firm's senior positions absolved the organization. From his perspective, the organization was

agnostic about whether someone who was up for a promotion was a man or a woman. It was, instead, more likely to be social constraints via "neighbors and family" that restricted Indian women from getting ahead professionally. As I showed in chapter 1, women across these sites were from similar socioeconomic backgrounds, often daughters of middle-class professionals, and were earning more in their first jobs than their fathers earned at retirement. Like their peers in law firms, they were also highly educated women who were living on their own in cities with a greater agency over their personal choices than most of their generation. It seemed unlikely that their "friends and neighbors" would have much say in how these women spent time outside their homes—and indeed, few women mentioned such pressure as a restriction on their professional success. But the fact that Bhavesh believed this was the reason his female colleagues were not getting promoted is revealing of the kinds of deep organizational bias that prevailed in these consulting firms.

Against this mostly defeatist background, the Indian law firm case assumes even greater prominence. Whereas consulting firms could afford to dismiss their failed attempts at creating gender-friendly organizations and blame them on the unsuitable conditions India offered, law firms had no similar global safety net. Unlike local offices of global consulting firms that could ride on the legitimacy of their parent organizations, domestic law firms believed they had to compete in a global environment where their legitimacy was at stake because they were not technically "global" institutions. It was to assuage this concern that Indian law firms engaged in what I term *speculative isomorphism* that led them to mimic the firms they wanted to be like without actually having a formal relationship with them. As one senior partner told me, referring to the evolution of his firm in the context of the Anglo-Saxon law firm model, "They have been doing this work for hundreds of years; for us, this is new. But we have learnt, we have managed." What he calls "managing" is what I theorize as "speculative isomorphism" in this book. Modern law firms—unlike multinational firms that existed with the privilege of global branding—felt the need both to differentiate themselves from their traditional peers *and* to signal that they were global. But while these new corporate firms had close proximity to the traditional litigation firms they did *not* want to be like, their institutional access to the foreign firms they were trying to emulate was less concrete. As a result, these locally managed but externally facing firms felt the need to adhere to and replicate what they thought were modern, meritocratic institutional scripts. And in trying to mimic these scripts, they often outperformed the ideals of the Western firms they sought to emulate. But this mimicking was neither committed nor fully researched—it was performative in a sense, and this performance was *speculative*. As new organizations trying to be legitimate, law firms did a range of things that would make them appear global: they had posh offices in high-rent business districts, they boasted fine art and embossed stationery, they had recruitment events at elite law schools that signaled their commitment to meritocracy and competence. Not discriminating on gender was just one more way in which they could signal modernity. But what exactly this needed to look like was a more emerging process that garnered legitimacy along the way.

"We Had to Learn You Know" Legitimacy Concerns

As I explained in chapter 1, while many elite law firms were founded by lawyers with successful pre-liberalization practices, it was only post-1991 that these firms' organizational practices began to mimic the institutional prototype of the Anglo-American corporate mega-law firm (Wilkins et al. 2017). This context placed these firms in a uniquely vulnerable position, both vis-à-vis their peers within the profession as well as with respect to other professional elites.

As chapter 1 tracks, before 1991, private investment in domestic industries was not allowed, and trade in general was heavily regulated. This meant that domestic lawyers mostly worked on domestic transactions. However, with liberalization, domestic law firms had to reinvent themselves to deal with a range of international cross-border transactional work (e.g., mergers and acquisition, private equity, international finance transactions). Balinder, an older senior partner who had left three decades of private practice to join his firm, described the change in work:

> You know how when they say "firms" before [globalization], they meant lawyers who did some testamentary property or company work . . . but it was not transactional. There were always Company Secretaries or Chartered Accountants in big companies who took care of things like that. It was only after 1991 that this began to change. . . . There was a good market, and auditors couldn't do work outside their company . . . and of course, then there were new regulations that expanded the scope for what lawyers could do . . . so the firms [he signals with air quotes] "adapted."

But it was not just new work, it was also who this new kind of work was being done for. Following the regulatory reforms of 1991, many smaller traditional law firms continued to do transactional work for existing domestic clients who were venturing into more sophisticated commercial transactions. But a small set of new law firms began to gain in prestige (in part because of the high profiles of their initial domestic clients), servicing international clients and large domestic conglomerates in globally significant transactions. Elaborating on a conversation about how liberalization had changed the organization of legal practice, Balinder described the change in exposure at this time of transition:

> Suddenly, there was exposure to the globe. In-house counsels could only do so much. But for [joint ventures], mergers, those types of sophisticated things—well, for those types of things, you know you need a lawyer. . . . The risk perceived was just that much more and these [international] clients wanted lawyers.

Thus, after liberalization, a lot of this transactional work, especially in the most prestigious of these firms (such as the one where Balinder had been a partner for more than a decade), began to include a strong international component where either the work or the clients were global.

Finally, since the piously defended nationalist monopoly of legal services following the 1991 reforms limited the entry of international law firms into the Indian market, these elite firms, unlike their counterparts in other Asian countries (e.g., Liu 2008), emerged without direct structural support or intervention of Western law firms. Partners (many of whom were involved in the original movement to oppose the entry of foreign firms) saw this as an opportunity to showcase their unique capabilities. Rahul Kumar, a senior partner who had transformed his practice from a handful of lawyers to one of the country's most "global" transactional law firms, seemed both aware and ready for this competition:

> There is no difference between [Major U.S. Law Firm] and us—if we are on a matter, we are as good as them. In fact, sometimes I think we have the better work product. . . . Because we are new, there is energy here. People are excited about this work—and this is where the magic is happening. India Shining, and all that.

But alongside Rahul's striking confidence was also some insecurity about the process, especially in terms of what it would mean when the market for legal services inevitably opened to international entities:

> There is that fear, we had no one teaching us, so we had to learn, you know? They have been doing this work for hundreds of years, for us, this is new. But we have learnt, we have managed. We don't really need them—if [International Law Firms] enter [the Indian Legal Market], they will need us.

A few things in this interview demand attention. The first is that there were no scripts readily available for Rahul and his peers to follow: "We had no one teaching us," as he noted. In addition, the process itself was highly uncertain and therefore offered ample opportunity for speculation; firms like his had to wade through a new environment with no tools for how to navigate it. At the same time, this was as much an opportunity as a disadvantage. Being the face of corporate legal practice in India meant that he was part of a niche cohort of firms with a monopoly in the market: a monopoly that could well be used to his advantage when the market for legal services became global.

But despite Rahul's display of confidence, these emergence conditions initially left elite Indian law firms in a tenuous position. They were organizing themselves in new ways, doing new work, facing sophisticated international clients, and they were doing all of this without the direct structural intervention of foreign firms. *And* by boisterously opposing the entry of foreign law firms, Indian law firms risked undermining their ability to signal a competitive global image to their competitors and clients alike. To strategically position themselves, firms adopted two dominant mechanisms. First, they separated themselves from the rest of their peers and made clear that they were unique, professional spaces not tainted by the old-school logic of their predecessors. And second, they started aggressively signaling that they were capable of being global firms. Both these approaches, especially the latter, required them to mimic norms of global firms, which they did in a variety of ways. But as firms without any real connections to these Western firms, this knowledge was asymmetric and the mimicry, as a result, speculative.

"We Are Not Traditional": Differentiation Logics

Key to this identity creation was that these firms represented a contrast to traditional law firms and legal practices that were mired in traditional, local scripts of nepotism, patriarchy, and old-boy networks (Gandhi 1988). But their projection to an external audience that included new global clients seemed predicated on a deep internalization of the organizational identity by associates and partners *within* the firm. Niyant, a young man in his early twenties and a rising third-year associate in one of these elite firms, described one common attraction for young professionals who wanted to join these firms:

> I really like being part of [Elite Law Firm]—it is a really professional. . . . There aren't other places in the profession with this sort of professional culture—it is shocking, but this is the sort of place where having connections can actually hurt you. . . . It is all based on merit—I can't see myself leaving for another firm. . . . This is not like out there [in litigation]—here, *[in air quotes]* "royalty" holds you back.

The "royalty" Niyant worried about was the fact that members of his family (which was active in business) knew some of the firm's partners personally, a connection that he feared would "hold him back" if his peers deemed it inappropriate. His worry was not unfounded. As I show in chapter 1, projecting the image of a deeply meritorious institution—particularly by recruiting on merit rather than social connection—was central to the way in which these firms distinguished themselves from their peers in litigation. It cannot have hurt Niyant that his parents knew the managing partner, but the fact that he was ashamed of it revealed something of the cultural image the firm was trying to foster. And it was not in vain. Nina, a young partner who, unlike Niyant, did not know anybody in the firm before she applied, told me mockingly that she, like many of her peers in her firm, "did not have to know Judge Uncle" to get her job—a reference to the tight old boys' network that still advanced the careers of many lawyers outside of these transactional law firms. Instead, as a graduate from one of the country's top law schools, she felt her career was based on merit in a way that legal careers often were not before the advent of these new firms. In her words, "Finally there was a route to a secure career [these firms] that I could get through merit."

But it was not just that these associates and partners *felt* that their firm was different from traditional litigation practice. As I explain in chapter 2, top law firms in the country recruited in local law schools almost exclusively on the basis of merit and invited their new associates to an environment that was both visibly and organizationally different from traditional legal practice. While litigation practices and smaller firms operated in decrepit old buildings, offices of large elite law firms in Mumbai looked and felt like international law firms. Located in prime real estate and designed to impress, these air-conditioned, fine art–studded offices felt distinctly different from the pigeon nest–lined buildings, with their old elevators, that housed older law offices. But it was not just how these spaces were experienced by associates that told how deeply ingrained this logic of differentiation was. Partners, many of whom had been central to the creation of these firms, were keen to highlight the ways in which their firms were unlike traditional legal practices in the country, especially when it came to how the firm treated its associates. Kamal, a senior partner who had seen his firm grow over the last two decades, made the comparison this way:

> In the courts, in litigation practice, nobody is treated equally—the judiciary still hasn't reached that level of maturity. The thinking used to be "Ah, the women will come, get married" or, even, "If they make a point [during court arguments] then it will be more emotional than substance." But all other things being equal, in a place like this [an elite law firm] women score over men. . . . Things like gender discrimination, gender harassment, that just isn't there . . . look, we have equal number of male and female partners. A thought like this doesn't even arise . . . The culture is just different here.

The "culture" Kamal mentioned is important because it set the tone for the kind of merit-based workspace that Niyant and Nina spoke about. The projection of being more "mature" than litigation firms (although, ironically, they were much newer) was central to elite firms' identity—as was the fact that gender would not be the yardstick used to discriminate. Instead, by maintaining high standards of merit-based entry, they saw themselves as being beyond the clutches of discrimination that plagued their more traditional peers. And this commitment was well received. For instance, like many of her peers, Lata, the senior associate we first encountered in the previous chapter, who saw her path to partnership clearly before her, felt there was a distinction between her firm and others. Recall her stating, "If I had been in litigation, it would have been different. . . . But not here [in an elite law firm]."

"We Are Global": Mimicking Logics

The emergence of the new Indian corporate law firm was also marked by another association—firms emerging as a response to what they saw as global expectations of performance and propriety. In my interviews, partners and associates alike spoke about "merit" and "egalitarian" norms in various ways, both to signal that they were no longer wedded to old notions of ascription-based advantage but also to signal that they were rising from this preexisting framework by being more internationally competitive and, specifically, meritocratic, "just like global firms." Thus, there was a dual categorization of merit: merit served as a way of signaling departure from the old but also as a way of merging with the global image these firms were attempting to foster. Several lawyers in these firms talked about the ways in which their firms had really become a function of the global clients they served. Sapna, a senior associate, explained that the price of working in a very prestigious law firm was that her work depended on the whims and preferences of her international clients. As an example of this dependence, she offered that the client's terms were really always primary (a strain that is discussed in greater detail in the next chapter):

> There is a definite difference between what we say to an international [private equity] client versus what we could say to a domestic client. There is no concept of an extended Indian holiday. We are not like the Courts where every national holiday is off—we are on 24/7/365. The only big break we get is Christmas, when the US and UK just shut down and work starts to slow down. There is no question of taking a similar break for, say, Diwali or Holi. . . . [Name of Law Firm] won't even allow us to ask if the client is OK with it. . . . When the client says "jump," you don't ask why.

Sapna's description of "when a client says 'jump'" may have been a bit extreme, but it revealed the sentiment that many of these lawyers expressed— that as new firms catering to international clients, elite law firms were subject to strong international scripts of practice and performance. Structuring work schedules differently for international clients, in a way that superseded their local clients' interests—or even their own (Diwali and Holi are both important Indian holidays)—was reflective of a larger institutional pecking order. And the culture around gender—beyond how these firms looked or how associates structured their work schedules—was one more way in which firms could signal this "global" attitude. It echoes Kamal's elaboration of what he thought accounted for the "difference in culture" in his firm:

> Exposure! Things have changed . . . [we are] keeping up with the times. It's not like the litigating offices where people have to worry about connections or gender—we are like any international law firm. Merit is everything.

Note that this explanation was not rooted in gender itself, but instead in the extensions of merit signaled by "keeping up with the times." Faced with new clients and new times (exposure), firms were charged with the task of dispelling preconceived notions about professional work in India. And they did this by both distinguishing themselves from their predecessors ("it is not like litigation") *and* aggressively signaling their assumed similarity to global firms ("we are like an international law firm").

I use the phrase "assumed similarity" here because this notion of international firms as capstones of meritocracy and gender parity was closer to an ideal type assumption than it was to reality. And this senior partner's statement was not an isolated reference—some version of the phrase "merit is everything" came up in other conversations about gender in these firms, confirming that even if they did not have structural access to global firms, there was a central assumption that the ideology of merit and equal opportunity was important to global firms. The pressure to "keep up with the times" demanded an aggressive reorientation that brought these Indian firms' own image in line with this prominent ideology, to show that they were serious global players. At the same time, as local firms without any real connections to the global firms they were trying to mimic, their knowledge of and response to these macro-cultural scripts was both speculative and, incidentally, more adherent. I use the term *speculative* here because there is no indication that firms thought gender equity was the only or even a central way to signal this global isomorphism. They were trying to do everything they could to gain legitimacy by being "modern" and "meritocratic": being gender-agnostic happened to be one way of accomplishing this. But importantly, all the ways in which they were trying to be "just like global firms" arose out of conjecture rather than actual knowledge. In fact, as the case of consulting firms revealed, actual knowledge was counterproductive to the gender project because, among other things, actual knowledge revealed that, globally, women were scarce in prestigious workforces.

Pandering to the ideal of meritocracy did not always mean that lawyers in Indian firms had little idea of how Western firms looked or operated. In exploring this theme in later interviews, I asked lawyers to explain the ways in which they imagined international firms: What did they think these firms looked like? How did they think their own firms compared? There was a lot of variance in this meaning-making process, especially given that different lawyers had different levels of exposure to Western firms. (A few, though not many, had spent a year in the United States or the United Kingdom pursuing a graduate law degree or had spent a few months on secondment in a foreign firm.) But while the lawyers I interviewed did not imagine Western firms in any uniform way, it was clear that most envisioned them as environments staunchly upholding the ideology of meritocracy and gender equality. A partner who was comparing her firm composition to that of international law firms seemed unsure (but optimistic) about the ways in which Indian firms measured up: "And the women? Well, it's the same as any international firm— India is changing, you know? In fact, maybe we have more partners who are women than in the U.S. . . . Is it true?"

In other firms, gender representation evolved to surpass global cultural norms. Although this relationship to global standards was not always articulated in comparison, toward the end of my fieldwork, a senior managing law firm partner gave a public interview[7] about the ways in which India's elite legal service firms were not just competent, but also better than firms in the West when it came to gender:

> The East, I think, has learned a lot from the West. I have learned a lot from the West in terms of how I've been able to lead and build this firm, but there are also a number of things which we can do differently. . . . I think the way we deal with diversity is very different. More than half our firm is women, including at the partnership level. And the environment that we have been able to create . . . sometimes not consciously, but it's just happened that way . . . I think we truly believe it's a meritocracy.

In other words, lawyers did not necessarily think that Western firms had equal numbers of women and men; instead, they saw meritocracy and equal opportunity as core ideals on which these firms were built—or at least saw meritocracy as an ideology (independent of outcome) that Western firms would find important and attractive. And in their need to aggressively signal both competence and competitive advantage in a global environment, meritocracy was the ideal norm they paid ceremonial deference to. In turn, their offices looked like the firms in whose image they emerged; they structured their partnerships with lockstep compensation, they hired from prestigious law schools in the country, with recruitment and internship cycles that resembled those of their foreign peers; and they promoted their women partners without attention to gender. This lack of attention to gender did not mean these firms were being gender-friendly, and this non-discrimination on the basis of gender did not mean that firms were substantively egalitarian. As I unpack in chapter 6, these conditions privileged different kinds of inequalities and reproduced a range of other hierarchies. But in being non-discriminatory on the axis of gender within a professional sector where this was highly unusual, these firms, almost inadvertently, surpassed the gendered outcomes of the Western firms they were attempting to ideologically mimic. As the senior partner above put it, these developments occurred "sometimes not consciously . . . it's just happened that way."

"It Does Not Matter" Whether You Are a Man or a Woman: Consulting Firms and the Standard Hurdles of the MNC Model

The underlying organizational nuance in the case of Indian law firms becomes clearer when they are compared with management consulting firms. Like the elite law firms, management consulting firms were new organizations that had similar ideological commitments to modernity and meritocracy. They recruited from similarly elite business schools, often shared office spaces in the same compounds as the law firms, and worked the same kinds of hours. But these were local offices of predominantly foreign multi-country professional service firms, and gender was experienced there in much more typical ways.[8] In these firms, women raised the standard issues that scholars studying gender in elite workforces have long identified as the persistent problem of sustaining egalitarian workplaces: gender-typed essentialism (Pierce 1996); sustainability of female careers (see Kay and Gorman 2008 for a review); lack of adequate mentorship (Epstein 2000; Blake-Beard et al. 2006); male-friendly partner composition (Chambliss and Uggen 2000; Gorman 2006); and overall gender-based stratification (Epstein 2000). Most female consultants started any conversation about gender with the blanket acknowledgment that they knew of no senior women with families who also had client-facing roles. Still, many insisted that this was despite the firm being completely committed to equality. The explanation offered by Subbu, a rising senior woman associate in the Mumbai office of an international consulting firm, was, simply, "India":

> As a company, [Name of Consulting Firm] is extremely committed to making gender a priority. I know they put a lot of thought into it and across the world, they've been more successful. But you have to realize, this is India—so no matter how many interventions you make, at the end of the day, it is going to be affected by how things play out in the ground. Most people at [Name of Consulting Firm] are those who are nice about it—but there are still people who will say something stupid or sexist and you have to learn to deal with that.

Subbu's explanation revealed a classic decoupling narrative: global organizations had the best intentions, they tried implementing as many interventions as possible, but "at the end of the day" gender equity was still subject to what were seen as inherently local hurdles. This narrative about the difficulty of translating ideas into practice "in India" contrasted strongly with law firms in the same India (and often in the same postal code) that continued to think of themselves as global despite their environment.[9] Another way in which professionals at consulting firms internalized this idea that their global firm was sullied by its environment was in the way they used the environment to justify the lack of senior women in their firms. Bhavesh, the rising consultant quoted earlier, worked in the same firm as Subbu. He told me the lack of senior female consultants was especially stark because the organization did so much to make them stay: "In fact the push is to encourage women to stay—but they still leave." When I asked him to elaborate, he went on:

> [Women] have a chance of choosing flexible work hours, they can certainly pick projects that are closer to where they want to be, but even with all that, women leave. . . . There is no difference between men and women—in fact, the only time it makes a difference, is in promotion. But that is because the amount of time you need to invest is more and so, then, it matters. But it doesn't matter to the firm—if you do as much work as a man, you'll get your promotion—but it probably matters to family and neighbors who will not want a woman to spend so much time at work outside the house.

Bhavesh's explanation reveals a particularly problematic repercussion of this narrative that "global progress doesn't work in India" in that it absolved the firm of responsibility: the firm had done everything it could do. It also does not take seriously (while simultaneously reinforcing) the increasing evidence that flexibility is a double-edged sword for women who choose it because of the double-bind it causes for them (Epstein et al. 1999). With this shifted burden of blame, what Subbu saw as a difficult path ahead for herself was to Bhavesh something that his firm could no longer do anything about. In his telling of the story, Indian women's personal hurdles were what kept them from moving ahead: "The push is to encourage women to stay—*but they still leave.*" Bhavesh's framing asserts that the firm was doing everything it could to help female employees but that the women chose not to take advantage of those opportunities, thereby absolving the firm and casting any gender disadvantage as his female peers' own doing.

In contrast, lawyers in elite law firms—women from similar socioeconomic backgrounds as those in Bhavesh's firm, women who were equally educated, women who were asked to work similar hours, women who arguably could have had the same kinds of neighbors and family, etc.—saw the work–life balance as something that *all* lawyers faced, which needed to be addressed more generally. Take the example of Girija, a partner at an elite law firm (whose husband was also a partner at the same firm) talking about the ways in which her family negotiated parenting responsibilities:

> I think in terms of how work and the mother thing has worked out, I was very, very, very apprehensive about being able to juggle it given the timeline. I spoke a lot to [name of managing partner], saying what do you want me to do? Flex hours? Something else? How do things work? Do you want me to go into non-transaction mode? Because on the one hand, I wanted to spend time with my child. But I also had clients— and the firm, well, the firm really just made it work.

Girija's explanation for how she "made it work" included long negotiations with her firm and her partner. She admitted that while she sometimes felt like she was "not spending enough time" with her child, she had a great support system both at home and at work. Girija did not have family in the city, but she had household help for most of the day: "I have a curfew time at 8:00 pm. So either my husband or I have to be at home." Importantly, she was not the only one who needed to meet this curfew: "we manage—we take turns, sometimes it's [my husband] and sometimes it is me, but one of us is there." The pressures on Girija to balance home and work were not vastly different from those probably faced by Bhavesh's peers at the consulting firm, and there is no indication that the resources available to Girija were not available to consultants as well. Everybody I interviewed had access to household help and the resources to fund it—and everybody made use of it. Yet what Girija and her husband saw as the price of being working parents, Bhavesh saw as a burden that lay solely on the shoulders of his female peers ("But it doesn't matter to the firm—if you do as much work as a man, you'll get your promotion").

Consulting firms' structural commitment to egalitarianism also contrasted strongly with the law firm story of gender parity as something that "just happened that way." Unlike consulting firms that adopted standard gender-friendly work arrangements (e.g., flextime options) from their parent firms, law firms did not have structural incentives that made it easier on the female professional. There were no "gender groups" or formal mentoring networks that helped women feel secure about their careers. There were no formal childcare arrangements, and boundaries around work and family were often muddled and negotiated on a case-by-case basis. For example, one partner told me, almost as a display of valor, how she had clients texting her as she was being wheeled in to the delivery room to have her first child. And of the eleven female partners in transactional law firms in my sample, four had children, and each of these partners had negotiated on an individual basis how they would construct their maternity leave and work schedule. And yet, despite these differences that should have structurally advantaged women in consulting firms, it was in domestic law firms that women felt the constraints of their organizational environment least.

This contrast did not go unnoticed. As I was wrapping up an interview with Tarunya, a senior female consultant on the partner track who seemed very invested in making consulting more "gender-friendly," she asked me if I knew what lawyers were doing "right," especially since consulting firms were "struggling to retain women at the top." Telling Tarunya what law firms were "doing right" was difficult because, as the senior partners themselves conceded, the emergence of law firms as gender-neutral spaces wasn't necessarily their "doing." In chapter 5, for example, I show how much of these negotiations were made possible by structure in addition to individual class advantages. Tarunya, like her peers in these law firms, might have had similar class advantages. She could have had proximate family, she certainly had access to similar kinds of domestic help and care. But other structural advantages helped her peers in law firms. As I set up here, their emergence offered them a certain kind of organizational culture and praxis, but they were advantaged by other kinds of temporality too. Because women in these firms were graduates from elite law schools who began their careers in their early twenties, their life course had advantageous synergies with their career trajectories. They could have children after they became partners in their early thirties, allowing for structural navigation of their careers to be on very different terms than other professionals who started their careers later and whose career tracks were more demanding of choice-making that conflicted with their personal commitments. Offering the argument that gender parity was a consequential empirical outcome of institutional emergence would not have done Tarunya much good, especially since there was no way to port these advantages to her own firm. But to organizational scholars, the variance in these fields' institutional emergence and their subsequent adherence to different ideological scripts might be a satisfying explanation.

Firm See? Firm Do. Firm Doesn't See? Firm Does Better

The variation in organizational emergence and structure offers a core explanation for the varied organizational identities—and, therefore, individual experiences—in these two similarly elite sectors. The need for legitimacy certainly led consulting firms to signal their "global" identity. But as firms seeking to emerge as global players, elite law firms with global clients found themselves in a unique position. Unlike their peers with domestic clients, they were facing external markets with new scripts and ideologies about professional practice; at the same time, unlike their other professional peers, they were facing these new scripts while emerging from a particularistic legal profession. And unlike consulting firms that were inherently global organizations, especially within the context of their audience (i.e., local clients), elite law firms were much more conscious of this need to emerge as global players. While consulting firms, with their clear global identity, could afford to blame the attitudes and culture in India for their failed implementation of equality initiatives and outcomes (e.g., Subbu's explanation that "you have to realize, this is India"), elite law firms were much more insecure about their global identity. As a result, as domestically managed firms with external-facing environments, Indian law firms could differentiate themselves from traditional frameworks of patriarchy (which plagued internal-facing domestic firms) *and* reach for new identities that would aggressively signal their competitiveness in global markets (which they needed to do because they lacked the legitimacy enjoyed by externally managed "global" consulting firms). Alongside the differentiation strategies already discussed (rejection of traditional scripts and adoption of global scripts), law firm identity was shaped by a third factor: they didn't have direct experience or knowledge of how global law firms actually lived out their scripts.

Elite domestic law firms, however, could not afford a similar decoupling. These elite law firms, as domestic monopolistic firms, were emerging from a regulatory climate replete with cultural associations of nepotism and gendered hierarchies. In short, they were starting from a place where the assumption was that they were *not* globally competitive. Starting from this place of questionable legitimacy meant that firms felt the need to overcompensate for their environment by aggressively signaling their global standing and ideology. This pragmatic legitimacy creation (Suchman 1995) happened in a range of ways— these new firms looked like elite foreign offices, they recruited associates like elite foreign firms, and they adopted strong meritocratic micro-cultures to match their aspirational macro-cultures.

However, Indian law firms also had to contend with the fact that they had relatively diluted knowledge about the workings of global firms. A few partners had spent time in international firms, and many more were constantly facing these firms as associates in transactions, but there were no formal flows of information between these firms. It is this asymmetric knowledge of macro-cultures, this relative naïveté, that set up the conditions for a form of "speculative" mimicking based on assumptive ideas about the global, and, ultimately, a form of signaled isomorphism toward this ideal type. I use the term speculative because the intention here was not specifically to make these firms gender-friendly, but rather, it was a zealous effort to be as close to the ideal type of a global meritocratic professional firm as possible. One way in which this convergence played out was in firms' vocal commitment to meritocracy—a commitment which, given the comparative professional spaces into which these women could have gone, offered a new haven for professional development for women lawyers in these firms. Thinking of this gender outcome as an incidental consequence of a much grander project of idealized organizational identity also explains why most of the partners who were asked about this unique gender outcome explained it away as something that "just happened" or something that ought to have been obvious given the fact that they were a "global firm." In turn, this created an environment which, while not actively gender-friendly, remained one within which women—senior and junior alike—did not feel like they were actively disadvantaged.

The early literature on neo-institutionalism reminds us that organizations adopt practices and structures not just for the sake of efficiency but also because their cultural environments construct that adoption as being proper, legitimate, or natural (Meyer et al. 1983). Through ritual performances, organizations struggle to preserve fragile meaning-giving myths in the face of inconsistent cultural demands and uncertain technical capacities. But what about organizations that are not sure what the myths and ceremonies are? DiMaggio and Powell (1983) tell us that over time, as an extension of this cultural sculpting, organizations will copy successful practices in an attempt to reduce risk and converge through a process of "mimetic isomorphism." But mimetic isomorphism assumes that the mimicking is happening in environments with access to the original type. What about new organizations that are trying to enter fields without such access and the scripts it provides?

The Indian elite law firm case shows us that sometimes, in the absence of these scripts, the isomorphism rests not just on mimicked scripts, but on *imagined* scripts. And in cases where the mimicking was based on assumptions rather than knowledge or experience of the original type (e.g., in law firms), the resultant convergence was even stronger than in cases where the forms were being replicated (e.g., in consulting firms). In turn, these findings give us new context for understanding the processes of coupling in global organizations—especially in transitional economies that are overcompensating in ceremony for the disadvantage of their emergence environments.

Yet, no matter how essential organizational environments are for the creation and sustenance of internal stratification, institutional inquiry offers only one set of explanations. Significantly, it doesn't take into account the other meso- and micro-level processes that might also be at play. For instance, the role of cultural sorting and matching (Rivera 2012) in determining good fit for these organizations could be crucially relevant for telling us how class and elite credentials operate in this emergence.[10] Additionally, while this research can give us some insight to the process and strategies that firms employ in reorienting their identity in a globally competitive market, it doesn't provide similarly comprehensive information about clients.[11] As a result, it cannot tell us much about the effectiveness of this mimicking. Further still, despite the comparative nature of this study, the gendered "level playing field" in law firms could be theorized through the lens of relationality vis-à-vis other sites in the legal profession: i.e., the conditions of parity in elite law firms offer a haven for women, but they also mean women do not have the same opportunities as men upon exiting these firms, thereby prejudicing the substantive equality the firms purport to offer at first glance. Despite these caveats about their ability to fully explain gender differences across firms, the institutional mechanisms at play in the Indian elite law firm case still hold valuable lessons for theorizing about global legal orders and the ways in which logics of emergence and isomorphism can produce heterogeneity across similar kinds of professional actors. Finally, these findings also remind us that globalization is a two-way process wherein institutions are changed at the global level by norms and adaptations taking place at the national and local levels. Socio-legal scholars have described similar relationships between the global and the local at macro-institutional levels (Halliday and Carruthers 2007; Halliday 2009; Halliday and Shaffer 2015), but while isomorphism can operate in a bilateral dynamic, this has not been a primary focus of this scholarship. Law firms and consulting firms alike offered perspectives on the muddling of the global as interpreted by the local. But, in their efforts to "be global," local law firms were changing what it meant to be global in very different ways than local offices of global consulting firms. It is this reiterative recursive process, rather than evidence of a straightforward mimicking strategy, that makes this process valuable to observe.

Site Variations and the Local Advantages of Global Imaginations

This chapter highlights the second important dimension of incidental construction of the gender outcome in elite law firms—the specific organizational emergence conditions that incentivized these firms to signal a particular brand of modernity to their assumed audiences. Elite domestic law firms were trying to do everything they could to gain legitimacy by being "modern" and "meritocratic": being gender-agnostic happened to be one way of accomplishing this. But importantly, many of the ways in which they were trying to be "just like global firms" arose out of conjecture rather than actual knowledge. In fact, as the case of consulting firms revealed, actual knowledge was counterproductive to the gender project because, among other things, actual knowledge could reveal that women were ill represented in most elite global workforces.

The research design of this project, as I established in chapter 1, offers us a unique micro-perspective that complicates our understanding of the mimetic isomorphism of global firms. Institutionalization of global norms is not usually observed at this level because data on individual experiences in firms like these are often unavailable to scholars interested in the transfer and impact of norms. The variance in these professional cases also provides a quick snapshot of the imperialist possibilities of the Western professional model. Not only do structural and environmental differences cause firms to emerge differently, they also afford very different experiences of globalization. *Three* kinds of structural conditions accounted for the variance in gender outcomes across these sites. As I highlight in the last two chapters, first was the novelty of the field and practice area. As new firms doing new work, all firms had the potential to renegotiate preexisting frameworks of identity and propriety (Ridgeway 2011). But the Indian corporate law firm had the further advantage that, in addition to being a new subfield, regulatory restrictions also required that it be domestically owned and managed. Together, this primed a second structural condition relevant in bringing about greater parity—global exposure.

As I highlight in chapter 1, unlike consulting firms and IT firms that "do" globalization in a standard MNC manner, elite corporate law firms are domestic firms *responding* to a foreign market of clients and competition, which makes them structurally different in the ways they absorb and replicate international cues and standards for emergence. This placed on them an additional onus to respond to standards of international meritocracy. While large corporate law firms did some work for domestic clients, their primary focus was servicing international clients. Their monopoly on the legal service market meant that they were not only emerging in a market where they had to negotiate their legitimacy, but that they were also interacting with sophisticated actors who did not prime gender in the same ways that those facing more traditional clients were likely to face. As I lay out in this chapter, senior partners in law firms were seriously flummoxed when I asked them about the gender composition in their firms. The most common answers were some combination of "why would gender be diversity?" and "it is just like a foreign law firm—gender really doesn't matter." Part of this explanation was rooted in information asymmetry, especially since the assumption that these firms were "just like foreign law firms" was not actually true. Yet, these firms were so keen to differentiate themselves from traditional legal practice (e.g., "gender is no longer relevant—it might matter in litigation, in the courts, but not here!")—that the end result was not so much the championing of gender as it was a marking of modernity through deployment of meritocratic scripts. Here again the accidental assumptions about modernity and meritocracy in the ideal type firms that these new law firms were trying to mimic set up the possibility of egalitarian outcomes.

A third structural condition that remains relevant in the construction of gender-friendly outcomes is the barriers to entry in these professional workspaces. As chapters 1 and 2 illustrate, corporate law firms are significantly aided in creating egalitarian environments by the ways in which their supply pool is recruited and socialized in the prestigious law schools that emerged alongside these corporate law firms post-liberalization. The gender-egalitarian pool of graduates produced by these schools creates an elite supply that differs significantly from that available to consulting firms, which recruit from established elite schools that are more traditional and deeply gendered. In the case of IT firms, the vastness of the field also means that barriers to entry are relatively lower and more variant. While here too, the firms are new and the work is new, the hiring pool is riddled with strong gendered biases. Central then to this claim of unintentional gender egalitarian outcomes—*accidental feminism*—is the strong and growing commitment in India to an education-based labor market where women can—and do—outcompete men. Men and women from middle-class, English-speaking, urban families enter new, elite, high-status law schools that offer them a certain kind of liberal education. This is the first stage where the possibility of a relatively gender-neutral experience is created. To the extent that a commitment to meritocracy drives change, it works in favor of these women entering both new kinds of neoliberal law schools *and* firms. Unlike engineering and business schools that are still steeply male-dominated, law schools that admit men and women in equal number socialize both women *and* men to treat gender as a relative non-issue. This socialization, of course, does not carry over wholesale to every kind of firm these men and women enter. And graduates of elite schools who join traditional law firms continue to face roadblocks to professional success. But the combination of this socialization along with new firms that do not fixate on a gendered ideal worker together creates this space where women can negotiate their position more favorably.

Finally, the capacity to maintain this otherwise unlikely environment is driven in large parts by the clients and families who sustain and support the firms' existence. The fact that these clients are not—as I highlight in chapter 4—predisposed to priming gender in their interactions reinstates the possibility for relative gender-neutrality to exist in these firms. As does the support of these women's larger families. Here too, as I argue in chapter 5, the temporal advantage of these structures is rooted not in an agentic social movement, but in the fact that such a movement did *not* exist in the preceding generation—allowing women to take advantage of relational communities (in the form of extended families of women who are not in the workforce) while accessing rewards from an individualist market economy.

Together, the ways in which gender plays out in these different professional spaces give us one slice of the relevant structural characteristics that set up the different strands of globalization story that is at the center of this book. In the IT sector, the more diffused and *mainstream* version of globalization reaches more people and assumes a more general format of what is assumed to be "international" or "global." In turn, this vast proliferation and its assorted allied assumptions allow gender hierarchies to be renegotiated in the name of being "global" *and* "moral." But the broad scope of the field results in a much less concentrated pool of professional women, especially at the more senior levels. Consulting firms are advantaged by field and practice novelty, but because their clients are mostly local, women distinctly feel gender primed in interactions. Thus, while institutionally similar to IT in terms of being a product of neoliberalism, consulting firms are sites of *fringe* globalization. Not only do these sectors operate on different scales, these firms are also much less a part of mainstream professional consciousness as fewer people realistically aspire to enter and succeed in these firms. Indian corporate law firms, as new firms doing new work but within regulatory restrictions that inhibit access by foreign corporate firms, emerge in an interesting vacuum that bodes well for their professional inhabitants. On the one hand, they are new sites doing new work without steeply gendered expectations of the ideal worker (Acker 1990). At the same time, regulatory circumscription mean that these firms are emerging under the *expectations* of globalization rather than with the express rewards of it—setting them up to be competition-fearing organizations with strong hurdles of legitimacy to overcome. As new firms with no global associations to lend them weight, these law firms depend on promoting their modernity in the international market to remain competitive. This *responsive* globalization is possibly borne out of an organizational commitment to be competitive in international markets; their overcompliance to gender neutrality is one way in which they appease these assumed concerns.

In highlighting these responsive modes of capacity- (and culture-!) building, this book uses these comparative genesis findings to illustrate the ways in which globalization of work has introduced new professional spaces for the contestation of prestige and power. I argue that professional spaces that are built on institutionally settled organizational forms are likely to be different from those that emerge independent of a Western prototype. Similarly, older professions with set institutional scripts differ from professional spaces that have emerged as a response to neoliberal demands in the marketplace. Each of these contexts yields different outcomes for gender representation and parity. While each relies on globalization and global impetus to some degree, the ways in which they translate this into internal accounts of stratification are distinct. The findings in this book give us one method by which to begin to dissect the ways in which reorganization and adaptation of professional frameworks and assumptions happen in one emerging country context. But the findings have legs beyond India. Thinking about globalization not as a static, unidimensional cultural process, but rather as a recursive process, sheds a new light on the relationship between law and society.

As this chapter argues, over the last three decades international businesses have been important sites where we can unpack the working of globally integrated and transnational organizations (Bartlett and Ghoshal 1989; Prahalad and Doz 1999; Palmisano 2006) because their emergence underscores the ways in which a range of hybrid "glocal" cultural codes get legitimized and cemented (Meyer et al. 1983) to provide a survival antidote to adopters in uncertain environments (Powell and DiMaggio 1991:69). One way to gain such legitimacy—and, as I show here, the way in which firms in India *do* gain legitimacy—is through a process of institutional mimicking: adopting cues from peers and ideal types to signal and enhance their institutional membership and standing (DiMaggio and Powell 1983). This ambitious—and often ambiguous—reaching toward ideal scripts of modernity as having better results than the prototypes they seek to mimic is a novel finding for scholars of globalization. At the same time, recognizing that the conditions that set this mimicry in motion are speculative (in that they had no idea that having good gendered representation could be seen as modern, and it certainly was not the only kind of modern legitimacy they were trying to achieve) rather than strategic, or even ideological or aspirational, reminds us of the role of intention and the nature of accident that set up the reinforcing conditions that produced these firms.

Alongside these accounts that explain convergence or isomorphism at the organizational level, socio-legal scholars have described similar hybrid relationships between the global and the local at more macro-institutional levels (Halliday and Carruthers 2007; Halliday 2009; Halliday and Shaffer 2015). Halliday and Carruthers (2007), for instance, argued that the globalization of legal institutions (similar to the aggregate "organizational field" in neo-institutional theory) has happened through recursive, reiterative cycles of law- and norm-making at the national and global level respectively. Thus, change in legal systems (and by extension in other systems that are based on legal systems) is not so much a unidirectional response to global cues but rather an interrelated and relational process by which the local and the global interact and integrate with one another. The sociology of law literature has since expanded on the implications of this recursive relationship between the local and the global, offering one more lens through which to conduct a nuanced consideration of the emergence of India's law firms (e.g., Dezalay and Garth 2010; Plickert and Hagan 2011; Wilkins et al. 2017). In particular, this approach encourages us to think of institutional change in emerging economies not just as a straightforward mimetic process of isomorphism, but also as a two-way process wherein these institutions are changed at the global level by norms and adaptations taking place at the national and local levels. India offers an especially rich arena for investigating these negotiations around legitimacy and convergence from an emerging country perspective. As the markets change to include actual—rather than speculative—competition, these distinctions might become starkly different; they'll certainly have to contend with the reality rather than the imagination of the other. Still, for now, it provides an organic setup for studying natural variations in organizational motivations and ideological positions vis-à-vis global cues.

Of course, there is a potential counternarrative. It is possible that the entire story of advantage could be conflating a deeper class dynamic: women in global law firms do better because they self-select from an elite pool of similarly qualified and socially advantaged women. As many lawyers seemed to suggest, their ability to signal class position often guaranteed that they would not be seen as a secretary or paralegal. But beyond visibility, as I show in chapter 5, this advantage of class was particularly salient when it came to balancing family and work. While women across sites spoke about having to navigate choices and paths about children, it was clear that certain kinds of women were best able to achieve this balance. Typically, these women worked in cities where they had many social ties and large networks (often, these cities also happened to be their hometowns). This often also meant that they had certain class advantages, including the cultural freedom to marry partners of their choice and make their own decisions about starting (or not starting) families. Thus, one possible explanation could be that these women are not priming and championing a gender narrative at all—they might be championing a class narrative. Even so, women from a certain strata with class advantages have always existed (and continue to exist), and my broader research on elite professional women shows that not all elite firms—including other kinds of new elite firms—advantage women in the same ways. It is something about *these* firms that seems to offer elite women a particular advantage. This is not to say their class frame does not advantage them; rather, their class frame alone has not been enough to advantage them in the past, or even now, in other contexts. This movement away from a simplistic understanding of why some women are doing well in India is central to the dismissal of these findings as a purely class-based story. The middle-class, first-generation, elite professional mobility that I highlight in this book is central to what is novel about the findings in my research and about these women's careers at this specific point in time more generally. In other words, when holding the individual-level advantages constant, women across different work spaces continue to be differently advantaged upon entry into these different firms, and it is this novelty of advantage—even if only to a cross-section of the population of lawyers capable of leveraging it—that sets these new and elite law firms apart.

Further still, the extensions for temporality could have other limitations and other perspectives on how we code this equality within firms. As the first generation of women who have made it in firms, senior women can have expectations from following cohorts that may be experienced by junior women as structurally nonfeminist or gender-friendly (Staines et al. 1974; Kanter 1993). As one male partner offered, one can have a kind partnership that is visibly equal but still gendered. And if what is being generated is a generation of women who have made steep sacrifices during a time of limited opportunity to make the most of their situation, the intergenerational impacts of such an inheritance could be complicated.[12] In particular, if gendered success within the firm is received as an achievable end without specific regulations, women who have gained such success might have no incentive to rework the support systems that would allow others after them to navigate the same terrain.[13] Besides, if exits from the firm have different outcomes for men and women—and indeed for different kinds of women—that attrition also tells us something about the ways in which women are forced to overperform to maintain the veneer of "equality" within these firms. If women have reason to think that marriage and children will affect their career prospects differently than their male colleagues, then one can imagine that their choices (to the extent these are clear choices) reflect this institutional evaluation.

I had no explicit data to support this framing—answers to "why" questions are rarely useful in terms of shedding light on actual mechanisms at play— but the many retrospective and reflective conversations I've had with lawyers both within and beyond my sample following my years in Mumbai have given me reason to imagine that this might well be another underlying inequality that affords a semblance of advantage. The women who left these firms offer at least as much of the story of success as those who stay. I did not have a robust attrition sample with enough variation to make a streamlined argument about why people left these firms. Some left for personal reasons (often, but not always, related to a male partner in a different city or country), a few left to go to smaller firms or smaller branches of firms in other cities, and fewer still left to pursue further credentialing that they believed would help them navigate other careers.[14] Still, at least one common theme was their inability to balance work and family responsibilities because of institutional limitations—either the lack of a proximate family support system, or lack of "good" carework,[15] or, more commonly, the lack of an independent relationship with a senior mentor who could vouch for the need for a specialized renegotiation of this balance. Sailaja, a lawyer who was on partner track in her late twenties, left the firm when she had her first child to focus on being a parent, but was ready to come back (and did) in a few years when she felt the transition was more manageable. As suggested by other scholars who study gender in the legal profession, mentorship and the ability to help navigate careers from a position of power is a striking advantage for junior women,[16] and what made Sailaja's reentry manageable was not just that she had a domestic partner who supported her vision of how to manage these conflicting demands and a set of helpers who could help with responsibilities at home, but also that she had a senior partner in the firm who was a committed mentor who felt that "loyalty to the firm was really important and not something that could be replaced if one were to recruit similar talent in the market." This meant that Sailaja had a protective cover of sorts, offered by someone who both had a stake in her personal development as well as the power to pitch such return as tactical from the firm's perspective. While stories about interpersonal relationships like this were numerous in my fieldwork, their fragility lay in their exceptionalism. Thoughtful (and strategic) partners who will extend themselves to ensure the post-baby renegotiation of a younger associate with serious potential, or those who will aggressively cultivate junior careers, are useful; but only inasmuch as they are also rare. Further, as independent (and often uncommon) individual actors, they were, on their own, not enough to secure sustained equality within these firms.

Even with these caveats, institutional mechanisms at play in the Indian elite law firm case still hold valuable lessons for theorizing about global legal orders and the ways in which logics of emergence and isomorphism can produce heterogeneity across similar kinds of professional actors. As neo-institutionalism framework reminds us that organizations adopt mainstream and vetted practices and structures for both efficiency and legitimacy, and that the ritualistic performance of scripts allows organizations to preserve the meaning making myths in the face of inconsistent cultural demands and technical capacities (Meyer et al. 1983). The Indian elite law firm case shows us that sometimes, in the absence of these ritual scripts, the isomorphism rests, not just on mimicked scripts, but also on imagined scripts. And in cases where the mimicking was based on assumptions rather than knowledge of the original type (e.g., in law firms), the resultant convergence was even stronger than in cases where the forms were being replicated (e.g., in consulting firms). But this pattern is not meant to be seen only as an extension to a body of literature, or a way to theorize about the Indian case more thoroughly. Instead, these findings give us new tools and context for understanding micro inequalities in global organizations more generally—especially in transitional economies that are overcompensating in ceremony for the disadvantage of their emergence environments. Seen this way, the variations in globalization processes that these cases illustrate offer us new ways of thinking about the everyday lived consciousness and experience of macro institutional processes more generally.

But while explanations at the individual and organizational levels are useful for setting up the context, they are still only part of the story. Institutional inquiry, for instance, does not shed light on the ways in which other interactions—with clients, peers, and family members[17]—play out in these firms and the ways in which these relational expectations help produce the unlikely outcomes I speak about in this book. These micro demographic stories were crucial at the individual level—both in terms of who these professionals were engaging with professionally (i.e., the people who were holding a mirror to their professional success) and the kinds of dependencies they had in their familial life that buttressed their ability to have these work personas. It is to these interpersonal dynamics and the ways in which they were negotiated, navigated, and legitimized that we turn in the next two chapters.

FOUR

FACINGS

My Clients Prefer a
Woman Lawyer

NEW RETURNS TO ESSENTIALISM

AS I LAY OUT in the last chapter, the organizational variations that were crucial for explaining gendered outcomes were also predicated on the power of broad and diffuse ideological constructs. Yet, broad and diffuse ideas—and, more specifically, common understandings of concepts like meritocracy and modernity—do not occur in vacuum. Rather, they are created and maintained by individual actors across a range of interactions. Sometimes this was reassurance from a partner that the firm was internationally competitive. At other times, it was between colleagues who were trying to navigate their environment with accepted scripts about what it meant to work in a certain sort of firm. But importantly, notions of what it meant to be a modern firm or a merit-forward and equal objectivity–focused firm mattered in interactions with clients who remained powerful gatekeepers.

Following a line of feminist research that suggests that gender is not merely a variable, but a process that is recursively "done," I analyze in this chapter the variations in the way women professionals experienced these interactional environments. In the process, I shed light on the ways in which essentialist assumptions about gender were valued in these varied work contexts. A robust body of research highlights that professional women get judged for *not being men* before they get judged as professionals. That is, over and above biased organizational structures, women are also judged for actions and interactions they are part of at the individual level. This focus on individual navigation of pathways is not to alleviate the embedded structures within which women (and other minority actors) are placed, but it does offer one more way in which workplace inequality persists. And because these acts are seen as "done," these individual choices and preferences, cultivated over years of socialization within a range of gendered structures, are seen as legitimate reasons to discriminate (Correll 2001; Cech and Blair-Loy 2019). Particularly, research also shows that, for professional women, the choices are either to lean into doing more male work or to self-select out of jobs that valorize male actors and traits. These choices might seem agentic. Yet, at their core, they are illusory because they hurt women in different ways while simultaneously relieving their organizational actors of responsibility. Because male work is more valued, women internalize professional norms that encourage masculine behavior and modify and model their actions and networks to match their male counterparts (Davies-Netzley 1998; Blair-Loy 2009; Ramarajan and Reid 2013; Reid 2015; Reid and Ramarajan 2016). At the same time, women who exhibit hegemonic male traits are subject to double standards and backlash (Rudman and Glick 1999, 2001), requiring them to balance on a precarious tightrope between "able" and "liked" (Williams and Dempsey 2014). The most common example of this difficulty is that women are expected to be deferential, cordial, and undemanding in organizations, but these same organizations reward "male-typed" qualities like aggression and ambition. The double standard makes it hard for women to heed advice like "if you do not speak up, you only have yourself to blame" (Babcock and Laschever 2003), because when they do speak up, their boldness is not received positively (Bowles, Babcock, and Lai 2007).

In line with this global evidence, essentialist assumptions about gender and work were omnipresent across the professional cases in my data. For example, women lawyers in litigation firms felt flagrantly discriminated against by their traditional—often domestic—clients, who did not see them as aggressive enough to be effective in the courtroom. Similarly, in the consulting firms, women often felt the pinch of benevolent sexism in that they were both treated better *and* respected less than their male peers by older men in local industry (their typical type of client). Essentialist assumptions were also present for women in elite law firms, but they worked in different ways. Even though these women worked primarily with international and what they described as "sophisticated" domestic clients, their interactions were still rife with rigid assumptions about what men and women were better suited to do; unlike in the other sites, however, this essentialism furthered rather than inhibited gender-egalitarian outcomes. Adding to the suggestion in chapter 2 that novelty was crucial in debunking background identities of the ideal worker, this chapter shows how the lack of preexisting frameworks helped women to be appreciated by powerful interactional actors even as they continued to be essentialized. For example, women in these law firms were still seen by clients as less aggressive than their male peers, but in the new work context, aggressiveness itself was not highly valued. Similarly, being polite, communal, and "good with clients" were all descriptions of an ideal worker, but because the work itself was not predetermined to be associated with a specific gender, these qualities, often feminized and devalued in other contexts, were not viewed as "weak." As a result, essentialism didn't exclude women outright.

It is this unlikely valorization of gender that is the crux of this chapter. This positive valuation of a female trait within a high-status workplace—and this unconventional valorization of a still strongly gender-typed identity— extends conventional understandings of gender and essentialism by reviewing its potential for variation in new employment contexts. And, in introducing this third mechanism of accidental feminism—interactions with clients and peers—this chapter challenges the standard assumption that gender egali- tarianism and essentialism are inversely related. A rising strain of research has pushed for organizational valorization of these "feminine" values and strengths (e.g., John Gerzema and Michael D'Antonio's *The Athena Doctrine*), but empirical progress has not matched the enthusiasm of such advocacy. In highlighting this case of new firms, this chapter suggests that gender desegre- gation is better achieved through novel organizational structures and changes in the labor market rather than ambitious agendas to modify cultural atti- tudes about women. At the same time, by unpacking the variations in external audiences across firms (i.e., elite law firms were domestic firms with mainly sophisticated, international clients, whereas consulting firms were interna- tional firms with local, domestic clients), the chapter reveals the limitations of this important structural condition. Organizational novelty could offer new environments for work, but without interactional support, their potential remains unrealized.

The Relationship between Essentialism and Work

As I have suggested earlier in this book, women are constantly brushing up against the norm of an ideal worker. Thinking of these essentialist hierarchies as products of rigid cultural frameworks is useful, but what about cases where cultural associations and values regarding the ideal worker are still in the early stages of being defined and negotiated? If pervasive understandings of who is best qualified to do a certain job are still in flux, could there be some leeway for who is seen as an "ideal" fit for these positions? Particularly in work contexts, when gendered meanings of work are not yet so set, can cultural understand- ings of male and female traits become valorized in different and perhaps more egalitarian ways?

A robust body of research suggests the collinearity between essential- ist gender stereotypes and unequal outcomes within organizational settings (Fiske 1993; Steele 1997; Kray, Thompson, and Galinsky 2001), and profes- sional work environments have provided an influential site to dissect the ways in which these micro inequalities persist and reproduce (Epstein 1993; Kanter 1993; Pierce 1996; Chambliss and Uggen 2000; Schultz and Shaw 2003; Gor- man 2005, 2006; Kay and Gorman 2008; Gorman and Kmec 2009; Rivera

2012). Within these work environments, women who wish to succeed either are left to become better at doing what is considered to be "male work" (Jackson 1998) or are excluded entirely by self-selecting out of these jobs (Baker 2003). As a result, there is an under-rewarded and unidirectional convergence into female-friendly work (England 2010) rather than an egalitarian essentialism where both male and female work is valorized equally (Cotter, Hermsen, and Vanneman 2011).

To explain the persistence of these social categories like gender that beget unequal outcomes, scholars have moved away from understanding gender attribution as a cognitive or biological bias (Taylor 1996) and instead have adopted the critical view of essentialism as an ideological tool that legitimizes power relations in any given context (Hacking 1999). Such a perspective explains the way that many advanced industrial societies share a cultural image of most high-status professional work as being male-typed and women as being less naturally suited for the tasks at hand (Collinson and Hearn 1996; Powell, Butterfield, and Parent 2002). For example, Lyness and Heilman (2006) demonstrated that even when women enter large financial corporate spaces, they are evaluated more harshly than men generally and especially in jobs that carry a "male typed image" like production and sales. Elizabeth Gorman's (2005) study of the hiring criteria used by large US law firms in the 1990s revealed that stereotypically masculine traits (e.g., assertive, ambitious) were more commonly listed than stereotypically female traits (e.g., cooperative, friendly) and that, unsurprisingly, the more masculine the criteria, the more likely it was that a man was hired for the job. Similarly, in her ethnography on American law firms, Jennifer Pierce (1996) showed how women professionals were expected to perform more emotional labor than their male peers and also how positions within the firm were constantly embedded with gendered meanings. While male lawyers, as "Rambo litigators," were pardoned for bad behavior—and even expected to display it—women were expected to be "ladylike," often garnering "criticism, disapproval and even ostracism" if they attempted to be adversarial. Women, Pierce revealed, were best served when they "split" their identities and stayed aggressive in court but were caring and mother-like with their subordinates. Pierce's nuanced elaboration of this firm was jarring because it reminded readers how not that much had changed from the 1950s' suburban American model of gender roles—women were still doing the caretaking, only now they were doing it in professional firms. Almost two decades after Pierce's study, O'Neill and O'Reilly (2011), who studied elite business school graduates over eight years, found that women still had to do this balancing act to leverage gains in their work environments. In their study, women who were most rewarded in the workplace were those who could embody masculine traits (defined as aggressiveness, assertiveness, and confidence) while also being able to "self-monitor" their behavior. Successful women were often those who could be "chameleons," i.e., those who could fit into their environment by assessing social situations and adapting their actions. These patterns of gendered roles and expectations, while certainly not specific to the global north, remain much less thoroughly investigated in other emerging contexts, where the mainstay of the literature on women and work has remained focused on jobs that are either deeply "female-typed" like nursing (e.g., Burawoy et al. 2000) or low-status and process-driven like factory labor (e.g., Salzinger 2003).

The "No Problem" Problem: Intra-Firm Peer Dynamics

As chapter 2 suggests, an understanding of preentry socialization is integral to comprehending the interactions within law and consulting firms. All these firms recruited from largely homogenous pools of professionals—a homogeny that, I argue in chapter 6, is at the root of perpetrating this structural equality. However, in contrast to the gender-equal compositions of elite law schools that trained most of these firms' lawyers, consultants were mostly trained in male-concentrated elite engineering and business schools. Senior male consultants like Bhavesh, the rising star consultant quoted in chapter 3, saw these environments as more gender-equal than the schools they graduated from (e.g., "yeah, it is male heavy—but not as bad as IIT") and their firms as agentic institutions working hard to be egalitarian. Women consultants, on the other hand, saw these firms as having inherently gendered tracks, especially after they had spent some time in them. Sridevi, a senior consultant, explained the ways in which she felt gender play out in intra-firm dynamics—something she didn't expect to be the case when she first joined the firm. She admitted to initially having seen "no reason" for one of the firm's women's groups because she did not feel any different from the men she was working with. But at the time of our interview, in her fifth year as a consultant, she agreed she had shifted from that initial stance. She explained her change of perspective this way: "we didn't think we were any different from the men we were working with and there was no difference in the way we were being treated, so it didn't matter . . . But [emphasis], over time, we've realized the criticality of the initiative."

Sridevi's explanation for the usefulness of women's spaces within her organization was rooted in gender difference, especially given the way she saw gendered categories playing out in her firm and the kinds of affect that grounded interactions and hierarchies:

> [the] thing is more senior you go, you will come across one cocky junior who thinks he is so awesome and is just the rock star of the company (he?) is working for—and he will look at politeness and softness—in terms of how you speak—to mean lack of capability and you need to shed your inhibitions and reluctance and face this person and take it

head on [and say] "you might like it or not / but you are working for me." If someone is cocky, [they] might be that way with anyone, but if [they try it with] a male consultant, he will fix it on day one and say "Dude, what is wrong with you? Fix it." But as a woman, I feel like I'll wait for many subtle ways before I actually have that conversation. I'll try telling him more subtly that he is working with people who have more experience that he has to learn from.

Sridevi's account of these gendered interactions with peers is, at least in part, dictated by the strong male presence in her workforce. And her predicament is in line with what other gender scholars have identified as a core predicament for women's organizational success—the constant tightrope between untenable and contrary characteristics like nice, able, liked alongside confident, aggressive, and forceful (Rudman and Glick 2001; Brescoll and Moss-Racusin 2007; Rudman and Phelan 2008; William and Dempsey 2014). As chapter 2 reveals, women are constantly judged against prescriptive stereotypes, which hurt them both when they are too accommodating and when they are too aggressive. And independent of how it is received by peers, many women resist such aggressive forthrightness because they feel it is inauthentic to their natural selves. Sridevi's account confirmed that this was the case for her too, offering not just a portrait of a "cocky, rock star" male junior who was likely to listen to a more forthright male colleague but also a sense of how being less subtle (and saying her equivalent of "Dude, what is wrong with you?") was hard for her personally:

Sure, you have to power through and steamroll a person in front of you—but it is difficult to change personal style—although I've done this with clients and in front of others, it leaves a bitter taste. It's not who I am and it's hard to do it. How do I keep personal style and keep up with the situation? It is difficult if you are a woman, for sure.

Being subtle, as Sridevi suggested, might be an inherent, even authentic, part of her "personal style." But this brand of authenticity—or this hesitation to unnaturally change one's personality in order to navigate workforces—is by no means a trait found only among Indian women. In other work on women navigating gendered workspaces in US organizations, colleagues and I show that this authenticity is central to the ways in which women think about their place in organizations across different contexts (Ballakrishnen, Fielding-Singh, and Magliozzi 2019). As Sridevi laments, being inauthentic in the workplace takes a toll on many women, and even if they do act in a way that goes against their personal style, it leaves a "bitter taste." This parallel research, from a very different cultural context (a large organization in the Western United States), shows that—despite any advice and training that suggests they "lean in"—women are more likely to reject executive, self-promoting leadership styles in favor of more communal styles to feel more authentic: a strategy we termed "intentional invisibility." Staying behind the scenes, or in Sridevi's case being subtle, irrespective of its actual long-term career advantages, may offer women a valuable tool for aligning their personal values and professional demeanors. In fact, it could be the only tool they have.

At the same time, despite the taste Sridevi's account offers for gendered interactions among organizational peers, it is not meant to suggest that internal dynamics were key to creating the internal environments in consulting firms. Although there were variations in the ways in which women across sites described their work environments, professionals across sites seemed to enjoy some similar advantages from a comparable level of background homophily. Women and men alike in these firms went to similar schools, were all part of a similar middle-class background, and were comfortable in gendered interactions because they did not have a reason to be triggered in them. Most women across organizations spoke about how, "behind the doors" of the office, "everyone was the same" and people were "very chilled out" even if they were the "only girl around." At the same time, it was clear that there were tensions around gender—especially in consulting firms given the ultimately inegalitarian outcomes—even if not overt discrimination. Take this nuanced explanation from Tarunya, the emerging senior consultant from chapter 3, who noted that background homophily was useful in avoiding overt problems in peer interactions, but still disadvantaged some women consultants because they didn't "bond" as well with their male peers:

> Within [my firm] people you work with—up and down, both—well, communication-wise it's not a problem. There are no cases of discrimination *per se* because all these people are from same [socio economic status], so they've gone to similar schools, they all speak the same sort of English, like similar things like that. But what does happen, is that there is a concept of a *sutta-club* [cigarette club]. I don't even think they smoke anymore, but they are just men who bond together in the cigarette hallways or take breaks together. And they just bond with each other easier than they bond with women.

Tarunya's admission that there were varying levels of interactional comfort but "no cases of discrimination *per se*" speaks directly to what organizational scholars have referred to as the most persistent obstacle for gender equity in modern workspaces—a *second-generation gender bias* (Ibarra, Ely, and Kolb 2013) or the "*'no problem'* problem" (Rhode 1991). Essentially, women are struck in their careers by not one direct obstacle of discrimination, but rather by a complex network of more subversive hurdles. Ibarra and colleagues argue that the main problem is no longer a deliberate exclusion of women from the workforce, but instead, a set of subtle and often invisible barriers that inadvertently benefit men while putting women at a disadvantage. Rhode's argument is that we are so committed to revealing our lack of direct discrimination (the "no problem") that we are oblivious to more entrenched inequalities that have taken their place. Similarly, Tarunya's exclusion from a *"sutta club"* illustrates how, for many women who were no doubt included in obvious ways within the organization, there were still sites of exclusion. In *Hamilton*-speak, they were simply not in the "rooms where it happened."

This invisible discrimination played out in the differential access men and women had to mentoring networks. In traditional litigation practice, it was a stark function of numbers: There were so few women at the top that it created a troubling oligopoly where there were a few accessible mentors, and those who were available were likely to be very senior men or women who were too stretched as visible minorities to have enough social capital to share with possible junior associates. As Kanmani, a litigating lawyer in her late twenties, explained:

> The perception is that you don't have enough female mentors, so the trajectories are defined by people who are [already senior]. And these women get a major minority complex so they don't go out of their way to help other women because no one helped them—so it is not a very healthy environment for a junior woman.

In consulting firms, senior women were more common than in traditional practice (although there were almost no women partners). But rising juniors still felt the pressure of these networks of homophily that excluded women. As noted in chapter 3, Tarunya felt that, in spite of their strategy and planning, consulting firms were unable to replicate the successes of women lawyers in elite law firms. Later in the same interview, she brought up how her consulting firm had structural tools in place to change this culture, but had had trouble implementing it because senior partners (most of whom were male) found it "easier to interact" with male colleagues:

> So there are a lot of workshops around for senior male partners and principals who find it hard to interact with junior women probably from an attempt to be more professional. But the thing is, it still hurts the women they are not mentoring. . . . The other side of it is that junior men are also better at reporting to male bosses and they are weird about really respecting female partners—I mean, we don't have female partners yet, but it is still something that is hard for them. Girls—at least here in India—are also more likely to sit around and wait for things to work out if they do their jobs well. But because of how [Consulting Firm] is set up, it's about how you present yourself upwards. Just sitting around and waiting for it is not going to produce results. If I don't tell my partners what I did or toot my own horn, they are not going to know me. And without that, they don't know who the

hell I am. I know these are complete generalizations and I try to avoid it, but it is just the way it is.

Other researchers who study diversity in organizations have observed similar obstacles for women and minorities in mentoring relationships (Blake-Beard et al. 2006; Rhode 2011; Pearce, Wald, and Ballakrishnen 2015). In general, people feel most comfortable around others like themselves and, absent significant intervention, will gravitate toward assisting them (Wilkins and Gulati 1996; McPherson et al. 2001). At the same time, minorities must constantly contend with implicit bias (Johnson et al. 2004; Ridgeway 2011; Roberts, Mayo, and Thomas 2019). If "girls in India," as Tarunya said, are "more likely to sit around and wait for things to work out," not only are they excluded from mentorship opportunities, but it also means that those women who *do* "toot their own horn" are likely to experience backlash for being agentic. The trouble with homophily and its reproduction of implicit bias patterns is well documented, especially in the case of professional firms (Levinson and Young 2010; Weatherspoon 2010). And closed mentoring networks such as the one Tarunya described above are the inevitable fruit of these latent mechanisms. But because consulting firms did not see these biases as problems—"there are no cases of discrimination per se"—finding solutions for them was not a high priority.

Yet, not all interactions were rife with second-generation biases. And even when they were, they were not the only determining interactional factor for gendered professional experiences. Beyond internal dynamics and biases, the more pressing ways in which gendered navigation occurred in professional service firms was through interactions with clients. Seen as powerful interlocutors, clients were central to reinforcing existing gendered biases, and in even more cases, introducing new kinds of legitimacies for gendered expectations and, as I show below, gendered exceptionalism.

Making the Client Comfortable: Facings Outside the Firm

The importance of client influence in professional work has been well documented (Nelson 1988; Suchman and Cahill 1996; Beckman and Phillips 2005; Gorman 2006; Liu 2006; Wilkins 2009). And it isn't surprising that cultivating a good "fit" with clients was a consideration for senior partners and associates across the board. Just as mentoring was more comfortable and successful between like peers, external interactions were improved by facings with clients who were "similar." This penchant for homophily in itself is not unexpected, as it sets up important mechanisms of trust, favor, and comfort (Heinz et al. 2005; Rivera 2012). But it does suggest an important mechanism governing the ways in which these different professional settings conducted external interactions. As I have already shown, elite Indian law firms were advantaged by their structural innovation and new kinds of work, which distinguished them from traditional legal practice but made them comparable to new consulting firms. In addition, they benefited from the new pool of professionally trained workers they recruited and these workers' exposure to global clients—both advantages that management consulting houses, as internally facing firms staffed mostly with engineers, did not have. As firms doing work for international clients, women lawyers in elite law firms leveraged the advantage of *speculative isomorphism* as I suggest in chapter 3 as well as a moderation of *gendered frames* that operated in other, more gender-typed professional work like litigation as I suggest in chapter 2. Here, I focus on a more limited mechanism—the differences in their interactions with clients. Independent of the ways in which gender was primed *within* the firm, external interactions were strongly influenced by the type of client these professionals were most likely to encounter.

ESSENTIALIST HURDLES IN HIGH-STATUS WORKSPACES: TRADITIONAL LITIGATION PRACTICE

Accounts of interactions across sites were fraught with expectations for women to be careful, cordial, and nondemanding. And for women in traditional litigation practice, these gendered expectations meant that they had to prove continuously why they were good fits for the job at hand. Kanmani, a litigating lawyer in her late twenties who had a successful practice but still felt that she had to "manage her image," described it this way: "If you are a woman, you are not taken seriously. If you are a young woman, you are really not taken seriously." Clients in particular were crucial to setting these unrealistic standards because they were a relevant audience that moderated the construction of this identity. Mohan, the senior litigating lawyer, who was first introduced in chapter 2, explained that in his practice, "gender did not matter," except when clients felt uncomfortable dealing with a woman, at which point he "did not have a choice" and assigned the client to a male attorney:

> Gender does matter for old clients, who are orthodox, but that is because they have reservations about the interaction. . . . When a client has a problem, we don't have a choice—I don't think it is because they are trying to do a disservice, it is just that they are not comfortable with interacting and dealing with a woman.

The endeavor to make his client "comfortable" *was*, of course, a "disservice" because it meant that Mohan's female colleagues were constantly dealing with (and curtailed by) prescribed essentialist assumptions about their professional identity. And young women in particular felt they had to negotiate this identity doubly since many of their clients were older men who did not take their professional position seriously. Male lawyers like Mohan did not deny that women had to balance this identity negotiation, but their explanation for why an older, "orthodox" client might not want a young female lawyer was rooted in structural reasonableness: i.e., such selection was fair "given the nature of the job." As Mohan explained, women just did not fit the "client's perception" of what it meant to be a good lawyer, especially in court:

> There is some perception about what clients want in court and essentially it is something like this: [*speaking in Hindi*] "a lawyer should speak loudly, he should be able to show the other side in poor light." Clients want a performance, . . . they are not lawyers, they don't understand the case and its merits, they want someone who can shout and give the sort of performance that will make them win the case. . . . They [male lawyers] are seen as more powerful, more dominating, and it is difficult for a woman to come up to that level, at least, it is difficult in this sort of courtroom.
>
> *This is one in which you need to be loud—so [you] can put down [insult] someone in court. You need to be rude.*

Performance might seem distinct from success in courts, but oftentimes they were not disparate mechanisms. Clients cared about a performance because it was indeed a better indicator of success in courts, which positively valued aggressive lawyering and repeat lawyers before the bench. Yet, this was not the only way in which women were excluded for what were construed as "just" reasons. Women in litigation routinely spoke about interactions that were "uneasy" or "uncomfortable" because the clients (usually described by them as "local" or "traditional" men who were not used to interacting with women) did not initially feel comfortable discussing their personal matters with someone new. Take the example of Archana, a lawyer in a small litigation practice that dealt mainly with what she described as "local men" because her practice area (tax law) mostly encountered business clients (who were predominantly men). Like many women respondents, she described the discomfort that local clients, especially from small towns, felt when they had to deal with a female firm lawyer:

> He was like . . . from Rajasthan and he came to the office with his son. . . . But this gentleman wouldn't look me in the eye. And he was one of those conservative . . . men. So he was talking to me like this [*turning her face to the side*] . . . and while he was talking to me like this, and I couldn't see his face—he said, [*Speaking in Hindi*] "Is nobody else there?" . . . I was really pissed off.

Archana went on to explain that this particular client's initial dismissal of her made her want to work twice as hard as she might otherwise have worked on a case like this. Although she was given the option to be relieved from the case by the partners in her firm, Archana asked to be staffed on it to be able to prove herself and eventually, in her own words, "won him over" to a point where he would specifically request her services when he came to the firm. Of course, this need to doubly prove one's self despite an initial discriminatory interaction might be specific to Archana (and it was something that served her well in this case), but it can hardly be what we expect from minority actors more generally in the face of similar friction. The partners who nudged her to excuse herself from the case might have been looking out for Archana, but they certainly were thinking about the long-term implications of the client's comfort and satisfaction. Perhaps if it was a more prestigious client, or a client who was less likely to be "won over," the import of the interactions might have looked different. Independent of how it worked out for Archana personally, what stays relevant is that, in being able to root the explanation for this discrimination in practicality rather than prejudice, senior men like Mohan could explain their staffing and hiring decisions as ones in which their hands were metaphorically tied and where they "did not have a choice." I also highlight these here to illustrate how the persistence of background frameworks of gender and work were not just cemented by clients who had strict gendered notions of what it means to be an effective lawyer in court. In litigation the nature of the work and steeped history of the field meant that women were constantly encountering gendered interactions where they fell short of the ideal male worker, often just by existing and before they had a chance to prove themselves. But these ideas of gendered work were just as culturally embedded in non-litigation environments where clients were wary of women in professional capacities. In some ways, then, categorical discrimination and gendered coding of women as ineffective lawyers was just as detrimental for women's careers as shy clients who were uncomfortable about dealing with women in professional capacities just because they were not used to it.

NECESSARY BUT NOT SUFFICIENT: MANAGEMENT CONSULTANTS AND THE ADVANTAGE OF NEW WORK CONTEXTS

While litigation was typically described as a "man's world," accounts of such dynamics in consulting were much less stark. And while women were not always staffed on cases, there seemed to be a general agreement that this was the result of prudence rather than gender preference. For example, women were sometimes not staffed on cases that required travel to rural sites without "facilities" because firms neither wanted to inconvenience their workers nor become liable for them. Yet, this did not mean gender was absent from everyday experiences, and not all choices could be explained with the "nature of work" rationale alone. Instead, in consulting firms, women had to contend with another form of practical sense-making used to rationalize essentialism— clients who treated them fondly or "better" than their male colleagues, but, at the same time, did not take them very seriously.

Unlike litigating lawyers such as Archana who had to deal with hostility rooted in discomfort, or Kanmani who had to "manage her image" to prove she was on par with an ideal (male) lawyer, women in consulting had to deal with a different variant of sexism: *benevolence* (Fiske and Glick 1995; Glick and Fiske 2001; Barreto and Ellemers 2005; Barreto et al. 2010; King et al. 2012). Tarunya, like many of her peers, attributed this to the general demographic of the client base—older Indian men who had set expectations about their business allies:

> It comes down to the way clients perceive you. This is the other thing— it is generally hard for 50–60-year-old men, who have been around in the industry longer than you've been born to take advice from you. And clients are generally who make or break you—so it is harder for them to take it from a girl. I've had difficulty with clients who basically refused to talk to me because they were like "what would I know as a young girl." Especially in places like a hard-core engineering company, I had a rough time because I was a girl and not an engineer, [which were] two things they don't respect very much. But on the other hand, [I] also have had clients who have been very fatherly—you know, 60-year-olds, I could have been to school with their daughters or they wanted their daughters to be like me—and they feel like they have to make my life easier so [they] treat me much much better than my male colleagues.

Even though Tarunya described her experience with these "fatherly" clients as generally treating her "much much better" than they treated her male peers, the paternal perception behind that treatment did not always serve her best professional interests. She was, for instance, one of three mid-tier consultants who were "on track" to the still all-male partnership in her firm. And, like other woman consultants, she felt simultaneously better treated and less valued than her male peers by her clients and colleagues alike. Clients, for example, thought she was not confident enough or aggressive enough in transactions, both male-typed traits that plague women's advancement universally:

> One feedback we hear a lot—especially at a more senior level—is that guys are more confident and [their] presentation skills are much better. But what they don't get is that it is particularly difficult for women—how do you make yourself be heard without being aggressive? How do you make a presentation where the room is looking for a guy? That's the hard part. If you crack clients, you have everything else sorted. If a client likes you, you are golden.

But "cracking clients," as Tarunya put it, was not exactly straightforward. Women consultants often felt they were not being true to themselves when they were aggressive or forthright, a conundrum that their male colleagues did not share. Further, the women who were aggressive had to deal with being deemed unapproachable and difficult or, as Bikram, a male consultant with more than a decade of experience suggested, "bitchy":

> One defense mechanism [women] use . . . is that they are unapproachable. If you talk about how nice a person is, it won't always be a woman . . . and senior consultants are always the bitchiest. The guys are nice, you can goof off with them. But women, because of the journey they've had to go through, are very protective of themselves.

Bikram's description of a "journey that [women] have had to go through" refers to a larger, more diffuse expectation of what women in India must go through. And while it was not always quite as simplistic as one singular journey that all women went through, the dilemma inherent in navigating these professional careers was often echoed in women's own accounts of being torn between their inclination to be their "authentic selves" (Eagly 2005) and their need to be taken seriously. If they were all business, they were seen as unapproachable. If they were relational in their dealings, they might be "authentic," but they were not seen as legitimate leaders. Further, for some women, being "too nice" sometimes was read as an invitation for more personal contact. Sridevi, the senior consultant mentioned earlier in the chapter who highlighted the gendered variations in affect in confrontation, was also someone slated to be on the partnership track. Her track if she "played her cards right" set up the base essentialist assumption that underlined her workplace interactions in some sense:

> As a woman, you are very different from the men you work with and you are different in many ways and the first reason that comes to mind is how you deal with confrontation. As a woman—and I think it's a woman trait—I'm more likely to not get into confrontation or find ways to avoid it than get into it head on. I find male counterparts do it more confidently and get into an argument or debate. That would be my last resort.

Sridevi's predicament helps unpack one of the many frustrations inherent in this "journey" that Bikram alludes to. It is also in line with what other gender scholars have identified as a core balance for women's organizational success—the tightrope between contrasting expectations of being "nice" or "liked" alongside "competent" or "able" (or, less appealingly, "bitch" and "bimbo") (Rudman and Glick 2001; Rudman and Phelan 2008; Williams and Dempsey 2014). As professionals constantly judged against prescriptive stereotypes, women consultants were hurt in their workplaces both when they were too accommodating *and* when they were too aggressive. This combination of factors left women feeling that they were constantly struggling to find a professional style that was both authentic *and* advantageous (a dilemma that has been a constant threat to women's careers) (Eagly 2005; Lewis 2013).

Women consultants felt especially stuck. Sridevi, for example, went on to describe how she understood that a "cocky, rock star" male junior or client would be more likely to listen to a "confident male" but also that being aggressive was hard for her personally. This is similar to Tarunya's lament: "how do you make yourself heard without being aggressive?" Unlike Sridevi, Tarunya did not expressly describe herself as unable to be aggressive, but her question is telling of the grander social expectations that she straddled: "how do you make a presentation where the room is looking for a guy?" This question, of course, drives home a sentiment not unlike Mohan's description (see chapter 2) of the ideal male lawyer in the courtroom. At first glance, the "old, orthodox" clients in Mohan's litigation practice or the Rajasthani client who could not bear to look at Archana might seem more blatantly sexist than the older Indian man who treated Tarunya in a fatherly way. Yet in both cases, disadvantageous gendered assumptions cemented professional identities.

Finally, women in consulting felt the circumscription of the Indian context more starkly than did their peers in elite law firms. As Rasheeda, a senior consultant, explained, the speed at which globalization had transformed these professional spaces was significant in determining the tensions in these interactions:

> Then there is also the Indian context—where this [gender in client interactions] gets more exacerbated. I've spent a fair amount of time working outside of India—4–5 years, actually. So in the Western context, because of your attire and dress, even if you wear trousers and a top, you could be older and wearing that—what you wear doesn't talk to age that much. But in India, if you are an older woman, you wear a *sari*. Or you wear a *salwar khameez*. Again, [there is a] cross point of conflict between what you wear—and it's not just what you wear, more like how you look—and the traditional systems of perception. I mean, this is a society for several years that has worked a certain way and suddenly—perhaps in the last 10–15 years—you are in a position where things are changing very rapidly and people are still trying to come to terms with that.

A few things in Rasheeda's description demand attention, especially in contrast to other sites. Women in litigation practice often dressed in a sari or salwar khameez but never saw this as a function of clients' preference, perhaps because they took it to be a given in traditional practice. Women in elite law firms spoke about attire and client perception sometimes, but it was usually seen as a tactical decision based on specific clients and, specifically, a strategy that was useful for domestic and regulatory clients when they had them. Consultants, however, were left with a conundrum. Unlike lawyers in elite firms who were exposed to international clients (or peers in large domestic corporations who were their own age and trained in schools similar to theirs) and lawyers in traditional litigation practice who were exposed constantly to traditional interactions both within and outside the firm, consultants' internal environments were infused with global influence while their external client facings were riddled with the India that they had worked so hard to escape by working in an elite multinational corporation (MNC). Because of these contradictions, they felt the pressure of globalization more than their peers. As Rasheeda put it:

It's also the contexts where this is happening. Mine is a MNC, so we have a fairly global culture. But this is not representative of everyone outside these microcosms of global culture. Because you work in a certain firm and you have the friends you have and you hang out where you hang out, there is a certain assumption that the world is a certain way, and so you become used to it—it's your lifestyle and everything. But the minute you step out of it, outside is a starkly different local culture.

[SSB: Can you give me an example of this diference between global and local culture?]

For example, for me, it is easier to wake up and not wear a sari, and only bother wearing it if you have time to do it . . . But when you don't wear it, [the clients] are likely to think of you as much younger. And our firm interacts [with clients] from an age or era, which is long gone.

Rasheeda's sari-versus-trousers predicament gives us a palpable example of the ways in which clients—the external audience of these interactions—might be crucial in dictating the work environments of these professionals. Of course, it might seem simplistic to make a distinction between actors based simply on their perceived response to physical attire. It certainly does not do justice to the levels of nuance that might dictate the day-to day-perception of these women. But it is worth noting that the classic engagement for women in elite law firms was with either highly sophisticated clients who had themselves internalized these global scripts of presentation, or international clients who had no context for this differential. While the sari *might have* represented something to the older men Rasheeda refers to, lawyers in elite firms were less likely to engage with a similar demographic as clients. And it was to highlight this selection difference that I offer this example.

POLITE NEGOTIATORS WHO GET THE JOB DONE: WOMEN IN NEW, TRANSACTIONAL LAW FIRMS

The experiences of women professionals being circumscribed by gender essentialism in litigation or management consulting afford us a relevant comparative framing to the case of elite transactional lawyers. Women in these elite firms continued to be essentialized in interactions, but unlike in the other cases, they were seen as well suited for the job *because* they were "hard-working," "responsive," "careful," "dedicated," and good at negotiations. Unlike women in litigation who felt that they were managing persistent perceptions about an ideal male worker, or women in consulting who had to navigate benevolent sexism, elite law firms did not subject their employees to similar interactional pressures.

Lata, the senior associate from chapter 2, was right when she described her career to be on the "same track" as the male colleagues she joined with. About half of the partners in Lata's firm were female. Thus, unlike women in litigation and consulting who had few role models, women in elite law firms felt institutionally supported and represented. However, even though they were relatively reluctant to characterize their gendered experiences as a disadvantage, there were suggestions that essentialist assumptions were at work in these spaces as well, although they operated unlike those found in traditional litigation or consulting. In particular, some of these core essentialist assumptions seemed to positively shape the women lawyers' interactions. For instance, women in elite firms, like those in traditional practice, were thought of as "polite" negotiators—but in the elite firms, politeness worked to their advantage as well as their clients'. Lata, for example, shared a story about her interactions with clients, to showcase how women associates were not just safe from discrimination in her firm, they were actually preferred:

> I was talking to a client about our [female-heavy] team and he said, "Oh, it is good you have that composition because I would much rather have a woman partner or senior associate because that ensures quality.
>
> *[SSB: What do you think they mean by "quality"?]*
>
> Clients that tell me that they want women lawyers also tell us that women work better in negotiations . . . (they are) not taken aback by the antics of the male lawyer.
>
> *[SSB: What kind of "antics"?]*
>
> Compare two situations: a man and a woman in a boardroom works better than two men or two women on opposing sides . . . because, then, the ego crops up and everyone is immediately on edge—everyone wants to show who is boss. But when there is a man and a woman, everyone is more polite. Substantively, what you are saying doesn't change but the politeness helps the transaction.

Similarly, many transactional lawyers shared a version of this story about how clients preferred having a woman on the case because women were more reliable, or "diligent" and that clients liked the "comfort that everything is being taken care of." Sudha, a mid-level associate who was on track to partnership at a transactional law firm, described this care logic as a simple matter of efficiency—women, according to her, were just seen as more likely to "care" and therefore, to better ensure "quality":

> they are very open about it [for example, they'll say]–"I really want a woman on a team because then it gives me the comfort that everything is being taken care of. She is diligent and hardworking. . . . [clients say] "I want women on my team. Guys are careless and overconfident." . . . it does not mean that women are under confident but women are more careful with their work. *They care.* (Emphasis added)

Similar to this care logic was the idea that women would "get the job done." Take, for example, rising elite law firm partner Sita's explanation for why gender did not matter to her clients:

> In fact, a lot of my clients tell me that they prefer a woman because women are a lot more intelligent . . . and that they will get the job done . . . and I have heard this from more than a few of my clients.

It seems unlikely that women entering law firms (as opposed to other firms) are unusually or particularly "caring," "diligent," or likely to "get the job done." Instead, these sites differ in their baseline expectations of what constitutes an ideal professional. Whereas litigators faced client expectations that framed the idea of a good litigator in ways that disadvantaged women, Sita and Sudha were not similarly circumscribed in their professional spheres. Of course, one part of it was that clients who could afford transactional lawyers' hourly rates were socialized in similar kinds of organizations (e.g., large corporate houses, banks, private equity firms) and unlikely to expressly prime gender as a factor for exclusion. But even beyond expressed niceties, gender was simply not the most relevant criterion for rationalized discrimination in these law firms. As a relatively small field within the grander legal profession (Papa and Wilkins 2011; Wilkins et al. 2017), these law firms hired exclusively from elite law schools in the country that had high standards of entry and a gender-equal graduation rate. Hiring and retaining women in these firms was often explained by senior partners and clients alike as the "obvious" rational choice given the nature of those credentials.

Yet, consultants were hired from elite business schools too—why were they not similarly advantaged? Over and above the structural differences between elite law and consulting firms, transactional lawyers were also advantaged because they were dealing with work that privileged certain "feminine" traits. One can articulate a functional explanation for this outcome if we were to accept the essentialized attributes as fixed: when the work demanded attention to detail and the ability to negotiate with a "cool head," the aggressive male lawyer who was "careless and overconfident" was not the ideal choice. In contrast, these new law firms were advantaged by a particular—and incidental—coupling of factors: a particular cross-section of highly trained women employed within a workplace not already male-dominated, where the characteristics of an ideal professional were not already set, and where the tasks at hand could be rationalized by stakeholders (external and internal alike) as being well suited to "feminine" traits.

Senior male partners concurred, often referring to women lawyers as "hard- working," "careful," and "dedicated." And although this representation was not always in the rhetoric of preference in reference to men, there was certainly an agreement that these traits were desirable for staffing certain transactions. Elite law firm lawyers worked on transactions where qualities like care and dedication mattered more than a kind of deliberately masculine presence that Mohan, for example, believed successful litigators were required to have. In general, this characterization of women as careful, dedicated ("get the job done"), and understated in interactions ("not taken aback by antics") is not uncommon, but that these were coded to be positive characteristics in a high-status work environment draws attention.

Structural Benefits: Retention and Institutional Privilege

As I argue in chapter 3, in any organizational emergence story, building truly innovative workspaces is difficult because old frameworks of operation and management always attach themselves to new forms. In this case, conventional logic would assume that any new firm would typically adopt the same hierarchies found in the environment in which it is embedded—in other words, these new law firms should have been as steeply gendered as the professional framework from which they sprouted. But as I reveal above, this was not always the case—and it was particularly not the case in deliberate ways that disadvantaged women. Essentialism was still consistently relevant in shaping women's career experiences, but it did not always do so in ways we might have predicted. So, the question arises: *What were the ways in which these law firms managed to differentiate themselves from the more gender-bound legal profession in general?*

The overarching persuasion in this book is to consider that the curation of gender-advantageous organizational spaces in India has not been an active, agentic process with feminist leanings. Here, I forward one more explanation—that it is a set of structural qualities of facings in these elite law firms that are particularly conducive to the construction of new gendered hierarchies. A set of structural conditions shaped not just client expectations but also the specific form of client relationships, which in turn had important impacts for women's experience of their negotiated careers.

An organization's exchange partners—which in the case of professional firms are their clients—can have an impact on its demographic composition.

Damon Phillips (2005), for example, shows that law firms with women-led cor-porate clients were more likely to have female partners, especially if the firm's client pool was small. Phillips's theory that the vitality of inter-organizational relationships rests on homophily and dependence has lessons for these Indian professional firms. Unlike the US law firms that Phillips studied, the Indian law firms were not dependent on a limited market, but the variance in struc-tural position between different kinds of firms did impact their internal organ-ization. First, their ability to do new work for new clients meant that they were mainly concerned with international transactional work, which was both new (and therefore frameless) and also unlikely to be seen as personal. Thus, even if an elite firm did recruit clients who were "not comfortable speaking to women,"[1] the nature of the matter was not personal enough to make the interaction especially awkward. Second, the fact that it was done for large, important, and world-renowned corporate clients meant that transactional work was instantly viewed as prestigious, in addition to being new and frame-less. Client facings were especially advantageous to women lawyers in elite law firms because these organizations were structured to have repeat, retained clients who were dependent on these firms. Together, this set of synergistic structural mechanisms, while intention-agnostic, came together to form a pro-fessional oasis in an otherwise strongly demarcated environment. I detail each of these conditions below to explain why this was so.

REPEAT CLIENTS: ADVANTAGE OF RETENTION

When asked whether gender was salient in interactions with clients, respon-dents often replied that "clients don't care" or that "clients *want* women lawyers." The seemingly gender-neutral work atmosphere these women enjoyed appeared not just egalitarian but even at times advantageous to women. In part this was because of the importance of repeated transactions in this work. Unlike the one-off transactions that characterized litigation and consulting work, transactional work in elite law firms consisted of repetitive matters that benefited from having the same people work on subsequent trans-actions. Women in these elite firms constantly spoke of how clients were not just happy with them, but often requested them to be staffed on matters. Cli-ents, for their part, spoke highly of the women counsel in these firms because of the value of having people who knew the transaction well.

At least in some part, the structure of transaction staffing and client recruitment remained central to the kinds of advantage that women in elite firms enjoyed. And it speaks to the explanations that women lawyers gave for why they were preferred by clients—lawyers who "ensure quality" and "get the job done" were more likely to be requested by repeat clients. Take, for example, Lata's recollection about how her client "would much rather have a woman partner or senior associate because that ensures quality." Similarly, another partner at the same firm recalled how a lot of her clients preferred her because they knew that with her team, "the job would get done." And yet another partner agreed that while sometimes it was a bit of a hurdle to handle traditional male clients who had never worked on a transaction with a woman lawyer, it all changed once they began working together: "Sometimes the most traditional clients—they wait till they are sure—but once you have them, they won't leave you."

In contrast, litigation practices had long-standing clients (because their matters often stayed in court a long time) but few repeat transactions. Domestic law firms had repeat transactions, but their clients were often local, smaller businesses; senior partners at those law firms believed that client comfort was all-important in dictating who would get staffed on a matter. Gupta, a senior lawyer who mainly did advisory work for what he called a "traditional, value-conscious firm," told me that women did superbly well and that he had never thought it weird that he could have a female boss, because, naturally, it wouldn't be anything different. Yet, when he spoke about his clients and their capacity for chauvinism, there was some evidence that not all interactions with clients and attorneys were always gender-neutral. He said he was blessed with "good clients" but simultaneously insisted that when those clients preferred a male lawyer, this was not discrimination so much as a reflection of their level of comfort with a given professional.

Staffing in consulting firms was similarly dependent on client preferences, but it was also aligned with a range of internal processes and dynamics. Staffing typically took place over three bids, and the matching process depended on what the consultant bid for and what was available. Despite the organizational setup, however, consultants agreed that in practice staffing was pretty informal and unscientific, and was largely organized around assumptions of fit determined by "just word of mouth." As a young consultant in his twenties told me, determinations about fit were much more informal and depended on the "word getting around very fast" about who was most likely to be comfortable working with whom. And for this fit too, consultants' personal opinions within these firms about peers and superiors—and, over time, intra-firm "public" perception of those opinions—mattered both for choosing and sorting purposes. Project histories and working styles—for example, who was a micromanager, who had a high level of efficiency—mattered for these bids and matches. Equally important were the "style conversations" that managers had with teams at the start of a project to brief colleagues about the cultural specificities regarding how a project was likely to run beyond the actual logistics of it. As a result, consultants bidding for projects make decisions and choices based on what they know of the staffing or lead managers (e.g., "I don't want to work with the micromanager") and those staffing or leading projects made decisions based on who they thought would be well aligned with their working style (e.g., as one consultant explained about the sorting, a self-aware micromanager might not want to work with someone they know to be a "free spirit" because of the obvious clash in styles).

Thus, while elite lawyers were staffed based on the clients' request for someone who knew them from historic transactions, consultant staffing was likely to depend on internal dynamics such as whether one was a good fit internally. At the same time, having shorter-term projects that had to be staffed anew for each client meant that prescriptive stereotypes of both the clients and the peers affected the ways in which women were staffed on these transactions. Clients were less likely to be repeat clients, which meant the advantage that law firm women enjoyed (i.e., of clients feeling comfortable with their working relationship and requesting it) did not extend as naturally to them. One-time transactions also meant that women could not depend on a single client being their primary source of reinforcement within the firm. Since consultants also prided themselves on their ability to work *across* a breadth of substantive contexts (unlike lawyers, who were more likely to gain expertise by focusing on their knowledge fields and practice areas), the constant revolving doors with a range of clients meant that they were starting afresh with each one of them and had to prove themselves anew across contexts.

But alongside the staffing decisions and client choices was the fact that the Indian legal market for commercial transactions was an oligopoly. Elite law firms had a repeat cohort of clients because there were only a few full-service elite transactional firms; further, the closed market for legal services meant that all and any transactions that included an Indian party required the assistance of an Indian firm. For the lawyers working within these firms, this meant that, unlike their peers in litigation, they did not need to recruit clients—a task that women found decidedly difficult to do while navigating conflicting gender expectations. Consultants in particular struggled to walk this tightrope between being friendly enough to retain a client and being perceived as too "modern" for their clients' cultural tastes. Rasheeda, the senior consultant quoted earlier, explained the ways in which activities that involved client bonding left her in a sort of Catch-22 situation:

> The other angle is that building connections with guys [clients] also poses some challenge. If you are an extrovert, you end up speaking better with other people. But sometimes as a woman, you don't have that avenue—especially if you don't smoke or drink. Because the standard is to go out and get a drink and if you don't do that, it just means that somehow at the back of the head, you are not part of the clique that do all of these things. That's the other challenge: to be able to do the same stuff as guys when you don't want to do those things. And I am not passing any good or bad judgment on this—and smoking is very common. . . . But even if I did [smoke and drink], [the] assumption is that very few women in India smoke and drink.

Rasheeda's distinction between her private and professional personas provides insight into the negotiations required of women who had to actively retain clients. She discusses socializing with clients over drinks as something she excludes herself from for personal reasons ("to be able to do the same stuff as guys when you don't want to do those things"), but also that this is a choice that hurts her as compared to her peers who build client relationships with such socialization. Later in our conversation, she confides that "consulting ends up being a bit of a lifestyle" and that those who do not lend themselves to it organically have to pay the price. It was not so much that people were forced to drink and smoke, but not being in the in-group of social events (that implicitly included these activities) alienated women differently and interfered with their ability to build rapports with clients. But the more subtle extension is the double find that her account resurfaces. In recalling her choice to not be part of the clique (even as it hurts her interactional social capital), she simultaneously shows the trouble encountered by the women who *do* socialize and how they are likely to be judged by the same traditional domestic clients ("But even if I did [smoke and drink], the assumption is that very few women in India smoke and drink").

Women in elite law firms had to build client relationships too, but the frustrating double bind did not affect them in the same ways because of the nature of client access and retention within their firms. In contrast, not having to actively recruit clients meant that elite lawyers could focus on dealing with the transaction without having to deal with the hostility of the greater gendered environment that this recruitment was likely to bring. Instead, they just had to show that they could "take care" of the transactions they were in charge of. And they were in charge of a consistent train of transactions because the market placement of their firms deemed it so. Further, even in the cases where these client relationships demanded socializing beyond the negotiation table, elite women lawyers could draw solace from the fact that their average client was not likely to judge them for socializing in ways deemed out of bounds for many Indian women.

INTERACTIONS WITH THE FIRM: INSTITUTIONAL PRIVILEGE

Another structural factor that helped reduce set assumptions of gender was the fact that the institutional prestige of the firms themselves helped offset any reservations clients might have had about their advisers being women. Smaller firms and litigation practices had to contend with clients' set preferences (which were often gendered), whereas elite law and consulting firms had the advantage of institutional credibility that replaced individual identities when it came to client representation. As a result, clients in elite firms felt comforted by the firms themselves being at the face of these interactions and saw individual lawyers as extensions rather than as independent actors.

I asked Dilip, a relatively young and new law firm senior partner, what he thought was the big difference between the elite firm where he had previously worked and his current, smaller firm (where he was a founding partner) with regard to clients and their perspective on gender. His response:

> Well, [we] have a lot of new companies, medium companies. At the same time I do some of the mid-level transactions with smaller businesses, firms . . . I have to kind of work quite hard at approaching clients. And once I do, there is a fairly long lead period before they start trusting us, giving us work and then coming back to us. And this is where the difference is—in the sense that . . . someone put it very beautifully, one of the general counsels had made this comment. He said "Look, the element of these exchanges between client and firm is simple. When I hire [Elite Firm A] or I hire [Elite Firm B] and if they screw up, it's their problem. But when I hire [your firm] and if you screw up, it's *my* problem."
>
> I think this is the biggest challenge for a small firm. You have to generate your own business, there is a lot of inertia involved, which you kind of have to work on constantly. It wasn't like that when I was in [Previous Elite Firm]. As that GC [General Counsel] says—there, even if [clients] have doubts about me as a personal lawyer—they saw me as a [Previous Elite Firm] lawyer. When you see it like that, the gender thing goes away.

That elite firms enjoyed this kind of institutional privilege was not surprising, but its creation of nonchalance regarding gender in the elite law firm case was novel. I didn't speak to many law firm clients during my time in Mumbai, but the handful of interviews I could schedule confirmed this connection between gender and organizational privilege that Dilip highlighted. For example, a private equity client referred to me by a senior partner in an elite law firm (a lawyer who, like Lata above, insisted that her clients preferred women lawyers on their matters) said he was "consistently impressed" with his team at the law firm:

> I don't think of them [lawyers] as men or women—in fact, it doesn't even strike me. Instead, I think whether they'll be competent—and I know that since they are from [Elite Law Firm], they'll be competent. I have a very high opinion of and am consistently impressed by the two women lawyers who have handled almost all our transactions at [Elite Law Firm]. That is what it is—you are not calling a man or a woman, you are calling [Elite Law Firm]. I see no difference as long as I get what I want for my product.
>
> *[SSB: And what do you look for in a lawyer—what is "getting what you want."]*

Well, quality within the profession is of highest concern. I care about someone [who] has met the standards for quality, is responsive and has that personal touch. And after a while, when you know you are working with someone, it's nice to be able to know her background and connect with a person. And at the end of the day, you know you are getting that quality when you work with [Elite Law Firm A] or [Elite Law Firm B]. Who the lawyer is doesn't matter, you already know they have been trained and are meritorious.

This assumption of merit and quality applied more to the firm than to the individual professional. And both elite law and consulting firms had the organizational status to leverage it for themselves. However, because of a range of other interactional factors that came together, women in elite law firms were more likely to feel its benefit than women in consulting. In contrast, smaller and less prestigious firms had to contend with institutional legitimacy vis-à-vis domestic clients; they felt that taking on too many women who make their clients "uncomfortable" was risky and they didn't feel they had the institutional bandwidth to overcome that.

Thus, in consulting firms and traditional law practices, even when intra-firm dynamics were gender-neutral, external interactions with clients were likely to typify a hostile, gendered experience. In contrast, in elite firms, as a result of a set of structural factors and especially the fact that so many of their clients were international, the experiences of women were fundamentally different. In turn, this created a certain kind of reinforcement mechanism that was in play across these sites. Elite law firms with global and sophisticated clients were sites least likely to reinforce gendered frames because women in these firms were least likely to have these kinds of interactions with clients likely to prime them. In contrast, other sites that tried to de-essentialize gender had to contend with the fact that their clients (domestic, traditional men who are not used to interacting professionally with women) would reinforce traditional gendered hierarchies. Thus, even if they managed to overcome the ways in which gender played out internally within their firms, they were forced to—as external facing firms—deal with external role expectations. And this external world was an uncontrollable environment where women felt the double bind between making the client comfortable and appearing to have crossed a line.

Together, these structural conditions—none of which were put in place to consciously "do" gender differently—distinguished elite law firm interactions from those in other elite professional spaces. The idea of pandering to the "client's comfort" was a main theme in the accounts about interactions that professionals shared with me. Given that these were professional service firms, it is not that surprising that client preferences mattered, but the ways in which these preferences prefaced interactions with these firms—and therefore, these lawyers—was a relevant part of the explanation for why women lawyers in these elite firms experienced their environments differently from their peers.

New Returns to Essentialism

These comparative sites offer some leverage to rethink the role of new contexts in negotiating the relationship between gendered ideals and the professional workplace. The cases of traditional law firms and consulting firms, to different degrees, illustrate the ways in which cultural expectations about gender plague most professional firms. The findings from traditional litigation, especially, fall in line with what other scholars have theorized to be at the core of gender inequality in organizations. As I argue in chapter 2, if the idea of "success" in these firms is crafted around a masculine ideal, it is not surprising that women in these sites—like in other similar workplaces around the world—are seen as less "ideal" fits (Acker 1990). Yet, this research also offers some confirmation that new organizational spaces can help displace essentialist gendered ideals. And to the extent we think of these essentialist markers as culturally set (Ridgeway 2011), newer professional spaces with less entrenched historical meanings did offer some reprieve. In new consulting and new elite law firms alike, the new work sites offered fresh fodder for cultural ideologies because they were not saturated with old meanings of fit and form. Of course, this is not meant to suggest that organizational novelty automatically produced equality (Padgett and Powell 2012) or that new organizations could magically resist persistent gender stereotypes (Ridgeway 2011). Neither is it meant to advocate for the use of stereotypical feminine traits in these organizations. This research, instead, reveals the ability of new sites to successfully—and organically—implement the advantage of existing gendered frameworks that typically hurt women. In particular, it suggests that in contexts where ideas about fit between worker and organization are still in flux—i.e., in new organizations where the idea of the ideal worker is not yet embedded into cultural understandings—there could, to the limited extent offered by other structural and individual sources of inequality in these contexts (e.g., cultural imperialism) (Afzal-Khan 2010; Tomlinson 2012), be some leeway in negotiating these identities and spaces anew. One such negotiation could be a more positive valuation of what is considered "feminine" in professional work.

Whether stereotypically feminine traits were construed as positive depended on the co-constructive process between the clients and the stakeholders within the organizations who used client perspectives to justify their own internal decisions. In litigation, senior lawyers felt justified in not stepping in when clients "preferred" men who could talk a certain way and perform appealingly in court. In consulting firms, women consultants were often treated with relative benevolence, yet nevertheless found themselves trapped beneath the glass ceiling because they could not, as Tarunya put it, "crack clients." Women in transactional law were better positioned to field the expectations of their professional position, but here too clients were paramount in buttressing their status. It was clients' impressions about who was best to "get the job done" that were commonly used to explain the success of women lawyers. This sort of practical sense-making by professional organizations around client preference is not uncommon (Heinz and Laumann 1978, 1982; Sandefur 2001; Phillips 2005; Liu 2006), but it is interesting that in addition to standard hurdles for gendered career trajectories (i.e., blatant and benevolent sexism), this rationalization also could, to some extent, explain positive outcomes for women. It is in unpacking this contrasting finding that this research offers three different—but interrelated—theoretical strands for the study of global professional stratification.

First, client structure offered some part of the explanation for the variations in experiences women had across these sites, by creating an environment where feminine traits were valued within the professional workplace (Heinz and Laumann 1978, 1982; Phillips 2005; Liu 2006). In addition, variations in organizational emergence histories have also influenced preferences and hierarchies, as suggested by the work of Padgett and Powell (2012). Whereas consultants worked for "global" organizations that serviced a predominantly local—and male—client base, regulatory requirements positioned transactional lawyers to work within local organizations that had a diverse, global client base. Unlike lawyers in litigating practice or consultants who pegged client perception as an insurmountable hurdle, women in elite firms described their clients as "modern, international companies and firms" that "do not care if their lawyer is a woman" and were "obviously used to seeing women in the workplace." This, especially in comparison to firms where women had to interact with more traditional clients, marked an important interactional advantage between these sites. The takeaway here is not that all global clients are gender-blind. Beyond the firms' imagined cultural expectations of clients, the clients' actual positioning vis-à-vis these professionals was key in dictating hierarchies among them. Unlike litigators who had to source their own clients, women who worked in large consulting and law firms had clients who were "theirs" because they were retained by the firm; many of the women spoke about the ease of completing repeat transactions with long-standing clients. If these conditions were different and careers in these elite firms were more dependent on one-off transactions and solo-client recruitment, it is possible that these dynamics might not look quite as gender-neutral.

Second, in addition to the variation in actual client demographics was the interaction between those demographics and the nature of the work. Other scholars have alluded to the importance of this interaction between client type and nature of work (Sandefur 2001), but it has typically been conceptualized in terms of "professional purity" or the nature of work most prestigious within the internal structures of a given profession. Thinking of this theoretical interaction beyond professional prestige gives us one more way of understanding the valorization of gendered work. Clients were important, but so too were the tasks they were trusting women to do. Women were viewed as less suited to argue aggressively in courts or as lacking in confidence when they had to make presentations to large companies as consultants. But in commercial transactions that were predominantly based on technical legal tasks, such as drafting contracts and legal memos or negotiating deals with a "cool head," women were considered ideal fits for the job. It is this renewed valorization of essentialist tropes that demands our attention. The client who described his ideal transactional lawyer as someone with a "personal touch" or Lata's argument that women were actually preferred in negotiations are both alluding to gendered traits but, unlike in litigation or consulting, these feminine traits were evaluated favorably. However, this preference did not overturn base essentialist principles or dichotomies. Quite the contrary: men continued to be deemed innately aggressive and overconfident ("the ego crops up and everyone is immediately on edge"), but this dominance was not regarded as useful in the setting at hand.[2] Internal stratification in these professional fields, then, was dependent on a combination of client preference and the actual tasks at hand—except here, instead of professional prestige, the markers were variations in what were considered "gendered" work and who was best equipped to do it.

However, and third, for these particular clients and work contexts to be relevant, having a professional field with diffuse cultural meanings about the ideal worker, as I highlight in chapter 2, was crucial. If it were purely a case of client preference based on a classical efficiency model, these gendered assumptions would have systematically advantaged women transactional lawyers in corporate law firms across the world. Yet this is notably not the case given the general gendered representation in global firms. This can hardly be because "having a cool head" or "not being aggressive" are unhelpful traits in transactions universally. Long-held cultural expectations become hard to replace in established professional spaces where the idea of an "ideal worker" is already set. What allowed women lawyers in elite Indian firms to gain an incidental advantage was a combination of client valuation and gender essentialism within a specific context where the background framework of an ideal corporate lawyer was still diffuse.

These findings that women can be viewed as competent because of (rather than in spite of) their feminine traits, especially against the context of a persistent system of gender segregation, complicates our understanding of the relationship between essentialism and egalitarianism. It reveals that while new surroundings can be useful in allowing new meanings about gender and work to emerge, novelty alone is not enough. This research shows that the positive valuation of gendered traits arose from a combination of work that could be advantaged by "feminine" traits as well as an environment where this advantage would not be rejected because of preexisting assumptions of gender and identity. Organizational scholars who pay attention to gendered outcomes have been arguing for the better valuation of many traditionally "female" tasks and traits (Rosener 1990; Eagly and Carli 2003; Post 2015), but this push has been difficult to implement in practice. Other kinds of professional work (e.g., nursing) have positively valorized essentialist feminine traits, but these subfields are rarely prestigious or especially favorable to women (England 1992). In highlighting a case that is prestigious as well as advantageous for women, this research offers one lens through which to view the potential for gender desegregation. These findings are at odds with the larger literature on gendered roles in elite work (e.g., Epstein 1993; Kanter 1993; Pierce 1996; Chambliss and Uggen 2000; Schultz and Shaw 2003; Gorman 2005, 2006; Kay and Gorman 2008; Gorman and Kmec 2009), but especially so within the particular empirical context of India, where women make up less than 10 percent of all lawyers (Michelson 2013). However, the takeaway here is not to suggest that new sites are altogether devoid of proscriptive gender traits. Even for women in elite transactional law firms, interactions were rife with rigid assumptions about what men and women were each better suited to do. However, unlike in the other sites, this essentialism sometimes improved rather than inhibited women's lived professional experiences. For example, women in these law firms were still considered less aggressive than their male peers, but in a work context that called for reasoned deliberation, aggressiveness itself was not judged to be very rewarding.

Yet, it is hard to feel too optimistic about the implications of such a finding. Organizational validation of "feminine" traits is only progress when there is also space for women to *not* exhibit these traits. One could assume that if elite law firms were faced with tasks that called for aggressive negotiation or performances before a larger audience outside the firm, women, even in law firms that were seemingly more egalitarian, would go right back to being disadvantaged. Such hypotheticals illustrate the precarious limitations of any advantages flowing from essentialism. Besides, while these findings illustrate dominant narratives about gender essentialism in each of these sites, my data can only go so far to explain how much of this behavior was organic and how much was structured to respond to client preferences—a paradox that further complicates the import of these findings. These findings similarly extend a line of research that suggests that, while gender is certainly a pervasive social identity, it is necessarily shaped by other intersectional status identities like class, education, and, importantly in the Indian case, caste. These coexistent statuses were clearly sources of empowerment for my respondents. As this book reinforces, these were a very specific strain of enabled actors—most professionals I interviewed were from middle-class families, often from urban cities, and educated in prestigious schools. That the women I interviewed were seen as good fits—rather than "women professionals"—in contexts that were

Western facing (i.e., transactional law firms with Western clients) helps better illuminate the other structural conditions at play here, especially in light of research that shows the complicated interplay of the "local" and "global" with gender in "cosmopolitan" work settings (Al Dabbagh, Riley Bowles, and Thomason 2016). It also reminds us that these phenomena rest stoutly on other forms of innate inequality: some women were advantaged, but only when they were already in a position of relative advantage.

In constructing the cumulative claim of *accidental feminism*, this chapter argues that the valorization of traits traditionally devalued as feminine within traditionally sexist and high-status work contexts was not a product of a bias-free environment. And it certainly did not flow from an intended commitment to create feminist organizations. Rather, the return to gendered roles followed from legitimate, market-friendly ideologies based on underlying power relationships between these organizations and their clients. Additionally, in presenting these incidental circumstances that created this unusual perception of the ideal worker, this research diversifies how we theorize returns to essentialized workplace expectations in a few ways. First, this positive valuation of female traits within a high-status context offers fresh empirical insight for scholarly and business writings that have advocated for such valorization with little success (Rosener 1990; Eagly and Carli 2003; Gerzema and D'Antonio 2013; Rezvani 2014; Serano 2014; Post 2015). Second, it adds to the scholarship on cultural frames (Ridgeway and Correll 2004; Ridgeway 2011) by revealing that although cultural codes may be hard to undo, new market and organizational conditions could offer tools to disrupt their weight. Finally, in highlighting some of these conditions of relevance—i.e., the type of client, the variations in nature of work—this research confirms earlier arguments about organizational incentives for professional work (Sandefur 2001) while extending their application to new settings.

FIVE

FAMILIES

It Is (Not Always) Difficult
Once You Have a Family

WORK, LIFE, AND BALANCE

OVER THE LAST THREE CHAPTERS, I've tried to suggest that the socialization of professionals before (elite law schools), within (homogenous peer interactions), and outside (facings with clients) these firms set up a cyclic mechanism of incidental advantage for women lawyers in elite firms. In this chapter, I investigate the non-firm mechanisms at work in creating this unique setup for these elite legal professionals. After all, socialization and reinforcement are not a function of schools and firms alone. Imperative to this inquiry are the other institutions that shape engagement, especially at the individual level, defining many of their everyday choices—particularly around their personal lives and families, both the ones they came from and the ones that they were choosing to create. It is these negotiations that form the core of this chapter.

The empirical data on lawyers in most late industrial economies confirm that family choices are significant moderators of women's professional life outcomes since parenthood is simultaneously penalizing for mothers and rewarding for fathers.[1] Not only are men more likely to be married than women, but marriage and family yield bonuses for men: married men with children earn more than both their unmarried peers and their childless peers (Dinovitzer and Garth 2004:59). As I argue in chapter 2, given what sociologists have identified as persistent "cultural meanings" that get attached to gender and work (Ridgeway and Correll 2004; Ridgeway 2011), it is not surprising that this is so. We are so strongly socialized to attach gendered meanings to life course patterns that even when women are included in organizations, most actors within these organizations cannot help but to see them as inevitable mothers and caretakers who will (and should) ultimately prioritize their family over their careers (Ridgeway and Correll 2004). In turn, this assumption makes them less than "ideal" for the workforces they join (Acker 1990; Hays 1998). In some ways, women confront the "maternal wall" (Crosby, Williams, and Biernat 2004; Williams and Dempsey 2014) even before they are mothers and even in organizations where men and women are told they enter as gendered workers; assumptions about how they are likely to manage work and family expectations vary drastically, and often to the detriment of the female professional (Pearce, Wald, and Ballakrishnen 2015). As I set up in chapter 2, some of this has to do with our expectations of what an ideal worker must stand for, i.e., often a man who will prioritize work and drop everything else at a moment's notice to meet these commitments (Acker 1990). Of course, this unrealistic expectation of an ideal worker who will "drop everything at a moment's notice" is not actually couched in empirical evidence. For example, Epstein and her colleagues show that "face time" at work is not necessarily associated with worker performance and productivity (Epstein et al. 1999). Similarly, Bielby and Baron (1984) show that to the extent work commitment is measured by the importance people attach to work, there is no difference in commitment between mothers and non-mothers. Even so, cultural logics about how gender and life course choices affect commitment to work remain ingrained and problematic for working women. When negotiations between the identities of "ideal worker" and "good mother" (Correll, Benard, and Paik 2007) are problematic for women in Western countries who have been contesting workplace gender stratification for more than half a century,[2] how are these women professionals in India managing the balance differently?

This chapter begins by employing an institutional approach to understanding these emerging relationships between law, work, and family (Albiston 2007, 2009) to reveal, as it does with other structural mechanisms in this book, that it is not agentic social movements for women's equality in the workplace that have advantaged new Indian lawyers, but rather, a more incidental advantage conceived by a range of specific structural factors that have come together within the context of a particular cultural moment in history. At the same time, in understanding the institutional context through the lived experience of individual lawyers and their relational dependence on their families and other systems of support, this research recognizes important factors at the individual and interactional levels that buttressed this advantage.

Particularly, I trace the role of families and life course in determining the unlikely gender outcomes found in these elite law firms. I find (as in other chapters within this book) that the origin families that most professionals come from are deeply homogenous (middle-class, high-caste, urban) but that similar class and caste advantages did not always translate into gender advantages in other elite professional careers. I argue that the distinct advantage of the legal profession in India was that its specific career trajectory incidentally allowed for a more progressive work–family balance in certain kinds of practice. Specifically, while women in litigation were often dismissed for being unsuitable given the "nature of the job," women in new elite law firms instead experienced their trajectories as more aligned with their life course choices. For instance, typically, transactional lawyers in these firms started their careers in their early twenties and were in a position to become partner by their early thirties—a timeline to promotion that allowed these women to be in relative positions of power when they did in fact negotiate childcare and maternity leave.

At the same time, successful professionals were also advantaged by a support system of intergenerational family members—mothers and in-laws who were available to help with household work and childcare. And here too, relative timing of institutional factors was key in explaining some of the advantage. As often was the case with first-generation professional women, these women lawyers were uniquely positioned to access the hybrid advantage of access to traditional household structures (family as support systems) *and* modern professional opportunity that was closed to the generation that preceded them. Finally, inherent in all of this was the advantage of class. Professionals had access to a large, affordable service labor force—*domestic help*—that managed much of their house and childcare. While India's dependence on domestic help is not confined to its uppermost class (Ray 2000a; Ray and Qayum 2009), it still reflects the underpinnings of a rigid caste system.

This chapter adds to the continued and layered reveal in this book to suggest that the incidental timing of events at different levels of analysis was central to framing the advantage women could leverage within new and elite law firms in India. This advantage of temporality, when dissected in different ways, affords a new way of thinking about the interconnectedness of a range of otherwise disparate factors. Gender scholars have long alluded to the importance of observing the workings of gendered meanings across different levels of analysis (West and Zimmerman 1987; Ridgeway and Correll 2004; Risman 2004; Albiston 2009). The Indian case, as I show in this book more generally, naturally lends itself to these multipronged observations. And in revealing the importance of temporality, it offers a new lens with which to weave these different—but interconnected—prongs together. When thinking about inequality, timing is often used as an individual-level variable (e.g., age, cohort). In treating it instead as a structural variable, this research extends the ways in which we can deploy its analytical purchase.

Balances of Work and Family in Traditional Law and Management Consulting

Beyond shedding light on gender and work dynamics, professional careers have been fertile landscapes to observe, across different cultural and geographical settings, the circular effects of gendered career and life course choices (Menkel-Meadow 1986; Epstein 1993; Schultz and Shaw 2003; Rhode

2011; Dawuni 2016). Particularly, we know that childbearing and -rearing responsibilities affect women differently than they do men (Hochschild 1979, 1997; Ridgeway and Correll 2004; England 2005; Correll et al. 2007), creating "second shifts" of responsibilities that cumulate rather than alleviate women's workloads (Hochschild and Machung 2012). As a result, even as women and men enter in similar proportions, women trail behind professionally following childbirth and other family-centric choices (Chambers 1989; Kay and Hagan 1995, 1998; Hagan and Kay 1995; Seron and Ferris 1995; Korzec 1997; Reichman and Sterling 2001, 2004, 2013; Hakim 2006; Kay and Gorman 2008; Dinovitzer, Reichman, and Sterling 2009; Wald 2009; Walsh 2012; Sterling and Reichman 2016). And this is not singularly a reflection of direct discrimination between mothers and non-mothers (Fuegen et al. 2004; Correll et al. 2007). Scholars across disciplines have offered a wide range of mechanisms to explain gender divergences at the workplace, including, for example, implicit hiring biases (Blau and Khan 2000; Goldin and Rouse 2000), sex differentiation (Reskin 1988; Fausto-Sterling 1992), socialization (Dodd-McCue and Wright 1996), organizational structures and norms (Acker and VanHouten 1974; Acker 1990), and choice-based essentialism (Trauth 2002; Crompton and Lyonette 2005). But while the actual theories differ, most (if not all) of these mechanisms for sex segregation converge on the problematic assumptions of gender-based life course priorities: men and women are expected to make different choices when it comes to managing work and family.

What was true for women across these varied contexts remained true for many of my respondents. Most professionals agreed that while gender did not matter initially, marriage and childcare responsibilities changed career trajectories differently for men and women. But there was a variance in how this played out in different firms. Dilip, the litigation partner in chapter 4 who thought the "gender thing went away" when clients could base their decisions on organizations, still saw gender as a main divider in his ability to retain attorneys after a "certain point," i.e., once the women in his firm got married and had children. Dilip was a graduate of one of the National Law Schools himself and was quick to remind me that this difference was rooted in practicality, not a vestigial remnant of a traditional approach to women in the profession. In his words, despite a commitment to merit, the pressures were just *different* for a female lawyer:

> Gender is one hundred percent an issue. When you are looking at the first five years, it's not really an issue, but post that, it's something you have to tackle head on. I have not had to deal with that yet, because we are a small firm, but we will soon have to start thinking about policies of leave and how to structure it. And the truth is, most firms do not make the distinction—it's all merit based, but once we have a family, if you are a female lawyer, the pressures are different.

The explanation Dilip gave me later in the interview for why these pressures were different for the women in his firm was similar to a narrative I heard across many sites, especially in smaller types of private practice that felt they just did not have the institutional support to counter what they saw as ingrained differences between male and female professionals. Smaller firms had no dedicated human resource wings, and policies like day care and flexi-work schedules were not something they could afford to do without severe repercussions to their own precarious standing in the market. Dilip reminded me, almost in explanation, that he was not employing double standards: "My own wife was working and she just had a kid and it has been hard to just get back to work and pretend like that was not an issue." Even if there was personal frustration, however, it was not enough to mitigate the cost to the firm. As long as individuals could figure out a way to balance their work and family with their own set of resources, firms were open to privileging merit, but this negotiation had to happen at the personal level, it was not—or, at least, not consistently—institutionally supported. Even in cultures that are seemingly more gender-egalitarian, research confirms that women do more housework,[3] more childcare, and bear the brunt of parenthood more steeply than their male partners (Silbaugh 1996; Thébaud 2010; Collins 2019), even when actors wish to have different institutional arrangements (Pedula and Thébaud 2015). In turn, women who do well have had to "take gender out of the equation" and become more like their male peers (Bender 1988). This has meant choosing professional and personal lifestyles that do not prime other responsibilities and do not prime the "double bind" in the workplace (Stanford 2009). These unreachable, "nobody can truly have it all" standards have made women adopt different strategies than men and, by extension, have made them leave elite career tracks at rates distinctly disproportional to men. Notably, the bigger problem is not that women leave but, rather, that we attach certain assumptions as to *why* they leave. Persistent explanations include that women leave because they are "wired that way" or "they want to" or "cannot take it" or "just choose to." In turn, these structural assumptions about men and women continue to absolve organizations from being responsible for this attrition, leading them to fall down a "visibility-vulnerability spiral" (Kram and Hampton 1998). In Dilip's words, "As long as you have [childcare] sorted and have a support system, the firm does not care. But not everyone has that support system."

Dilip's explanation sets out standard road blocks that other scholars have identified as problematic for the sustainable inclusion of women in the workplace—the complexities in constructing viable policies and infrastructure that can retain women, the lack of personal support systems, and the inevitable attrition when women have to make decisions involving family responsibilities. But his explanation for why his firm could not accommodate post-parenthood women was particularly revealing of how he—and others lie him—saw their predicament. Dilip, like his peers, saw firms as "inherently meritocratic" *until* this negotiation around families had to be made ("most firms do not make that decision"). This inclination to seeing firms as organizations with clean hands and workers within them as defaulters is problematic because it works on a subtle cultural assumption that it is working women—and not their (often male) personal companions—who should bear the brunt of managing work *and* family (Pearce, Wald, and Ballakrishnen 2015). This "difference-blind" standard that seemingly "meritocratic" firms set for both their women and men did not intentionally or even explicitly discriminate on the basis of gender; but it did something else that had the same effect—it forced women to meet standards not designed for the average female professional (Acker 1990, 2006) and absolved the firm for having created these expectations.

And it was not just senior male partners who thought of gender representation as a function of agentic choices made by women. This invisibility of the firms' implication in all of this was clear in the ways women described the manner in which gender played out in these firms too. Saraswati, the senior consultant in a management firm we first encountered in chapter 2, saw the firm where she worked as "pretty egalitarian" even while admitting in the same sentence that there were no senior women consultants in her firm with both children and client-facing roles:

> There are very few actual situations where it feels like man v. woman. . . . The only difference, however, comes in getting to the higher levels. There is not a single senior consultant with a client-facing role who has a child. So that makes it hard to aspire to even if it feels pretty egalitarian.

Saraswati's relative disregard for the gender variation in promotion ("in getting to the higher levels") is significant in that it shows how promotion—perhaps the single most relevant threshold for career advancement—was still seen as a minor (or, at least, inevitable) exception rather than as a fundamental problematic difference between men and women professionals in her firm. It also reveals the deep diffusion of the myth of equality—men and women alike across firms saw themselves in modern organizations that were "doing all they could" and the women as simply "not cutting it" despite fair standards: a classic example of the "no problem" problem (Rhode 1991). Alongside this problematic ideology of blaming the worker instead of the firm, women in most of these professional sites were also disadvantaged by the lack of serious role models and mentors. Saraswati and others like her had trouble seeing themselves as senior partners within the firm because there were no obvious pathways for people like them, even if they might have otherwise personally wanted to make more balanced choices between their careers and personal life. Most consulting firms had not advanced any (and certainly not many) women with children to senior client-facing roles, and junior women saw—as researchers of gender and work have shown elsewhere (Seron and Ferris 1995)—opportunities like flextime as a double-edged sword that accommodated women while also pigeonholing them. Unlike their male peers who were supported by partners who helped them "maintain their married lifestyle," women instead were pushed to make more serious either / or choices when it came to their career possibilities. The trouble these women had with seamlessly seeing themselves as senior professionals within the firm is telling of the inherent structural disadvantages in which they were embedded. For women like Saraswati, there were simply no role models to show how senior positions could be managed post-motherhood and they felt necessarily stuck between two choices—either to not have a child and stay on track or to have a child and then quit or take on an internal—less prestigious—role. As I show in the previous chapter, many women across these contexts felt their interactions within firms were buffered by certain kinds of class privilege and social capital—they went to the same schools, came from similar cities, etc.—but no matter what they felt in surface-level interactions, decisions that balanced personal and career choices together felt more tumultuous and most female consultants believed it was not viable to move too far ahead in their careers without making serious personal sacrifices.

A Multilevel Temporal Approach to Understanding the New Law Firm Advantage

Women in elite law firms were advantaged, especially when compared to their peers in other kinds of professional practice, across very different—but still related—levels of analysis. At the individual level, factors of socialization continued to be important, but for many lawyers in these elite firms, early socialization in elite law schools meant that they came into these firms with a certain expectation of equality. On being among similarly socialized peers and colleagues, these expectations went on to be reinforced in ways that women in smaller law firms (even with the same socialization) or women who went to consulting firms following degrees in engineering and business did not enjoy. Interactions also mattered in other ways—women with different kinds of social capital felt entitled to different capacities of negotiation for work and personal trajectories alike. Embedding these advantages at the micro and meso levels was the institutional advantage of *timing*. As I show below, elite firms had a career life course that worked well in sync with the personal life course of women in these firms (or at least, in plausible sync in ways that other career trajectories were not). This allowed women in elite law firms to reach partnership before having to make serious decisions about marriage and children—an incidental mechanism that allowed for a renewed power in their ability to negotiate their standing within these organizations. Finally, at the structural level, this was all engulfed in two structural conditions within the broader Indian society—a caste-dependent labor force that supplied affordable housework and childcare, and a penultimate generation of close female family members who were not in the workforce themselves and who were available to provide free and reliable household support. I highlight the importance of each of these below to show how they worked together to offer these peculiar conditions for gender equality in the Indian law firm case.

"DAMN YOU, GRANDMA": SOCIALIZATION PATTERNS AT THE INDIVIDUAL LEVEL

To the extent that we think of the "ideal worker" as being omnipresent and "always there" (Williams 2001; Blair-Loy 2009), there is an implicit understanding that such a commitment takes precedence over any family obligation (Epstein et al. 1999; Williams 2001). Working women suffer more than their male peers because they are subject to the competing requirement of also being "intensive" and "good" mothers (Kobrynowicz and Biernat 1997; Hays 1998; Ridgeway and Correll 2004; Johnston and Swanson 2006; Blair-Loy 2009; Collins 2019). This paradox was no doubt institutionally created and reinforced, but its material result was that it resided as much within the women themselves as their employers. Other scholars who have tracked this balance confirm the "inevitability" of this guilt for even contemporary working mothers, independent of their geographic placement (Collins 2019), and professionals in my sample spoke about the ingrained internal struggles with these choices that they had to maneuver, even when they had husbands and family that understood about the pressures of balancing work and family. Take for example Behag, a young lawyer in a smaller litigation practice who was in her mid-twenties and had just graduated from an elite law school a few years before I had met her. Married to another lawyer—a relatively common pattern—she now worked for a small startup firm in Mumbai—a metropolis not unlike her own hometown. Behag's reaction to how gender plays out was an interesting insight into how deeply prescribed these work-family negotiations were for many of these women: she had just gotten married and her husband, who she called a "solid guy" that "ran the house" (i.e., coordinated domestic chores that the maid was responsible for doing over the course of the day), an arrangement that caused her deep guilt:

> I just got married. My husband used to work for a firm but now he works for [a company] and I work for [practice name], so again—now I'm back to not being the one who is home early. So he gets home at 6:30. And he's a good guy. He's a solid guy. So he does not mind running the house. But I have guilt. I have a lot of guilt. When I get home at 9:00 he has also worked all day, and he is home at 6:30 and he's ordered all the groceries and he has made some calls with the maid and coordinated

everything. And my bed is made. This all sounds really awesome, but I have guilt. So I think that's just . . . well, that guilt is just . . . damn you, mom. Not even mom. Damn you, grandma. I think that's hard. I think that's not going to go away.

Behag's "guilt" and her preoccupation with her own failings as a partner was, by her admission, dictated not by actual dispensation of labor, not by her partner's own hesitation about sharing the labor, but by her grandmother's imagined, internalized disapproval. Her "damn you, grandma" is significant because it speaks to the persistence of cultural contexts, even in the face of multiple conditions working in one's favor. An understanding partner, a maid who took care of all her household responsibilities, and a job that she really enjoyed could not shake that feeling of guilt in her head that she had retained from her childhood assumptions about gender roles. I also highlight this case because Behag was one of the few women in my sample who had a working professional mother as a young girl. When I asked her to explain her provocative (even if in jest) "damn you, grandma" comment, Behag explained:

I think that's why lawyers marry a lot of lawyers. And it works. But there is a lot of guilt, knowing that he is home. And he does not care. So it's obviously in my head.
   [SSB: You just said, "Damn you, grandma." Why did . . . is that—]
   I think there is some amount of socializations that happens there. My mom worked, always.
   [SSB: What did she do?]
   She's a scientist. So she was always away from home for as long as I can remember, 9:00 to 7:00 she was out. My dad was out similar hours. But my grandparents were home. My grandma [her father's mother] was home. And she always said to me when I was young that she [her daughter-in-law, Behag's mother] should have been home. So I grew up thinking that.

Behag's response seemed self-aware that this was an effect of deeply embedded socialization, yet in tracing it to socialization, she offered another indication of how timing interacted with socialization in her particular context. Most women—as first-generation professionals—had to learn this balance of managing work and life anew. And while that was exceptionally daunting, it also meant that they had the advantage of a fully functional support system at home who, unlike Behag's mother, were often outside of the formal workforce and eager to have a chance to raise their grandchildren. As I discuss in the next sections, this advantage of familial networks was integral to helping successful women balance expectations of work and family. Being in the workforce was less likely to attract the sort of dismissal that Behag's mother faced a generation ago from her mother-in-law ("And she always said to me when I was young that she [her daughter-in-law, Behag's mother] should have been home. So I grew up thinking that"). And being in a certain kind of work-force at this particular juncture in India's history meant that for many of these women, there was access to both these traditional familial advantages as well as more modern scripts of gender parity that they felt equally entitled to.

THE FIRM REALLY JUST MADE IT WORK: INDIVIDUAL-LEVEL ACCOUNTS IN ELITE LAW FIRMS

In contrast to women in smaller firms, litigation practice, or even larger and global consulting firms, women in elite law firms felt the pressure of manag-ing both work and family, but did not feel that having a child necessarily pre-cluded them from staying on in the firm or continuing to be "on track" toward partnership. Existing partners and senior associates with children set prime examples of how this could be done, and mid-level women felt confident in aspiring similarly for their future selves—especially given the general hostil-ity of the larger profession toward mothers. And the handful of partners who did have children felt surprisingly well received in their Indian professional contexts. Ambika, a law firm partner with two school-age children explained her own situation while commenting about the irony it posed vis-à-vis West-ern firms that seemed more structurally competent to help women overcome these hurdles:

> I think firstly, foreign firms are far less hospitable, even though they have all these programs and systems for women partners. So I guess it must be far less stressful and far more also organized there, if there is no family support, then you have to depend on day care, etcetera. That's one. Then in terms . . . I'm just thinking. I do not think they have as many women as we have. So it's kind of ironical, actually. On one hand, we do not have that many things [except the] institutional help [refer-ring to domestic help] that we are getting. But still, I think the reason to my mind has to be because number one, there is family support here. And number two, there is good domestic help. You need something, and the *bai* [hindi for maid] is there. In India, they really do most of the work at home. You rely on them completely. Number three . . . liv-ing in a city like Bombay is a very expensive thing. Buying a house is very expensive. I believe that this helps because most of the help that come to work here from other places can not afford to live here, so you get live-in help. And that helps a lot.

Ambika's reliance on domestic help was not unique and most professionals (parents and non-parents alike) similarly expressed the inherent advantage in having domestic help as a natural strategy for balancing work and family. I deal with the larger systemic problems of this reliance later in the chapter, but

Ambika's specific reasoning for why she was advantaged in her firm vis-à-vis "foreign firms" did not explain why women in other kinds of Indian firms who had similar advantages of family and domestic help could not leverage these work returns. When I pushed her on what might make this distinction more understandable, she offered a fourth reason for why she and others like her have managed to make this balance work—spouses and partners who meet them halfway:

> And to a large extent the younger boys are very supportive of wives working, other than the going in for women who are not working. . . . I guess the tricky part is when they have kids; how supportive are they going to be in terms of actually helping out rather than just saying, "I'm there." Will they be coming and helping [the kids] in their studies? Will they be coming and helping with homework? Will they be coming in to help for the doctor's appointments? All of that. So I was lucky my husband did a lot of all of that, whenever I was busy or had to be at a client meeting . . . So, for example, if there is something to be done on Saturdays obviously I am going to try and make it, because we officially do not work Saturdays, but if a deal is closing and I have to be here, I have to be here. If it's a weekday, if my kids have to go to an appointment or if they had something, then more often than not my husband would go rather than I. Which has worked well, also, because my kids have a great bonding with him because of that. He actually helps in the kids' studies, also, because he realizes that academics in India are such an integral part of the kids' life—that if you're not part of it you are kind of away from them.

This description of a partner who is "more likely to take the kids to an appointment" than herself is not unlike Girija, the law firm partner from chapter 3 who explained that her firm helped make the negotiation between work and family possible to navigate. Girija, who was in her late thirties when I spoke with her, admitted to having felt anxious about the prospect of negotiating childcare and family but, in reality, felt like between her husband and domestic help, she could "make it work." Girija's explanation for how she "made it work" included long negotiations with her firm and her partner. She admitted that while she sometimes felt she was "not spending enough time" with her child, she had a great support system both at home and at work. Girija did not have family in the city, but she had household help for most of the day: "I have a curfew time at 8:00 pm. So either my husband or I have to be at home." Importantly, she was not the only one who had to meet this curfew: "we manage—we take turns, sometimes it's [my husband] and sometimes it is me, but one of us is there."

Contrasting the way Ambika and Girija talk about their families to the earlier limp resignation that consultants faced is useful to understand why a career "once you had a family" was not such an impossibility for all women. The differences of course did not neatly categorize across organization type, a lot of individual level factors and support networks mattered. Even so, organizational cultures were crucial to reinforcing internal expectations and anxieties about balance. Tarunya, the consultant from the previous chapters who felt that gender was salient across her interactions, saw advancement within her consulting firm as a mythical goal because she was not a man with someone at home to "maintain his lifestyle." In contrast, Ambika, Girija, and their peers saw people around them doing it and believed they could repurpose their environments to work for them.

The pressures on Girija to balance home and work were not especially different from those faced by her peers at other kinds of firms, and there was no indication that the resources available to her were not available to other professionals. Women in elite law firms, like women professionals across the country, had access to domestic help. But what they also had to their advantage were partners who met them halfway and did not place set, traditional expectations on them. Their reference points were, of course, to more traditional men who, as Ambika describes, "might choose wives who are not working" or who would not actually help with childcare ("how supportive are they going to be in terms of actually helping out rather than just saying, 'I'm there'"). In a country where household work and childcare could be dependably outsourced, having supportive partners made the bigger difference. Women in law firms still felt the pressure of their long work hours and having to be client-facing over weekends and holidays if the deal demanded it, but knowing that it was something everyone felt took gender out of the equation—at least for women who were advantaged by a set of other factors and could afford it to be so.

IN INDIA FAMILIES ARE IMPORTANT: RELATIONAL BUFFERS IN INDIAN LAW FIRMS

Even so, cultural assumptions, while sticky, were not all bad. There is increasing global evidence that work and family conflicts are not just something women have to navigate. Although mothers face special hurdles, the balance between work and personal commitments is taxing for *all* professional actors. Alison Wynn (2018) for example, argues that this "everwork"—i.e., constant expectations of work availability among professionals—has different kinds of avatars for different kinds of employees based on institutional assumptions about their roles: men and women without children are "quit intenders," mothers are "tightrope walkers," and fathers are "reluctant sacrificers." And women (and men) across these sites did "everwork" in that they worked hard and long hours, oftentimes without weekends and holidays. As Sapna the lawyer, in chapter 3, said about her domestic firm servicing international clients, holidays—especially with calendars that did not converge—did not matter: using her half-serious allegory, when a client said "jump," one did not ask why.

Yet, at the same time, it was in these domestic firms that women experienced a sense that their predicament was understood. Nipun, a general counsel of an international conglomerate and a senior lawyer who had previously worked at both an Indian elite law firm as well as an elite firm in the UK, spoke directly to this difference and the ways in which Indian cultural norms played out in the workplace, especially around family negotiations:

> Just because I am not at [an elite law firm] anymore, it is not like 6:00 [pm] is the magic number. You stay late when you have to . . . And I really think it's easier in India supporting the guys I do because I think it's an Indian man thing that I need to get home for my child at X pm and that if my mother is sick, I'll be home. And it is not just me, that family thing applies to [my husband] too. Even now, when I walk out and meet [ex law firm partners from her old firm], they still ask me about my family, the kids. And it is not just a formal "hi, hello." These things matter here. Being personal is just a way of being here. I would never get that kind of understanding in, say, [name of a corporate house in the UK]. There is just no way it would work. So . . . I think it's less about institutions themselves and more about just India. The fact is that you have a mother-in-law at home more often than not. And the other side of the transaction table has one too. So when you say it, you do not have to explain it.

It is not the "personal" reception with more than "formal 'hi, hello's'" or the benevolent sexism ("it is an Indian man thing that I need to get home for my child by X pm") that make the cultural assumptions that attach to Nipun work for her. Instead, it was the grander cultural assumption of what family meant in the Indian context that a-gendered this equation. Not needing to explain family obligations—or at least extending the expectation that men and women might *both* be called on to balance it—somehow made the negotiation more egalitarian. It did not mean that she could afford to meet lax standards because she was a woman or a mother. But since "family" care was such an extended obligation, it was not seen as just a woman's balance. Similarly, Niharika, another partner at an elite law firm who had previously spent time in a foreign law firm in the UK, saw family upbringing and the expectations around this in Indian culture as a significant difference, especially when considered cross-culturally:

> I think in Western firms, as soon as you know a woman is married. . . . There is always that debate. You probably know it. "She [is] eight years [into the firm], qualified [to practice law in the UK]. She's married. Is she going to pop a baby, or not? Do we make her up before the baby

or after the baby? What's it going to be? And if you make her up and then she pops the baby she's not going to be pulling her weight as a partner." All this debate happens . . . [In India], I do not think that they view whether a woman is going to have a child or not as an issue. And I think it's because in India families are important. And I think it's almost expected that a woman will get married and have children at some point. . . . Maybe I'm not saying this [is] the right way. It's not expected that you are going to get married and have kids. But if you get married and have kids it's not viewed as a negative on your career . . . I think in a UK context society is a little bit more individualistic, if I can put it that way. And I think that has an effect.

That there are cultural differences between work and balance expectations between the UK and India is not surprising. Still, the idea that a foregone expectation of fertility choice will *not* be "viewed as a negative" on one's career is an interesting extension to that expectation, and one that tracks with the kinds of bizarre essentialist returns than chapter 4 exposes. Yet, at the same time, not all women thought this balance between work and family was borne equally between men and women. Sunanda, a senior consultant, for example, agreed that in the Indian context, family obligations did not stop with children. However, even though men and women both had the same familial obligations toward parents, in-laws, and extended family, their response to them depended significantly on socialization:

> I do not have a child and I have no plans on having one anytime soon. But particular to the Indian context is that family just does not mean children—you are also responsible to a larger family. Your parents are old, they require a certain level of support. Then you have your husband's parents who also you want to check-in on. And this might be only a once a week phenomenon if you do not live with them, that is— but it is still once a week when we have only a day or two off. So, at the end of the week, when you take stock, you realize you do not know where the time has gone. Sometimes, a large part of family commitments is that you can not get out of it, but also that you do not want to get out of it—you want to be there to take care of it. And I think this is very, very particular to Indian women. I do not think Indian men feel it quite as much.

When I asked her to explain this difference between Indian men and women, she backtracked a little to a distinction that was rooted in upbringing and socialization more than gender:

> Maybe it's a matter of gender—or maybe it's upbringing. My brother, for example will be equally committed to our [parents'] needs. We both grew up in a disciplined environment, we were taught to listen early

and not argue. So my brother and I will both respond to our parents in exactly the same way. With my husband, it's the way he was brought up—he learnt early on that it was ok to push back and be stubborn and as he grew older, he puts himself first and he puts logics first. And he'll do whatever is right based on what is logical even if it requires an uncomfortable conversation. He's like that—he will comfortably have an uncomfortable conversation if it means he does not have to do something. I am not like that. I find myself incapable of having these conversations.

Across cultures, gendered role expectations and institutional adjustments remain integral to understanding workplace dynamics for men and women alike (e.g., Aumann, Galinsky, and Matos 2011; Humberd, Ladge, and Harrington 2015; O'Connor and Cech 2018; Padavic, Ely, and Reid 2019). In India, independent of whether individuals actually followed through on them, these multifaceted familial obligations were generally accepted cultural understandings. Childcare was important, but so was parental care; and these cultural premises attached themselves to men and women alike. Particularly, the fact that such filial duty was equally expected of both men and women is significant to our understandings of how the negotiation between "ideal worker" and "good mother" played out in the Indian context. As I show later in this chapter, the "good mother" responsibility was not attached specifically to a mother being personally available for her child. With access to intergenerational living arrangements and proximate family, childcare—which traditionally was thought of as a communal responsibility—did not hold women hostage, in a sense, quite as much as it did to female parents and caregivers in the West. To the extent those family responsibilities mattered and interfered with work, there was a general cultural informality, especially among domestic firms that understood this to some extent. What was more, they understood it for both men and women who were committed in family obligations that conflicted with firm time. Much like Nipun's comment that since "you have a mother-in-law at home more often than not," no additional explanation was necessary (especially since men and women alike had mothers-in-law, even if those attachments were differently associated), Sunanda blamed it on the built-in psyche of the Indian "guilty conscience":

I think it's an Indian thing because you live with your parents longer than you do in the West—so the kind of expectations they have pass on to you. You see your parents take care of their parents for a better part of their life / so brought up with certain kind of behavior / so even if it's not spoken about and expectations are not worded, you are expected to put family first and it's part of your psyche and it's in your head. It's amazing—they [Indian parents] make you feel guilty so tactfully that I have a perpetual guilty consciousness.

On inheriting this blanket guilty conscience, it was not just an ideological role war between "good mother" and "ideal worker." And in the war that included multiple family dimensions of "good son/daughter/in-law/brother/sister," everyone—regardless of gender—was implicated. Having these extra responsibilities did not organically make it easier for professional women—and men—to navigate demands at work and home. In fact, it was far from it. But in the multifaceted juggle that they were called to do, men and women were both contestants, no matter how they each responded to it.

PARTNER BY THIRTY: INSTITUTIONAL ADVANTAGES OF A FIVE-YEAR UNDERGRADUATE DEGREE

One of the key factors that benefited women in elite law firms was the temporal advantage they enjoyed as young professionals in new firms. As law graduates from these new five-year undergraduate law programs, women in these firms were already on a tenure track to partnership by the time they were in their early twenties. As a result, they were well poised to work the regular twelve- to fifteen-hour shifts, pull all-nighters for transaction deadlines, and make allied sacrifices traditionally expected from early associates so they would be on partnership track by the time they are in their late twenties. They were also advantaged, as I argue in chapter 2, by the fact that unlike their peers in consulting for example, they were socialized in gender-equal law schools to believe that in many ways "gender did not matter" and that they were as capable as their male peers, a value that would be appreciated in the modern and meritocratic firms where they were seeking employment.

Furthermore, since these firms are still new and eager to bulk up their middle management, partnership tracks are between seven and ten years—a short duration when compared to litigation careers, which typically demand a fifteen- to twenty-year practice before being considered for seniority. Women in consulting, in contrast, typically started after a graduate degree in business and had longer paths to partnership because fewer partners were promoted every year, and being a bottom-heavy organization actually worked for the business.

This career temporality had implications for personal life course decisions and choices that these professionals across sites believed they were in a position to make. Women in law firms, for example, were already in senior positions by the time they had to contend with decisions of marriage and children. And the women who were not yet at the position to personally think of these choices did not feel the same threat their peers in other firms did. Take for example this senior associate in an elite law firm who was recruited at the end of her last year in law school:

> In *our* [emphasis applied, "our" referring to other elite firms] interviews, they never ask questions about children or families. . . . They ask

question(s) that might get at ambition, I guess, but I do not think the questions they asked me would have allowed them to judge whether I wanted a child or family. At least the way they interviewed me, I do not think it was something they could gauge.

Other interactions with similarly positioned senior lawyers spoke to the advantage that distance from parenthood gave these women. As young lawyers recruited at a time when marriage and parenthood were not foremost in their minds, they managed to navigate the early years of being a firm lawyer without gender issues coming up as necessary priorities. Ganga, a senior lawyer on the verge of her thirtieth birthday who had still not decided after a few years of marriage if she wanted to have children, spoke to this relative distance that women in law firms seemed to enjoy from parenthood trajectories and choices that seemed more rigid for women outside these firms:

> We [referring to her peer group of senior lawyers] are at a stage where there are many women but most of us do not have children and are not immediately planning on having children. There is no immediate sense of this *parenthood culture*. (She says this with emphasis, using air quotes.)

While many of the women I interviewed were in committed partnerships or early marriages, a much smaller number had children. The lack of what Ganga calls an "immediate sense of parenthood culture" afforded women like her who were on the path to partnership and childless, a break from needing to juxtapose roles of "ideal worker" and "good mother." In turn, it allowed other women to navigate these compromises from a position of power—i.e., as partners. At the same time, they did not think that this sacrifice of putting off decisions about parenthood until they reached their early thirties involved too much of a risk.

I intentionally use the terms "sacrifice" and "risk" here. Almost all the mothers I met in Mumbai had children when they were in their thirties and in senior positions within the firm that allowed them to negotiate the terms of the arrangement. Having children in your thirties might seem par for course for professionals, but in a country where the average age of first birth was 19.9 years, this was still unorthodox. Ganga's environment that lacked "parenthood culture" was not something women outside these firms enjoyed. It was not like women within these firms were uniformly unperturbed about how they were going to navigate having children and staying "on track" within these firms. As Makhija and Raha (2012) show in their report on women professionals, marriage and parenthood continued to be real and persistent barriers to entry and success within the larger profession, especially in cities outside of Mumbai.[4] Yet, at the same time, given their own advancement and the example of other women ahead of them, they felt better suited to negotiate these decisions than they might have been in traditional law firms or earlier in their careers.

I Get By with a Little Help from My Family (and Maids): Interconnected Dependencies at the Structural Level

Even if women like Sunanda blamed their Indian guilty conscience for overextending their weekends with family commitments, the flip side of this relationship was that proximate family and close ties to them was pertinent to helping professional dual-career couples manage work and childcare. Almost all the successful professional women with children had family that lived in the area and those like Girija who did not have family nearby had full-time help to assist with childcare. Aruna, one of the few senior women in an elite law firm who had children before she was thirty, spoke to how having a family that was close to work was a crucial factor in being able to continue working and managing her client obligations. Between her husband and herself, Aruna had three retired parents who either lived with them or within a twenty-minute car ride (which, as she shared, was practically "next door" for Mumbai standards) that she could trust with childcare. And this was in addition to two full-time maids and a driver, all of whom worked in the house. This multitiered support system allows her husband—another elite professional—and her both to manage and negotiate their careers without having to feel guilty about not being present in their young son's life:

> We chose a house close to office so I could continue working. My mother lives here. She took care of my son full-time for a year and a half after he was born. If I did not have these factors, I am pretty sure I would not be working.

But it also highlights the obvious disadvantage for women who could not similarly rely on parental support and proximity to work. Kaveri, an inhouse counsel of a prominent MNC in Mumbai, attended the same kind of law school that Aruna did and worked in "midtown" Mumbai, a few blocks away from Aruna's law firm, in a new building that—similar to Aruna's own workplace—looked and felt like a New York City skyscraper. Kaveri's daughter is not much older than Aruna's son, but the experience of managing work and family is different for her:

> I do not believe that in India it's easy to be a working woman . . . I have friends in London and New York. For them it's a lot easier because they have the facility where they can drop their child off in day care. . . . My daughter travels one hour away to school. I travel one hour in the opposite direction to work. So logistically it's a nightmare. . . . Socially it's a

nightmare because unless you have family in the area, there is no-one you can depend on . . . I do not have anybody who lives in Bombay. My mother-in-law comes and goes at her will and fancy. But it's not like I can assume that she is going to be around. Up until six months ago my husband did not get home before 10:00, 11:00, 12:00 at night from work . . . I'm very, very happy for women who have husbands who are there and who help. Up until [now], the buck [has] stopped with me.

The difference in experience was, of course, exacerbated by the firms they actually worked for. Aruna, who worked for an elite Indian law firm, believed that her seniority and relationship with partners put her in a position to navigate motherhood because the firm "got it" when she needed to leave at lunchtime to pick up her son, or take a call midway through a meeting when it was from her son's school. On the other hand, Kaveri, who worked for the Indian office of a global conglomerate, felt that being a woman at such a senior position put her in an especially vulnerable position to negotiate motherhood:

I think it's important for women not to use womanhood as a crutch, but to demonstrate that "you know what; I bring accountability and responsibility to the table." It has to be a give and take. When people see that "you know what; she's responsible, she gets the work done"— they will be OK with not having you [physically] be at work. Because they know that if they give you the job, if that means you will come in early and get it done, or if it means you log in from home and get it done—but you will get it done. . . . So at [Name of Last Employer], thankfully—because I had been there for as long as I had and because I had been able to build credibility, I had the flexibility of coming and going at my own choice. But you need to actually be around to build that sort of credibility . . . Which is when it becomes a little easier. But otherwise, the buck stops with the woman. Here, it is a one-woman show—I can not go home and use the motherhood card, because they probably expect me to and if I do, working out of it will be impossible.

Yet, it was not just the work environments that made it easier for Aruna than it did for Kaveri. Their differences in experience were also predicated on the variance between their respective support systems. Aruna benefited from a working relationship with her law firm, but she also enjoyed personal relationships in her home (proximate family, a partner with whom she could afford to buy a home that was walking distance from her office), which buffered the extent of her advantage. In contrast, for women like Kaveri, holding on to careers was a more solitary task. Her mother, who lived exactly halfway across the country, was a professional herself and was not available to help with childcare, unlike most other women who managed work and family. Her mother-in-law lived in a small town a four-hour flight away from Mumbai, and while she helped with Kaveri's daughter when she visited, it was not a reliable support system. Even though she, like every professional I met during my time in Mumbai, had full-time help and a driver, the lack of family support that could supplement this made, as she says, "the buck stop with her."

Kaveri was not the only Mumbai transplant for whom navigating this work and family balance proved difficult. For professional women who moved to Mumbai for work, sourcing domestic help was easy enough, but finding "reliable" outsourced domestic help, especially for childcare, was riddled with other problems. Maya, a lawyer in her early thirties, painted a very different picture from the one Aruna (a Mumbai native) did about their outsourced support at home:

> Sure, I guess technically, options are available—there are, for example, crèches. You can have people take care of your child when you are at work. But when you are not from Bombay, it is hard to find someone who is same background or at least someone who understands your mindset. . . . There just is not a professional market—so most of the women are not educated, they come from lower income backgrounds. So it is not like you get people with recommendation or that there is a placement agency. If you find someone you are comfortable with and you like her, great, but there just is not a market for it. So you cannot even get someone who is a 12th pass [Indian equivalent of a high school diploma], and this matters if you are leaving a child alone with someone all day. Imagine, even to just take the child to a hospital, they are not likely to have that frame of reference—it's something as simple as that. So if you do not have family here, even if you are willing to pay, it is hard to find someone.

Maya's fear that she'd have to leave her three-year-old with someone who comes from a "lower economic background" and who does not have a high school diploma speaks to an underlying (and perverse) structural advantage that most women with proximate family signaled but did not directly speak about—the fact that family and domestic help served very different, caste-specific roles in helping balance work and childcare. Across sites, without exception, people had a reliable network of paid help that took care of household chores. However, when it came to childcare, the efficacy of this caste-dependent labor was under more scrutiny. Domestic help in India are not employed only in high socioeconomic households, but the distinction between doing menial labor and not is still imbued with caste dependency (Frøystad 2003; Ray and Qayum 2009). As Raka Ray and Seemin Qayum (2009) offer, the main distinction between the Indian middle class and the domestic worker is not just economic difference and distance, it is also an inherently "caste-infleccted social structure" where lower-caste women are forced to perform manual labor that is customarily associated with menial work and servitude outside the home.

Nobody really spoke of it expressly in this way—caste privilege, after all, exists most blatantly in its performed invisibility—but the distinctions in the kinds of tasks that were delegated reaffirmed some of these patterns. While tasks like cooking, cleaning, washing dishes, doing the laundry, driving the employer to work were in line with caste-dependent expectations of servitude, being the primary caretaker of a child introduced some problems to this reliance. Having family that would take care of one's child meant that most of the child's socialization was managed by people the parents trusted and whose homogeneity with their own selves could be assured. Not having family to take care of a child brought back this worry about not being a "good parent" if one was not at home—and women balanced this negotiation more than men. Maya had, for example, left the elite law firm after trying for a year— unsuccessfully—to find "suitable" help that met her expectations for childcare. She hoped to return when her son was in kindergarten but felt like in the years that the child needed full supervision, relying on someone who did not have the same "frame of reference" as she did was simply not an option. In contrast, for women like Aruna who had access to both family that shared their "frames of reference" for socialization purposes as well as a set domestic labor force that could meet the requirements of servitude, the setup was complete. Nipun, who spoke about how Indian workforces were just culturally better for working mothers, spoke to this preferred (but much less talked about) synchronicity:

> My parents live in Bombay, yes. They are both working though, so they have less time to pitch in, but they are around—they are not like unavailable. If I need my mother to take care of my daughter for an afternoon, or pick her up from school, I just have to coordinate it, but it is not impossible. But that aside, I have fantastic support. I have no complaints. . . . I have a full-time nanny. I actually have my husband's nanny, who is living with us—I know, it is fantastic. And I have my in-laws coming in and out. She [the nanny] supervises everything at home [Nipun and her husband also employed three other people to help with housework, whom the nanny supervised]. And she cooks amazing food. It's amazing. I'm sorted. I have no complaints. Other than the fact that no one seems to know how to read a thermometer at home [*laughs, because she has just told me her son is running a fever and she feels bad leaving him at home*]. But that's OK.

As a Mumbai native whose partner was also from the city, Nipun's family had access to not just extended family and personal networks, but also a familial long-standing workforce (another marker of privilege, but one that necessarily complicates understandings of servitude and dependence) that they could trust and rely on to supplement her own investments in mothering. Together, these were all factors that, presumably, she could not have managed to align in the UK where she previously was a lawyer. Many of the lawyers I spoke to were very cognizant of the incidental patterns that advantaged their careers. They recognized, as one of them mentioned, that *a certain kind of woman* indeed did do well in the Indian professional elite environment. But this woman is also likely to have been predisposed to unlocking a set of relational advantages that was, as I show in the previous chapters, unpredictably reliant on variations in their organizational destinations. Close family and traditional networks of domestic support were indispensable—especially to those who were already predisposed to having this access. But so were where they worked, and *when.*

Temporality and the Contingencies of a Specific Cultural Moment

Scholars of gender and leadership have a strong theoretical grasp on why most women typically do not attain top leadership positions but only a weak command of why some women do (Bowles 2012). By exploring the career paths of successful professional women in India through their negotiations of family and firm, these data reveal how these women embedded in steeply hierarchical social structures manage to repurpose their environments to their advantage. In doing so, it advances the way we think about so-called traditional mechanisms, the importance of temporality in discussions about gender and work and, together, the systemic reproduction of new kinds of hierarchy.

This chapter follows the rest of the book in that it unpacks an optimistic surprise finding—of these women lawyers achieving new kinds of professional success—first with celebration for the extension of mobility that success affords, and then, more critically, to reveal its much less shiny underpinnings. In approaching these rewards with circumscribed celebration, this research reveals one set of structural conditions that have fortuitously come together to create environments of emancipation. But, as I allude to, there are other factors that come together to perform this kind of "accidental feminism," including organizational novelty, the imagined forces of globalization, a particularly receptive audience. But they all remain framed within the temporal contingencies of specific cultural moments.

Women in elite law firms, for example, were advantaged by the incidental co-emergence of both the law schools that produced them and the law firms that hired them. Similarly, women across organizations were advantaged by the fact that they were the first generation of women entering these professional labor enclaves at the time they were entering them. Unlike countries in which the feminist movement's agenda to funnel women into the workforce has been a dominant social framework for almost a century, India's gender politics, while rich and diverse, has had little focus on women in professional workspaces before liberalization in the 1990s. As a new cohort of women entering new kinds of workforces, many of these women were dealing with mature versions of these feminist scripts without sharing the inherited stories that produced them in the first place. As I show in chapter 4, firms in newly global India, especially domestic firms responding to increasingly global markets, were keen to signal their "global" thinking, and this often was represented by their commitment to egalitarian and modern gender scripts. Inherent in this process of adopting modern scripts is the fact that what was modern at the time of adoption was a particularly evolved global script of what it meant to be a woman in the workplace. If India had adopted these global scripts for what professional equality ought to look like more than a few decades ago, or if this pattern of liberalization had developed earlier in the timeline of the global movement for gender equality in the workplace, the inherited scripts might have been differently adopted. Instead, as women who were entering the Indian equivalent of a global elite workforce at a certain point in time when ideas (even if not reality!) about equality in the workplace were more settled, women in firms that were "reaching" toward these ideals were well placed to receive its aspirational rewards.

In other ways, temporality of the larger women's movement advantaged women across firms. It is self-evident that no writing about gender is complete without acknowledging its intersections with other sorts of inequality. Still, this chapter offers new extensions to existing debates. In India, class historically was signaled by women *not* needing to enter the workforce (Caplan 1985). And while high-class women were more likely to be better educated, to the extent they undertook paid employment outside the home, it was likely to be non–labor intensive (Ray and Qayum 2009) and sector-specific (e.g., teachers, clerical workers; Caplan 1985). Part of this inherited social movement without a shared history was the fact that they could—as first-generation female professionals in their family—depend on a cohort of women from a preceding generation (their mothers, in-laws) who were *not* in the workforce and who were ready and willing to help with childcare. These women from the previous generation were not uneducated; they were simply not women who contended with the same demands on their time between work and family as this current cohort of women did. Not only did this earlier cohort feel comfortable with the idea of communally helping with their grandchildren's care, they *expected* that they would be involved in doing so. Out of the handful of women who had mothers in the workforce, most of them were teachers or worked in a bank—professions historically known in India as jobs that would help women balance home and family while maintaining their financial independence. In turn, this gave this small sample of women a hybrid access to traditional relational advantages *and* modern scripts of what they expected from global, feminist workplaces.

Recall Behag, the lawyer who said she felt guilty about leaving her husband to coordinate housework because she had her "grandma's voice" in her head that socialized her to not be like her mother. Similarly, Kaveri, the lawyer who felt like the "buck stopped with her" and whose mother was a doctor, told me how different growing up with a professional mother was as a child in the '80s: "I was one of those weird kids who had dual parents working way before it was cool to have it," she told me, suggesting that her family arrangement—where her father did not mind taking care of the kitchen when her mother had to be at work, was in some ways, for the time "unthinkable." This is hardly to suggest that her mother was not socialized with traditional notions of marriage herself. As Kaveri lamented later in the interview, "now, when I tell my mother I have fought with my husband, her response is usually something like 'what did you make him for dinner' or 'you've spent enough time on your career, now take care of your family.'" Kaveri's response, though, is legitimately defensive, "What she does not realize is that her career was supported by her husband and a large family that lived in the same building as her and helped out whenever she needed them. I have not been that lucky—I have not had that."

And Kaveri indeed does not have what her mother had when she was a child. But the way in which she describes her mother's advantage is not far from the advantage other peers in this generation—successful women in this book—have when they rely on their familial support systems. As women who were entering the professional workforce at a time when it was not considered to be too radical, they were also less likely to face the kind of wrath that Behag's mother faced for leaving her to be cared for by her grandparents. It is not that unrealistic to speculate that if the generation that preceded this cohort of professional women had a feminist movement that had focused on getting women into the workforce (rather than the range of other significant commitments and strides it did make, as I lay out in the preface), this advantage of family support might have looked very different. Instead, the timing of this social movement's inheritance helped women with scaling the maternal wall, without actually having been set up to do that.

Naturally, this set of factors around the work and family balance is still only one part of the explanation. For instance, as I have elaborated in chapter 4, the importance of the kinds of external audiences these women deal with were central to dictating the environments they navigated. Particularly, while consultants and women in litigation had to deal with much more traditional domestic clients, women in elite law firms were doing work for what they described as "sophisticated" global clients who did not prime gender in the same way that they were used to. Yet, these organizational variations were only relevant over and above factors at the individual level that reinforced base advantages these women had. Still, this research reminds us that relationships between gender and work cannot be understood without also paying attention to the ways in which gender operates in other contexts, and that invariably these patterns bleed into each other. It confirms that to understand how gender works at one level of analysis also requires an introspection into how it works at other levels, oftentimes reinforcing its impact across levels as a reiterative structural factor.

Together, these negotiations between work, family, and gender offer a new nuance to our understandings of the social reproduction within the global legal profession. As other scholars have suggested, there are systemic inequalities that get recursively reproduced (Dezalay and Garth 2002, 2010; Dinovitzer 2006; Dinovitzer and Garth 2007; Sandefur 2007; Dinovitzer 2011), but here, not all of these transmissions were quite as straightforward. Different kinds of social and cultural capital continued to be important for these women professionals, but it was paying attention to this value in a temporal context that gave us leverage over their resultant differences across context. Middle-class women of the previous generation were educated but seldom employed. And the proliferation of new kinds of education and professional opportunities meant new kinds of possibilities and futures for women of the current generation who had access both to their new brand of capital *and* to a generation of close women before them who had not accessed it before them. This new access was certainly class-dependent to a certain extent, but it was also particularly time-bound. Together, it gives us a new agenda for understanding the textures within these movements—*who is adopting them? At what stages, and in what contexts? And, most important, for how much longer?*

SIX

FUTURES

Now What?

WHAT DO WE DO WITH THE ACCIDENTAL?

THE EPISTEMOLOGICAL UNCERTAINTY with the root for the word "accidental" was cause for much joyous intellectual looping as I anguished over this book's title and framing. Peter Goodrich, who has been my constant companion in these deliberations, initially thought that the root of the word accident was in *occidere*—which means to kill. Just as I was about to get attached to that framing—to run with the idea of *occidere* as to fall down and kill, perish (here, to kill a preconception, an old way of thinking, perhaps, with a fall)—research revealed that "accident," much like "incident," while coming from the word Latin "to fall" (*cedere*), does not include the meaning to kill. Incident comes from *incidere*—to fall upon, to happen to, while accident is from *accidere*—to fall toward. While they have synergies and merge at *cedere*, the choice of accident over incident is in the direction of its tendency. It is where we fall facing, what our fall can effect, that holds promise for the trip, so to speak. A fall could be a result of a trip up, perhaps of old complacency. But it is in the repair that follows that its eventual promise garners traction. As a theory, it allows for us to extend what this could mean for equality more generally. Accidents cannot be replicated, but they can give us new tools to pay attention to ripe sites and plan for the necessary process of converting accident to intention. And the first step of that might have to be our slow but deliberate acknowledgment of more uncomfortable allies and framings. How we merge narratives with our unlikely allies might determine the course of our futures.

In the past, scholars have used the legal profession as a case to illustrate the detriment of looking at gender as a singular analytical category (Menkel-Meadow 1989). And in trying to unpack these layered relationships, more recent scholarship about gender and work more generally has illuminated the importance of a multilevel approach (Risman 2004; Ridgeway 2011). As I illustrate across this book, there is a rising consensus that it is not enough to look only at how gender operates at the individual level; or gets "done" at the interactional level (West and Zimmerman 1987); or even to recognize that gender, like other systems of inequality, is embedded within persistent and problematic social structures (Acker 1990, 2006; Kanter 1993; Hull and Nelson 1998; Albiston 2007, 2009; Rhode 2011). Instead, it is critical that as feminist scholars we pay attention simultaneously to all three levels and their macro-interactions with each other.

In taking this meta-approach, this research reveals that while relationships with proximate family and available care workers for the house and home were crucial at the interactional level, micro identities like class and sociocultural capital were imperative across levels of analysis. Moreover, these intersections were embedded within specific contexts of organizational emergence and existing scripts of social stratification. Together, beyond a global empirical exploration on women in the legal profession, this research makes three theoretical contributions. First, these findings add to the broad literature on cultural contexts and the globalizing legal profession (Dezalay and Garth 2002, 2010; Halliday and Carruthers 2007; Liu and Halliday 2009; Silver 2011; Wilkins, Khanna, and Trubek 2017) and extend that literature further by offering a more concentrated gendered analysis of these interrelated contexts. Second, this work adds nuance to current understandings of social reproduction theory within the legal profession (Dezalay and Garth 2002, 2010; Dinovitzer 2006; Dinovitzer and Garth 2007; Sandefur 2007; Dinovitzer 2011). While advantages of class and capital were useful in the Indian context, they do not always operate in linear ways, especially for women. Finally, using the case of women in these new global law firms offers temporality as a useful lens to studying interconnected relationships between women, work, and family across levels of analysis. In particular, it reveals that while new kinds of palatable equality often rest on other kinds of stratification, these underlying inequalities are not always historic in the ways we expect.

In each of the preceding empirical chapters, I have attempted to make the case that it is the alchemy of structural conditions—and not targeted law or intentional policy—that has allowed for advantageous gender outcomes in the case of these select elite Indian professionals, while leaving others to experience their gendered environments much more explicitly. The overarching argument of this book is that several interrelated factors aligned to create a set of circumstances that created a relatively novel environment for its actors. Specific characteristics of the regulatory environment I describe in chapter 1 created a blank slate enabling certain kinds of cultural frameworks, and it was this, as I show in chapter 2, that allowed firms to reframe their cultures against the rest of the larger legal profession. The lack of background frameworks illustrating who was a "good" or "ideal" corporate lawyer allowed a new—and a-gendered—avatar of corporate lawyer to emerge, one that renegotiated existing hierarchies even as it aligned and stratified across new lines. Other extensions of liberalization buttressed this individual advantage, particularly the exaggerated imagination around ideas of global meritocracy standards and the specific kind of speculative mimicking that I highlight in chapter 3. Firms could demonstrate their embrace of the global through hypersignaling their commitment to meritocracy. By not expressly disadvantaging women, especially within a larger professional environment that was generally pitted against them, these firms created an organizational vacuum with its own promise and potential. But none of this commitment could have had substantial (or sustainable) standing if it was not reinforced by client preferences. And as I show in chapter 4, egalitarian opportunity arose not so much as a function of commitments to diversity but rather from structural conditions within certain kinds of firms—and with interactions and facings outside the firms, especially with clients—that were predicated on deeply essentialist tropes and reliabilities. Finally, as chapter 5 describes, support systems and networks *outside* these firms enabled women to balance work and family in new ways.

What is central to all of the factors I highlight above—and throughout this book—is that they were *not* about feminism or gender or even intentional parity. In addition, none of these factors could have produced such outcomes in isolation. They had to work in tandem with each other to produce the environments that they did, and this happened in some firms but not others. As the comparison with different, similarly prestigious professional practices shows, this advantage was an accident specific to a certain coordination of factors at a specific point in time. Together, this analysis sheds light on how gender-egalitarian change can blossom in environments that are accidental or unintended; it also shows that such conception flows out of a conjuncture of seemingly minor and perhaps even inconsequential institutional characteristics. Women professionals across the board, for example, shared the advantage of mothers and domestic help to assist them with balancing the responsibilities of family and home. Yet, it was only women in elite law firms who, armed with the subtle structural advantages provided by the other factors I highlight here, unlocked that advantage to the fullest. This suggests that conjunction of a set of narrow-gauge arrangements can—in some specific cases—generate big change. The fact that ostensibly similar firms could not offer the same parity, even with agentic intention, reveals the crucial role of the accidental in creating this kind of gender parity in elite Indian law firms. And it is this *butterfly effect*[1] of accidental, happenstance feminism that this book tries to unpack.

Finally, if egalitarian outcomes can be created and supported without explicit intention, what are the costs of this success? What giant shoulders of inequality do these successes stand on? And is this success sustainable, and if so, in what ways? This relationship between costs and sustainability is important because it uncovers the precarious modifiers that complicate what looks like the success of equality in these firms. In doing so, it reveals the importance of valorizing such success within the limited example of these firms, as well as for any external extensions we may choose to draw from them. In the preceding chapters, I have highlighted the ways in which this unintended parity has been buttressed by other inequalities inherent to the Indian case, including class-based socialization that modeled an ideal type of professional (chapter 2) and advantaged them in interactions with peers and clients by assuring a certain kind of "fit" (chapter 4), as well as the rigid caste system that underwrote frameworks that professionals across the board could depend on for housework (chapter 5). In this concluding chapter, I consider the sustainability of this advantage. What can we expect this accident to produce? And, to the extent we can predict it, how much will this early advantage influence the path dependency these firms are likely to instill in their future genealogy? Of course, without time series data, predictions about the actual sustainability of this advantage (i.e., how much longer we can expect an accident to produce equitable outcomes given market forces) are moot at best. But in considering them through a range of related lenses, I argue that this "accident" could have important implications and extensions, even if only for a small cross-section of the profession. Specifically, I'd argue that this case of elite Indian legal professionals offers fresh insights not only into the global legal profession, but specifically to larger relationships between mobility, merit, gender, and globalization. While this research appears to focus on a singular occurrence that is best preserved for its own policy extensions, I'd argue that its true value lies not in its own self-extensions, or even in its direct portability, but rather in its ability to inform us about the optics and effectiveness of diversity, representation, and inclusion more generally.

What's the Deal with Merit Anyway?

Two broad and somewhat contrary patterns influence the trajectory of global wealth segregation. On the one hand, inherited, ascribed advantages have been central to the reproduction of hierarchy—so most elites are predetermined. Yet, at the same time, post-Enlightenment logics have opened up new access to elite spaces and pathways, diversifying who can constitute the elite class. Thus, although wealth remains concentrated, the demography of individuals who control that wealth has changed both geographically and racially (Domhoff and Zweigenhaft 1998). However, although we know legacy patterns are no longer the only routes to aristocracy and that self-made attainment is on the increase (Piketty and Saez 2003; Edlund and Kopezuk 2009; Khan 2012), distinctions between "meritorious" and "inherited" remain murky (Brooks 2012; Khan 2013; Laurison and Friedman 2016; Naudet 2018).

In India, as in other countries, socioeconomic status has long been a function of ascribed factors. For example, in 2015, India ranked third globally in its number of billionaires, second only to the United States and China. Of these, only 5 percent (in contrast, for example, to China's 61 percent) reported being "self-made," and even this small cohort admitted to having had a "help-ing hand" from their parents.[2] And this is not just about billionaires: Nau-det and Dubost (2017) show that regional, caste, and family ties are at the root of the dense directorate networks in the country's largest listed compa-nies. Thus, unlike the more coherent distinctions between "self-made" and "inherited" that characterize traditional elites in the United States and Europe respectively (Khan 2012), elites in India attain and retain elite status through a more checkered process. The "self-made" elites of India remain deeply rooted in inherited wealth and status advantage—chief among this, caste—and in cultural capital that is tightly maintained through consolidated networks of power, exposure to urban environments, and expert micro-socialization. In her research on businesswomen within the non-brahmin but elite Agarwal community of North India, Ujithra Ponniah (2017) showed that despite inhab-iting modern contexts, women in family businesses reproduce cohesive caste identities through traditional mechanisms like marital matches and "fictive kinship ties" with other elites through business opportunities and activities that could be viewed as "social work." Parul Bhandari's ethnography on *kitty parties* among elite Delhi housewives offers evidence of a more layered social reproduction. Bhandari argues that elite women are not limited to domestic power or even obvious consumption, but rather a more complicated relation-ship to capital, its management and its performance, that is "wrought with feelings of fear, anxiety, pride, competition, and gender role performance" (2019:276).

Elite professionals offer yet another dimension into this textured process of understanding mobility: as actors who are accessing elite rewards through means other than ascribed status of birth or its ascribed extension of elite mar-riage, the women who move into this space of elite praxis further complicate our understandings of gender, inequality, and selective mobility. Other schol-ars have highlighted professional spaces as environments ripe for investigating the "sociological heartlands of culture, monopoly, closure and stratification" (Macdonald 1995). And in the Indian case, scholars have offered new ways of thinking about access to elite networks historically predetermined by log-ics of caste and kinship (Jodhka and Newman 2007). But while professional elites in other countries have been the subjects of sociological interrogation (e.g., Hagan and Kay 1995; Sommerlad 2002, 2011; Dinovitzer 2011; Rivera 2012), investigation in India has focused mainly on the more limited ques-tion of professional work as a means of mobility into a stable middle class (e.g., Fernandes 2000; Deshpande 2003; Fernandes and Heller 2006) and, to a smaller extent, the implications for women in these spaces (e.g., De Neve 2005; Patel and Parminder 2005; D'Mello 2006; Mukherjee 2008; Nadeem 2009; Radhakrishnan 2009; Bhatt, Murthy, and Ramamurthy 2010; Donner 2012; Vijayakumar 2013; Fuller and Narasimhan 2014; Upadhya 2016; Bhatt 2018).

One reason for this lack of inquiry is that professionals in India have not always been considered "elites"; until fairly recently an "elite professional" would have been someone born into a wealthy family who happened to acquire professional training. And even for this sub-cohort, the label "professional" is not exactly apt. Although second-generation elites are increasingly diversifying their professional portfolios and obtaining international graduate degrees,[3] many continue to inherit their wealth and status as they stick with the family business. And for these second- or third-generation elites, professional credentials offer a hand-wave toward meritocracy, another tool to legitimize their inheritance.[4]

Another reason Indian professional elites have not been widely studied as "elites" is because professionals in the Indian context are *not* always elite. As chapter 1 sets up, the professional women described in the vast research on IT professionals, for example, are not elite workers in the same way that senior corporate lawyers making US$200,000 a year are. Still, these parallels between the software sector and the challenges faced by women in my consulting sample are consequential for our purposes of thinking about selective mobility and new directions to the flow of capital. Whereas studies of the software sector focus on the attainment and retention of middle-class status, this book examines a different kind of mobility—a gendered mobility into an elite professional class whose praxis is at odds with the middle-class origins of many of its members. In unearthing these women's journeys, this book offers a snapshot of a particular type of mobility that globalization offers; it also joins a rising strain of literature (e.g., Maqsood 2017) that probes new extensions to traditional understandings of the relationships among modernity, mobility, and gender in global contexts that are traditionally viewed through development-forward or linear postcolonial lenses.[5] Thinking of scripts of modernity as based outside of the West offers us a new way to think of transnational circulation of culture. These portrayals of global south mobility are important not just because they offer new understandings of class emergence globally, but also because they counter the linear ways in which postcolonial emergence can play out for women in global contexts. As I argue, a key difference between the professionals described by other accounts and the professional elites I study in this book is the relative distance the elites have in their everyday lives from these middle-class concerns of domesticity, nation, and feminine morality. Not only are they in a salary bracket that far outstrips that of the average IT or outsourcing professional, they inhabit spaces and praxes that are at direct odds with a middle-class ethos that situates itself *against* rather than among the governing rich and powerful. Many women in my sample had a sense that their very mobility had placed them in a unique bubble where traditional balances between modernity and morality seemed less stifling. At the same time, while this book anatomizes a particular kind of mobility, it is not oblivious to the ways in which such mobility is gained. It is to these costs and underlying mechanisms that buffer these advantages—particularly the steep charge of whitewashing accidental and inherited advantage alike as meritocratic—that I turn next.

A Certain Kind of Woman Does Well

This research confirms the persistence of gendered frameworks across organizations, even in new and modern workplaces. At the same time, it also offers some hope for the curation of more gender-egalitarian professional sites, especially through the socialization offered by early gender-equal institutional structures. The law firms I examine here may not be feminist firms, they might not even be equal firms. But in seeming to have parity, they are at the precipice of affording a different kind of opportunity to Indian professional women. The cultural malleability of new work is influenced heavily by its workers: as chapter 2 argues, the earlier that professionals are socialized into frameworks of gender parity, the better prepared organizations can be for resisting the plaque of persistent gender inequality. But this resistance was hardly a matter of certainty, and it certainly did not extend itself to all women equally.

As this book highlights throughout, many of the "advantages" or underlying mechanisms that produced visibly parity-favoring outcomes were cascading structural accidents that were unintentionally intensified by synchronicity. Women in elite law firms were best set up to reap the rewards of this structure because they were incidentally advantaged across multiple levels of analysis—they had a built-in class advantage (as did their peers) but in addition to that, they were socialized in a certain sort of law school. That socialization was reinforced when the women entered firms that were predominantly populated by people who shared it. The women had interactional advantages too—they were in domestic firms that "got" their cultural assumptions but also had an organizational bandwidth that allowed them to accommodate the women they wanted to. And over all of this, there was the distinct institutional advantage of the ways in which their personal life course interacted with their professional life course. As women with the chance to become partner *before* they had to make serious negotiations about family and marriage, these women were better suited than their peers to negotiate from positions of power.

At the same time, these women, like all professionals studied here independent of organizational context, depended on systems of structural inequality: an affordable workforce took care of all the domestic labor that in other situations might have been borne centrally by working women and not their partners. And here too, incidental factors mattered in addition to the strong buffers of structural violence. As chapter 5 reveals, the women who were most successful in navigating what is otherwise seen as a "maternal wall" (Crosby, Williams, and Biernat 2004) were those who not only had elite graduate degrees with sympathetic partners, but could also complement that with a familial network to help with household work and childcare. But what further advantaged domestic law firms was a certain kind of sympathetic understanding about this work-family divide. India's intrinsically family- focused cultural ideology influenced the ways in which these commitments bore down on every worker—and not just women. Since the balance of "work versus family" was not limited to childcare alone, men and women both had to negotiate these commitments. Adding to this pattern of traditional structure with surprise outcomes was, of course, that it was domestic firms and not international conglomerates that "got" these cultural assumptions that surrounded family and started negotiations from a position of understanding.

Yet, this privilege was not always visible because, in addition to these many layers of advantage that women drew from, they also saw their advancement as legitimate within the more dominant framework of meritocracy and track-dependent achievement. One of the female law firm partners I interviewed told me that I should not be surprised by the number of women in law firms who were doing well, because, as she put it, the women who were there had already "been on track to becoming partner." At the time she said this, I remember thinking that she probably was going to talk about caste or class homogeneity—a clear theme that I was beginning to garner from my fieldwork. Instead, she offered a more individualistic explanation of how success operates:

> A certain kind of woman does well in a firm that looks like [Elite Law Firm]. It is not just anyone who can become a partner or even be on partner track here. It is not like being a partner in [Domestic Law Firm]. It means something here—so a certain kind of person is already on track to becoming partner here. This sort of woman is more likely to know about all of it or want it—and therefore find ways to be able to have it. She'll juggle work and family. Sure, the firm matters—but it is mostly the kind of people who self-select into this track.

This notion that a driven, individualistic woman could "find ways to be able to have it" no doubt had some personal resonance for the partner in question. But it did not do justice to the resources these women had that allowed them to "juggle work and family": the family support systems, the cultural capital, the invisible accretion of advantage.

Cultural capital and the ways in which it allows old inequalities to take new forms is a striking strain in mobility research in general (Bourdieu 1972), but it takes on special relevance as a mode of analysis for interrogating professional contexts in emerging economies (e.g., Trubek and Santos 2006; Papa and Wilkins 2011; Garth 2016; Liu, Trubek, and Wilkins 2016). In the Indian context, Ajantha Subramanian's work on elite engineering graduates (2015) lays out the ways in which the social life of caste has been predicated on the legitimacy of modern meritocratic capital. She notes that upper-caste individuals think of themselves as "modern subjects" with "sincere commitments to universalistic ideas of equality, democracy and rationality" without always paying attention to the "history of accumulated privilege" that affords them that perspective (2015). These "meritocrats," Subramanian argues, then produce a "castelessness" that allows them to present their access to elite education and the experience within elite schools as distinctly legitimate in ways that it might not have been had their access been solely inherited. This kind of credentialism is not always the norm—for example, Jules Naudet and Dubost (2017) show how Indian business elites, unlike Western elites, do not feel the need to perform legitimacy through top global credentialing—still, other work on professional elites who are trained in the STEM fields in India offers similar explanations for the new avatars of caste and class privilege as they inhabit new positions within postcolonial spaces. Fuller and Narasimhan (2014) similarly remind us that modernity or being able to perform its affective access has consistently been employed by those already advantaged (Tamil Brahmins, for example) to legitimize their positional advantages in new and old professions alike.[6] Such research into elite workers and their trajectories rarely offers an optimistic gender analysis. Yet it does reinforce some of the central findings of this book that positional privilege and the various kinds of social and cultural capital it offers naturally leads to various other advantages. Recall from chapter 5 that the women from families that either were from Mumbai or could afford to live there—in itself, a marker of class—were the ones who could be supported substantively with childcare. And even for those with families in Mumbai, class connections mattered. Aruna, who with her husband had moved to an apartment within walking distance from work, had parents at home and a full staff of domestic help, but she also had the ability to negotiate with the managing partner of the firm about a schedule that worked for her and her family. In her words: "It all comes down to what your relationship with them is, *yaar.*" In her recollection, how she negotiated time off from the firm, how she planned her return, how she responded to client-facing roles before and after childbirth, were all a cordial, peaceful discussion. One cannot help but assume that her comfort in these negotiations was a function of her "relationship" with the firm. It also appears that this relationship was buttressed by a range of social and cultural factors that she felt no need to articulate because they were so inherent in their advantage. Maya, on the other hand, who we encountered in chapter 5, had been a lawyer at the very same firm but had more difficulty structuring these negotiations because as an outsider, she saw the problem of her work-life balance as entirely her own. In the absence of strict rules and policies for structuring these balances, negotiations were determined by comfort in these interpersonal relationships. What empowered some women who felt like they were in a position to access this interactional capital, left others in the lurch.

This book has also tried to show that class in and of itself does not guarantee women the same kind of experience across sites: even when keeping class constant, environments can change experience. Although most—if not all—of these elite professionals were second-generation middle class, their relative compatibility and fit within these elite life chances came from a conjunction of factors: going to the graduate schools they did, at the particular time in history that they did, and the ways in which these two things were valorized by the institutions they joined upon graduation. Variation in these three factors afforded very different kinds of experiences even within this seemingly tight class of first-generation elite professionals.

What Do We Do with the Accidental?

As I illustrate in different ways across the book, structural conditions that rewarded novelty and timing were central to the creation of these advantages for women in elite law firms. But newness and temporality also made this advantage less sustainable. New institutions, after all, are not always going to stay "new," and with interaction and exposure to surroundings, "accidental" structural advantages can begin to fray at the edges. In the case of elite law firms, their small scale makes the advantages they confer especially precarious to the changes wrought by growth over time. Because of the innate inability to "replicate" accidents, the unique advantage enjoyed by women in these elite firms is not likely to extend to firms beyond those that currently offer it, and it remains to be seen whether it will be sustained when these firms grow beyond their current size. In a country with more than one million lawyers, firms like these that routinely employ from 200 to 500 lawyers in each office are a small subset. Of course, this corporate elite (Papa and Wilkins 2011) has been central to the expansion and globalization of the industry and holds much of the market share for corporate transactional work, but they are still only a small part of a larger, deeply gendered profession.

Ironically, their very novelty may pose a detriment to their structural advantages. As new firms, elite law firms offer a good contrast to preexisting hierarchies, both because of their novel structure and work but also because of their ability to attract a concentrated group of gender-socialized professionals. Since both the elite firms and the law schools that supply them have a homogenous population, they allow for this commitment to merit (not gender!) to reinstate itself. With an expansion of these firms—inherent as the market expands—this clean pipeline from elite law school to elite law firm might inevitably be affected. The top five National Law Schools each graduate 80–130 students a year, and each of the top two law firms typically recruits the top 15–30 candidates on the job market every year. With expanded recruitment possibilities, the supply of gender-socialized professionals will also need to simultaneously grow for a stable model. That is, if the number of gender-egalitarian elite firms competing for these top-tier graduates increases, the supply of such gender-socialized professionals will also need to increase or the model will become unstable.

Further, while it is certainly promising that these firms are egalitarian in their early days, we will have to wait and see what happens as India's global legal landscape continues to expand and change. Currently, these firms are domestically owned and foreign-facing, factors that I show are integral for the kind of imaginative mimicking that results in gender-egalitarian outcomes for their members. With impending liberalization of these firms—a debate that has been gaining momentum over the last half decade—foreign firms could well merge and acquire these firms. The extensions of this globalization for firms will be an interesting time to observe gender patterns within these firms. On acquisition, will these newly global law firms—like their MNC consulting counterparts—become truly global but lose the accidental advantages they currently capitalize on? In particular, with the inevitable extensions to partnership tracks that will come with expansion, are women condemned to lose out on the timetable advantage that currently works in their favor?

Finally, many of the structural advantages that have predicated the success of women lawyers in this book rests heavily on other violent inequities inherent in the Indian system. This book uses the Indian professionals case as one way of teasing out the ways in which inequalities get reproduced, repurposed, and replaced in new global sites. For instance, the reason that work–family conflict is not as stark for a select set of Indian women is because, as I argue in chapter 5, it relies on a strong caste-dependent setup of household help and a previous generation of women who did not participate actively in the workforce and are available to help with childcare. Thus, while this research might propose a new kind of feminist mobility that renegotiates existing hierarchies, that mobility also creates new hierarchies that depend on the sticky resilience of old inequalities—like a rural, uneducated domestic labor class and a preceding cohort of educated but unemployed grandmothers who can help with negotiating the double bind. Such a position—accessing the advantages of globalization but also reaping benefits from traditional structures—is, as other scholars suspicious of similar gendered professional success (e.g., Sommerlad 2002) have warned, an unsustainable premise at best.

Even so, this exercise of looking at the emergence of a new field of accidental parity both as a surprise outcome of a nonexistent social movement as well as an introducer of new hierarchies gives us a more holistic way to analyze the impact of globalization in the developing world. More broadly, this research reminds us that wins for gender equality in workspaces can, as in other cases (Phillips 2005), happen unintentionally and may be couched in other, more broadly conceived and supported movements. The success of the Indian law firm case has not been as much about a feminist movement as it has been about legitimacy and economic opportunity. As I argue in chapter 3, in emerging from an environment steeped in hierarchy and particularistic assumptions about gender, a big condition for creating this parity was that these law firms saw local differentiation and global mimicking as useful strategies to signal their competitiveness in new markets. A prominent part of this signaling process was the ideological commitment to being "meritocratic"—a catchall phrase that was prominent in respondents' explanations of gender parity in their firms. The relative ambiguity of the explanation was crucial in determining the specifics of their performance of meritocracy. While some lawyers thought that they were mimicking global firms, others saw this performance as showing that they were better than global firms in conforming to the ideal type. In both cases, though, as firms with no connections to Western firms and logics, these elite law firms were using assumed external myths and overcompensating in their performance—thereby converging with an imagined set of global norms through what I call "*speculative isomorphism*" in chapter 4. In contrast, local offices of global firms did not feel the same threats to their legitimacy and saw their inability to substantively implement gender-egalitarian workspaces as a frustrating but understandable extension of being in a country "like India."

Altogether, these chapters suggest, these were not women who would identify as feminist or whom other feminists (rightly so) might claim as doing the work of the movement. Still, the egalitarian outcomes in these firms might bear the promise of potentially feminist futures. It is this inclusion of unintended feminism—or a thing that looks like feminism produced by structural conditions rather than committed contract—that this book calls attention to. As I note at the start of the book, this inclusion does not feel organic and, indeed, being able to code unintentional actors as movement propagators has its own costs. But it does lay before us a way to make sense of the accidental, as well as an urgency to track its progress and find ways to tap into its inherent possibilities for creating other promising and innovative practices, or even resultant "new, radical utopias" (Cooper 2014).

Over the years that I have presented this work, I've been asked what purchase the term "accidental" gives us to understand these phenomena. What meaning or extension can this work have if I write away all my analysis as accidental? As an early reader of this manuscript asked me, "What *can* you do with 'accidental'? Where do you go from there? It seems so pessimistic." The quippy response, of course, is that socio-legal scholars cannot afford to be in the business of offering comforting portrayals of the world. Calling progress "accidental" may not be very hopeful, but it does aid in explaining the incidental nature of this phenomenon. And it offers a note of caution against assuming that this outcome deserves to be claimed by the actors who might wish to claim it as intentional. At the same time, while an "accidental" development may not be immediately extensible or replicable, it does leave room for limited—and, decidedly, cruel (Berlant 2011)—optimism. As other scholars have suggested, early blueprints, no matter what their intent or genesis, are vital for organizational culture. Historic emergence patterns are crucial for organizational histories, and even if the accidental feminist advantages of these firms are time-circumscribed, there is hope that at least some patterns of this feminist organizational makeup will carry over to the futures of these firms. At the time of this book's writing, firms were reporting partner representations and promotions for 2019–20. In the firms I studied, although women moved between cities and firms, they remained as well represented in these partnership tracks as they had been at the time of my initial data collection and fieldwork years. What was more, although women's partnerships across all firms in the country were close to global averages (in that they skewed male), blogs and legal sites reporting on these partnership decisions highlighted representation—paying attention to gender in partnership data or noting the prevalence of "growing minority" partnerships. This kind of reinforcement and continued progress offers some optimistic possibility for future path dependency.

This focus on incidental and independent factors that have come together to create unusual spaces of parity for elite legal professionals also deviates from more causal understandings of the relationship between law and social change as well as broader theories of intention. Further still, it urges our understandings of intentional feminist intervention to have a different kind of critical, self-reflexive introspection. The rejection of Western models of feminism and the w(e)ariness of hegemonic orthodoxies they offer has been a strong thread in radical global south resistance (Mohanty et al. 1991; Abu-Lughod 1998, 2013; Grewal 2005). And beyond rejecting the Western lens, or dismissing hegemonic orthodoxy's diminished ability to truly speak on behalf of the transnational subject, some of this resistance has been aimed at the weight of these categories themselves. As I start this book by suggesting, calling a thing feminist not only attaches a fundamentally scripted and normative understanding of that category; it also claims for itself a certain political weight. One can imagine that if the law firms described here claimed a feminist identity, or if they were viewed as being spearheaded by feminist actors, they could have garnered counterproductive attention.

At its core, this book asks—can we see and theorize the role of intention anew, can we queer the ways in which we understand its lack? "Accidents" have not always been seen as harbingers of positive possibility since unintended consequences, when realized (and theorized), are usually negative outcomes that are at odds with the profitable premise or noble intentions they start with. Scholars have been attentive to the unintended consequences of *intentional* institutional changes ever since Merton's classic article on latent functions of social action (Merton 1936), and critical organizational scholars have paid attention to the ways in which historical productions of opportunity and equality within firms have been subverted (Dobbin 2009; Ahmed 2012). It is now established across a range of sites that different actors may have possibly good intentions to create good social institutions, but the actual lived experience of their intention could deviate dramatically and changes within them require a constant "coming up against" these institutions (Ahmed 2012:186). While this line of analysis is meant to accommodate functional and dysfunctional consequences alike, less attention has been paid to *positive* unintended consequences (and even less to such consequences following unintended action).

Yet, historically, accidents have played roles in setting up feminist frameworks, even if the focus of their recall has not been just on the lack of intention. For example, scholars long have argued that the word "sex" was added to the list of protected categories to employment discrimination, not because Howard Smith (a Virginian segregationist and leader of an anti–civil rights coalition determined to block the act) cared about the possibilities it had for gendered emancipation, but because he saw it as a "poison pill" that would kill the Act (Dierenfield 1981; Purdum 2014; Thomas 2017).[7] This incidental addition of "sex" to the Civil Rights Act of 1964 (even if it then meant gender) also has clear implications for current transgender rights and debates—a path dependency that certainly could not have been predicted at the time of this inclusion, poisoned or otherwise. Similarly, the entry of women into professions like medicine—which they were traditionally kept out of—was a function of not lobbied demand but a market condition that was irreplaceably altered with World War I (Greenwald 1990). Women were also introduced into the formal economy at rapid rates through most nations involved in World War II, because of changes in market circumstances and material need rather than states' commitments to women's movements more generally. While feminist movements were still key in finagling this entry, the opportunity itself was a product of circumstance.[8]

Even so, this renewed push to focus on lack of intention or accident is not meant to valorize it. To reemphasize, this book's reliance on the crutch of the accident as a theoretical tool is not meant to replace the work of intention. Instead, it is to afford spaces of engagement and inquiry where things can be seen through a different lens, to establish a queer practice of reassigning the reinforcing ways in which we use words and frameworks. It certainly is not a call to embark on new searches for accidents. After all, the dearth of attention paid to accidents is not surprising—how would one even go about looking for accident?

The more salient question, rather, is what this discovery offers. On the one hand, unlike the *ceder* etymology I struggle with above, we could afford the Aristotelian etymology of the accident and trace it back to a root in relative uncertainty. An accident is not a modal part of what produces an outcome, but rather, one possible way in which one could invoke the possibility of such outcome's production. Yet, if we see the accident as already having happened—as in this case—as a thing that is real and doubtless but one whose necessity[9] we are not yet aware of (or, in Aristotle's terms, cause), our ability to contend with it has more power. Instead, if we think of the accident as deserving of repair or cure, I hope the usefulness of this framing offers more agentic tools. Once you unearth a positive accident, what do you do with it? How do you contain and crystallize the main sources of its advantages? And, most important, how do we replicate such accidents with more intention? In the case of these law firms, it might be a more agentic recognition of the advantage parity offers and its symbolic potential for shaping institutional cultures well beyond the firm. In other words, it is a hope that this synergistic parity allows for more intentional feminist commitment to future path dependency. It could, for example, start with clearer policies and active development opportunities that are women-focused, or it could introduce better holding patterns for institutional equity and diversity more generally. The time to make this shift from accident to intention is certainly *now* for the firms I study. Even if gender is not what offers feminism focus (Butler 2004), and even if feminization itself is not a worthy response for a better legal profession (Menkel-Meadow 1989), the turn from accident to intent can be fruitful for future generations of lawyers: with more women attorneys in senior positions, the likelihood of their implementation could be better leveraged, and with more implementation, the creation of an organizational culture could be further cemented.

It is worth stressing that even as it focuses on positive outliers in ways that are important for this particular demographic of the world, the accidental feminism described in this book does not lend itself to expansive policy implications—after all, demanding institutional dissonance to achieve gender parity seems both unsavory and nonportable. In fact, even as the above partnership decisions were announced in India, halfway across the world, the large US law firm Paul Weiss also declared its year's partners—eleven white men with a sole (white) woman at the end of the 2*6 matrix, tucked away at the bottom right of the photo grid made public on Twitter. The lack of diversity in the firm's cohort of new partners made central a gaping problem with representation in the US legal profession. But I offer this contrast to highlight beyond the importance of optics and the frustration of ideological decoupling more generally. The US legal profession, as other scholars have laboriously argued, remains deeply hierarchical and impenetrable (Epstein et al. 1999; Dinovitzer and Garth 2004; Wilder 2007; Kay and Gorman 2008; Nelson et al. 2009; Dinovitzer et al. 2014) with accounts of new kinds of diversity confirming old theories about exclusion and social reproduction (e.g., Reynoso 2004; Postar 2011; Escontrias, Moran, and Nelson 2016; Headworth et al. 2016; Ballakrishnen and Silver 2019), especially around gender (Sterling and Reichman 2012, 2016; Kay 2016; Olson 2016). Notwithstanding any commitments to diversity the firm actually might have had, these optics and the uproar it raised among critics and commentators remind us that diversity need not just be done, but that it also needs to be *seen* as being done. Of course, this imperative comes with its own limitations—having specialty programs and aggressive performative recruitment strategies for people of color and glossy brochures to attract diverse candidates cannot be just (just!) ways to acquire the notional (and useful) badge of inclusive excellence. Incentivizing firms to be better vessels for their different and diverse institutional actors is meaningless if it is just about optics. Focusing on entry and not sustainable flourishing of diversity in these firms results in exactly the sort of second-generation biases and no-problem problem that were rampant in the consulting firms I studied: firms that felt like they were off the hook because they had done enough institutionally to accommodate a range of professionals. And although ideological commitment to equality is not enough, it is simultaneously true that, left untended, unintentional opportunity for women too can be unsustainable and/or short-lived. If we were to remain committed to pessimism (as most stratification scholars have been, with good reason[10]), the paradox could be pretty straightforward: neither intention nor its lack is likely to guarantee or bring about sustainable equality.

Simultaneously, neo-institutionalism gives us some hope. Where *imagined* beliefs matter, ritual and symbolism can have long-lasting substantive impacts that, in turn, produce new cultural scripts. No matter what the initial incentive to create these structures may have been, firms with gender-parity partnership are likely to have at least one effective weapon in their arsenal—an early script of gender egalitarianism which, by extension, can be instrumental for future generations of egalitarian firms and professional identities. By creating institutions where women are not inherently fighting the sort of bottleneck that is standard in other parts of the profession (and in high-status careers more generally), what might be a one-cohort advantage can still have positive ripples in later generations, even without intention. In particular, the concentration of women at senior positions in these firms could set the tone for the way future entrants see and seek entry into these firms even if the representation itself does not substantively invite such entry.

Beyond gesturing at possibly replicable policy, the socio-legal intervention this research offers extends our understandings about gender and the workplace in the neoliberal developing world. In particular, it gives us tools to dissect the impact of global markers—both assumed and imagined—in shaping institutions in emerging economies, with their widely varying iterations of diffuse Western cues. It also gives us a way to think about new histories and concurrent anthropologies of women in the emerging world and their relative advantage in being able to negotiate hierarchies independent (and sometimes, *because*) of preexisting frameworks. Research on emerging economies has, understandably, concentrated on a development perspective that traditionally ignores elites in these economies. Rethinking our focus on these economies and introducing some heterogeneity in our research agendas, especially at a time when gendered understandings of the region—and the global souths more generally—are painted with a broad brush, is not just meaningful but necessary. The unveiling also offers us a different glimpse at the persistence of inequality. The number of complicated (and happenstance) factors that have had to come together to afford a certain kind of equ(al)ity in this case, reminds us that the building of truly egalitarian firms cannot be done with just the wave of a well-intentioned and diversity-hopeful magic wand. There is enormous work ahead if we are truly committed to building these spaces. And even then, what looks like failure might still have hopeful progress waiting to be discovered and to learn from. The Indian law firm case might not be replicable, but attention to processes in other "failed" sites (Massoud 2013) might reveal new oases and give us novel ways to think about progress, especially if we are willing to concede the limitations of categories and questionable dichotomies.

The experience of the women lawyers in my study might not have been intentionally curated, but that experience, simply being what it has been, has set the tone for a certain kind of law firm to emerge. To these extents at least, *Accidental Feminism* offers a ray of hope: sustainable frameworks can be birthed out of accident. And in this sense, whatever passes for chance, also passes for truth.[11] Ultimately, beyond the immediate contexts of its inquiry, the larger questions about intention that this research nudges us to think about are also, at their core, questions about the possibilities of focus. *If what we see is a function of how and where we look, perhaps the real call is to look and see differently.*

Research Methods

DESIGN, DISCIPLINE, DISCURSIVE DISTANCE

MY DATA ARE from 139 semi-structured, in-depth interviews (table 5) conducted between 2011 and 2015 with professionals across these three main theoretical cases in Mumbai, India (table 4), accounting for variations in organizational types and novelty of emergence (table 6). As I explain in chapter 1, data were analyzed in three critical stages—first after the pilot in 2011 to establish the parameters of the study (including kinds of actors, organizations, and location); then in 2012–13 after the first stage of the interviews investigating the experience of gender across different organizations and confirming that in fact gender played out differently in a small oasis of elite law firms (table 7); and finally, in 2014–15 after the addition of the third comparative case of consultants.

Even though the main focus of these interviews were successful women across organizations, several allied interviews set the tone for interpreting their narrative. For instance, although I oversampled women, the men in the sample were crucial for placing the women's responses in context since they provided an interactional peer and structural perspective to understand their journeys. Although my focus was on specific kinds of legal careers and organizations, narratives of those in other sites (e.g., lawyers in public interest firms and nongovernmental organizations, or in general counsel offices and positions, whom I encountered in early stages of the study) and cities (i.e., lawyers in Indian cities that were not Mumbai) were crucial to placing these findings in relative context. Similarly, clients were central to confirming the ways in which women spoke about their experience. Finally, relevant to understanding the "success" cases was the attrition sample in my study, of women who chose to exit these firms. Thinking about the "kinds of women" who did *not* make it in these firms—and their reasons for being able to navigate these environments with the same kinds of rewards as others—were critical to valorizing

Table 5. List of all interviews ($N = 139$)

Gender	Pilot (2011)		2012–13		2014–15		Total	
	F	M	F	M	F	M	F	M
Traditional legal practice	7	3	16	4	23	5	46	12
Transactional law firm	15	3	20	6	4	2	39	11
International banks and consulting firms	—	—	5	—	16	6	21	6
Gender totals	22	6	41	10	43	13	106	29
Other informant interviews (clients, industry reporters)	—		3		1		4	
Total Respondents	28		54		57		139	

the narratives of those who did stay. Although these triangulated and added texture to the import of my main data, they were not complete in their analytical variation and served much more of a key informant and narrative buffer purpose. For instance, I did not systematically vary these additional respondents' characteristics (e.g., kinds of clients, reasons for different kinds of attrition respondents' leaving these firms) and indeed, during the years I was in the field, professionals left and moved between organizations, another set of changes and nonstatic data points that this research does not systematically capture. Similarly, although consulting firms offered an important comparative case for the experience of these women in elite law firms, the ability to comprehensively profile their professional experience was limited by this focus on using them primarily as a reflective case study.

As a financial capital with an established presence of both older and newer professional service firms, Mumbai was a prime city to locate this analysis. To identify respondents, I first wrote to a random selection of law firm partners in the five firms in Mumbai that had been ranked consistently as the top legal firms by global ranking agencies over the last five years. This is a standard typology of the organizational stratification within the Indian legal profession (Gupta et al. 2017). In the years after this research, this cohort of "elite law firms" now includes six firms, following a split among one of them. However, it does not affect this sampling since the organizational split was geography-based and did not affect the "elite firm" category among Mumbai's law firms. Over the course of the first field visit, I met with seven of the fifteen partners I contacted. Once the first connections were established, however, internal networks that these senior lawyers were embedded in made it easier to contact and interview more respondents. These partners were influential contacts who connected me with junior colleagues and peers in their own firm, shared

Table 6. Field and firm emergence for major Indian professions

Field	Post-1991	Global Organization	New Organization
Consulting	●	●	●
Accounting		●	●
Banking		●	●
Law			●

Table 7. Comparative gender representation in legal profession

	% Female	
	United States (2013)	India (2013)
Legal profession	34	5
Elite law firms (private practice, entry-level)	44.8	55
Elite law firms (private practice, partnership)	20.2	48

Notes: For United States Women in Legal Profession statistics, see American Bar Association Market Research Department, April 2013. For Indian women in the legal profession statistics, Michelson (2013) reports census data indicating that women make up just 5 percent of all lawyers, about half the number in bar council admission records for a similar time period (table 1). Note, however, that most Bar Council records report all law graduates registered with the Bar. All data on elite private practice are collected by author and reflect entry and partnership rates at two of the largest transactional law firms in the sample at the end of data collection. Note that data on private practice for US lawyers in private practice includes associate and partner numbers in all law firms. This offers a conservative comparison since retention and partnership in large law firms is typically much lower than in smaller law firm practice. For more general detail on the limitations of demographic data on the Indian legal profession, see Ballakrishnen 2020.

with me details and contact information for lawyers in other professional firms, and connected me with colleagues in banking and consulting practices.

For most of the interviews, I spoke to women and men in each of these firms, for 40 to 90 minutes each. Interviews were initially designed to probe a set of predetermined areas, including: family history, professional schooling experiences, career trajectory, career aspiration, everyday experiences, and barriers to progression. Preliminary interviews offered a range of open-ended biographical data, allowing for more structured inquiry in subsequent interviews. Early interviews also helped explore emergent themes (Spradley 1979) and subsequently became more streamlined to include specifics about, among other things, personal and professional interactions with clients and the ways in which those interactions shaped exchanges and experiences. All interviews were in English, except for the odd word in a vernacular language, usually used for effect. For many of my respondents the primary model for being interviewed was the press, and most were pleased (and many, required) that I not reveal their identities in published research. Some respondents were uncomfortable with being recorded, so I took notes in shorthand during interviews and transcribed them immediately afterward. When recorded, the interviews were professionally transcribed. Over the course of the data collection—and to some extent, in the years since I have been thinking of and writing this book—I would meet some of these respondents for shorter meetings to update the original transcripts. While these follow-up meetings were useful to confirm the data in some ways, they were not routinely recorded or transcribed and their use was mostly just to frame the analysis and clarify, as necessary.

As the case selection process in chapter 1 reveals, the reiterative design of this study was central to this project and findings from these early field visits were used to theoretically sample professionals across sites. All interviews were coded initially around thematic categories that motivated the interview questions across three levels of analysis: individual (life and career biography), interactional (socialization at school; relationships with mentors, peers, and clients), and institutional (organizational hurdles; external cultural influences). These interviews focused mainly on professionals who were in the process of mobility in their field rather than those for whom scripts about these firms were more set (e.g., named partners in law firms and more famous professionals who were profiled often in the news). This reluctance to include more set and public actors was rooted in a range of reasons: for one, I was interested in mobility and process; and because of the popularity of more established professionals, their narratives about their careers were likely to be more fixed, and therefore include less revealing data. Further, because their biographies were more known, it would have been hard to anonymize them within the "studying-up" setup[1] of an already small and high-status population. At the same time, although they were not the focus of these data, these ideas and narratives that were publicly available (e.g., content analysis of their news articles and public appearances and interviews both before, during, and after these data were collected) were key informant nodes that shaped the main ways in which I analyzed these findings.

The emergent data were further analyzed for similarities and differences that were interpreted based on existing research on institutional theory, organizational innovation, global mobility, and workplace gender dynamics. This led to a more focused coding around themes at different levels of analysis that afforded these similarities (e.g., mobility into an elite professional class, dependency on domestic help) and variations (e.g., learned behaviors at school, organizational culture, reception by clients). While underlying mechanisms emerging from these themes are interrelated, I relied on different variations for unpacking mechanisms at different levels of analysis. For example, in chapter 3, which deals with organizational variations, I relied mostly on the differences in organizational structures and influences across cases to high-light variations in the ways in which firms created and received their individ-ual cultural narratives. These variations were a subtheme that emerged from the more focused coding of the data on "organizational history" and "external cultural influences." Similarly, in chapter 4, which deals with client-prompted rewards to specific kinds of essentialism, I relied primarily on the differences in client and peer experiences across cases to highlight variations in gendered assumptions around work, a sub theme that emerged from the more focused coding of the data on "reception by clients."

As other critical scholars have noted (e.g., Gustafson's *Critical Methodol-ogy* 2011:189), all of these interactions and capacity for access were symboli-cally influenced by my own identity and engagement. I present as female, and am an Indian-born, dual-trained lawyer with experience in international transactional law; and these interviews were conducted when I was affiliated with prestigious Western schools in different capacities as scholar, fellow, and graduate student. These titles were important because, although many of my respondents thought this was a project for school, others knew me by profes-sional association. These networks were crucial in granting me access to these busy professionals, yet it is possible that their representations to me were in response to my then-current professional and academic affiliations. Despite the interpretive implications and limitations of these subjectivities, I hope this research also offers perspective on how presentation of self is moderated when respondents engaged with external expectations and standards.

Simultaneously, although the source of data is purely at the individual level, the analysis and the impact of their theorizing necessarily implicate the organizations and professional fields they inhabit. The rich theorization of glo-balization offers important perspectives about the ways in which institutions transfer and port across geographic boundaries. Yet, much of the evidence for this line of research comes from macro-level data. Focusing on profession-als gives us one way of perceiving how individuals and their actions scale up to organizational outcomes (Thornton 1999). Particularly, in paying atten-tion to the ways in which professionals working in these firms understood and experienced their surroundings, my research offers some purchase on how organizational actors read and respond to cues in their naturally occur-ring contexts (Weick 1985). This research cannot—and does not claim to—give comprehensive detail about all the mechanisms at play in (to the extent such disparate dichotomous categories exist) global or local organizations. It certainly cannot relay entire narratives about professional fields, or even the specific organizations it studies. It simply was not designed to make those claims and it is the central reason why I do not describe or offer extensions at the organizational level in this book. While I hope it has some extensions for thinking about reframing organizations, the choice to keep the specific organ-izations in the study ambiguous is—contrary to the running theme in this book—very intentional. *This is not about how firm X or organization Y can or has created a certain kind of organization.* It is much more about how subjective experiences of individual actors can afford us windows into meaning-making processes for organizations more generally. It is the hope that these rich subjective details may offer meanings of organizational processes that its actors hold and the rational extensions this has for the environments in which they find themselves (Morrill and Fine 1997). And that, in turn, it will allow for emergence and progress narratives that can be adapted by organizations beyond the ones actually in question in this book.

Despite (and perhaps because of) a reiterative design that was constantly conscious of its field assumptions and positionality, this project and the analyses of these data went through several theoretical reframings, especially over the course of writing this book. This modification of theoretical assumptions when encountering field patterns is not uncommon, particularly for long-term projects, but I highlight the particular processes that came up for my consideration in the event it might be useful to other scholars seeking to study similar (*newly global* or *global newly*) sites with similar (interdisciplinary) lenses. Three main themes were relevant to the framing and reframing of the kinds of analyses that produced this project—*design determinations, disciplinary agoraphobia,* and the *temporal advantages of different kinds of distance.* I highlight these interrelated themes below to help frame their import.

Design. As a study that was first designed in graduate school, the initial considerations that determined this project were straightforward—it had to be a project identifiable within the discipline for which I was completing my PhD, and it needed to be feasible (practically, within the time period and with the amount of research money I could allot for it). Yet, a decade ago, global and transnational sociology would not yet be a prominent subfield within the ASA, and those who were working on projects that could serve as research frameworks were mostly looking at emerging economies and markets in India from an emancipatory or development perspective. Perhaps also significant was the fact that I was not in a department that socialized me directly into thinking about international sociology outside the political economy framework. Rather, the kind of work that inspired me in my immediate surroundings was work on organizational emergence and inclusive inequality that my advisers and mentors were doing in other sites at the time. I highlight these socializing factors because they were central to modeling my design determinations. Perhaps if I was at a different school, with a different cohort, at a different time (e.g. if the school had a global law and society program or scholars that were more organically aligned to working on critical global sites), my project would have been differently structured. For example, instead of being motivated by the research on studying elites more generally (Hertz and Imber 1995), I might have determined or framed this project to respond to existing priors within the study of women in developing markets in a certain sense. Instead, studying these women in these specific kinds of sites as beyond exceptions to the theory priors of women and work in the emerging context, offered a new approach to thinking about these actors and the import of their narratives. More generally, beyond the immediate case of gender and professional firms, it forced me to interrogate the ways in which method and theory intersected, to consider possibilities that would allow for movement past exceptionalism. Because I was not trained in the lenses that traditionally were employed to dissect these sites, I was forced to ask how we could use other methods and grounded theories to move past existing frameworks of reference that theorized these global sites. I am not suggesting that graduate students necessarily go in search of departments that do not lend themselves organically to their research questions. I am only highlighting the ways in which my research was strengthened by years of having to pitch it to an audience that did not automatically find synergies with it. I offer, instead, that in retrospect, this accident of falling outside frameworks has invigorated a larger hope that we can move beyond scholarship and method while also speaking to them. In that sense, these seemingly blasé ideological priors have been crucial to the structuring and questions that produced this book, and they have added poetic resonance to its theme.

Discipline. Accompanying these design determinations is what I call the *disciplinary agoraphobia* that accompanied this project at different stages. As I note above, being socialized in a specific kind of department, at a specific moment in time, was central to the research design. But at different stages, exposure to new kinds of thinking and framing offered a way to return to the work and its implications differently. New kinds of audience perception and reception also introduced new kinds of struggle. As an interdisciplinary scholar trying to speak across theories and research, I found myself constantly trying to engage, usually from a liminal position, the shape-shifting nature of my audience. Thinking through this kind of struggle with audience is perhaps essential for method in global studies more generally (Darian-Smith and McCarty 2017), but I highlight them here because I think agoraphobia can be a compelling method as one retreats and revises a project's contribution. Over the past decade that I have been involved with some version of this project, I have had to defend it and make it attractive and compelling to differently placed scholars and policy makers that I have wanted to be in conversation with. My training in—and constant community within—legal scholarship carved out its primacy as a central audience. But having borrowed so much from theories in organizational sociology, gender, and globalization studies across disciplines, I was equally interested in how these findings implicated (and complicated) larger debates in work and diversity, studies in identity and social movements, and scholarship on global transformation.

Still, alongside this excitement to engage, I worried about usefulness and relevance of this research. Specifically, at the core, I questioned what it meant to be a global south scholar writing about "one's own" (Shami 1988) and who it would serve. Over the course of becoming the scholar that could produce this work, I have had to contend with the difficult and frustrating contradictions of relevance dictated by this positionality. I have had to accept that being visible to a global audience and being able to make interventions in global scholarly debates and questions necessarily makes a contribution less useful for those it is written on the backs of. Of course, this case about researcher positionality and ethics of usefulness has been made across sites, but it felt especially peculiar to make it on behalf of the elite professionals who I felt I was studying "up." These complicated relationships about method, usefulness, and service are not much different from the frustrations that I highlight for other processes in the preface to this book, but the fear of it producing a "bleached out" academic (Wilkins 1998) in me remains real and recurring. These various influences might have also made the project elliptical at different points, perhaps even audience-pleasing and distracted. I imagine that the unease of these liminal spaces might be shared by other scholars who are (or identify as) third culture or positioned between spaces that they are trying to work between. To graduate students or early career scholars who might be reading this, I emphasize the potential that frustration, *feeling*, anxiety, and exit can offer ethnographic methods. My notes about affect and emotion during different parts of this fieldwork were important parts of my praxis and have been central to noting what resonated and why at different stages of this research. My states of anxiety about both the conversations I wanted to be part of and the ones that I knew I could not fully respond to were both very real, but they were important tools in demarcating what and who I consistently wanted to engage with. And the exits from known narratives that framed this project, while frustrating, were precisely what shaped it ultimately to stand on its own.

Distance. Finally, and alongside this urging to embrace these praxis of alterity, I also offer some hope—*discursive distance* and the gains of temporality. One's relationship to a project alters and shape-shifts not just in response to audience, but also in response to one's self, over the course of writing it. I am not the graduate student who started working on this project, my uneasiness with the kinds of naming and claiming that I outline at the start of this book are now mediated by many new and different considerations. Still, because I have presented and revised and reshaped this work for a considerable period, my associations with these initially destabilizing and disorienting pulls to my research have shifted. In response to these intersecting conversations across these different fora, I have had the chance to see what remains, what still holds true. As a result, the more I have sat with the process, the more convinced I am that this feeling of not saying enough about all the things you find interesting is a useful way to let emerge the intersecting themes that do consistently come up in the research. *Agoraphobia, then, even when exhausting, can be an effective method over time.* And timing itself can change the design of the project. In addition to disciplinary pulls, this project has also lived in (and been shaped by) a range of other projects and institutional environments and these new places and interactions have offered their own kinds of opportunities for reframing. While my inspirations in graduate school were subject-forward, my associations with professional networks (most centrally, the Law and Society Association) and my time in Abu Dhabi changed the ways in which I thought about the place and contribution of a study like this, offering it yet another layer of discursive method—distance. The more time one spends away from data collection, the more layers the findings can offer, allowing insight to the sometimes *speculative* (more poetic resonance!) fervor of the initial design that the ultimate framing of research is trained to hide. Yet, those kinds of tensions—of all (and none of) the synergies one's work has with other work—are central to any project.

So, the last note on method is a call to be kind to one's journey with temporality in the research process. Past selves and framings, even when they fall away, perform important roles in allowing data to emerge and diverge over time, and this capacity for alterity and ability to parse meaningful difference could be central to analytical (re)framings. Similarly, just as reframing has followed initial understandings of a project, future selves might complicate whatever we take for granted at a given point (as this book goes to press, COVID-19 is changing relationships to work that might make the theoretical core here newly and differently irrelevant). Perhaps what this ultimately calls for is a new kind of relationship to sites, data, and method, with more patience for distance that can offer meaningful exits from expected conclusions, with more space for being unsure, with more acceptance for the limits of what our theories can do and who they can reach. Of course, many of our disciplinary ideologies and professional timelines do not make room for this kind of productive anxiety that can serve as method, which is even more reason to stress the gift of temporal exchange and interactional buffer at various stages that were at the invisible core of this project's methodological toolkit.

"Pāri! Pāri!" the bards chant,
feting him as the One
who protects the world;
but Pāri is not alone—
there is also Rain.

*—Puranāṇūṟu 107**

* The *Puṟanāṇūṟu* ("Four hundred poems") is a body of classic Tamizh poetry from the Sangam period (first–second century CE to third–fifth century CE), composed by 157 poets, at least ten of whom were women (14 were anonymous, and possibly also women). As one of the earliest surviving works in the language, it offers impressive accounts of war, politics, and public life during these times, usually in the form of short vignettes and conversation. Modern publications of these works from palm leaf to paper started with Swaminatha Iyer's first resurrection of text along with notes in 1894. Since then numerous translations have followed, including three that have influenced my own engagement over the years: Hart and Heifetz's *Four Hundred Songs of War and Wisdom* (1999), Venkatachalapathy's *Love Stands Alone* (2010), and Tamil scholar Vaidehi's translations on her *Sangam Translations* blog. This translation is more literal and less eloquent than those of these illustrious scholars, but it is a product of conversation and many short exchanges, staying true to the spirit of the genesis and meter of the *Puṟanāṇūṟu*. Special thanks to Kalpana Kannabiran, Swaroop Mamidipudi, and Alex Streim for indulging in these dialogues.

ACKNOWLEDGMENTS

I'VE PUT OFF WRITING this note to the very (very!) end because when you have worked on something for this long, attributing gratitude becomes an overwhelming, paralyzing task. Still, for a book that tentatively valorizes accident, the turn to intentional appreciation offers apt closure.

The most inextinguishable debt here is to the pseudo-named respondents whose stories build the core of this book. I could never pay them for their time (literally), candor, and generosity of insight; and I hope I have done them justice in this academic representation of their lives and worlds.

The ideas, terms, and language that form this representation are mine, but only inasmuch as any writing is just one's own. For training me to use people's careers as a way of thinking about global stratification, law, and policy, I thank David Wilkins, Marc Galanter, Rebecca Sandefur, Bryant Garth, and Carole Silver. Nothing in this book would have been written if David had not urged me to apply and come to Harvard Law School fifteen years ago. It was through him that I met Marc (who taught me, by example, to study what was interesting *to me* even if it was not "sexy" to anyone else), Becky (whose law and inequality research was the singular reason I applied to a Sociology PhD program at Stanford), Bryant (whose vision and career reinforced my faith in unique trajectories), and Carole (whose passion for international legal education redirected my research agenda). For someone who studies careers, the deliberate power of this form of mentorship is not lost on me: David's faith in my voice molded me to trust my instincts as a young academic, introduced me to the web of law and society humans who remain my primary intellectual community, and changed the course of my life.

If my law school mentors taught me to see legal careers as a site of critical inquiry, it was the sociologists who framed the ways in which it actually could be conducted. I first admired the power of the discipline to dissect social meanings while still an undergraduate in Kalpana Kannabiran's class in NALSAR, and it was Kalpana's voice that I relied on to guide me through the politics of the personal in these stories. In graduate school, David Grusky, Woody Powell, Tomas Jiménez, and Stephen Barley joined Becky to be the kind of interdepartmental committee that gave this project its initial structure. David's eye for big inequality questions helped me place my own reproduction of hierarchy theses in context and gave me a way to speak about this work within the stratification literature. Tomas and Stephen were key in training and reviewing my ethnographic methods, and it was really in class and conversation with Woody that I saw how my data were slowly emerging into *findings*.

[185]

Alongside this formal committee, I remain grateful for the nudges, inspiration, and advice from Cecilia Ridgeway, Shelley Correll, Michelle Jackson, and Corey Fields during my time at Stanford. Cecilia and Shelley were crucial to my theorizing around *background frameworks* (chapter 2) and it was in classes with them that I first pitched these data of an Indian exceptionalism argument. Michelle's and Corey's comments in workshops to lean more into the repercussions of client expectations and the value of comparisons were central to the essentialism framing in what is now chapter 4. At various stages, conversations with Brooke Bass, Binyamin Blum, Lorena Castro, Koji Chavez, Marrion Coddou, Adam Horowitz, Karina Kloos, Priya Fielding-Singh, Devon Magliozzi, Karen Porowznik, and Bobbi Thomason helped guide the project's design and core. Alongside these disciplinary leanings, conversations during this period with Ting Chen, KJ Cerankowski, Agnes Chong, Sacha Feinman, Vinita Jacob, Amita Katragadda, Sandile Hlatshwayo, and Sharika Thiranagama put in motion other kinds of lives my data could have in the world. These people trained me to reach ambitiously while staying grounded with the motivating questions, a balance that was especially hard when I was in graduate school and unable to see the life of this beyond a dissertation. In the years since, their sage advice and commentary have lent important direction as I've returned to this work with different kinds of perspectives.

David Grusky's parting gift was to push me to apply for a postdoctoral fellowship at NYU Abu Dhabi. It felt crazy at the time, but in retrospect, it was the soundest pathway to transform myself from a student to a scholar. I remain grateful for David's vision and to Hannah Brückner and Hervé Crès, who made the decision to bet on me as they did. My time at NYUAD was when I truly started making sense of my data, and it was where I unpacked the intersectional positionality that would eventually weave together its implications. If I had not spent those three years of solitude in the desert, I don't know if *this* is the book I would have written. My gratitude for the very specific ways in which colleagues and conversations at NYUAD influenced my thinking is rife in the references and notes within this book. But it would be remiss to not mention explicitly how much the intellectual community there shaped my writing. Large parts of this manuscript were written and rewritten in the Gender, SRPP, and Social Science workshops where comments from Eman Abdelhadi, May Aldabbagh, Elisabeth Anderson, Rachel Brule, Linsey Bostwick, Saba Brelvi, Andrew Bush, Kanchan Chandra, David Cook Martin, George Jose, Daniel Karell, Saba Karim Khan, Raya Lakova, Marc Michael, Henriette Mueller, Jaime Napier, John O'Brien, Zeynep Ozgen, Laila Prager, Surabhi Sharma, Peter Stamatov, Lexi Suppes, Rana Tomaira, and Deepak Unnikrishnan were crucial to clarifying my writing and argument. Similarly, Mark Swislocki's Global Asia program at NYUAD introduced me to interdisciplinary scholars who worked on other meta-Asian contexts, and conversations with Nora Barakat, Fiona Kidd, and Mark shaped broader possibilities for positioning this work as a glocal study beyond India. Parts of the book also had the absolute boon of being read and commented on by Paula England, Peter Goodrich, and Alejandro Portes, who were each visiting NYUAD during my time there. Their macro-field perspectives allowed me to see the analytical work that different parts of the book could do within distinct disciplines. Finally, conversations with other visitors (especially Arjun Appadurai, Uma Chakravarti, Gayatri Gopinath, Nighat Said Khan, Sana Odeh, Arvind Rajagopal) complicated critical categories like the global south that were at the core of this book. Together, these alliances produced both the *agoraphobia* I mention in the research appendix, and with it the soul of this book.

My time in NYUAD was also buoyed by the time that it allowed me to be *away* from Abu Dhabi. My visiting positions at the Clayman Institute at Stanford, the Center on the Legal Profession at Harvard, and the American Bar Foundation in Chicago allowed me to balance the perspective this time away from the United States offered with interventions that kept the project relevant to a US audience. In particular, comments, feedback, and reactions from Bernadette Atuahene, Marianne Cooper, Ronit Dinovitzer, Bryon Fong, Terence Halliday, Sida Liu, Ajay Mehrotra, Beth Mertz, Bob Nelson, Laura Beth Nielson, Jothie Raja, Chris Schmidt, Susan Shapiro, and Alison Wynn from these institutions over the years were crucial to editing several chapters in this book. Similarly, being part of the Wilkins-spearheaded Harvard GLEE project located my research centrally within the globalization and legal profession literature, and it gave me a precious chance to think through the work with old friends like Shamnad Basheer, Jonathan Gingerich, Vik Khanna, Jay Krishnan, Pavan Mamidi, and Nick Robinson.

Beyond formal institutional affiliations, over the years, several conferences and research communities have elevated the potential of this project. Scott Cummings, Bruce Green, Russ Pearce, and Deborah Rhode were part of a central group of legal ethics scholars whose work and friendship trained me to speak to legal questions with my empirical work. The Harvard IGLP workshops have been a source of great instruction about writing from the margins, and colleagues from these meetings have stayed interlocutors over the years. Particularly, for reading drafts and pushing back on ideas at different stages, I'm grateful to Alejandra Azuero Quijano, Cyra Choudhury, Ratna Kapur, Maryam Khan, and Genevieve Painter. I was a late ASA adoptee, but I have since come to appreciate its resonance as a venue for my scholarship thanks to exchanges with Rina Agarwala, Grazi Dias da Silva, Cynthia Epstein, Fiona Kay, Ann Morning, Carroll Seron, and Leslie Salzinger. Similarly, several smaller conferences have offered me new communities for dialogue and discussion. Of these, invitations to Grietje Baar's Critical Corporations talk at City University London (2015), Usha Natarajan's Law Workshop Series at the American Univeristy in Cairo (2016), Jules Naudet's Elites conference in CSH Delhi (2016), Esra Burak Ho's Protecting the Weak conference at the Lingnan University Hong Kong (2017), and Peter Stamatov's and Sebastián Rojas Cabal's Comparative Sociology Speaker Series at Carlos III de Madrid (2018) were most central to this book.

My LSA community is too large to name, and it has many overlaps with my other intellectual homes, but I'm particularly grateful for the chance it has given me to build two research networks that spilled over to this project: the legal education CRN (19) shaped my understandings of comparative legal education and its built-up inequalities, and the IRC on Invisible Institutionalisms that allowed me to build, along with Sara Dezalay, a ground-up project on globalization and law with scholars who would engage in framing questions across disciplinary difference. These scholars, who form the core of my book with Sara (2021), were key in teaching me how projects never have fixed boundaries. This might be a book about professionals in India, but it is only as much about that as it is also about the many other projects I was working on simultaneously over the years. In particular, my work on the *Lawyers in 21st Century Societies* chapter (edited by Rick Abel, Ole Hammerslev, Hilary Sommerlad, and Ulrike Schultz), the Intentional Invisibility project (with Priya Fielding-Singh and Devon Magliozzi), the chapter on India's women legal academics (with Rupali Samuel), the book on gender and privacy jurisprudence (with Kalpana Kannabiran), research on transnational migration (with Hannah Brueckner), and the ongoing research with Carole Silver on legal education all offer(ed) different refractive slants to help write this book. The significance of these collaborations is seeped into its architecture.

Although the idea of *Accidental Feminism* was theorized afresh in this book, the manuscript works from the foundations set in earlier journal articles. The argument in chapter 2 about preentry socialization was first developed for the *Canadian Review of Sociology* (2018), the argument in chapter 3 about speculative isomorphism first appeared in the *Law and Society Review* (2019), and chapter 4's theorizing about the new returns to essentialism was the core of an article that appeared in the *Journal of Professions and Organization* (2017). I am indebted to these journals for giving these thoughts their first home and to the many anonymous peer reviewers who were in conversation with this work well before it was *work*.

These publications also reinforced my resolve to keep writing from these data. This research is beholden to the committed institutional funding that supported it for many years (chiefly through the Juan Celaya research grant, the National Science Foundation dissertation improvement grant, fellowships from the Vice Provost for Graduate Education, Diversifying Academia by Recruiting Excellence, and the Center for South Asia at Stanford, and grants from the Globalization, Lawyers, and Emerging Economies and the Institute for Global Law and Policy projects at Harvard). But it was in the reception by these journals, first by the editors and anonymous peer reviewers (many thanks to Sida Liu, Tracey Adams, Susan Sterett, David Brock, and Mike Saks respectively for soliciting these reviews and for their own comments) and then by the micro-communities that valorized this work (the JPO article won the best article award in 2018, the CRS piece won the best article award in 2019, the LSR article won an ASA best article honorable mention in 2020) that I started to trust that there was enough *there* here for a book project.

Of course, the steps that would build this book would well precede my own comfort about its value. It was Woody Powell who first pushed me to get my proposal before presses, and along with Lynn Mather and Deborah Rhode, gave me invaluable advice about the process before I knew what I wanted from it. I also learned much from pitching this project to various editors, and the reviews I got from Eric Schwartz and his team at CUP in particular were extremely helpful as I started writing this manuscript. Still, I think this book only really started to become a book when I sat huddled with Meagan Levinson, my editor from Princeton University Press, in a secluded corner of an ASA meeting venue in Toronto and saw her eyes become large with understanding as she *saw* what it could be. Meagan has since breathed life into this project when it has most needed it for almost three years. Her ability to get to the core of my dithering, to calm me with her surety about its purpose, and to read keenly, are just some of the reasons I'm so grateful she's who I get to bring this book into the world with. Her all-star team at PUP kept the project on track at different stages and made a range of hurdles feel manageable. Jackie Delaney, Kate Hensley, Dorothy Hoffman, Erin Suydam, and Debbie Tegarden were crucial to providing the structure and support that coordinated the many moving pieces of production from draft to public launch, Karl Spurzem *got* and transformed my vision for the book's cover, and Karen Verde's sharp eye and diligent focus during copyedits helped turn this from manuscript to book. For allowing me to use the most perfect visual allegory to (literally) hold this work, I am indebted to the estate of the late Zarina Hashmi, the Luhring Augustine Gallery in New York, and to Meghaa Ballakrishnen, my soundest Teacher, who introduced me first to Zarina's life, spirit, and work. I am still not sure what I did to deserve the privilege of these overlapping conditions, but it feels aligned with the governing logic of this research, and I'm so very grateful.

At UCI Law, where much of this project has coalesced to become the book in your hands, many people have been crucial to its production. UCI is special for many reasons, but a key one is that it gave me the chance, after years of friendship, to teach with Bryant Garth before he retired. BG might be the only person in the world to have read and workshopped everything I have ever written at least once, and his invisible hand is all over this book. The Center for Empirical Research on the Legal Profession that I now co-run with Bryant and Ann Southworth, and the first year Legal Profession class that I teach with Ann and Sameer Ashar continues to make central my initial call to use the legal profession as a site for thinking about processual and reinforcing inequ(al)ities. Similarly, other classes I've taught at UCI on gender (GUILT, as I explain in the preface), and in NYUAD (Accidental Equality) have been important spaces to work through concepts with students. Treating the classroom as a recursive learning space has been a deep resource to this project, and I am grateful to the many students over the years whose reception of these ideas have helped me calibrate their weight.

Conversations with several colleagues have enriched this book's substance, especially as it applied to a legal audience. Special thanks to Alex Camacho, Eve Darian Smith, Vic Fleischer, Michele Goodwin, Kaaryn Gustafson, Dalié Jiménez, David Kaye, Stephen Lee, Ji Li, Philip McCarty, Omri Marian, Sasha Natapoff, Song Richardson, Trilby Robinson-Dorn, Greg Shaffer, Catherine Sameh, Jane Stoever, Shauhin Talesh, and Emily Taylor Poppe for conversations and notes on the article that became the base for chapter 4. Many thanks to Tendayi Achiume, Asli Bâli, Devon Carbado, Scott Cummings, Nate Ela, Cheryl Harris, Sung Hui Kim, Rachel Moran, Meghan Morris, John O'Hare, Jeffrey Omari, Asad Rahim, Joanna Schwartz, and Jonathan Zasloff for comments on a draft that ultimately shaped chapter 5.

At several stages, I've relied on friends and colleagues to tighten the manuscript, make it more legible, and catch glaring errors. The alchemy between the administrators (especially Laura Castillo, Saru Gameel, Angie Middleton, and Diana Pangan) and librarians (especially Jeff Latta, Jessica Pierucci, Dianna Sahhar, Christina Tsou, and Jessica Whytock) across institutions has been essential to keep up with the research queries and trails that have accompanied this writing, and Deborah Lewites's transcriptions and notes helped me mine the data for more each time I was stuck on an issue.

In India, I owe a special debt to the resourcefulness, verve, and kindness of Shankar Athimber, Sai Bharathan, Mohsin Bhatt, Nikhil Chandra, Veena Ganesh, Vivek Holla, Shekhar Iyer, Rohan Kaul, Rahela Khorakiwala, Deepa Vaidyanathan, Anusha Venkatraman, and Akshay Venkatachalam who at different stages (and ways) made the field accessible to me. In California, Dubai, and New York (both during fieldwork and for the years after when I was writing up these data), I am grateful for the homes, meals, (hairdryer-ed) beds, families, and generosities of the Dearmas-Jacobs, Gohil-Ashars, Hlatshwayo-Andersons, Korula-Sethis, Krishnamurthy-DiBellos, Pearces, Pal-Mathurs, Sudeep Srivastava, and the Zahines. Many friends offered necessary reminders over the years that sociology is often just empirically vetted common sense. For this particular strain of their expansive friendships, I thank Amar, Cherry, Divya, Koshy, Feefs, Kavi, Minnah, Raghav, Ranji, Sanky, Samru, Skoo, and Sumi. Still, for reminding me, when I needed it the most, that a good pitch *was* Peggy's life, Suryapratim Roy will always have my unwavering respect.

Countless times over the last few years, Bella Furth and Raya Lakova have read the manuscript with the kind of keen eye I just do not possess and pushed me to be clearer about my positions. For this trusting space they offered, and for their engagement without judgment on many of my *meh* drafts, my gratitude knows no bounds. In these last stages of writing, the thoughtful discernment that Rina Agarwala, Mehrsa Baradaran, Carrie Menkel-Meadow, Carole Silver, Ann Southworth, and Susan Sturm brought to their reviews made me refine many key concepts that I had taken for granted. These kinds of deep reads take time, and the book is deeply enriched by their interventions. Similarly, the generosity of sight with which Maya Alison and Shruti Gohil engaged with the book helped me think of its possible life outside the disciplines it tries (and is tired) to live within. Still, as my nervousness about this book's release rose (I remain terrified about letting this text go), I burdened friends to read for its authenticity in relaying *my* affect and tone. While I owe May, Sameer, Peter, and Rabie for the time and energy they spent on this, the real solid due to them is for knowing me as they have to *know* this was the book I'd be OK letting out into the world. Needless to say, perhaps: despite the riches of these exchanges and influences that this book greatly benefits from, any and all slips and errors remain, assuredly, mine alone.

Book writing is solitary, but real and nourishing solitude is contingent on the knowledge of community. These pages make the last decade seem devoid of any conversations that did not involve kernels of what would eventually become this book. While some version of this is true, it is also as true that I have only had the luxury of this mind space because my daily life has been buttressed with expansive soul and life connections. I'm lucky to navigate this world with humans who drink (single-origin cortados, spiked kombuchas, craft cocktails, all forms of bubbles), eat (parupu sadam, tacos, a certain pasta, fried potatoes, sichuan spice), and share (orchids, homes, secrets, beach sunsets, meaning-making, tiny humans) with me in ways that make me feel *seen*. They don't always overlap and they are mostly not visible, but it is in the depth of our relational crevices that my ability to burrow deep draws its core strength.

Speaking of *visible* strength, I end this book with the same people I started it with. David Wilkins once told me that the farther I am from my family, the closer I could be to the dreams they have for me. It has never felt truer than it does now as I send this book to press in the middle of a global pandemic. But it is also true that near and far are muddled categories. I have not lived *at home* in more than two decades, but my family remains the grounding orientation to my days and lives. Choochoo, Thatha, and Thathi have passed, in a sense, but I never feel far from their loving energy. Ram (the uncle my grandmother was carrying in the opening image), Sudarsan, and our #2 dining table with Shiva, Fudge, and Uglee together under it still form my most calming recalls of Madras. That Alex, Agni, Mani, and Baali will join in memory making when the world returns to some sort of normal, is already cause for celebration. Distance cannot diminish these potent virtual intimacies that have comforted me through this writing process and, as a constant *pravasi*, my life.

Amma, Appa, Magi—this is where this book ends for a reason. If this were about thanking you, I'd both struggle to start and be incapable of knowing when / how to end. Instead, I'll just quote, from that tiny frame that hoverd over our heads in *Sudarsan*, paraphrasing poorly from *The Gita*: you are never lost to me and, therefore, never I to you. None of this means anything if it can't be shared with you. I love you and I am so proud to be yours.

Preface. Can Feminism Be Accidental?

1. In her book, *Third World Women and the Politics of Feminism*, Chandra Mohanty clarifies that the use of the term "third world" here is cognizant of the kinds of implicit problematic categorization it embeds. Mohanty et al. argue categorically (1991:74–75, n.1) that "terms such as *third* and *first world* are very problematic both in terms of suggesting oversimplified similarities between countries labeled thus, and in implicitly reinforcing existing economic, cultural, and ideological hierarchies which are conjured up using such terminology. I use the term 'third world' with full awareness of its problems, only because this is the terminology available to us at the moment. The use of quotation marks is meant to suggest a continuous questioning of the designation. Even when I do not use quotation marks, I mean to use the term critically." My use of the term feminist and feminism here, as I hope to convey through this note, follows in that wake, with trepidation, with central acknowledgment of its limitations, but nonetheless critically, even when not used within quotation marks.

2. If anything, Ahmed's *On Being Included* (2012) lays out clearly how she is *not* thinking of diversity in organizations and its connection to intention as the same kind of "turn to the difficult" as I use here. Chapter 6 makes this connection between accidental and intentional more deliberate.

3. I'm indebted to the many feminist and queer intellectual communities with whom I've had the pleasure to think through ideas over the years, as well as to the collaborators from other projects whose conversations have helped shape this meaning-making. Early in this project's inception, colleagues at the Harvard Institute for Global Law and Policy (especially Ratna Kapur, Maryam Khan, Grietje Baars, Alejandra Azuero Quinjano, Usha Natarajan, Genevieve Painter, Cyra Choudhary) read and debated with me about many of these ideas and raged together about the limits of neoliberal constructions of these identities. Invitations from them for further exchange through talks (Baars to the Critical Corporations lecture series at City University London in 2015, Natarajan to the American University in Cairo in 2016) and round tables (Baars, Choudhury, and I have since continued some of these conversations in critical queer round tables at the *Law and Society Association Meetings*) cemented many of these ideas. During the writing of much of this book, New York University Abu Dhabi offered community in allowing me to create a critical gender workshop that I hosted over three years (2015–2018). Conversations in those meetings (especially with May Al Dabbagh, Eman Abdelhadi, Maya Allison, Fawzia Afzal Khan, Marzia Balzani, Nora Barakat, Hannah Brueckner, Saba Brelvi, Linsey Bostwick, Gayatri Gopinath, Raya Lakova, Laila Prager, Jamie Napier, Sana Odeh, Lexi Suppes, and Rana Tomaira) and in allied events that were with members from it (e.g., the Making Space workshop that May Al Dabbagh curated with colleagues at the NYU Tisch School of the Arts and the Transnational Feminisms "long table" that Fawzia Afzal Khan and I co-hosted in conversation with scholars like Uma Chakravarti, Nighat Said Khan, Bishnupriya Dutt, Omnia Amin, and Tina Rosenberg) similarly were crucial to giving these categories their required global and local south extensions. Critical collaborations within law school networks and communities now at UCI School of Law, the American Bar Foundation, E-CRT, and Yale Law and Political Economy colleagues have helped me to think about extensions to these lines of thinking in other contexts, including other kinds of identity categories that

mark experiences of peripheral actors (e.g., asexual inclusion in queer normativities, Muslim identity as the new legitimized racism, etc.). See the appendix on research methodology for the ways in which this meaning-making followed differently aligned trajectories and my own complications with theory-building.

4. Critical feminists have long contested the limits of feminist displays by hegemonic actors at different levels of analysis and inquiry. At the institutional level, the liberal hegemony of feminists from the global north, especially toward local actors and their movements and assumed exits and emancipation, has been a ground of important critique. Mohanty, for example, in her book with Russo and Torres (1991) on *Third World Women and the Politics of Feminism*, calls attention to the persistence of the "western eyes" that control narratives of women by wielding power over both the regions studied as well as the women who are seen as "universal dependents" within them (58–60). They argue that this is centrally problematic because it does not allow women to "theorize and engage with the feminist politics of the third world women" on their own grounds, an understanding that calls for us all to "respond rigorously to the challenge of our postcolonial condition) (39–40). Note that several scholars have intrinsically answered this call for a more critical interrogation of these conditions on their own terms in the Indian context, e.g., Geetha (2006, 2007); Chakravarti (2003); Menon (2004, 2012); Ray (2000b) and several others have built scholarly communities that have further cemented the criticality of these interrelated connections, e.g., Loomba and Lukose (2012); Arondekar and Patel (2016); Kannabiran and Swaminathan (2017); Kathuria and Bhaiya (2018); and Nagar's (2019) multi-method and cross-disciplinary *Hungry Translations*. Similarly, critical scholars have pushed back against the use of feminism as a placeholder for state intervention and justification on the grounds of "governance feminism" (Halley et al. 2018) or state-sanctioned gender progress (e.g., Al Dabbagh and Gargani 2011; Carvalho Pinto 2012; Le Renard 2014; Al Dabbagh 2015; Prager 2018) as a model of feminism that offers a "liberal rights regime" that remains incapable of offering "true freedom" for its purported subjects while simultaneously reaping the benefits of such posturing. (See Kapur 2018 more generally about the imaginary possibilities of freedom's alterity in this critique of state-sponsored human rights and its resultant regimes.) Scholars have also demarcated logics of inclusion based on ideological views seen as "progressive" by hegemonic liberal actors, especially against what are seen as "traditional" practices that stand in the way of gendered empowerment and emancipation. Examples of these are rife, especially in portrayals of religious women, particularly from "gender-unfriendly" parts of the world (at least from the lens of "advanced" nations). See, for example, Abu- Lughod (1998, 2013); Suad Joseph (1999); and Mahmood (2011). This puts scholars who want to push back against these singular narratives in a complicated position because it might simultaneously call upon them to be apologists in ways they do not mean to be. For the complications that this brings up in the field and in research more generally, see Altorki and El Solh (1988); Visweswaran (1997); and Abu-Lughod (1991). The appendix to this text offers insights into variations of the internal struggles these complications extended to this research more specifically.

5. Sameer Ashar recently reminded me that even using this term without explanation of what it is meant to mean could be a kind of postured privilege. As always, I'm grateful for his kind candor and for this type of intellectual nudging that demands re-markation of subsumed interactional hierarchies that can otherwise get brushed under the proverbial rug of subjective shape-shifting category ambiguity. So, to clarify, I use the term "queer" here to suggest its emphasis on the praxis of alterity, marginality, nonconformity, and deviance beyond rigid categories of sexuality. Queer theorists in the humanities have long used deviance (including of method and archive) as part of their subversive inroad into theory-building (e.g., Rubin 2011), but I am inspired especially by Heather Love's call for thinking through the analytical possibilities this affords social scientists, especially in their

inquiry in the fields of gender and sexuality studies. As Love would offer, I identify—and
see my academic lenses broadly as a product of—this "queer ordinary" category "beyond
traditional fixed categories of gay, lesbian, and bisexual in favor of a more general category
of social marginality" (Love 2015). I feel most solidarity and resonance with Preciado's
post-dream articulation of the trans condition in his book *An Apartment on Uranus* (2019:
29). I empathize (from my own varied trans position) most dearly with his articulation on
what it means to be "Uranian": "I am not man and I am not a woman and I am not het-
erosexual I am not homosexual and I am not bisexual. I am a dissident of the sex-gender
system. I am the multitude of the cosmos trapped in a binary political and epistemological
system . . . I am a Uranian confined inside the limits of techo-scientific capitalism." On
deviance and sexuality more generally, especially as a product of method, in the Indian
context of gendered personhood, see Mitra (2020) on the theorization of the working pros-
titute as deviant only as a product of social scientific delineation of the time (6); Gopinath
(2018) on queer aesthetics as a new method to interrogate new kinds of temporal, space,
and relational queer praxis; and Arondekar (2009) on the presumption of deviance in the
queer feminist archive.

6. Despite any personal narrative and identifications I might claim from deviance both
locally and globally as a person of color who has led a life (in)consistently—as queerness
demands—in equal parts choice and chance affording successful "queer failure" (Halberstam and Halberstam 2011), I use this term "local north" to make central the many advantages and "successes" both ascribed and achieved that have been offered to me. The bane
of my myriad secular *Savarna* privileges that culturally and socially shape and lubricate
my experiences in the world, even when removed from India. Crucially, of among other
possible perceived categories, the privileges of caste and class that I enjoy as a cisgendered
presenting (still gender-queer identified) Brahmin from an urban Indian city, who was
raised by multiple college-educated adults, all of whom communicated in English to them,
was central not only to my local socialization and success within private and public educational opportunity, but also to my relatively seamless socialization into American urbanity
and academy. To give this term theoretical significance and weight, I borrow from scholars of globalization that push against the logics of a linear or even a clearly demarcated
global "north" and "south" to understand power, culture, and praxis in the increasingly fluid
world we inhabit. Ong and Collier (2005), for example, remind us that capital, markets,
and geopolitics of culture frame local and global stratification in unprecedented ways that
easily allow for "global assemblages" of domination at different levels that bleed into each
other. Appadurai (1996) would credit these dynamic global cultural flows as central to the
production of local meanings, images, and representations that produce a sort of post-
territorial modernity. Scholars of legal globalization have taken these to be much more
specific to the condition of law's work and the positionality of legal actors to inhabit positions of eliteness locally even as they claim accommodation for their relative peripheral positions in more relative and relational global contexts. For the theoretical underpinnings of this
approach, see, e.g., Silbey 1997; Santos and Rodriquez-Garavito 2005; Darian-Smith 2013;
Halliday and Shaffer 2015; Santos 2016; Darian-Smith and McCarty 2017. For empirical
illustrations, see, e.g., Dezalay and Garth 1996, 2002, 2010; Klug 2000; Merry 2009, 2011;
Wilkins, Khanna and Trubek 2017. Over the last few years, I have been working with Sara
Dezalay to bring together more contemporary interpretations of this approach and its
extensions by working with scholars and practitioners across temporal and spatial norths
and souths to more critically examine their location and position and critical relationship
with the framing of their work. A book of collected and conversational reflections from this
endeavor is forthcoming (Ballakrishnen and Dezalay 2021).

7. I've been thinking about this as a kind of "Brahmin or *Savarna* fragility," to borrow
and build from DiAngelo's construction of *white fragility* (2018)—which makes speaking

on behalf of caste difficult both when it is and is not done. There is a certain inadequacy and guilt entrenched in the narrative—a summon to use privilege to call the self out on one's own positional advantage *and* a chide to be sure not to let it seep into a counternarrative that has more agency. But alongside this "resistance and culpability to check one's privilege"—thanks to Chris Williams for helping me think of this like that—is the cost of space that such pontification even takes. If *Savarna* feminists like me with an access to so much global space and network and resources don't use those spaces to talk about intra-group solidarity beyond our own, that feels like one kind of violence. And to find— using those very same privileges—spaces that will take our narratives more seriously or as more "nuanced," "accessible," or "meritorious" because of a set of cultural factors that we have inherited feels just as violent. Yet, the luxury to debate which is more violent, to ponder and agonize about which is doing more damage and for whom, and to feel entitled to an audience that will empathize or sympathize with what feels like such legitimate— if dramatic—indecision, feels most violent of all. The violence, I think, is manifested by capacity to demand sympathy for the agony that this deliberation produces, of claiming space to work through one's position and assume there'll be an audience that will witness such narcissistic intellectual self-flagellation (to the extent some things are more of these than others in academic writing, that is). It is this Brahmin fragility that I am naming, claiming, and self-shaming here. It is perhaps not unlike male writers who think they have no wins within patriarchy because they are seen as flawed when they write—and do not write—about and on behalf of women subjects. They are indeed flawed when they write about women (since they take away opportunity and voice from women writers who can speak on their behalf and do not have the same voice in publishing) and they are flawed when they do not engage with women (given how much more is written about male subjects than female, for instance), but they are most flawed when they claim sympathy within patriarchy for the impossibility of this choice. In any event, this self-hating but conscious fragility is being theorized in this tiny footnote rather than in the main text (of a perhaps peripheral part of this book) as a small measure in acknowledging the luxury of agony that shrouds the space-claiming fragility of a Brahmin academic writing in the middle of a global pandemic, safe and warm and healthy (for now) in one of the few jobs that could structurally benefit from these socially distant material conditions.

8. I am thankful for many instances where Oishik Sircar's delightful company and keen insight into the human condition have given me perspective. But this articulation of middle-aged queerness and identity while drinking hot beverages in a Swiss pub mid-conference is one that has provided so much layered use.

9. I self-identify with—and within—this queer category of citizenship with the kind of belonging that is typical of my (now) diasporic identity. But the journey to this citizenship has made me think more critically about the use and usefulness of claiming identities—and the work it can do in different contexts, and certainly for different kinds of actors. In some ways, I could argue that I was no more or less queer twenty years ago because I did not have the words for the experience, but words and meaning-making do have power. Even if I were to suggest that living what might have presented as a cis-straight-heteronormative life (or even seeking it) does not take away an individual desire for gender and other bending, it is certain that my perceived historic identity—or even the usefulness of my claiming an alternate one—felt then as a distinctly different personal or political act. Pockets of LGBT organizing certainly predated my own journey of claiming this identity, and the writings of many critical scholars who formed the movement—most notably those who set up the Alternative Law Forum in Bangalore when I was a law student at NALSAR—influenced my scholarly interests, commitment, and, later, pedagogy as a legal academic. Still, I did not always feel comfortable claiming these identities for a combination of factors—India was still very much vocally and viscerally homophobic (a regressive colonial law, Section 377,

which criminalized homosexuality in the country, would remain for well more than a decade after I left the country), even in its most "progressive" and "elite" spaces. Despite navigating what was once such academic space as a student, I received slur notes when I tried to do a project on decriminalizing homosexuality as a law student, and advice from a well-meaning (and practically progressive) mentor to be less radical in my approach to writing if I wanted to make effective change as I "swam upstream" in these currents. I did not have close queer mentors—certainly not mentors who identified vocally with queerness in ways that I have since come to embrace—and I was not systematically part of these circles of organizing that I admired from afar and learned so much from when I lived in India. But more than any of this, it was just that I did not, at the time, find the kind of "imagined community," to use Anderson's (2006) term, that would offer me useful citizenship within its boundaries until I truly embraced the communal, social, and collective "effervesance" (Durkheim 1965: 241, 247, 250, 469) that *queerness*—rather than identity based on sexual praxis and performance—could offer. In the decades since, I've come to be on more comfortable terms with this kind of "flexible citizenship," as Ong (1999) would call it, as one that is not uncommon for transnational and diasporic queers, especially from South Asia. Specifically, as Gayatri Gopinath (1996) cautions, thinking about categories as direct products of Western (or other hegemonic) movements and markers does not do justice to locating people and their praxis, and it is particularly not straightforward for South Asians. Since citizenship itself is fragile, claims to queerness have to be "constructed at the interstices of various strategic negotiations of the state regulatory practices and multiple national spaces" (121). On perceived choice making and its received visibility among community—or even interactional partners—as not always in contradiction with one's own inherent tendency toward alterity or my subsequent urgency in needing to claim it, see Nelson (2015).

10. For example, the temporal histories of queer movements in the global south, especially in non-western contexts that are not seen as "modern," offer us important insights into the ways in which we code "success" of movements and the usefulness of movement politics to emancipate the actors on whose behalf it professes to rally. In the Indian context, Dave's (2012) research on the progress and politics of the queer movement makes the argument that its success or even political identity is often inseparable from its current framing neoliberalism. Thinking of queer inequality in these contexts as both produced by colonialism (i.e., vestiges of colonial law) and subsequently dismantled on terms that are framed by neoliberal scripts is a framework that alludes to the particular violence that these "successes" could produce. Identity—when seen as a neoliberal script—may well not be what offers the "freedom" that these movements profess to encourage, and as Kapur (2018) might argue, it could reinforces yet another liberal paradigm of inaccess, especially for actors who do not seek such identity progress and whose narrative of experience is beyond the frameworks of these metrics. This view of modernity and progress as necessarily within a dichotomous logic of success and failure has been criticized as intellectually orientalist and with a view to determinately dehumanize "the other" on its own terms (Said 1978). In the context of queer movements and assumptive realities, critical scholars have questioned the usefulness of the "putative singularity of an assumed global gay subject that seems to underpin some contemporary Western LGBT activism" (Roy 2015, drawing from Mohanty 2003 on feminist movements). Massad (2007), in particular, goes beyond the complexity of this dichotomous straight/gay narrative in contexts outside the Euro-American West and demands an anti-identitarian framework that allows for non-western subjectivities (Massad 2008: 41–43). On the Indian history of these movements, especially with respect to their over- and under-application of queer umbrellas to peripheral actors who do not share the same kinds of privilege in their access (e.g., the hijra communities), see Narrain 2007, 2009; Tellis 2012; Sircar 2017; Sheikh et al. 2018; Kannabiran and Ballakrishnen 2021.

11. GUILT, an upper-level law class in its first year of teaching at the time of writing, stands for Gendered Understandings in Law and Legal Theory. In addition to prior syllabi from my years of teaching about law, society, inequality, and gender, the course draws inspiration from, among others, classes offered by Professors Dean Spade, Deborah Rhode, Kathrine Franke, Janet Halley, and Catherine McKinnon. Engagement with students in this class, especially around limits of feminism (Jamison), agoraphobia (Carson), defection (Aziz), and the possibilities of alternate feminist futures (Yasmeen, Al, Maggie, Lya) offered central reflections that bled into this book. Special shout-out to chosen kin Rabie Kadri for helping me come up with the acronym and for thought community through its process and conception.

12. In addition to Mohanty et al. 1991 and Mohanty 2003 regarding global feminisms (see note 4), see Roth 2004 on the separate fragmentation of Black, Chicana, and White Feminist movements within the US second wave of feminism; Crenshaw 1990 and Carbado et al. 2013, on the work of identity politics for women of color and their everyday violence as not embodied by larger mainstream feminist movements. For more contemporary examples of social movements that can change value and texture when perceived from the perspective of the peripherally located actors, see Spade and Willse (2015) on the impossibility of normative LGBT rights around marriage equality as not doing true justice to queer unions and patterns of commitment. See also Sameh (2019) on activism and feminist solidarity by Iranian women activists in the face of what she describes as the "process and relationality" of the decolonial, and the renewed meanings of community and progress that their own internal logics can afford them when obscured from a linear Western gaze.

13. Sociologists have theorized at length about social movements and their relationship to identity work and relationships between networks (e.g., Snow and McAdam 2000; McAdam 2003) and on the cleavages and spillovers (Meyer and Whittier 1994) in social movements more generally. Still, while identity and ideology bifurcations have been central to these cleavages, these tensions have come under particular scrutiny for the Indian feminist movement in the wake of #MeToo. Not only did it provide a new node of inquiry to gauge inter- and intra-relational understandings of the movement, it also brought into sharp focus the positional disparities between its movement actors. Feminist scholars writing about India saw this movement as crucial to revisiting the "waves" of this movement (Roy 2018), but also as an opportunity to critically examine its potential for decolonization (Lukose 2018) and reckon with the political accounting attributable to actors' silence as performance within it (Tambe 2018). For many of the movement and policy "entrepreneurs" (Earl and Schussman 2003; Anderson 2018) themselves, the moment brought out a chance to bring to focus the inherent disparities in (caste, class, voice) positionality between generations of feminists. In 2018, following Dalit activist and student Raya Sarkar's *The LoSHA List* with crowdsourced names of Indian men in the academy who were being accused as sexual predators, the note about process, the pitfalls of "fingertip activism," and movement boundary marking by one of India's prolific feminist academics, Nivedita Menon, became the site of unpacking this generational tension and the layers of the movement embedded within what was seen as a larger umbrella movement. The LoSHA (List of Sexual Harassers in Academia) was compiled in October 2017 by Sarkar and made publicly available on Facebook. Following the viral post, Menon's statement on behalf of a group of prominent Indian feminists was hosted on an activist collaborative blogspace Kafila: Menon's (2017) statement (the "Statement") started another viral set of "fingertip" conversations and debates around positionality, voice, and movement politics, especially on the grounds that the Statement was signed by mostly forward-caste liberal feminist academics who were seen as removed in experience from the movement's younger actors, who were viewed as "*Savarna* apologists." It is worth noting that in addition to personal projected identities, actors were implicated in relational paradoxes too: some of Kafila's collaborative mem-

bers have since been associated with #MeToo allegations. See the Statement at "Statement By Feminists On Facebook Campaign To 'Name And Shame,'" Kafila, October 24, 2017. A revised updated statement in Menon's personal defense—rather than as speaker of the group—followed a few days later and continued to relay the tensions between the positions among generations about the process, solidarities, and futures of the movement. See "From Feminazi to *Savarna* Rape Apologist in 24 Hours," Kafila, October 28, 2017. For responses to the Menon (2017) post, see Meghana T, "A practitioner of finger-tip activism responds to Nivedita Menon," *Feminism in India*, March 13, 2018; Rakshita Arni, "Dear Nivedita Menon, Contemporary Feminists Are More than Just 'Fingertip' Activists," *Youth Ki Awaaz* (Voice of the Youth), March 21, 2018. For a review of 2017 and its "watershed" moments for Indian feminism, see Sumati Thusoo, "From #MeToo to #HerToo: A Feminist Review of 2017," *The Wire*, January 21, 2018. For a review of the larger embedded hierarchies critically, see Geetha 2017; Kannabiran 2018; Bansode 2020; and Kannabiran and Ballakrishnen 2021. For *Savarna* politics in modern India and the paradoxes of identity marking more generally, especially in the name of modernity, by privileged academic actors, see the important work of Dalit writers and activists like Tenmozhi Soundararajan and Christina Thomas Dhanraj: see, for example, Dhanraj, "The Modern *Savarna* and the Caste Is Dead Narrative," *Feminism in India*, September 13, 2017, and "MeToo and *Savarna* Feminism: Revolutions Cannot Start with the Privileged, Feminist Futures Must Be Equal for All," *Firstpost*, November 18, 2018; Soundararajan and Varatharajah, "Caste Privilege 101: A Primer for the Privileged," *The Aerogram*, February 10, 2015. Also see Soundararajan's web-based community space that is described aptly as a "political home for South Asian progressives," https://www.equalitylabs.org/, which includes, among other things, access to resources about caste and diaspora. See https://www.equalitylabs.org/research.

14. Actors and agents across intellectual and ideological divides—even within the same larger movement—can have strategic incentives for distancing themselves from the terms of the more central or mainstream understandings of a movement. In the US feminist context, for example, conservative and radical women alike have resisted the generic feminist tag and associations with it, although for different reasons. Dr. Betsy Cairo's 2016 TED talk about being an "equalist" and leaving the term feminism because of its gender binary implications that do harm even as they sound pro-women is one such example. Similarly, Jessa Crispin's manifesto (2017) does the work of rejecting the "rebranded banality" that she argues feminism has become. Crispin's rejection of the term evolves from her view that the term has long been co-opted by centrist liberals, leaving her no power other than that of a "self-help tool." Conservative women have similarly rejected feminist markers (e.g., Margaret Thatcher's famous statement that she "owed nothing to the women's movement," even as they have done the work that might be seen as gender-progressive for their limited communities (to the extent that term is used to signal progress in lived experiences and demands of themselves and women they are advocating for). See, for example, Johnson (2019), who argues that female evangelical leaders played essential roles in the Christian world but did so without alienating / stifling men in the religion, as a strategic choice, and certainly framed themselves as actively at the forefront of the anti-feminist movement. Similarly, Kate Bowler (2019) unpacks the importance of the powerful invisible women who are behind large spiritual empires and the ways in which they used their respectable identities to gain influence without acknowledging (or seeking acknowledgment) for their power as juxtaposed to these external logics of emancipation. As Bjork-James (2020), who reads these two works together, argues, the history with feminism for these women is complicated and its projection is often at odds with its intent: "white conservative Christian women helped make patriarchy safe after feminist successes but also relied on the feminist movement to create a patriarchy much kinder to women" (Bjork-James 2020: 598–599). Feminism as a term has also been "irrelevant" for women depending on

their global location. Abu-Lughod (1998) reminds us that women in the Middle East have had to remake and reclaim spaces of modernity, and feminism, because of the persistence of the Western gaze that has left them as toothless as other forms of patriarchal oppression. This "rejection of feminism," as Nour Hassan points out, "is not because [Arab women] don't need it, or aren't aware of the implications of the lack of feminist ideals, but to put it simply—we struggle with feminism for several reasons. As a Western born concept, feminism as we see it in the media is tailored to very different needs than our own." Nour Hassan, "5 Reasons Arab Women Struggle with Feminism," *Mille*, February 22, 2018. Hassan's rejection also highlights an important difference in the generational voice of dissent. See note 13 above re: similar generational divides in India. Also see Scharff 2009, more generally, on young women's disassociation with feminism. Similarly, Nigerian pop star Tiwa Savage created a stir when she went on record during an interview to reinforce gender difference as a product of divine order: "I don't think that is how God created us, especially in a household anyway. So . . . we (females) can be strong in our career and stuff, but when we are home we have to realize that the man is the head of the house." Following this interview, Florence Otedola, a popular disc jockey who goes by the stage name DJ Cuppy, admitted that women were "really powerful" but declared that she "doesn't consider herself a feminist anymore" (Otedola was 26 at the time!) to explain that she would "never come out as feminist" because she was in a male-dominated industry with scenarios that required her to "deal with men on a day-to-day basis and realize that they are always going to think they are better than women." Both these statements by celebrities were hotly debated on the Internet, but they are relevant here because they highlight the specific conditions wherein vocal membership of a movement might be the kind of posturing that is irrelevant and even hypocritical to the lived reality. See Damilola Odufuwa, "Nigeria: The Women Who Reject Feminism," *CNN*, October 8, 2018. For new theorizing about cross national feminist experiences in elite work, look out for research by Jaleh Taheri at Lund University.

15. This kind of "speaking," of course, is not just about structured movements. And the feeling of misplaced agency is an infliction experienced beyond the academy. As the twenty-seven-year-old "non-fiction novel" author (and Bourdieu-esque French social commentator) Édouard Louis says about this tendency to write about processes that have distanced one from the material conditions they write about, especially for audiences who are not similarly placed: "Sometimes I have the feeling that the books I am writing are a party for the people I used to live with, but that they cannot attend" see Elisabeth Zerofsky, "I Always Write with a Sense of Shame," *New York Times Magazine*, March 31, 2020. For the pushback that this kind of distance and proximity navigation has produced, see the review of Louis's first autofictional book, *The End of Eddy* by Sam Metz, in *The New Republic*, June 8, 2017. Simultaneously, the *New Yorker* reviewed such a potrayal of past and current conflicted selves and meaning-making on behalf of one's communities between truth and fiction as an "act of solidarity and an act of vengeance." See Garth Greenwell, "Growing Up Poor and Queer in a French Village," *The New Yorker* Books Section, May 8, 2017.

16. The strategy of not naming has been employed by actors intentionally across political and ideological divides (see note 14 above). And it is an especially useful strategy in a tense political situation with embedded meanings. In this sense, non-naming—even if not strategic at inception—could have usefulness in its ability to not attract the kind of backlash that could accompany identity politics and association (e.g., the case of conservative and radical feminists alike who seek disassociation for the wrath of ideologically being located alongside actors they see as non-allies).

17. Particularly, the long and important history of the Indian feminist movement has been buttressed by its commitment to the struggles of other actors (e.g., Kumar 1997; Ray 2000b; Anagol 2005) and I remain cognizant of the precociousness of asking such a movement to extend its nomenclature to individualistic actors that have not even, as Srila Roy

argues, "co-opted the term for themselves" (2018). This book addresses the critiques of neo-liberal adaptations that do what Kapur (2012) calls feminism "lite" (e.g., Roy 2011). Still, the distinction that emerges from the narratives in this book, as I lay out in this preface, is the lack of *claiming*.

18. Another COVID-19 example seems relevant to illuminate this distinction between intentional and incidental governance (even if only because it is the fundamental landscape of organizing one's intellectual inquiries at the time this book is going to press). In March 2020, in the middle of India's reckoning with the (start of?) the COVID-19 crisis, Prime Minister Narendra Modi directed "pleas" at his citizens to "clap hands" and "shine torches" at specific parts of the day to communally show solidarity with fighting the lethal infectious disease, including a request on April 5, 2020 to turn off the lights for "9 minutes at 9 pm" and "light a lamp" to "move past darkness and uncertainty that has been created, and go towards the light." These actions were similar to requests in other parts of the world, calling for solidarity from communities for careers and workers. But it was also centrally different in that this was a "plea" from the country's head of state, rather than the product of a viral organic campaign started by a local social entrepreneur. It also was monitored in state-sanctioning ways (e.g., teachers, on Modi's orders, in central board–funded schools wrote letters to parents to remind students to collect these lamps, and collected data on such compliance), and cemented an underlying majoritarian political agenda in the guise of a secular "unity call" (lamp lighting has been interpreted as a modern-day version of a collective *yagna* or collective ritual practice, and the timing and call have astrological significance that have not been missed by the Hindu right). While these actions could have given some (or even many) people comfort during scary times, in the Indian case, this wool-pulling over the nation's collective eyes was clearly to distract from the larger problems of public health, population, and poverty that could dismantle any response the country had to the pandemic. One can see that this is a clear governance model—a liberal, communal, citizen-friendly request that does the work of fascism while seeming benevolent. But one could perhaps also argue that it is distinctly different from other kinds of tribute models from which this gains legitimacy (e.g., home-grown social movements in Italy and France that Modi uses to justify the call) even if they too might still appear to be institutionalized tributes because of the involved actors' powers and positions at the time of the call for solidarity.

19. I do not mean to suggest that clarity is better than ambiguity for theory-building. Even so, unlike the nervous association leaps I make by extending Ahmed's logic to hierarchical law firms, the applications here to naming and claiming a queer identity are jumps I make with more clarity and confidence. Ahmed tells us that feminist theory was a series of "continuous clicks" for her—and coming to layered queered identity and theory was similar clicking for me, often (and especially with) frustration and failure. Drawing from Lorde again (Ahmed 2016 citing Lorde's *Sister Outsider* 1984:152), Ahmed makes the case that racism and sexism, although they are "grown-up words," are words that we experience before we know how to name. Words, she says, "can allow us to get closer to our experiences, words can allow us to comprehend what we experience after the event. We become retrospective witnesses of our own becoming." Just as sexism and racism are "given names that tend to lag behind their problems," so too is my relationship with queerness and (perhaps as an extension) with categories more generally.

20. It remains important to distinguish between mobility through work and professional mobility because of the kinds of relationships that have been navigated, especially by new actors, into these landscapes. Davies (1996), for example, argues that the gendering of organizations and bureaucracy is not so much a product of *excluding* women from work defined as professional as much as it is their routine inclusion in ill-defined supported roles *within* professions that are already deemed to be masculine framed and typed. I make a

comprehensive extension to this argument in chapter 2 about gendered frameworks and the framing of professional work in the contexts this book examines.

21. In an essay that pays homage to his late mother, Mukul Kesavan, the Indian historian and political essayist, reminds us of the possible universality of this paradox: that this contradiction of modernity and convention, optics and personhood, are not peculiar to just my mother, or one particular time period. Essaying his parents' life and work histories, he revisits the distinction I call attention to here (*infra*) between work and a career: recalling the "Superwoman" who was his mother, an acoustical engineer whose pioneer status was predictably better served in historic retelling by her son than through her lived experience of sexism, Kesavan offers: "Her career was constrained by the routine sexism that all women encounter in male preserves, made worse by the fact that she was something of a pioneer. It must have irked her, but she didn't complain. . . . She worked a demanding nine to five job, drove a car, ran the household, controlled its finances, cooked, sewed, knitted and finally, built a house for her family. My father had the career, she had a job. It was not a perfectly fulfilled life—few lives are—but it was a remarkably productive one." See Mukul Kesavan, "A Different Slogan: In Praise of Indian Mothers," *The Telegraph*, March 26, 2016.

Introduction. The Accidental Emergence of India's Elite Women Lawyers

1. When I asked her if she would entertain the idea of an arranged marriage, she merely scoffed at me. Dealing with scoffs is an occupational hazard for the qualitative sociologist, but the question itself was not out of turn. Arranged marriages are still widely the norm in India, and Sitara's parents—like most people in their generation—had been married in their twenties; by both of those standards, Sitara's unmarried state was unusual. Her mother, as Sitara had told me earlier, had married right out of college and had three children in middle school by the time she was Sitara's age. Yet, there was neither malice nor regret in Sitara's scoff; instead, she chuckled—she worked hard, when would she have the time? Note that arranged marriages have been a crucial mechanism for cementing caste hierarchies across class lines in India. Yet, despite an increasing trend toward agency in spouse selection (Banerjee et al. 2013) and elopements for "love" marriages (Donner 2002; Chowdhry 2007; Grover 2009; Allendorf 2013), arranged marriages are still pretty much the norm. The 2005 Indian Human Development Survey, for example, shows that less than 5% of all Indian women had a primary role in choosing their husbands and only 22% knew their husbands for more than a month before they got married (Desai and Andrist 2010). These numbers do not fully represent India's young, urban, and increasingly global population, but they are useful as context to understand any variation. On Indian intimate relationships beyond traditional logics of arranged and choice or "love" marriage, see Bhandari 2020.

2. In his pioneering book unpacking the concept of social class, Portes (2010:97, 106) argues that elite workers are distinguished by their ability to improve their class position through the "selective marketing of rare and desirable skills." In new economies, then, where skills that are in demand become relevant, it also becomes class confirming. Thus, even if in a Marxist sense the skills are not "productive," they still do the work of production because they lift their possessors across a class divide in a capitalist society where their skills are deemed to be valued. The mobility itself is tied to its class position, but in exceptional cases, might reach the ranks of true capitalistic achievement, especially if the individual has the ability to negotiate the kind of compensation that will allow for economic autonomy. Portes specifically includes as an example a "lawyer who makes partner in a famous firm" (2010:85).

3. Scholars of the professions use this term "feminization" to mean, explicitly, the increase in number of women, typically in fields that were historically male-dominated.

As other scholars (whom I agree with) have pointed out, this does not speak to the texture of such entry even if there is some consensus that such demographic change could impact the cultures of work over time. See, regarding this paradox, Bolton and Muzio 2008, and Sommerlad 1994, 2011. Feminization is an incomprehensive term because, while it has the effect of being optimistic, historically it has not followed through in effect. Instead, feminization has typically devalued subfields over time (Reskin 1988; England 1992, see chapter 3) and creating cultures of hyper-essentialism (e.g., Pierce 1996) that have a range of adverse effects for women, even if they do not feel that way at first brush (e.g., chapter 4). Carrie Menkel-Meadow's early work (1985, 1989) expresses the well-grounded cynicism for the impacts of these numbers more generally, i.e., the actual work feminization in numbers can do for the legal profession (in terms of better gender justice and rewards for women over time). For feminization of the legal profession more generally, see Sommerlad 1994, 2002; Hagan and Kay 1995; Schultz and Shaw 2003; Michelson 2013; and the *After the JD* Studies. It should be clear that while this book uses the case of this small victory to explore the possibilities of extensions, it by no means is meant to suggest that feminization in itself could be an absolute reward.

4. I am aligned with the theorization that Santos offers, for example, that there is no one single kind of "cosmopolitan legality" (2005) but that solidarity between those that are marginal across sites require an alternate solidarity that affords a particular kind of coordinated cross-border citizenship that binds them (Santos and Rodríguez-Garavito 2005:14). This kind of "epistemology from the south" (Santos 2016) requires us to not just theorize about these factions, but also to include such theorization as we sit with its resultant praxis. Yet, applications of this theory are usually thought of as a development praxis, an approach that I push back against in this book. Instead, the line of inquiry is to ask how we can occupy these spaces of liminal global peripheries to subvert understandings of law and legal institutions, and what that kind of framing could look like in the context of a globally subversive yet locally cosmopolitan gendered process. On geopolitics of gendered location and identity more generally, see Mohanty (2003) and Jayawardena (2016).

5. The shaping of the neoliberal state has important political economy extensions, but in this book, I use it as an (inadequate) marker for the specific changes that the "opening up of markets" in 1991 has had for markets and cultures of work. I'm particularly interested in the work of the implications such neoliberalism has at the individual level of the worker and the kinds of inequalities they institutionally legitimize in the performance of what was considered global merit and modernity. The focus on work and interactional culture through observation as the central point of analyzing the work of neoliberalism in this book is intentional. It follows what Appadurai terms a "future-oriented development logic" that is rooted in the conviction that aspirational capital (or the "capacity to aspire") is central not just to development and poverty (as Appadurai argues; see Appadurai 2004) but also to creations of new kinds of class formations and elite mobility. Similarly, the focus on the individual worker and her narratives is to offer a bottom-up narrative of the construction of this kind of neoliberalism, to offer evidence of its stickiness through people's lived praxis and expectations. As the Comaroffs argue, new waves of capitalism, offer, for new kinds of elites, neoliberal conditions that "obscure the rooting of inequality in structures of production, as work gives way to the mechanical solidarities of "identity" . . . which, like citizenship, is increasingly measured by the capacity to transact and consume" (Comaroff and Comaroff 2001:15–16). On the emergence of the post-independent neoliberal state more generally, See Goswami 2004 and Gopal Jayal 2013. On the development of capital and market governance in India that allowed for this trajectory of "neoliberal enthusiasms," (Birla 2009:23), see Birla 2009, 2015.

6. Fernandes (2006), for example, argues that while benefiting from new sources of economic capital, the "new middle-class" labor market is characterized by increasing job

insecurity, higher employment of contract workers, and higher intra-segment distinctions within the country (90–91) which in turn create a field that "crosses traditional analytical boundaries between cultural and structural variables." She pushes back against the generic idea that economic possibility and potential—available only to "new rich" within the middle class—represent a holistic view of middle- class mobility for all Indians more generally. I agree with this analysis of liberalization's impacts on the middle class, and would argue that the professionals in this study might have come from the middle-class Fernandes describes, but in achieving this kind of elite worker status, they transcend the capacity for their stories to be generalizable to a larger middle-class narrative about India, mobility, and globalization.

7. I define success here to be both the actual organizational outcomes that women achieve (i.e., entry and accession to senior levels of partnership within these firms) but also the ways in which these outcomes allow them to navigate their personal and professional lives more generally. It is this praxis of success that is the focus of much of this book. As I detail in chapter 1, this cohort of "first-generation professional elites" relayed very specific narratives of their lives that were at odds with the class narratives they emerged from as well as other accounts of professional women and their navigation of middle-class morality and modernity (e.g., Radhakrishnan 2009). Similarly, I highlight the variations in these experiences as my respondents dealt with peers (chapter 2), clients (chapter 4), and families (chapter 5). It is the synthesis of this visible attainment along with the lived extensions of its experience that I term here as "success" and, in turn, a feminist outcome.

8. I deal with the possibility and limitations of this intersectional approach across the different empirical chapters of this book (chapters 2 through 5) to show how similarly placed women with comparable positionalities continued to have different kinds of professional experiences depending on their organizational environments. For a review of the theory of intersectionality this extension draws from more generally, see Crenshaw 1990; Carbado et al. 2013. For a review that extends this specifically to the contemporary Indian context, see Roy 2018. On intersectional variations in the global legal profession, see Williams 2014; Wilkins and Fong 2017; and Tomlinson et al. 2019.

9. See also note 10 in chapter 1 and notes 4 and 5 in chapter 2.

10. Following the admission of Cornelia Sorabji (India's first woman advocate) to the Allahabad Bar, the Legal Practitioners (Women) Act of 1923 was passed, allowing women a statutory right to practice law. However, this did not immediately bring about much change in gender demographics. The Bar Council of India (BCI) estimated the total number of female legal professionals to be fairly negligible at the start of liberalization in 1991 and not unlike the pattern for decades before (table 2b).

11. Based on representation among law students, some research predicted that women would make up about 40% of the profession before 2005 (Sharma 2002:97). And while the specific demographics of India's lawyers are hard to track for particular reasons (see note 12 that follows; also see Ballakrishnen 2020), these numbers seem far outside even the most optimistic representations. Almost a decade after this projected due date, women still constitute about 10% of all lawyers registered with the BCI (table 3).

12. The cumulative numbers of bar admissions or lawyer demographics—however discrepant—are still useful to gain a sense of the wide profession, but numbers these large are incomplete in other ways too. In 2015, the BCI embarked on a verification drive to check the validity of "genuine lawyers" in the country—an effort that reportedly outed close to half the profession's population as nonpracticing lawyers (Garg 2017), including in the country's capital (and most densely lawyer-populated region), Delhi (Azeem 2016). Here too, numbers are speculative—news reports claimed anywhere from 45% (Garg 2017) to 60% (Sarda 2017) of lawyers to be "false," and this range highlights the problem of discerning practicing lawyers from those with law degrees who do not actively practice law (as well

as those who practice law without a valid degree). See BCI Chief Manan Kumar Mishra on the verification drive: "The number of practicing lawyers is about to come down [by] 55–60% after the completion of the verification process. This will certainly improve the quality of our legal profession" (Garg 2017).

13. Empirical research across various sites indicates that caste continues to matter for the litigating Bar (Nagla 2001; Sharma 2002; Mishra 2015). As earlier studies found (e.g., Gadbois 1969; Morrison 1972), forward caste Hindus and local elites continue to reap unequal rewards (Dezalay and Garth 2010; Galanter and Robinson 2014); and caste, kinship, and communal ties matter even in newer corporate ecosystems (Krishnan 2013; Nanda et al. 2017; Wilkins et al. 2017). Gadbois's recent book on the Supreme Court (2011), for example, shows much the same patterns he found fifty years earlier: 40% of Supreme Court judges were Brahmin, and another 50% were from other forward castes. Yet caste plays out differently in other contexts. For example, in 2014 in the Madras High Court in Tamil Nadu, a state with strong anti-Brahmin politics, fewer than 15% of judges came from forward castes, and the possible appointment of more forward caste judges recently generated unprecedented controversy. In 2014, close to 15,000 advocates stayed home from work, and Justice C. S. Karnan, a Dalit sitting judge of the High Court, impeded a courtroom in session denouncing "unfairness" when three upper caste names were included on a list of twelve recommended for judicial appointment by the high court collegium (Deccan Herald 2014; Legally India 2014). The Karnan court disruption has been controversial (Ramasubramanian 2015; Hindu 2016) as has his career trajectory following it. In May 2017, Justice Karnan (who, in 2011, had alleged victimization and discrimination by fellow judges before the National Commission for Scheduled Castes) was sent to prison for contempt of court (Yamunan 2017); and upon release, in May 2018, he floated a pro-women, anti-corruption political party from the BR Ambedkar Memorial House (India Today 2018). For commentary on courts and caste in the Madras High Court more generally, see Chandru 2015, and Vijayakumar 2015. In her recent ethnography of the judicial iconography in the Madras High Court, Khorakiwala (2018) suggests that "the issue of dalit (lowest caste) politics today engulfs the Madras High Court," as is evident in the Karnan case, but extends beyond it to politics around public statues of noted Dalit legal icon (and drafter of the Indian Constitution), Dr. B. R. Ambedkar.

14. See Soni Mishra, "I was sexually harassed in the corridors of the Supreme Court," THE WEEK (November 13, 2016), available at http://www.theweek.in/theweek/cover /interview-indira-jaising-senior-lawyer.html (Last visited on March 8, 2017).

15. Numbers do not do justice to the important work of eminent women, legal and socio-legal academics, in these schools. Other research further unpacks these nuances and sets up the complications in the narratives. Even so, only ten of 102 members of Academic Councils in what are commonly considered the "top 6" national law schools in the country are women. By contrast, in public schools, there are more women in leadership, and as of 2018, each of the three law departments at Delhi University is headed by a woman (Ballakrishnen and Samuel 2020).

16. In this resistance, it joins a line of rising strain of research that similarly queers sites and actors to realign their normative assumptions. See, for example, work that resists global south narratives about gender to focus instead on "hiphop" cosmopolitanism revealing layered "third world cultures" and black feminist intersectionalities in Dubai (Isoke 2013) and cyber-cosmopolitanism revealing new global masculinities and aspiration in Delhi (Dattatreyan 2020). Similarly, John O'Brien's work (2017) on Muslim teenage boys in California extends Mahmood's (2011) politicization of piety to re-invoke the important work of "coolness" that piety can also manifest. These reformulations of typically overgeneralized categories are crucial not only for the novelty of their perspective but also for the value for theory-building that they hold in their wake.

17. See chapter 1 as well as research notes in the appendix for how these data were collected and the logic of sampling these professionals. Note that the original research design was not meant to investigate gendered outcomes. I was interested in the globalization of work and professions generally and was looking to study organizational change and innovation following the 1991 liberalization reforms. As I argue in the following chapters, the finding that gender was, in my respondents' own words, "not an issue" in some of these firms came as a surprise given the background of these law firms' emergence and the position of women more generally in India. In some sense, then, the study itself was "accidental."

18. From the context of the sending country, intergenerational mobility in emerging economies is generally lagging behind rates of mobility in the high-income economies, but certain parts of Africa, Eastern Europe, and East Asia show some variation to the pattern (Narayan et al. 2018). There have been some accounts by liberal and market theorists alike that post-transition socialist societies offered new channels of mobility with an increasing ability for class fluidity, but Jackson and Evans (2017) reveal the limitations of these short-term analyses to reveal that they don't take into account capacities for market changes to reinforce old inequalities in new ways. Scholarship from the receiving country perspective offers synergies to these findings. Portes, Fernández-Kelly, and Haller (2009:1080–1081), for example, use the case of US immigrants to warn that while this single generation mobility into university-trained, upper middle class is certainly possible (and the aspirational norm), slipping the window of opportunity could pivot the second generation into an even further descent than their parents' original class because of the structures of old stratification that are embedded into the conditions they enter into: "for new entrants into the labour force, including the children of immigrants, this stark bifurcation means that they must acquire in the course of a single generation the advanced educational credentials that took descendants of Europeans several generations to achieve. Otherwise, their chances of fulfilling their aspirations would be compromised as few opportunities exist between the low-paid manual occupations that most immigrant parents occupy and the lofty, highly paid jobs in business, health, the law and the academy that these parents earnestly wish for their offspring. Without the costly and time-consuming achievement of a university degree, such dreams are likely to remain beyond reach."

19. Just in the Indian context, mobility following other kinds of regulatory changes not intended to impact individual mobility but nonetheless having the effect of restructuring stratification was most central during and following independence in the mid-twentieth century. And here too, background frameworks of caste and cultural capital tied to it were central to privileging new entrants into positions of administrative power (e.g., IAS officers who formed what Fernandes (2006) calls the "old middle class" jobs and lifestyles).

20. The Advocates Act 1961 §§ 24, 37 restricted the right of practice to Indian citizens and practitioners from countries offering reciprocity. And while the Bar Council has allowed a few individual foreign lawyers (all of Indian origin) from recognized universities to practice in Indian courts, foreign law firms are still excluded. See http://barcouncilofindia.nic .in/disk1/foreign.pdf for the Bar Council Resolution on acceptable reciprocal standards. Proposals to expand the scope of this reciprocity have met resistance within and outside the country. See ttp://economictimes.indiatimes.com/News/International_Business/NRI _lawyers_demand_removal_of_restrictions_on_working_in_UK/articleshow/3536849 .cms.

21. Using the broad theoretical proposition that variations in organizational history would be central to shaping experiences, my exploratory study focused on the differences between lawyers in old and new organizations (including old and new kinds of law firms, in-house corporate practice, solo practices, and public interest organizations) across different Indian cities that I thought would have different legal cultures (e.g., Delhi for its more litigation-heavy and regulatory influences, Mumbai for its finance and banking deals–

forward culture, and Bangalore for its proximity to technology innovation). The variations between sites and organizational types diverged starkly, and in the interest of observing cases that were analytically useful to my research interests, I made the decision to focus on organizational variation rather than inter-city differences in legal cultures. I imagine, as I elaborate in the research appendix, that if I had chosen a different design, the path dependency of this study would have been entirely different. Still, unlike the pulse of this book's theory, these design decisions were informed and intentional.

22. I also hypothesized that if this gender finding were just a response to newness and the organizational structure of these firms, then *all* new law firms would have the same advantages. To test this, I added a new case of lawyers in other new law firms that were not particularly elite and found that the gender parity did not play out in the same ways as it did in very elite law firms. In particular, I found that while elite law firms saw themselves as catering to and competing with a global standard for legal services, new but less elite law firms that did not face similarly sophisticated and global clients did not see themselves as international firms. In these less elite firms, women were still better represented than in traditional legal practice, but women felt their status differently than in the elite law firms.

23. According to 2017 data from the National Association of Software and Service Companies (NASSCOM), IT is one of the fastest growing industries in the country, and contributes revenues of US$160 billion, or 7.7% of India's GDP, a significant growth from 1.2% three decades prior in 1998, when it was first introduced as part of the country's national priority mandate by the Vajpayee government. But it is not just national significance that makes this industry prime for the study of global influences in professionalization—at 38% of all exports, IT also accounts for the single largest share of India's total service exports. And with a presence in more than fifty-two countries, five hundred global client destinations, and more than a thousand cross-border acquisitions and captive organizations, the IT sector has been a prime site of what I term elsewhere (Ballakrishnen 2016) as "mainstream" professional globalization.

24. Specifically, as India's highest impact sector, employing more than three million professionals, IT is also India's largest private sector employer—a drastic change from the pre-liberalization sectors that were predominantly publicly owned. Particularly, scholarship on the emergence of the IT industry (Evans 1995; Singh 2000; Chanda 2002; Dossani 2008) has marked the relevance of this move from public to private as an important factor in creating professional ideology at the level of the workers. Satish Deshpande, for example, emphasizes how the shifting of the developmental state has meant a shift in the emergence of the middle class—with differentiated elites becoming the predominant producer of ideologies that the middle class consumes (Deshpande 2003). Thus, the sector has been all-important in ushering in a new set of global ideologies in the public imagination that included bureaucratic norms and non-partisan management. Further, the newness of the IT sector influenced not only the move in ownership from public to private, it also introduced a new set of global actors—clients, investors, management, organizations, etc.—who were part of the framework of this professionalization. As a neoliberal industry with no preexisting frameworks in the domestic context, these professional spaces have been inherently embedded in their global identities. Nowhere else has the proliferation of global firms and industry infiltrated local conscience and economy to the same extent (Singh 2000).

25. The scope and nature of the sector's proliferation has meant that global scripts have influenced more organizations and workers in this sector than any other—resulting in a more mainstream transformation of what "global" means to workers, organizations, and even more common cultural parlance. It would not be a stretch to say that local professionalization, as a function of global influence, is more likely to be thought of in terms of this sector than any other. But this impact on globalization and private ownership did not mean changes at the macro level alone. And a prominent brand of recent scholarship has focused

on not just the institutional proliferation of these sectors but also the intermittent connection between these macro influences and micro identities (Nicholson, Sahay, and Krishna 2000; Van den Broek et al. 2004; Taylor and Bain 2005; D'Mello 2005; Chakravartty 2006; Radhakrishnan 2011; Nadeem 2013).

26. Lily King's "Euphoria," a fictitious account of Margret Mead's life, describes this sense of euphoria in a way that applies well to the way I felt in 2013: "It's that moment about two months in, when you think you've finally got a handle on the place. Suddenly it feels within your grasp. It's a delusion—you've only been there eight weeks—and it's followed by the complete despair of ever understanding anything. But at the moment the place feels entirely yours. It's the briefest, purest euphoria." The interview with Sitara occurred more than two months into my fieldwork, but it was exactly at the point where I was far enough in to entertain the delusion that I had a grasp on the workings of my site but was still shielded from the despair that would come soon after.

1. Foci: Market Liberalization and the Changing Nature of Professional Work

1. This book focuses on Indian mobility processes within the subcontinent, but these implications of morality and restraint that follow the accounts of gender, women, and work apply beyond the country to include the diasporic contexts as well. In her ethnography on Keralite nurses in the United States and their "dirty" status despite transnational migration, George (2005) argues that although they are major breadwinners for their families, highly skilled nurses from Kerala who have transnational careers do not have the same kinds of gains in social spheres like church and community because they are seen as doing the "polluted" or "dirty" work of touching unknown bodies. Almost a decade and a half later, Sonja Thomas's research (2018) on this community of transnational Kerala nurses shows the stickiness of these curtailed mobilities, even as it offered more nuanced ways to consider the intersections of class, caste, and community extensions of privilege that are embedded in certain kinds of minority experience. When dissecting this line of research, the particularity of women's status in Kerala is worth noting. The Indian state is not just a main sending locale for transnational migration, it is also the site of a stark "gender paradox." On the one hand, it consistently ranks at the top for gender empowerment measures and gender development indices (Kumar 1996). Yet, feminist scholars warn us that the gender gains declared in Kerala are illusory—that they claim to have more success than they in fact do (Devika and Mukherjee 2007; Kodoth and Eapen 2005; Sreekumar 2007). For example, female labor force participation is at the low end of the Indian spectrum (28% of women between ages fifteen and forty-nine were working in 2005, about 7% less than the national average and 17% less than the neighboring state of Tamil Nadu). One common line of explanation for this decoupling between state indicators and the everyday lived experiences of women has been the State's communist party agenda that, while paying lip service to gender parity, has maintained a strongly patrifocal political agenda (Arun 1999; Saradamoni 1983). Kerala is also an important state in terms of migration patterns. In addition to the transnational gendered migration that George studied, Kerala is the highest sending state to the Gulf for (mostly male) migrant labor workers. Prema Kurien (2003), for example, sheds important light on the supply-side micro-dynamics of these sending ethnic populations (e.g., boundary heightening among in-groups to maintain status) and argues that a community-specific nexus of religion, gender, and status shapes and is recursively shaped by migration. But while she discusses the importance of kinship and marriage dynamics (e.g., extended family, marriage practices, organization of the household, economic behavior), her unpacking of the gender differences focus more on the middle-class female migrant rather than families of labor migrants. (For example, she shows that

Ezhava Hindus and Mappila Muslim women were restrained by their background identities as homemakers and unable to participate in Middle East migration, whereas Syrian Christian women with different sociocultural resources were able to take advantage of many white-collar opportunities.) Kurien's strong case for the centrality of gender to ethnicity and migration processes was picked up by Aboobacker (2005), who notes the ways in which migration to the Gulf remains significant for gendered citizenship in the sending country. But while he alluded to the relevance of migration in creating these imagined identities for women's political participation, he didn't delve into the importance of family and kinship patterns. In some of my other research with Hannah Brueckner (Research and Empirical Analysis of Labor Migration Grant 2016), we explore the significance of these women "left behind" and what it means for thinking about labor, gender, and globalization from the perspective of actors not seemingly central to the process.

2. These gaps in unequal access and privilege have been at the center of public discourse with findings such as the 2019 college admissions scandal (or, for that matter, pandemics). Still, as scholars of educational inequality argue, it is not so much that these scandals reveal new inequalities, they merely emphasize already existing cracks that are inherent in the system. As Jessica Calarco argues, "in some ways [these scandals] show that it is harder to game the system. It takes a lot more than just a phone call or a $5 million donation for a celebrity or CEO to get their kid into a top school. And that is because celebrities and CEOs are not the only one playing the game. Today, parents with mundane amounts of privilege—white doctors, lawyers, college professors, accountants, and even teachers—are playing the admissions game" (see "When Their Kids Don't Make the Cut," *Inside Higher Ed*, March 22, 2019). For structural inequalities of access and equity that the COVID crisis has revealed across educational institutions (making them, in some subversive ways, "equally (or at least, more similarly) unequal," see Wunpinni Mohammed, *Al Jazeera*, April 7, 2020 (on Ghana) and Nicholas Casey, *New York Times*, April 4, 2020 (on two students in Haverford College returning to very different home environments from which to virtually access their education).

3. While some commentators have argued that this neoliberal advantage might not be novel—see, for instance, Indian Oxbridge students in the 1950s and 1960s—I contend that the Indian case is not embedded in the same kind of class—or gender—advantages. While educated Indian elites who attended Oxford and Cambridge post-partition were no doubt claiming legitimacy as meritocratic professional elites, they could only access those advantages because of their class position, since going to the UK as an Indian from the immediate post-colony required economic *and* political capital (i.e., they needed actual monetary wealth to be able to pay for the education in foreign exchange, and political capital and networks to know how to convert such wealth to foreign exchange, given the pre-liberalization laws). In contrast, the students who attended the sending schools in my sample (i.e., elite engineering, business, and law schools that trained those who would eventually populate elite law and consulting firms, did not come only from wealthy Indian families). For the most part, they came and continue to come from middle-class families with some but not necessarily all the class markings that could predict these outcomes. Further still, families with similar kinds of class positionality have not been able to leverage this kind of advantage in other kinds of "modern" firms, as is clear from the case of the women in consulting firms. Still, the cultural and social reproduction that is key, signaling the rewards to modern and a particular kind of professionally socialized urbanity—embedded in caste—is an inescapable mechanism in all of these narratives, similar to what other scholars of mobility have observed in these contexts (e.g., Deshpande and Newman 2007; Jodhka and Newman 2007; Jodhka 2012; Jodhka and Prakash 2016).

4. Organizational economists have used comparative institutional analysis for theory-building (e.g., Williamson 1991), but this is less common in sociological research

of neo-institutionalism, especially using qualitative methods, particularly in global sites. For a comparative organizational ethnography that built theory using structural variation and was an important model as I constructed this research, see Katherine Kellogg's work (2011) on hospitals and mobilization among medical professionals. For research on the legal profession that has leveraged the comparative advantage of global sites to theorize, see Plickert and Hagan 2011; Silver 2011.

5. This reference to New York City was often used by my respondents to describe Lower Parel, an area filled with banks, law firms, and consulting houses, as well as high-rise luxury malls, designer warehouses, jazz clubs, and wine bars. Many of the professionals I interviewed either worked in this neighborhood or had regular meetings with clients there. However, while the reference to New York is noteworthy, so is the erasure of the area's more textured identity. Lower Parel is an erstwhile working-class neighborhood that has, over the course of the last few years, been completely transformed into a high-rise corporate district. For an important review of this history and the archives of loss imminent in this new postmodern reframing of work and worker within uncertain neoliberal urbanscapes, see Finkelstein (2019).

6. For instance, this is a far cry from Radhakrishnan's respondents—also female professionals—who, even as sole breadwinners, remained deeply committed to the ethics of austerity, especially when it came to "consumer spending that was disconnected from family life" (2009:205).

7. The mobility in the IT sector, for instance, has been an important point of accessing global capital, and the women in these studies were no doubt breaking new ground in their family histories and trajectories by working away from home. Yet, despite leveraging symbolic capital, these women were still accessing—or in many cases, holding on to—quintessentially middle-class positions. In fact, as Radhakrishnan's rich ethnography shows, they protect the confines of this ideological class by their practice of "respectable femininity" (2009:201), a practice that straddles classic conflicts around sexuality, family responsibility, and consumption with a deep commitment to middle-class ideology. Similarly, Nadeem (2009), who used the case of the outsourcing industry to understand global professionals' aspirations for modernity, continued to situate the *kama-dharma* (pleasure-duty) balance as a crucial concern for the "new middle class" (2009:104). In Nadeem's analysis, women were riddled with middle-class anxieties about loss of status, especially as they came to terms with the contrast of their identities as "young, chaste women" being sucked into a global "den of immorality." The things that global work offered—discretionary income, casual interpersonal relationships that were not tied to familial duty, and alcohol—were, by this account, dangerous to these women's "precarious standing on the middle-class social scale" (2009:118). Unlike the world of women professionals described in Radhakrishnan's study of women professionals, the outsourcing industry as described by Nadeem has a misogynist undertone—in this sector women workers are viewed, at best, as the incentive for male workers to continue working so they can buy them "dresses, necklaces or flowers" (2009:111); some employers may view women workers as one of the many "non-monetary perks" that can retain male workers (ibid.).

8. According to the All India Survey of Higher Education in 2018, women were 53% of the undergraduate degree holders in the country, 69.6% of the philosophy degree holders, and 41.8% of all PhDs. This investment in education for its own sake, or possibly, for better returns in the marriage market rather than for employment outcomes, is crucial not just in the Indian context (e.g., Banerjee 1999), but has extensions to other global south economies (see Masood 2019 on Pakistani "doctor brides"; Kaufmann et al. 2013 on Chilean women's pre-marital investments to gain better quality of partner parity). For statistics on education more generally, see Government of India, Ministry of Human Resource Development, All India Survey on Higher Education 2017–18 (2018), table 35.

9. Per World Bank estimates, the rate of adult (over 15 years of age) female participation in the labor force is about (in 2018) 23.6% as compared to 78.6% male participation. See World Bank Group, Modeled ILO Estimates for India, September 2019, available online at https://data.worldbank.org/indicator/SL.TLF.CACT.FE.ZS?locations=IN.

10. The National Sample Surveys on Employment, India's most comprehensive employment survey, reveals that the country has one of the lowest female labor participation statistics in the world, higher than only nine other countries (Yemen, Syria, Iraq, Jordan, Algeria, Iran, Somalia, Morocco, and Egypt). This finding, that adult women are not working or seeking work, is attributable to a range of factors including a decrease in agricultural jobs (the main source of rural employment) to the impossibility of available urban jobs. But it could also mean that higher-class women are investing more in education and that women seeking (and performing) middle-class positionality are on routes of alternate forms of mobility that do not include labor that might otherwise be required of them. See the data publicly available online at https://data.gov.in/dataset-group-name /national-sample-survey.

11. Research firms like Statista and Global Research estimate that the management consulting market was between $1,062–$1,304 million, or $1,587–$1,872 million between 2013 and 2015 respectively. Modi's liberalization policies might have had a positive growth according to these estimates (of up to 9% leading to between $1,548 and $2,132 million in 2016–2017, the years following my fieldwork). But they are still meager when compared to the (much more comprehensive) data on the IT market share which, per the NASSCOM India IT Report yearly, estimated for the same years (2016–2017), was an aggregated total revenue of $160 billion with $99 billion in export revenue and $48 billion in domestic revenue.

12. The Indian legal profession is, in many ways, not that different than it was when reviewed by Marc Galanter back in 1969. The widely touted number of "over a million" lawyers in India is a close approximation to the truth—not far off the mark. The estimate offered by the Bar Council of India (BCI) has varied between 1.2 and 1.7 million (Legally India 2013). In 2011, the BCI reported that "approximately" 400,000–500,000 people were studying law and 60,000–70,000 were graduating annually (Ganz 2011). These numbers are both small in comparison to the population and large given the GDP. The ratio of one lawyer for every thousand people is comparable to that in many other countries, if far less than in the United States and United Kingdom. Similarly, the GDP per lawyer in India is about $1.4 million—a strikingly small amount, especially when compared to other lawyer-heavy countries (Ganz 2011). It The legal profession continues to be difficult to survey and most of its demographic characteristics are still approximations. Most research is historical (Paul 1991) or confined to specific facets: for example, the Amritsar litigating bar (Gandhi 1982), women lawyers in the Punjab High Court (Sethi 1987), Lok Adalats in Uttar Pradesh (Moog 1998), gender in the Delhi courts (Sharma 2002) or the Uttar Pradesh district courts (Mishra 2015). Even the most ambitious recent study (Wilkins et al. 2017) addresses only the corporate sector of the profession. Primary data are even harder to find. The Law Commission of India periodically publishes reports on lawyers and the legal process, but these usually focus on litigants and lawsuits. The Bar Council of India (BCI) no longer publishes the number and gender of enrolled advocates by state. Data requests to individual bar associations proved largely fruitless, and despite efforts to use new verification processes to collect more comprehensive data through new verification processes, they remain scarce and unreliable. In 2010, the Legal Education Committee and the BCI introduced new rules for admission to the bar, including passing the All India Bar Exam (AIBE); (see http://allindiabarexamination.com/). And the Bar Council of India BCI Certificate and Place of Practice (Verification) Rules, 2015, required State Bar Councils to collect and verify data about enrolled lawyers. A challenge before the Supreme Court is pending (*Ajayinder*

Sangwan v. Bar Council of Delhi, Transfer Case (Civil) No. 126 of 2015). But responses to applications under the Right to Information Act for lawyer demographics revealed that this information has not been collected systematically. A BCI response to a 2013 Right to Information request from Kush Karla, a Delhi advocate, revealed more comprehensive data (Ballakrishnen 2020). The estimate of 1.3 million lawyers is considerably less than the 1.7 million lawyers cited by the BCI chairman a few months before these data became public (Vyawahare 2013). For a fuller review of these demographic patterns, see Ballakrishnen 2020.

13. Whether BCI can require such an examination as a condition for admission to a state bar is before a constitutional bench of the Supreme Court. Meanwhile, examinations under the AIBE are still being conducted. For a case in favor of the AIBE, see https:// thewire.in/25073/in-defence-of-the-all-india-bar-exam/ (Utkarsh Srivastava, March 17, 2016). Shamnad Basheer, a prominent legal education activist, has argued that the AIBE requirement is unconstitutional without an amendment of the Advocates Act. See http:// www.livelaw.in/right-to-practice-law-is-a-fundamental-right-and-aibe-negates-the -very-right-sc/. Srivastava and Basheer are alumni of the five-year national law schools described below. See also Basheer and Mukherjee 2010.

14. BCI Chairman Manan Kumar Mishra said about the verification drive: "The number of practicing lawyers is about to come down to 55–60% after the completion of the verification process. This will certainly improve the quality of our legal profession" (Garg 2017). These phantom lawyers—and the BCI's characterization of them as threats to the health of the profession—are important reminders about the state of legal education.

15. Though the national ratio of 886 people per lawyer is lower than the thousand estimated by Ganz two years earlier, there is huge regional variation, from Delhi (309) and Punjab and Haryana (391) to Jharkand (3,369) and remote regions with serious problems of political integration (Assam, Nagaland, etc. 1,436). The reliability of these numbers was questioned when a 2015 BCI verification drive reportedly found that almost half the profession was not practicing (Garg 2017), even in the capital, Delhi (Azeem 2016). Here, too, numbers are speculative—news reports claim that anywhere between 45% Garg 2017) and 60% (Sarda 2017) of lawyers are "false," illustrating the difficulty of distinguishing licensed lawyers who practice from licensed lawyers who do not and unlicensed lawyers who do.

16. A term used by Prime Minister Dr. Manmohan Singh to distinguish the national law schools from the "sea of institutionalized mediocrity." See Prime Minister's Inaugural Address at the Conference of National Consultation for Second Generation Reforms in Legal Education (May 1, 2010), available online at http://archivepmo.nic.in /drmanmohansingh/speech-details.php?nodeid=889.

17. Gandhi (1988:381); http://www.prsindia.org/media/media-updates/profile-of-the -16th-lok-sabha-3276/.

18. Preparatory courses for law school cost between US$100 for online mock tests and about US$750 a year for more extensive training.

19. In the year since its launch in January 2017, MyLaw.net has had 12,000 unique learners, almost half of whom were from non-metropolitan Indian cities, reflecting a possible democratic expansion of quality legal education, which law schools have been unable to offer. See https://mylaw.net/.

20. In addition to critics disappointed by the failure of these schools to produce social advocacy lawyers, others fear that the schools are graduating an elite that will undo earlier progressive achievements. See, e.g., Kannabiran's response (*The Hindu*, October 12, 2015) to Anup Surendranath's comment that constitutional rights had been historically—and incrementally—compromised in India (*The Hindu*, October 9, 2015); available online at http://www.thehindu.com/opinion/letters/upholding-pluralism/article7750330.ece.

21. Proposals to expand the scope of this reciprocity have met resistance within and outside the country. See http://economictimes.indiatimes.com/News/International

_Business/NRI_lawyers_demand_removal_of_restrictions_on_working_in_UK
/articleshow/3536849.cms.

22. See http://www.lawentrance.com/recognisedunivs.htm for a list of universities.

23. See http://barcouncilofindia.nic.in/disk1/foreign.pdf for the Bar Council Resolution on acceptable reciprocal standards.

24. As long as the outsourcing entity (i.e., the foreign lawyer) can ensure the quality of the work and client confidentiality, the ABA is unlikely to view this as unauthorized practice. In India, the *A.K. Balaji v. Union of India and Others* (2010) decision held that LPOs were outside the purview of the Advocates Act because they were not engaged in "legal practice" (Khanna 2017; Singh 2017).

25. In 2013, a spate of complaints against members of the litigating bar began to surface, following public outrage at the December 2012 *Nirbhaya* rape case (where a young paramedic student was severely assaulted and gang-raped by six men inside a moving bus in South Delhi before being thrown out on the road naked, dying a few days later from her injuries). Some were concerned about sexual harassment (see http://timesofindia .indiatimes.com/india/Another-lawyer-opens-up-says-she-too-was-sexually-harassed /articleshow/26060769.cms). Others were public statements about how the bar was gendered, oppressive, and hostile to women generally. For example, members of the Calicut state bar (literally) threw chairs at a woman for writing a Facebook post about gender inequalities in her professional environments (http://www.ukmalayalee.com/kerala-news /news.php?id=MzIyOA). For a statement about the gender disparities and hostile environment confronting female advocates trying to find a voice, see Kalpana Kannabiran (January 18, 2014; http://www.thehindu.com/opinion/op-ed/lawyer-judge-and-aam-aadmi /article5587057.ece).

26. The IDIA Diversity Survey 2013–14 found that 69.11% belonged to the general category, 11.65% to the Scheduled Caste (SC) category, and 5.06% to the Scheduled Tribes (ST) category. About 59% of NLS students were upper caste, 2.3% Other Backward Classes (OBC), 14.9% SC, and 7.1% ST. 10.7% reported not having a caste, while 6% reported being unaware of their caste. Similarly, NLSIU data reveal that Muslims are underrepresented in these schools (Jain et al. 2016:30–32). SC, ST, and OBC are official classifications of the population of India. SC/ST are historically disadvantaged groups with special constitutional sanction (under Articles 341, 342). OBC is a collective category used by the Government of India to classify castes that are economically and socially disadvantaged but *not* by caste (there are forward caste OBCs, for example, as well as Muslim and Christian OBCs). According to constitutional orders in 1950, there are 1,108 SCs in 29 states and 744 STs in 22 states. SCs and STs comprise about 16.6% and 8.6% respectively of the total population (according to the 2011 census). In 2006, the National Commission for Backward Classes (NCBC) estimated that 5,013 castes were OBC, amounting to 41.1% of the population according to the National Sample Survey Organization (which took place the same year). In 2015, the NCBC proposed further classifications and an income ceiling (US$2,222 per year) within the category to ensure that its privileges were not being abused.

27. For example, Bhadbhade at ILS has the distinction of editing the 2013 edition of Pollock and Mulla's Commentary on the Indian Contract Act, a core text on contract law that has formed the basis for much judicial doctrine over the last century. However, even the publisher's catalogue does not mention her name; see www.lexisnexis.in/the-indian -contract-act-1872.htm.

28. For instance, the description of feminist spaces by Professor V. S. Elizabeth, one of the few women with academic tenure in a National Law School, is telling of the kinds of limitations that this freedom comes with for faculty and feminist-identifying students alike: "Most of the women students have been hesitant to openly proclaim that they are feminists fearing the backlash or worried that they will not be so popular with their male

classmates and friends or because they just do not think anything is wrong with the world as it is, having accepted the inequalities as a given. . . . Most people think of feminism in terms of the most radical feminists and most students who call themselves feminists would prefer a liberal feminist perspective, something that does not radically change the world they live in and are familiar with" (Mukhija 2016).

2. *Frames: Women Can't Match Up*

1. And beyond the cultures in institutions they join, and the resultant organizational assimilation, family socialization tempers the kinds of choices that women make and the negotiations they are able to replicate in the environments they join. See, for example, Glenda Flores's recent work (2019) on how parental messages about career and family dynamics more generally impact the gendered career opportunities that Latina physicians make. For familial socialization more generally and the ways in which it might impact high-profile career choices and negotiation, see, with regard to women who decide to run for political office, Fox and Lawless 2003.

2. The OECD data on "math comfort," for example, show some interesting divergences. Girls continue to overperform on reading and underperform in math across the globe, and have since the early 2000s (another reminder that perhaps globalization spreads opportunities but also gendered scripts), but the exceptions (i.e., where boys are significantly *more* likely than girls to feel uncomfortable solving a math problem) are all countries in the Middle East—Jordan, Qatar, and the United Arab Emirates. See interactive data and indicators at http://www.oecd.org/gender/data/notamathperson.htm. Yet, despite higher rates of STEM education than in other parts of the world (women achieve more science and math degrees per capita than their counterparts in the United States and Europe), women are unlikely to maintain careers in the field following this education. See Araine Osman, "Arab Countries Surpass US for Female Enrollment in STEM Fields," *About Her*, October 23, 2017. Sana Odeh (who runs the impressive global Hackathon and Arab Women in Computing program in NYUAD) and colleagues are currently collecting a comprehensive dataset on the region's important work on Gender and STEM.

3. Despite high levels of inequality, especially in the context of labor force participation and unpaid care work, projected growth possibilities for India in comparison to the larger Asia Pacific region are compelling. The 2018 McKinsey Global Institute report, for example, suggests an increment of 18% GDP increase (from current "business as usual" scenarios) or $770 billion to annual GDP by 2025 if the country were to take advantage of its total gender / women's equality opportunity. See Woetzel et al. 2018, exhibits 24, 25.

4. This decline in labor force participation is striking because it reads as a decline in women's equality while also projecting a class-based cultural mechanism in India: improved standards of living have stronger *negative* impacts on female labor force participation since class is performed by *not* needing to work. Along with the increase in education rates for women, these projections of increased participation in the future might depend on the capacity of institutions to create more opportunities for skilled seekers who are wishing to move away from work to "jobs" and eventually careers that they aspire to occupy. See Mehrotra and Parida 2017 on the labor force decline. For an explanation of the gulf between choice and opportunity, see Rukmini reporting on the Nandi Survey on female aspiration and achievement. Also see, from Rukmini, "Indian Girls Brush Up Against Reality," *LiveMint*, November 13, 2018.

5. For instance, there is much lower inequality in professional and technical jobs when compared to labor force participation rates more generally, and these vary drastically between states. See International Labor Organization, *Global Employment Trends*

for Youth 2017: Paths to a Better Working Future (November 20, 2017), figure 4.5 on sector, age-specific employment shares, and skill distribution for young women 2005–15. Also see Chapman et al. 2018, fig. 25, p. 71, on differences in formal and informal labor across states using National Sample Survey Office (NSSO) data 2011–12. Similarly, there is some evidence that women are seeking and moving into more nontraditional professional work like communications, but one can extrapolate from the aspirational gap research (Rukmini 2018) that these are not always uniformly available to all who might seek them, even if we assume that the knowledge of these jobs is universal. These broad variations in data and disparities between what is aspired and achieved are useful in terms of revealing that there is not just "one inequality" story in the Indian context, especially around labor, but they are less useful in being able to offer more descriptive accounts of precisely what type of mechanisms offer these variations. For an important account of informal labor movements across specific industries (e.g., tobacco, construction, domestic work) and the relationship of their varied actors to the state, including gendered movements, see Agarwala 2013.

6. Despite the decrease in labor force participation following liberalization, the majority of female labor remains concentrated in the agricultural and informal sectors (Naqvi 2011).

7. Of the 774 companies (varying from micro-sized firms to those employing more than 25,000 workers) that Chapman and colleagues surveyed, only 26% stated that they would hire female workers in job roles that they saw as having the most growth. Thirty-six percent of respondents stated that they would prefer to hire men, and only 53% suggested that gender was not a factor in evaluating applicants for jobs (suggesting that almost half the surveyed companies *did* think of gender as a factor in evaluating applications even if *only* a third of them actively stated a preference for hiring men). Marital status, age, and family backgrounds all added to the desirability of the applicant, no doubt hurting women's chances for progress differently from men's opportunity. Men are also seen as having the right to fill scarce jobs—presumably enforcing a gendered contract about roles of labor and housework that are implicated in this balance. See Chapman et al. 2018:49–50.

8. For a cross-national review of the status of women in the world's leading professions, see Schultz and Shaw 2003. For a more recent review of the literature on women in the legal profession, see Kay and Gorman's review that covers strides in legal education (301), organizational barriers at entry and hiring (303), perception (315), experience once within the firm (305) especially surrounding sexual harassment (307), and family choices (307) and final outcomes like promotions (309), wage gap (311–314), and quitting (316–317). See Kay and Gorman 2008. For specific accounts on the legal profession, see Kay and Hagan's work on women's disadvantages in collecting different types of cultural law firm human capital (1998). Also See Jennifer Pierce's work on "mothering" gender-based roles that women fall into while seen within organizational spaces like law firms (1996). One of the most foundational pieces of research on women within legal organizations and the barriers they face at entry, experience, and success is Epstein's early work on the subject that remains deeply relevant while trying to understand gendered trajectories within law firms. See Epstein 1993. Specifically, for a review of the barriers to entry and success faced by women in the Indian legal profession, See the recent Rainmaker Report on Challenges Faced by Women in the Legal Profession published in 2012, available at http://www.scribd.com/doc/102128508 /Challenges-Faced-by-Indian-Women-Legal-Professionals-Full-Report.

9. Frank and Cook (1995) argue that the dramatic rise income inequality in the United States over the last twenty years is, at least in part, attributable to the proliferation of "winner-take-all" labor markets, i.e., markets where compensation is determined by relative

performance. Frank and Cook conjecture that technological advances in assessing relative performance have led to the observed proliferation of these types of labor markets in fields such as law, education, banking, and technology, as well as their continued use in markets such as entertainment and sports.

10. Until very recently, there were no entry requirements for entering the legal profession, and graduating from a law university/college with an LL.B. degree was enough to enroll with the Bar Council as an advocate. As a result, these numbers might well be reporting men and women who are not "active" and practicing lawyers, but merely those who have a legal qualification to practice law. The census data, which Michelson (2013) uses, reports practicing lawyers instead of adults with law degrees who are enrolled with a national or state legal bar.

11. See https://insideiim.com/indias-most-gender-diverse-business-schools-iim -indore-xlri-lead-the-way/ and https://insideiim.com/has-the-race-for-women-in-iims -gone-too-far/?src=gendiv.

12. In 1991, the government shifted to a more open economic policy that included, predominantly, a greater involvement of the private sector and the first move toward codified foreign direct investment. For a 10-year review of the implications of these reforms on the country's economic policy, see the influential text by India's former Finance Minister on the subject: Ahluwalia (2002). With specific regard to the impact this liberalization has had on the legal profession and law firms in particular, see the recent work of Jayanth Krishnan that chronicles the history of law firms and legal organizations following the 1991 reforms. Krishnan, following his ethnographic research with different parts of the Indian Bar, casts light on how corporate law firms in India "have garnered great attention from domestic and international clients, academics and media . . . liberalization has enhanced the powers of these lawyers already at the higher end of the pyramid" (p. 4). Krishnan 2013; Indiana Legal Studies Research Paper No. 216. Available at SSRN: http://ssrn.com /abstract=2151529.

13. Indian professional education schools and law schools don't collect admission statistics based on gender generally, but the vertical reservation that was institutionally inserted to recruit women (in the event not enough applied) has never been used because admission is based entirely on an applicant's success on an entrance exam—which has traditionally recruited gender egalitarian cohorts.

14. See Krishnan (2013) at 13–14. Krishnan shows, using data from the British-based consultancy group RSG, that twenty-three of the top forty firms in the country were established post-1991 (eighteen of which were established post-2000). Krishnan does not note this but many of the other firms in the list of "Top 40" were local law practices that reorganized quite dramatically in the years following liberalization. While the oldest firm, Amarchand Mangaldas, was indeed established in 1917, few would argue that its current organization and style is anything like the small, partner-founder-and-family-run practice it was in the years leading to liberalization.

15. See, broadly, on the need for India to borrow from but not replicate this "global" education, Blochand Prasad (2006) at 172, where Block and Prasad talk about India's inability to historically borrow from Western models of professional organization. While clinical education within law schools is, in itself, not a way of training lawyers for large corporate law firm practice, it speaks to the methods in which Indian law schools have recently begun to reorganize in ways that recognize the value of international standards and curriculum following the globalization of the economic markets in 1991. Other prominent scholars of the global legal profession, like John Flood, have heralded India's more recent efforts in legal education (especially the setting up of these new schools) as the "most dynamic experiments in legal education" (24). See Flood 2011. Available at SSRN: http:// ssrn.com/abstract=1906687 or http://dx.doi.org/10.2139/ssrn.1906687

3. Firms: Just Like an International Firm

1. And, in fact, Silicon Valley has been notoriously *in* the news for its treatment of female professionals. Some of this is explained by Ridgeway's argument (2011) that for background frameworks of gender to not be imposing on women, novelty in organizations needs to be coupled with newness in field of emergence. Silicon Valley had new firms, but not a new field ("tech," the field within which it emerged, was still strongly male-typed). For the persistent frameworks of gender in tech, See Acker 1990; Correll 2001; Baron et al. 2007; Cech et al. 2011. For research highlighting the difference in gendered experiences between tech start-ups and biotech start-ups (which were new organizations in the relatively gender-neutral field of life sciences), see Smith-Doerr 2004.

2. There is new evidence that, despite institutional mechanisms in many schools (e.g., often unused vertical reservations that were structurally in place to assure gender ratios in law schools), gender ratios in law schools are become *less* egalitarian over time. The NUJS Diversity Report (Sharma et al. 2020) alludes to this drop in gender ratios, despite female law students continuing to do better than their male colleagues in terms of grades. As this book was in the final stages of edits, for example, *Legally India* published analysis of the National Institutional Ranking Framework data on how most law schools have a gender deficit at the undergraduate level. There are some exceptions to these data, but they skew in favor of male representation, especially in the top-ranked schools and in non-LLM programs. This is not surprising given all that we know about feminization and the tendency of sites and institutions to become male skewed as they get more and more prestigious, and it leads to much less optimism about the futures of these accidental sites of parity. See "Digging Through NIRF Rankings: Most LLBs Have Big Gender Deficit," https://www.legallyindia.com/lawschools/digging-the-nirf-2020-law-school-rankings-most-llbs-have-big-gender-deficit-except-ail-kiit-sls-nliu-makes-good-case-for-more-reservations-llms-dominated-by-women-except-nls-20200616-11485, June 16, 2020.

3. With the expansion of international business over the last three decades, new kinds of organizational forms, processes, and phenomena have emerged to sustain and supplement different models of global production. In particular, as I set up in chapter 1, in response to the demand for efficient and territory-agnostic services, there has been a rise in complex "transnational" (Bartlett and Goshal 1989) or "globally integrated" (Palmisano 2006) organizations that purport to blur the boundaries between the local and the global (Prahalad and Doz 1999). Many scholars have developed useful tools to dissect this global proliferation and integration, and especially to underscore the ways in which organizations around the world have begun to develop certain immutable cultural codes, institutional theories of legitimacy (Meyer and Rowan 1977), and convergence (Hannan and Freeman 1977; DiMaggio and Powell 1983; Meyer, Scott, and Deal 1983). From this perspective, global organizational convergence is explained by the various legitimacy concerns that modern organizations face. Global codes, norms, and organizational schemes, despite being less rational in structure for many local contexts, take root in globally competitive environments to alleviate local concerns of legitimacy (Meyer et al. 1983). From the adopter's perspective, this convergence offers an antidote to uncertain environments. That is, where "goals are ambiguous or where the environment creates symbolic uncertainty, organizations may model themselves on other organizations" (Powell and DiMaggio 1991:69).

4. Isomorphism refers to the similarity of the processes or structure of one organization to those of another. The theory was posited by Paul DiMaggio and Walter Powell in 1983 as a way of theorizing the increasing homogenization of organizations and institutions around the world. There are three main kinds of institutional isomorphism: normative, coercive, and mimetic. The first two, as the names imply, suggest that organizations begin to look the

same as a result of developmental conditions that suggest or require it. The third, mimetic, is a result of imitation.

5. Hannan and Freeman (1977) framed this as a competitive survival tactic: organizations feel the demands of their competitive environments and converge in order to stay ahead of or catch up with their peers. Later, DiMaggio and Powell (1983) argued that isomorphism can also serve as a marker of institutional viability. Regardless of the motivation, however, over time this dynamic will result in a field-level isomorphism as more and more organizations turn to the same scripts for legitimacy. This convergence might come at the cost of creativity and innovation, but it reduces overall risk and transaction costs.

6. In 1977, John Meyer and Brain Rowan theorized that despite the proliferation of organizational norms across the world following globalization, there were certain unavoidable gaps between formal policies and the actual organizational practices that followed in their stead. The scattered empirical evidence of this theory in understanding modern corporations offers a consistent and pessimistic picture: modern organizations undergo a process of institutional isomorphism (Kanter 1972; Aldrich 1979; DiMaggio and Powell 1983) because they seek power, legitimacy, and economic fitness (Powell and DiMaggio 1991, 66). However, despite their best efforts, they fall short in their mimicking of these global norms, because they are saddled with a "liability of foreignness" (Zaheer 1995), or because they pay lip service to technical rather than institutional rules (Meyer et al. 1983), or because their modeling makes them less, not more, efficient (DiMaggio and Powell 1983). I use "decoupling" here in a broad Meyerian sense, as a way of understanding this difference between the actual and the ideal.

7. Cyril Shroff's interview with Todd Benjamin for the International Bar Association, September 2013, available at http://www.ibanet.org/Article/Detail.aspx?ArticleUid =34f5ec5d-7a44-42ca-a1f9-0bdbaa0c716a.

8. Local independent consultants worked across a range of industries essentially as freelancers. But the main industry players were all global professional service firms with a renewed India presence following the 1991 liberalization.

9. The professionals in these firms were often from similar class and cultural backgrounds in that they were highly educated, urban, English-speaking, and middle class. To the extent that class was dictating their entry and experience, they should have experienced similar advantages across these firms. I consider the implications of these variations in fuller detail in chapter 6.

10. Having said that, all elite firms hire from similarly elite Indian institutions, and in each of the firms I studied, few (if any) partners had international credentials. There were, however, differences in the gender compositions of these elite schools as well as the kinds of education they offered. While elite engineering and business schools (standard for consultant and banking hires) typically skewed male, elite law schools (products, again, of a post-liberalization reform) graduated equal numbers of men and women. Further, unlike business and engineering schools, elite law schools in India exposed students to strong meritocratic scripts (like feminist jurisprudence, gender studies classes) which might also have played a part in the kinds of expectations these lawyers brought to their environments. See chapter 2.

11. While this research does not include comprehensive data about clients, the role of clients remained integral to respondents' market justifications for gender egalitarianism across these firms. See chapter 4.

12. The "queen bee" phenomenon in male-dominated organizations has long been theorized (Staines et al. 1974; Kanter 1993) as a way in which senior women distance themselves from junior women to legitimize gender inequality in organizations in ways that can protect themselves. As organizations that are not intrinsically gendered in typical ways, this phenomenon might play out differently here. Even so, it is worth noting that despite

its name, this is not a gendered organizational actor response as much as a minority actor response that is performed by other marginalized groups too (Derks et al. 2016). Further still, it is integral to view these actions—to the extent they exist—as *response* to hierarchical, gendered tendencies in organizations. For another kind of similar "response," see Ballakrishnen, Fielding-Singh, and Magliozzi (2019) on women performing intentional invisibility.

13. This was not a straightforward pattern or response. Even among senior women partners who had opted out of traditional relationships or had not had children, there were differences. One, for example, felt that she had worked hard to get to her position, and that the "younger generation" that expected to balance family and work seamlessly but left soon after she had invested in them for a few years in order to have children or move away for marriage, just did not have the same commitment. Others felt more sympathy—at least in their conversations with me—about this need for balance between work and family that those with children had to achieve that they themselves had chosen not to. Agency in choice-making, of course, is often retrospective. But I highlight it here because I think it helps frame narratives of deserved career movement and legitimate achievement.

14. But this assumption was not always to reinvest in local careers. As I show in other work (Ballakrishnen 2011), foreign credentialing was not common for corporate lawyers in India because it was not seen as essential in the context and it had a variable advantage that did not always have straightforward rewards upon reentry. It certainly did not guarantee a linear advancement within these firms upon return, although it might have had soft advantages in interactions with foreign clients.

15. Most professionals I spoke to conceded that they had really good support systems and were "spoilt" by the advantage of having domestic help (while comparing their positions with similarly situated women in other parts of the world), but they also saw it as an advantage that was common for most people in the middle class in India and not necessarily a structural advantage particular to them. Instead, what was common alongside this acknowledgment of help as being useful was that it was only useful to a certain extent and for specific kinds of work. Childcare, for example, was considered hard to outsource because of the lack of "proper" or "good" carework available given class disparities. *Ayahs*, for example, were good to help grandparents or other family members who stayed home with tasks such as cleaning and food preparation, but their lack of language proficiency (most domestic help do not speak English, for example) made parents—and mothers in particular—wary of seeing them as capable primary caretakers of their children when they were away. As one such mother, a lawyer who was debating leaving her firm job to work in-house because she thought the hours might be better for her children, "yes we have help, but if something was to happen, they cannot even call an ambulance or the doctor, they will not be able to communicate . . . leaving your children alone at home then is risky." This note about good carework might be a functional worry about risk, but it also highlights another form of cultural capital that parents seek to transfer to their children—a certain kind of expected socialization that domestic help were not deemed capable of offering. As chapter 5 suggests, this is what made the advantage of having proximate family—or family that could be made proximate—central to the support structures that parents could rely on to navigate this work and life balance. Parents—and especially mothers, who were not part of the workforce themselves—of professionals could offer that kind of "good" carework while also relying on labor from other hired help to do the chores necessary to keep the household running (e.g., Maya, as discussed in chapter 5). This splitting of high- and lowbrow tasks within the house to achieve the work/life balance offers additional evidence for evaluating the steep costs of this equality and the shoulders that must bear its brunt. On the "micropolitics of mothering" in other contexts, see Macdonald 2011. On intimate carework and support performed by senior familial women, see Utrata 2015 for a discussion

of youth privilege and grandmother support for single mothers in Russia. On nannies and the politics of class, labor, and boundary-making through language and other social capital markers, generally see Ehrenreich, Hochschild, and Kay 2003.

16. See Mobley et al. 1994; Ramaswamy et al. 2010; Wallace 2001 on mentorship and gender dynamics for women in the legal profession; See also, more generally on quality of mentor and kinds of relationships that can hold sustainable advantage for women, Ragins et al. 2000; Blake-Beard et al. 2006.

17. For instance, as I explain in chapter 5, many of the successful women I interviewed shared how much they depended on large family support systems, usually mothers and mothers-in-law who stayed at home with them and never entered the workforce. So, these outcomes were certainly buttressed by a micro-demographic story at the individual level.

4. Facings: My Clients Prefer a Woman Lawyer

1. This was a rare occurrence in my interviews with lawyers. Women in these firms rarely, if at all, brought up blatant interactions where they felt their clients were priming gender. In itself, this is not that surprising—discrimination is not often as blatant and biases are much more likely to be implicit. But seen here in the context of how it worked in other professional sites, the "comfort" for some women in relation to others was palpable. On the importance of "career referents" for evaluating satisfaction in framing self-narratives of navigation, especially for women, see Gibson and Lawrence 2010.

2. It is worthwhile noting that this strategy (or, if not active strategy, this recognition of usefulness) of deference was not just practiced by women. Men and women alike wished to distance themselves from being thought of as aggressive because of the ways in which it was coded both by clients and colleagues alike. A senior male partner felt similarly about his colleagues (other men who performed aggression in dealings with clients as well as their peers within the firm and had accumulated bad "interactional capital" because of it). Instead, for this partner too, "not asking" for unreasonable things and allowing these other aggressive actors to speak out instead was a useful way to navigate difficult negotiations, especially among his peers, because it allowed him to "protect his positive capital without attracting negative capital." His framing of these transactions as rooted in capital is of course telling too.

5. Families: It Is (Not Always) Difficult
Once You Have a Family

1. The After the JD (AJD) project is an empirical study of the career outcomes of a cohort of almost 5,000 new lawyers, offering both a nationally representative picture of lawyer career trajectories and an in-depth portrait of the careers of women and racial and ethnic minority lawyers. The AJD is the first and most ambitious effort to gather systematic, detailed data about the careers and experiences of a national cross-section of law graduates. It follows a large national sample of lawyers admitted to the bar in 2000 over the first decade of their career and is a unique source of information on the changing nature of legal careers. The AJD study design is longitudinal, following the careers of new lawyers during the first ten years following law school graduation; the first cohort "wave" of lawyers was surveyed in 2002, the second in 2007, and the third in 2012. In the first wave of these data, women were more likely than men to have delayed marriage and childbearing (Dinovitzer and Garth 2004). By wave two, where the same respondents had spent seven more years in their legal careers (Nelson et al. 2009), this dramatically shifted but the gender difference remained (17.9% of women were never married as compared to 15.2% men; 75% of women reported that they were in committed relationships compared to 7% of men,

and 54% of women had at least one child compared to 59% of men). By wave three, almost three quarters of the women and 80% of the men were married or remarried. Women in wave 3 of these data were also significantly more likely to indicate that they were working part time (15%) or not working (9%) in order to take care of children. In contrast, 96% of the men worked full time (Dinovitzer et al. 2014:68). The research by Plickert and Hagan (2011) suggests that while family formation and fertility have similar patterns across Germany and the United States, legal cultures valorize these choices differently. While the legal culture in Germany offers greater autonomy for parenting but reduced economic rewards, the meg-law culture of the United States offers the reverse (i.e., less autonomy for parenting but enhanced economic prospects). Altogether these data call for more nuanced dissections of career outcomes of high-status professionals as dissected by life course courses and choices (e.g., Plickert 2019).

2. In the United States, for example, the decade between 1963 and 1974 boasts the first set of legislative wins for this particular social movement. In particular, the Equal Pay Act of 1963 is seen as the first legislative victory for women's equality in the workforce, although its actual implications for equality have been contested since. Nonetheless this 1963 legislation along with Title VII of the Civil Rights Act of 1964, Title IX and the Women's Educational Equity Act (1972, 1975), Title X (1970, health and family planning), the Equal Credit Opportunity Act (1974) and the Pregnancy Discrimination Act of 1978 are seen as the first set of movement milestones. For a review of the early implications of the 1963 legislation, see Murphy 1970. For a review of the first comprehensive analysis of its implication for the theory of "comparable worth," see Treiman and Hartmann 1981.

3. Housework in the Indian context, as I show in this chapter, is a little bit more complicated. Professional women in my sample were in charge of housework management (i.e., in terms of employing other women to do such housework) but not in ways that pattern India's larger gender disparities in sharing such work. Wider demographic data on unpaid labor in India confirm that women do more unpaid daily housework than men, one of the highest in the world, second only to Mexico. Indian men, on the other hand, do some of the *least* unpaid daily work globally (more only than Japan and Korea). See OECD time use data available at https://stats.oecd.org/Index.aspx?datasetcode=TIME_USE.

4. See Makhija and Raha 2012. While firms were sampled in the report (29.2 %), they were predominantly Delhi-based firms (only 10% of the total sample was from the Mumbai Big Law Firm population). This also suggests that there might be something about the culture of these Mumbai firms that further advantages these women. For a fuller research methodology, see pp. 4–6 of the report. For information on demographics, including sectors and cities in the sample, age profile, experience, qualifications, income, and family structures, see pp. 6–13.

6. Futures: Now What?

1. The *Butterfly Effect* is a chaos theory explanation that considers the limitations in predictability. Specifically, it is meant to capture the sensitive dependence on initial conditions in which a miniscule change at one level of a system can result at a later stage in a large difference in outcome. The metaphorical example most commonly used (thereby coining the term) is the example of the details of a tornado (e.g., the time of its formation, its path, and following dependency) being influenced by seemingly insignificant perturbations such as the flapping of the wings of a distant butterfly several weeks prior to the actual event. See Lorenz 1995 (appendix 1) for a more technical elaboration. For ways in which its extensions in popular culture have been flawed, see Dizikes 2008.

2. The Hurun Global Rich List (2015) tracks billionaires globally. As per the 2015 Report, only 5% of India's super-wealthy were described as "self-made, but with a helping

hand from parents," while 9% "inherited a small business and grew it big time." In China however, the report said 61% of billionaires were "self-made," without any financial support from their families. See Patel 2015.

3. Only 3.5% of all next-generation family members globally want to take over their parents' firm directly after college graduation; 4.9% plan to do so five years later, according to a study, "Coming home or breaking free," published by Ernst and Young in 2014. See Mandavia 2016.

4. International degrees are especially crucial currency for family businesses that are on the verge of globalizing operations. See, for example, the kinds of management and other degrees from prestigious US universities that second-generation family business owners acquire prior to running international wings of their conglomerate business. For example, the son of pharmaceutical company might have studied molecular biology at a prestigious American University before being put in charge of international marketing.

5. For example, in her book on the new Pakistani middle class, Ammara Maqsood (2017) argues that global modernity has many strains of lived experience beyond Western mimicking. Maqsood's research reveals how in the context of urban Lahore, a visibly religious and pious upwardly mobile group performs a variant of modernity that eschews the Western norm of global. Instead, through community choices, piety performance, and even clothing, this new class does modernity through adherence to Saudi-inspired cultural capital.

6. Fuller and Narasimhan argue that this ability to leverage caste-related appropriation has been central not only as a way of retaining old hierarchies but also as a means of wielding new power over emerging hierarchies (2014:65–73). Much of their research for this project focuses on the ways in which Brahmins have been at the forefront of the IT sector—where, they suggest, contemporary flexible logics of work have allowed Brahmins to suggest that they are accessing caste-neutral new advantages while in fact maintaining the structural privilege of their caste piety by doing good and respectable work. This reframing of cultural capital as merit and the ability of newness to offer such potential is an important takeaway. Still, it is in their ability to offer historic extensions that their case shines. In their profile of C. V. Raman, for instance, their case rests on the fact that the acclaimed Nobel Prize–winning Indian physicist could afford to perform Hindu piety without it being seen as religious because he'd also claimed the identity of a nonbeliever (74). This ability to shape-shift is central to the performance of cultural capital, especially when legitimated in (and by) modern environments.

7. See McCammon et al. 2001 re: the implications this has for social movements and their ability to succeed within embedded possibilities. For an alternative history that argues that Smith actually saw gendered politics as aligning with his otherwise nonprogressive politics, and found synergies with suffragists Alice Paul and Martha Griffiths, see Louis Menand, "How Women Got in on the Civil Rights Act," New Yorker, July 14, 2014.

8. Although some participation fell at the end of the war in some sites and industries (especially if they were male dominated prior to the war, and high status), the war, a natural historical "accident" for the purposes of the movement, still set in motion a path dependency that would change the course of women's employment possibilities, cultures, and futures. See Meyerowitz (1994) regarding women and gender in postwar America and the cultures of their resultant institutions, including for immigrant workers. Brinton (1993) makes the case for how gendered employment participation was not a function of just late industrial development or an essentialist sex-role assignment, but rather a more direct connection of the social and economic institutions in postwar Japan. Brinton warns us that this was not something that "just happened," that it was purposive, but it was not without the institutional impetus of its postwar generation. As this book goes to press, the world seems engulfed in yet another kind of global historic moment—the COVID-19

Pandemic—that will threaten the fates of work and workers as we know it; it will remain to be seen what kinds of incidental outcomes and reconfigurations of gendered rights this will offer a chance to emerge.

9. Necessity, of course, is philosophically fungible, since one could—and Goodrich did, while discussing etymology—argue that it is merely an expression of the extents of our knowledge. We don't know we *need* a thing until we have it. Like most technology, perhaps, or, my favorite extension, the discovery of new (but still, necessarily, old) Love.

10. For the traditional theories of societal stratification as inevitable and functionally essential, see Parsons 1940 and Davis and Moore 1945. For critique and critical analysis, See Tumin 1953. For empirical predictions of the original theory and more contemporary evidence of the persistence of this "gloom" logic, See Stinchcombe 1963 and Grusky and Ku 2008 respectively.

11. A line from the poem "All Roads" in Billy Corgan's collection of poems, *Blinking with Fists* (London: Faber & Faber, 2004).

Appendix. Research Methods

1. As other qualitative scholars who "study up" (i.e., study sites and people who are structurally more powerful than they are) have argued, these hierarchies are complicated and not always linear (e.g., see Ortner 2010 re: studying Hollywood as an anthropologist living in the same city). The elite professionals I studied were more powerful than I am in some ways, but they were also made vulnerable anew because of how much of their lives they shared with me during this process and how much more easily they could be outed because of it than other more generalizable respondents. My interest in culling from these exchanges representative data had to be consistently balanced against the recognition that these individuals were harder to anonymize than those from other projects I was involved in. But these other projects (especially one in which I was doing fieldwork in Kerala studying families of migrant laborers) reminded me of the power exchanges inherent in access and use of data like these. It might have been easier in some ways to gain access to the sites I studied in this book than in an insular village in rural Kerala where people were (legitimately) suspicious of me in their midst. But once I did get the data, using it and analyzing it had different challenges. For thinking differently about this process of studying up, especially in critical gender outcomes within set institutions, see Priyadarshini 2003.

BIBLIOGRAPHY

Abel, Rick, Hammerslev, Ole, Sommerlad, Hilary, and Schultz, Ulrike. 2020. *Lawyers in 21st-Century Societies. Volume 1: National Reports.* London: Hart.

Aaftaab, Naheed Gina. 2012. "Branding a Global Identity: Labor Anxieties, Conspicuous Consumption, and Middle-Class Culture in Hyderabad, India." PhD dissertation, University of Minnesota, available at http://hdl.handle.net/11299/133072.

Abu-Lughod, Lila. 1991. "Writing against Culture." In Richard G. Fox, ed., *Recapturing Anthropology: Working in the Present*, pp. 137–154. Santa Fe, NM: School of American Research.

Abu-Lughod, Lila. ed. 1998. *Remaking Women: Feminism and Modernity in the Middle East.* Princeton, NJ: Princeton University Press.

Abu-Lughod, Lila. 2013. *Do Muslim Women Need Saving?* Cambridge, MA: Harvard University Press.

Acker, Joan. 1990. "Hierarchies, Jobs, Bodies: A Theory of Gendered Organizations." *Gender & Society* 4(2): 139–158.

Acker, Joan. 2006. "Inequality Regimes: Gender, Class, and Race in Organizations." *Gender & Society* 20, 4(1): 441–464.

Adams, Tracey L. 2005. "Feminization of Professions: The Case of Women in Dentistry." *Canadian Journal of Sociology/Cahiers Canadiens de Sociologie* 30(1): 71–94.

Afzal-Khan, Fawzia. 2010. *Cultural Imperialism and the Indo-English Novel: Genre and Ideology in RK Narayan, Anita Desai, Kamala Markandaya, and Salman Rushdie.* University Park, PA: Penn State University Press.

Agarwala, Rina. 2013. *Informal Labor, Formal Politics, and Dignified Discontent in India.* Cambridge: Cambridge University Press.

Ahluwalia, Montek S. 2002. "Economic Reforms in India since 1991: Has Gradualism Worked?" *Journal of Economic Perspectives* 16(3): 67–88.

Ahmed, Sara. 2012. *On Being Included: Racism and Diversity in Institutional Life.* Durham, NC: Duke University Press.

Ahmed, Sara. 2016. *Living a Feminist Life.* Durham, NC: Duke University Press.

Albiston, Catherine. 2007. "Institutional Perspectives on Law, Work, and Family." *Annual Review of Law & Social Science* 3 (December).

Albiston, Catherine. 2009. "Institutional Inequality" (November 12, 2010). *Wisconsin Law Review* 2009, no. 5.

Al Dabbagh, May. 2015. "Saudi Arabian Women and Group Activism." *Journal of Middle East Women's Studies* 11(2): 235.

Al Dabbagh, May, Bowles, Hannah Riley, and Thomason, Bobbi. 2016. "Status Reinforcement in Emerging Economies: The Psychological Experience of Local Candidates Striving for Global Employment." *Organization Science* 27(6): 1453–1471.

Al Dabbagh, May, and Gargani, Ghalia. 2011. "Negotiating Identity: New Perspectives on the Globalization and Identity Debate in the GCC." Dubai School of Government Working Papers, 11(4).

Aldrich, Howard. 1979. *Organizations and Environments.* Englewood Cliffs, NJ: Prentice-Hall.

Allen, Tammy D., and Russell, Joyce E. A. 1999. "Parental Leave of Absence: Some Not So Family-Friendly Implications." *Journal of Applied Social Psychology* 29(1): 166–191.

Allendorf, Keera. 2013. "Schemas of Marital Change: From Arranged Marriages to Eloping for Love." *Journal of Marriage and Family* 75(2): 453–469.

Altorki, Soraya, and El-Solh, Camillia Fawzi, eds. 1988. *Arab Women in the Field: Studying Your Own Society*. Syracuse, NY: Syracuse University Press.

Anagol, Padma. 2005. *The Emergence of Feminism in India, 1850–1920*. London: Ashgate.

Anderson, Benedict. 2006 [1983]. *Imagined Communities: Reflections on the Origin and Spread of Nationalism*. London: Verso.

Anderson, Elisabeth. 2018. "Policy Entrepreneurs and the Origins of the Regulatory Welfare State: Child Labor Reform in Nineteenth-century Europe." *American Sociological Review* 83(1): 173–211.

Appadurai, Arjun. 1996. *Modernity at Large: Cultural Dimensions of Globalization*. Vol. 1. Minneapolis: University of Minnesota Press.

Appadurai, Arjun. 2004. "The Capacity to Aspire: Culture and the Terms of Recognition." In Vijayendra Rao and Michael Walton, eds.,   *Culture and Public Action*, pp. 59–84. Stanford, CA: Stanford University Press.

Armstrong, Elizabeth A., and Hamilton, Laura T. 2013. *Paying for the Party*. Cambridge, MA: Harvard University Press.

Arondekar, Anjali. 2009. *For the Record: On Sexuality and the Colonial Archive in India*. Durham, NC: Duke University Press.

Arondekar, Anjali, and Patel, Geeta. 2016. "Area Impossible: Notes toward an Introduction." *GLQ: A Journal of Lesbian and Gay Studies* 22(2): 151–171.

Arora, Satish K. 1972. "Social Background of the Indian Cabinet." *Economic and Political Weekly*, 1523–1532.

Arun, Shoba. 1999. "Does Land Ownership Make a Difference? Women's Roles in Agriculture in Kerala, India." *Gender & Development* 7(3): 19–27.

Aumann, Kerstin, Galinsky, Ellen, and Matos, Kenneth. 2011. "The New Male Mystique." Hillsborough, NJ: Families and Work Institute. Report available online at familiesandwork.org/research/2011/the-new-male-mystique.

Azeem, Ahmad. 2016. "Delhi Has Maximum Number of 'Munnabhai' Lawyers, Verification Process Reveals." *India Today*, June 2. Available online at https://www.indiatoday.in/india/story/delhi-fake-lawyers-supreme-court-bci-12011-2016-06-02.

Babcock, Linda C., and Laschever, Sara. 2003. *Women Don't Ask: Negotiation and the Gender Divide*. Princeton, NJ and Woodstock: Princeton University Press.

Baker, Joe G. 2003. "Glass Ceilings or Sticky Floors? A Model of High-Income Law Graduates." *Journal of Labor Research* 24(4): 695–711.

Ballakrishnen, Swethaa S. 2009. "Where Did We Come From? Where Do We Go? An Enquiry into the Students and Systems of Legal Education in India." *Journal of Commonwealth Law and Legal Education* 7(2): 133–154.

Ballakrishnen, Swethaa S. 2011. "Homeward Bound: What Does a Global Legal Education Offer the Indian Returnees." *Fordham Law Review* 80: 2441.

Ballakrishnen, Swethaa S. 2012. "'I Love My American Job': Professional Prestige in the Indian Outsourcing Industry and Global Consequences of an Expanding Legal Profession." *International Journal of the Legal Profession* 19(2–3): 379–404.

Ballakrishnen, Swethaa S. 2016. "India (international) Inc.: Global Work and the (re-) Organization of Professionalism in Emerging India." *The Routledge Companion to the Professions and Professionalism*, 265–282.

Ballakrishnen, Swethaa S. 2020. "Present and Future: A Revised Sociological Portrait of the Indian Legal Profession." In Ole Hammerslev, Hilary Sommerlad, Rick Abel, & Ulrike Shultz, eds., *Lawyers in 21st Century Society*. London, UK: Hart.

Ballakrishnen, Swethaa S., and Dezalay, Sara. Forthcoming 2021. *Invisible Institutionalisms: Collective Reflections from the Shadows of Legal Globalization*. London: Hart.

Ballakrishnen, Swethaa S., Fielding-Singh, Priya, and Magliozzi, Devon. 2019. "Intentional Invisibility: Professional Women and the Navigation of Workplace Constraints (May 13, 2018)." *Sociological Perspectives* 62(1): 23–41.

Ballakrishnen, Swethaa S., and Samuel, Rupali Francesca. 2020. "India's Women Legal Academics: Who They Are and Where You May Find Them." In Ulrike Schultz et al., eds., *Gender and Careers in the Legal Academy*. London: Hart.

Ballakrishnen, Swethaa S., and Silver, Carole. 2019. "A New Minority? International JD Students in US Law Schools." *Law & Social Inquiry* 44(3): 647–678.

Banerjee, Kakoli. 1999. "Gender Stratification and the Contemporary Marriage Market in India." *Journal of Family Issues* 20(5): 648–676.

Banerji, Manjistha, Steven Martin, and Sonalde Desai. 2013. "Are the Young and Educated More Likely to Have "Love" than Arranged Marriage? A Study of Autonomy of Partner Choice in India." *Working Paper Series* (pp. 1–43). New Delhi: NCAER.

Bansode, Rupali. 2020. "The Missing Dalit Women in Testimonies of #Metoo Sexual Violence: Learnings for Social Movements." *Contributions to Indian Sociology* 54(1): 76–82.

Baron, James. N., Hannan, Michael. T., Hsu, Greta., and Koçak, Özgecan. 2007. "In the Company of Women: Gender Inequality and the Logic of Bureaucracy in Start-Up Firms." *Work and Occupations* 34(1): 35–66.

Barreto, Ilídio. 2010. "Dynamic Capabilities: A Review of Past Research and an Agenda for the Future." *Journal of Management* 36(1): 256–280.

Barreto, Manuela, and Ellemers, Naomi. 2005. "The Burden of Benevolent Sexism: How It Contributes to the Maintenance of Gender Inequalities." *European Journal of Social Psychology* 35(5): 633–642.

Barreto, Manuela, Ellemers, Naomi, Piebinga, Laura, and Moya, Miguel. 2010. "How Nice of Us and How Dumb of Me: The Effect of Exposure to Benevolent Sexism on Women's Task and Relational Self-Descriptions." *Sex Roles* 62(7–8): 532–544.

Bartlett, Christopher. A., and Ghoshal, Sumantra. 1989. *Managing Across Borders: The Transnational Solution*. Cambridge, MA: Harvard Business School Press.

Basheer, Shamnad., Krishnaprasad, K. V., Mitra, Sree, and Mohapatra, Prajna. 2017. "The Making of Legal Elites and the IDIA of Justice." In Wilkins et al., *The Indian Legal Profession*.

Basheer, Shamnad, and Mukherjee, Sroyon. 2010. Regulating Indian Legal Education: Some Thoughts for Reform (January 1. Available online at SSRN: https://ssrn.com/abstract=1584037 or http://dx.doi.org/10.2139/ssrn.1584037.

Baviskar, Amita, and Ray, Raka, eds. 2011. *Elite and Everyman: The Cultural Politics of the Indian Middle Classes*. Delhi: Routledge.

Berlant, Lauren. 2011. *Cruel Optimism*. Durham, NC: Duke University Press.

Bhandari, Parul. 2019. "The Secret Lives of Money: Understanding Elite Women of Delhi." In Surinder S. Jodhka and Jules Naudet, eds., *Mapping the Elite: Power, Privilege, and Inequality*. New Delhi: Oxford University Press.

Bhandari, Parul. 2020. *Matchmaking in Middle Class India: Beyond Arranged and Love Marriage*. Singapore: Springer Nature.

Bhatt, Amy. 2018. *High-tech Housewives: Indian IT Workers, Gendered Labor, and Trans-migration*. Seattle: University of Washington Press.

Bhatt, Amy, Murty, Madhavi, and Ramamurthy, Priti. 2010. "Hegemonic Developments: The New Indian Middle Class, Gendered Subalterns, and Diasporic Returnees in the Event of Neoliberalism." *Signs: Journal of Women in Culture and Society* 36(1): 127–152.

Bielby, William T., and Baron, James N. 1984. "A Woman's Place Is with Other Women: Sex Segregation Within Organizations." In Barbara Reskin, ed., *Sex Segregation in the*

Workplace: Trends, Explanations, Remedies, pp. 27–55. Washington, DC: National Academic Press.

Birla, Ritu. 2009. *Stages of Capital: Law, Culture, and Market Governance in Late Colonial India.* Durham, NC: Duke University Press.

Birla, Ritu. 2015. "Jurisprudence of Emergence: Neo-Liberalism and the Public as Market in India." *South Asia: Journal of South Asian Studies* 38(3): 466–480.

Bjork-James, Sophie. 2020. "Book Reviews of Johnson 2019 and Bowler 2019." *Journal of the American Academy of Religion* 88(2): 594–599.

Blair-Loy, Mary. 2009. *Competing Devotions.* Cambridge, MA: Harvard University Press.

Blair-Loy, Mary, and Wharton, Amy S. 2002. "Employees' Use of Work-Family Policies and the Workplace Social Context." *Social Forces* 80(3): 813–845.

Blake-Beard, Stacy, Murrell, Audrey J., and Thomas, David A. 2006. *Unfinished Business: The Impact of Race on Understanding Mentoring Relationships.* Division of Research, Harvard Business School.

Blau, Francine D., and Kahn, Lawrence M. 2000. "Gender Differences in Pay." *Journal of Economic Perspectives* 14(4): 75–99.

Bloch, Frank S., and Prasad, M.R.K. 2006. "Institutionalizing a Social Justice Mission for Clinical Legal Education: Cross-National Currents from India and the United States." *Clinical Law Review* 13: 165.

Bolton, Sharon, and Muzio, Daniel. 2008. "The Paradoxical Processes of Feminization in the Professions: The Case of Established, Aspiring and Semi-Professions." *Work, Employment and Society* 22(2): 281–299.

Bourdieu, Pierre. 1972. *Outline of a Theory of a Practice.* Cambridge: Cambridge University Press.

Bowler, Kate. 2019. *The Preachers's Wife: The Precarious Power of Evangelical Women Celebrities.* Princeton, NJ: Princeton University Press.

Bowles, Hannah Riley. 2012. "Claiming Authority: How Women Explain Their Ascent to Top Business Leadership Positions." *Research in Organizational Behavior* 32: 189–212.

Bowles, Hannah Riley, Babcock, Linda, and Lei Lai. 2007. "Social Incentives for Gender Differences in the Propensity to Initiate Negotiations: Sometimes It Does Hurt to Ask." *Organizational Behavior and Human Decision Processes* 103(1): 84–103.

Brescoll, Victoria, and Moss-Racusin, Corinne. 2007. "How to Walk the Tightrope of 'Nice and Able': Overcoming Workplace Challenges for Female Bosses." *Psychology of Women Quarterly* 31(2): 217–218.

Brinton, Mary C. 1993. *Women and the Economic Miracle: Gender and Work in Postwar Japan.* Vol. 21. Berkeley and Los Angeles: University of California Press.

Britton, Dana M. 2017. "Beyond the Chilly Climate: The Salience of Gender in Women's Academic Careers." *Gender & Society* 31(1): 5–27.

Brooks, Rachel. 2012. "Student-Parents and Higher Education: A Cross-National Comparison" *Journal of Education Policy* 27(3): 423–439.

Buddhapriya, Sanghamitra. 1999. Women in management. New Delhi: APH.

Budhwar, Pawan, Saini, Debi S., and Bhatnagar, Jyotsna. 2005. "Women in Management in the New Economic Environment: The Case of India." *Asia Pacific Business Review* 11 (2): 179–193.

Burawoy, Michael, Blum, Joseph, George, Sheba, Gille, Zsuza, Gowan, Teresa, Haney, Lynne, Klawiter, Maren, Lopez, Steve, Riain, Sean, and Thaye, Millie. 2000. *Global Ethnography: Forces, Connections, and Imaginations in a Post-Modern World.* Berkeley: University of California Press.

Butler, Judith. 2004. *Undoing Gender.* New York: Routledge.

Caplan, Patricia. 1985. *Gender and Class in India: Women and Their Organisations in a South Indian City.* London: Tavistock.

Carbado, Devon W., Williams Crenshaw, Kimberlé, Mays, Vickie M., and Tomlinson, Barbara. 2013. "Intersectionality: Mapping the Movements of a Theory." *Du Bois Review: Social Science Research on Race* 10(2): 303–312.

Carvalho Pinto, Vânia. 2012. *Nation-Building, State and the Gender Framing of Women's Rights in the United Arab Emirates (1971–2009).* Reading, NY: Ithaca Press.

Cech, Erin. 2015. "Engineers and Engineeresses? Self-conceptions and the Development of Gendered Professional Identities." *Sociological Perspectives* 58(1): 56–77.

Cech, Erin, and Blair-Loy, Mary. 2019. "The Changing Career Trajectories of New Parents in STEM." *Proceedings of the National Academy of Sciences* 116(10): 4182–4187.

Cech, Erin, Rubineau, Brian, Seron, Caroll, and Silbey, Susan S. 2011. "Professional Role Confidence and Gendered Persistence in Engineering." *American Sociological Review* 76(5): 641–666.

Chakravarti, Uma. 2003. *Gendering Caste Through a Feminist Lens.* Mumbai: Popular Prakashan. http:/books. google.com/books.

Chakravartty, Paula. 2006. "Symbolic Analysts or Indentured Servants? Indian High-Tech Migrants in America's Information Economy." *Knowledge, Technology and Policy* 19(3): 27–43.

Chambers, David L. 1989. "Accommodation and Satisfaction: Women and Men Lawyers and the Balance of Work and Family." *Law & Social Inquiry* 14(2): 251–287.

Chambliss, Elizabeth, and Christopher Uggen. 2000. "Men and Women of Elite Law Firms: Reevaluating Kanter's Legacy." *Law and Social Inquiry* 25(1): 41–68.

Chanda, Rupa. 2002. *Globalization of Services: India's Opportunities and Constraints.* New Delhi: Oxford University Press.

Chandrachud, Abhinav. 2014. "From Hyderabad to Harvard: How Law Schools Make It Worthwhile to Clerk on India's Supreme Court World." *International Journal of the Legal Profession* 21(1): 73–101.

Chandru, K. 2015. "Judges, Castes and Social Justice." *The Hindu*, March 16. Available online at www.thehindu.com/opinion/op-ed/judges-castes-and-social-justice/article6996279.ece.

Chapman, Terri, Saran, Samir, Sinha, Rakesh, Kedia, Suchi, and Gutta, Sriram. 2018. *The Future of Work in India: Inclusion, Growth and Transformation.* The World Economic Forum and Observer Research Foundation, Available online at https://www.orfonline .org/research/future-of-work-india/.

Charles, Maria, and Bradley, Karen. 2009. "Indulging Our Gendered Selves? Sex Segregation by Field of Study in 44 Countries." *American Journal of Sociology* 114(4): 924–976.

Charles, Maria, and Grusky, David B. 2005. *Occupational Ghettos: The Worldwide Segregation of Women and Men.* Stanford, CA: Stanford University Press.

Chowdhry, Prem. 2004. "Private Lives, State Intervention: Cases of Runaway Marriage in Rural North India." *Modern Asian Studies* 38: 55–84.

Chowdhry, Prem. 2007. *Contentious Marriages, Eloping Couples: Gender, Caste, and Patriarchy in Northern India.* New Delhi: Oxford University Press.

Collins, Caitlyn. 2019. *Making Motherhood Work: How Women Manage Careers and Caregiving.* Princeton, NJ: Princeton University Press.

Collinson, David. L., and Hearn, Jeff. 1996. Eds., *Men As Managers, Managers As Men: Critical Perspectives on Men, Masculinities and Managements.* London: Sage.

Comaroff, Jean, and Comaroff, John L. eds. 2001. *Millennial Capitalism and the Culture of Neoliberalism.* Durham, NC: Duke University Press.

Comaroff, Jean, and Comaroff, John L. 2012. "Theory from the South: Or, How Euro-America Is Evolving toward Africa." In *Anthropological Forum*, vol. 22(2), pp. 113–131. Routledge. Cooper, David, and Robson, Keith. 2006. "Accounting, Professions and Regulation: Locating the Sites of Professionalization." *Accounting, Organizations and Society* 31: 415–444.

Cooper, Davina. 2014. *Everyday Utopias: The Conceptual Life of Promising Spaces*. Durham, NC: Duke University Press.

Correll, Shelley J. 2001. "Gender and the Career Choice Process: The Role of Biased Self-Assessments." *American Journal of Sociology* 106(6): 1691–1730.

Correll, Shelley J., Benard, Stephen, and Paik, In. 2007. "Getting a Job: Is There a Motherhood Penalty?" *American Journal of Sociology* 112(5): 1297–1339.

Cotter, David., Hermsen, Joan, and Vanneman, Reeve. 2011. "The End of the Gender Revolution? Gender Role Attitudes from 1977 to 2008." *American Journal of Sociology* 117(1): 259–289.

Cotterell, Roger. 1998. "Why Must Legal Ideas Be Interpreted Sociologically?." *Journal of Law & Society* 25(2): 171.

Crenshaw, Kimberlé. 1990. "Mapping the Margins: Intersectionality, Identity Politics, and Violence Against Women of Color." *Stanford Law Review* 43: 1241.

Crispin, Jessa. 2017. *Why I Am Not a Feminist: A Feminist Manifesto*. Brooklyn, NY: Melville House.

Crompton, Rosemary, and Lyonette, Clare. 2005. "The New Gender Essentialism—Domestic and Family 'Choices' and Their Relation to Attitudes." *British Journal of Sociology* 56: 601–620.

Crosby, Faye J., Williams, Joan C., and Biernat, Monica. 2004. "The Maternal Wall. *Journal of Social Issues* 60(4): 675–682.

Currid-Halkett, Elizabeth. 2016. *The Sum of Small Things: A Theory of the Aspirational Class*. Princeton, NJ: Princeton University Press.

Darian-Smith, Eve. 2013. *Laws and Societies in Global Contexts: Contemporary Approaches*. New York: Cambridge University Press.

Darian-Smith, Eve, and McCarty, Philip C. 2017. *The Global Turn: Theories, Research Designs, and Methods for Global Studies*. Berkeley: University of California Press.

Dattatreyan, Ethiraj Gabriel. 2020. *The Globally Familiar: Digital Hip Hop, Masculinity, and Urban Space in Delhi*. Durham, NC and London: Duke University Press.

Dave, Naisargi N. 2012. *Queer Activism in India: A Story in the Anthropology of Ethics*. Durham, NC: Duke University Press.

Davies, Celia. 1996. "The Sociology of Professions and the Profession of Gender." *Sociology* 30(4): 661–678.

Davies-Netzley, Sally Ann. 1998. "Women Above the Glass Ceiling: Perceptions on Corporate Mobility and Strategies for Success." *Gender & Society* 12(3): 339–355.

Davis, Kingsley, and Moore, Wilbert E. 1945. "Some Principles of Stratification." *American Sociological Review* 10(2): 242–249.

Dawuni, Josephine. 2016. "To 'Mother' or Not to 'Mother': The Representative Roles of Women Judges in Ghana." *Journal of African Law*, pp. 1–22.

Deccan Herald. 2014. "HC Judges Create Flutter in Court." January 8. Available online at www.deccanherald.com/content/379389/hc-judge-creates-fl utter-court.html.

Demaiter, Erin, and Adams, Tracey. 2009. "'I really didn't have any problems with the male-female thing until . . .': Successful Women's Experiences in IT Organizations." *Canadian Journal of Sociology* 34(1): 31–54.

Dencker, John C. 2008. "Corporate Restructuring and Sex Differences in Managerial Promotion." *American Sociological Review* 73(3): 455–476.

De Neve, Geert. 2005. *The Everyday Politics of Labour: Working Lives in India's Informal Economy*. New Delhi: Social Sciences Press.

Dent, Mike, Bourgeault, Ivy Lynn, Denis, Jean-Louis, and Kuhlmann, Ellen, eds. 2016. *The Routledge Companion to the Professions and Professionalism*. London: Routledge, pp. 265–279.

Derks, Belle, Van Laar, Colette, and Ellemers, Naomi. 2016. "The Queen Bee Phenomenon: Why Women Leaders Distance Themselves from Junior Women." *Leadership Quarterly* 27(3): 456–469.

Desai, Neera. 1977. *Women in Modern India*. New York: Asia Book Corporation of America.

Desai, Sonalde, and Andrist, Lester. 2010. "Gender Scripts and Age at Marriage in India." *Demography* 47(3): 667–687.Deshpande, Ashwini, and Newman, Katherine. 2007. "Where the Path Leads: The Role of Caste in Post-University Employment Expectations." *Economic and Political Weekly*, 4133–4140.

Deshpande, Satish. 2003. *Contemporary India: A Sociological View*. New Delhi: Penguin Books.

Deshpande, Satish. 2006. "Mapping the 'Middle': Issues in the Analysis of the 'Non-Poor' Classes in India." In Mary John, Praveen Kumar Jha, and Surinder Jodhka, eds., *Contested Transformations: Changing Economies and Identities in Contemporary India*, pp. 215–236. New Delhi: Tulika Books.

Devika, Jayakumari, and Mukherjee, Avanti. 2007. "Re-forming Women in Malayalee Modernity: A Historical Overview." In Swapna Mukhopadhyay, ed., *The Enigma of the Kerala Woman: A Failed Promise of Literacy*, pp. 102–128. New Delhi: Social Science Press.

Dezalay, Yves, and Garth, Bryant G. 1996. *Dealing in Virtue: International Commercial Arbitration and the Construction of a Transnational Legal Order*. Chicago: University of Chicago Press.

Dezalay, Yves, and Garth, Bryant G. 2002. *The Internationalization of Palace Wars: Lawyers, Economists and the Contest to Transform Latin American States*. Chicago: University of Chicago Press.

Dezalay, Yves, and Garth, Bryant G. 2010. *Asian Legal Revivals: Lawyers in the Shadow of Empire*. Chicago: University of Chicago Press.

Dhru, Kanan. 2010. Entry Barriers to the Litigation Profession in India (Ahmedbad, Research Foundation for Governance in India). Available online at www.rfgindia.org /publications/Entry%20Barriers%20 to%20Litigation.pdf.

DiAngelo, Robin. 2018. *White Fragility: Why It's So Hard for White People to Talk About Racism*. Boston, MA: Beacon Press.

Dierenfield, Bruce J. 1981. "Conservative Outrage: The Defeat in 1966 of Representative Howard W. Smith of Virginia." *Virginia Magazine of History and Biography* 89(2): 181–205.

DiMaggio, Paul J., and Powell, Walter W. 1983. "The Iron Cage Revisited: Institutional Isomorphism and Collective Rationality in Organizational Fields." *American Sociological Review*, 147–160.

DiMaggio, Paul J., and Powell, Walter W. 1991. "Introduction to the New Institutionalism." In *The New Institutionalism in Organizational Analysis*, pp. 1–38. Chicago: University of Chicago Press.

Dinovitzer, Ronit. 2006. "Social Capital and Constraints on Legal Careers." *Law & Society Review* 40: 445–480.

Dinovitzer, Ronit. 2011. "The Financial Rewards of Elite Status in the Legal Profession." *Law & Social Inquiry* 36: 971–998.

Dinovitzer, Ronit, and Garth, Bryant G. 2004. *After the JD: First Results of a National Study of Legal Careers*. NALP Foundation for Law Career Research and Education.

Dinovitzer, Ronit, and Garth, Bryant G. 2007. "Lawyer Satisfaction in the Process of Structuring Legal Careers." *Law & Society Review* 41: 1–50.

Dinovitzer, Ronit, Reichman, Nancy, and Sterling, Joyce. 2009. "The Differential Valuation of Women's Work: A New Look at the Gender Gap in Lawyers' Incomes." *Social Forces* 88(2): 819–864.

Dizikes, Petyer. 2008. "The Meaning of the Butterfly." *Boston Globe*, June 8.

D'Mello, Marisa. 2005. "'Thinking Local, Acting Global': Issues of Identity and Related Tensions in Global Software Organizations in India." *Electronic Journal of Information Systems in Developing Countries* 22(1): 1–20.

D'Mello, Marisa. 2006. "Gendered Selves and Identities of Information Technology Professionals in Global Software Organizations in India." *Information Technology for Development* 12(2): 131–158.

D'Mello, Marisa, and Sundeep Sahay. 2007. "'I am kind of a nomad where I have to go places and places' . . . Understanding Mobility, Place and Identity in Global Software Work from India." *Information and Organization*. 17(3): 162–192.

Dobbin, Frank. 2009. *Inventing Equal Opportunity*. Princeton, NJ: Princeton University Press.

Dobbin, Frank, and Kalev, Alexandra. 2007. "The Architecture of Inclusion: Evidence from Corporate Diversity Programs." *Harvard Journal of Law & Gender* 30: 279.

Dodd-McCue, Diane, and Wright, Gail B. 1996. "Men, Women, and Attitudinal Commitment: The Effects of Workplace Experiences and Socialization." *Human Relations* 49(8): 1065–1091.

Domhoff, G. William, and Zweigenhaft, Richard L. 1998. *Diversity in the Power Elite: Have Women and Minorities Reached the Top?* New Haven, CT: Yale University Press.

Donner, Henrike. 2002. "'One's Own Marriage': Love Marriages in a Calcutta Neighbourhood." *South Asia Research* 22(1): 79–94.

Donner, Henrike, ed. 2012. *Being Middle-Class in India: A Way of Life*. Delhi: Routledge.

Donner, Henrike, and Santos, Goncalo. 2016. "Love, Marriage, and Intimate Citizenship in Contemporary China and India: An Introduction." *Modern Asian Studies* 50(4): 1123–1146.

Dossani, Rafiq. 2008. *India Arriving: How This Economic Powerhouse Is Redefining Global Business*. New York, NY: AMACOM.

Dürkheim, Emile. 1965. *The Elementary Forms of Religious Life*. London: Tavistock Publications.

Eagly, Alice. H. 2005. "Achieving Relational Authenticity in Leadership: Does Gender Matter?" *Leadership Quarterly* 16(3): 459–474.

Eagly, Alice. H., and Carli, Linda. L. 2003. "The Female Leadership Advantage: An Evaluation of the Evidence." *Leadership Quarterly* 14(6): 807–834.

Earl, Jennifer, and Schussman, Alan. 2003. "The New Site of Activism: On-Line Organizations, Movement Entrepreneurs, and the Changing Location of Social Movement Decision-Making." *Research in Social Movements, Conflicts and Change* 24: 155–187.

Edlund, Lena, and Kopczuk, Wojciech. 2009. "Women, Wealth, and Mobility." *American Economic Review* 99(1): 146–178.

Ehrenreich, Barbara, Hochschild, Arlie Russell, and Kay, Shara, eds. 2003. *Global Woman: Nannies, Maids, and Sex Workers in the New Economy*. Gordonsville, VA: Henry Holt.

Eisenhardt, Kathleen M. 1989. "Building Theories from Case Study Research." *Academy of Management Review* 14(4): 532–550.

Ely, Robin J., Ibarra, Herminia, and Kolb, Deborah M. 2011. "Taking Gender into Account: Theory and Design for Women's Leadership Development Programs." *Academy of Management Learning & Education* 10(3): 474–493.

England, Paula, Budig, Michelle, and Folbre, Nancy. 2002. "Wages of Virtue: The Relative Pay of Care Work." *Social Problems* 49(4): 455–473.

England, Paula. 1992. "From Status Attainment to Segregation and Devaluation." *Contemporary Sociology* 21(5): 643–647.

England, Paula. 2005. "Gender Inequality in Labor Markets: The Role of Motherhood and Segregation." *Social Politics: International Studies in Gender, State & Society* 12, no. 2 (Summer): 264–288; https://doi.org/10.1093/sp/jxi014.

England, Paula. 2010. "The Gender Revolution." *Gender and Society* 242(2): 149–166.

Epstein, Cynthia F. 1993. *Women in Law*. Champaign: University of Illinois Press.

Epstein, Cynthia F. 2000. "Women in the Legal Profession at the Turn of the Twenty-First Century: Assessing Glass Ceilings and Open Doors." *University of Kansas Law Review* 49(4): 733.

Epstein, Cynthia Fuchs, Seron, Carroll, Oglensky, Bonnie, and Saute, Robert. 1999. *The Part-Time Paradox*. New York and London: Routledge.

Escontrias, Pilar Hernandez, Margarita, Moran, Rachel F., and Nelson, Robert L. 2016. "The Future of Latinos in the United States: Law, Mobility, and Opportunity (A Project of the American Bar Foundation)." *Professional Lawyer* 24: 21.

Evans, Peter B. 1995. *Embedded Autonomy: States and Industrial Transformation*. Princeton, NJ: Princeton University Press.

Evetts, Julia. 2003. "The Sociological Analysis of Professionalism: Occupational Change in the Modern World." *International Sociology* 18(2): 395–415.

Faulconbridge, James R., and Muzio, Daniel. 2008. "Organizational Professionalism in Globalizing Law Firms." *Work, Employment and Society* 22(1): 7–25.

Faulconbridge, James R., and Muzio, Daniel. 2012. "Professions in a Globalizing World: Towards a Transnational Sociology of the Professions." *International Sociology* 27(1): 136–152.

Fausto-Sterling, Anne. 1992. "Building Two-Way Streets: The Case of Feminism and Science." *NWSA Journal* 4(3): 336–349.

Fernandes, Leela. 2000. "Restructuring the New Middle Class in Liberalizing India." *Comparative Studies of South Asia, Africa and the Middle East* 20(1): 88–104.

Fernandes, Leela. 2006. *India's New Middle Class: Democratic Politics in an Era of Economic Reform*. Minneapolis: University of Minnesota Press.

Fernandes, Leela, and Heller, Patrick. 2006."Hegemonic Aspirations: New Middle-Class Politics and India's Democracy in Comparative Perspective." *Critical Asian Studies*, December.

Finkelstein, Maura. 2019. *The Archive of Loss: Lively Ruination in Mill Land Mumbai*. Durham, NC: Duke University Press.

Fiske, Susan T. 1993. "Controlling Other People: The Impact of Power on Stereotyping." *American Psychologist* 48(6): 621–628.

Fiske, Susan T., and Glick, Peter. 1995. "Ambivalence and Stereotypes Cause Sexual Harassment: A Theory with Implications for Organizational Change." *Journal of Social Issues* 51: 97–115.

Flood, John. 2011. "Legal Education in the Global Context: Challenges from Globalization, Technology and Changes in Government Regulation." University of Westminster School of Law Research Paper, 11–16.

Flood, John. 2017. "Theories of Law Firm Globalization in the Shadow of Colonialism: A Cultural and Institutional Analysis of English and Indian Corporate Law Firms in the Twentieth and Twenty-First Centuries." In Wilkins et al., *The Indian Legal Profession*, p. 335.

Flood, John. 2018. "Professions and Professional Service Firms in a Global Context: Reframing Narratives." In Mike Saks and Daniel Muzio, eds., *Professions and Professional Service Firms: Private and Public Sector Enterprises in the Global Economy*, pp. 26–45. London: Routledge.

Flores, Glenda M. 2019. "Pursuing Medicina [Medicine]: Latina Physicians and Parental Messages on Gendered Career Choices." *Sex Roles* 81(1–2): 59–73.

Fox, Richard L., and Lawless, Jennifer L. 2003. "Family Structure, Sex-Role Socialization, and the Decision to Run for Office." *Women & Politics* 24(4): 19–48.

Frank, Robert H., and Cook, Philip J. 1995. *The Winner-Take-All Society: How More and More Americans Compete for Ever Fewer and Bigger Prizes, Encouraging Economic Waste, Income Inequality, and an Impoverished Cultural Life*. New York: Free Press.

Freeman, Carla. 2000. *High Tech and High Heels in the Global Economy: Women, Work, and Pink-Collar Identities in the Caribbean*. Durham, NC: Duke University Press.

Freeman, Carla. 2015. *Entrepreneurial Selves: Neoliberal Respectability and the Making of a Caribbean Middle Class*. Durham, NC: Duke University Press.

Friedman, Sam, and Laurison, Daniel. 2019. *The Class Ceiling: Why It Pays to Be Privileged*. Bristol, UK: Policy Press.

Frøystad, Kathinka. 2018. "Failing the Third Toilet Test: Reflections on Fieldwork, Gender and Indian Loos." *Ethnography* 21(2): 261–279.

Frøystad, Kathinka. 2003. "Master-Servant Relations and the Domestic Reproduction of Caste in Northern India." *Ethnos* 68(1): 73–94.

Fuegen, Kathleen, Biernat, Monica, Haines, Elizabeth, and Deaux, Kay. 2004. "Mothers and Fathers in the Workplace: How Gender and Parental Status Influence Judgments of Job-Related Competence." *Journal of Social Issues* 60(4): 737–754.

Fuller, Christopher. J., and Narasimhan, Haripriya. 2010. "Traditional Vocations and Modern Professions Among Tamil Brahmans in Colonial and Post-Colonial South India." *Indian Economic & Social History Review* 47(4): 473–496.

Fuller, Christopher John, and Narasimhan, Haripriya. 2014. *Tamil Brahmans: The Making of a Middle-Class Caste*. Chicago: University of Chicago Press.

Gadbois Jr., George H. 1969. "Selection, Background Characteristics, and Voting Behavior of Indian Supreme Court Judges, 1950–1959." *Comparative Judicial Behavior* 221–256.

Gadbois Jr., George H. 2011. *Judges of the Supreme Court of India: 1950–1989*. Oxford: Oxford University Press.

Galanter, Marc. 1969. "An Incomplete Bibliography of the Indian Legal Profession." *Law & Society Review* 3(3): 445–462.

Galanter, Marc, and Rekhi, V. S. 1996. "The Impending Transformation of Indian Legal Profession." December 23. Draft with author.

Galanter, Marc, and Robinson, Nicholas. 2014. "India's Grand Advocates: A Legal Elite Flourishing in the Era of Globalization." 20 *International Journal of the Legal Profession*, 1–25.

Gandhi, J. S. 1982. *Lawyers and Touts. A Study in the Sociology of the Legal Profession*. Delhi: Hindustan.

Gandhi, Jogindra Singh. 1987. *Sociology of Legal Profession, Law, and Legal System: The Indian Setting*. New Delhi: Gyan Publishing House.

Gandhi, Jogindra Singh. 1988. "Past and Present: A Sociological Portrait of the Indian Legal Profession." In Richard L. Abel and Philip S. Lewis, eds., *Lawyers in Society: The Common Law World*, pp. 369–382. New York: Beard Books.

Gandhi, Jogindra Singh. 1989. *Law and Social Change*. Jaipur: Rawat.

Ganz, Kian. 2010. "NUJS-ers Threaten Outlook and India Today Law School Rankings with Press Council Complaint." *Legally India*, August 20. Available online at www.legallyindia.com/201008201213/Law-schools/nujs-ers-threaten-outlook-a-india-today-law-school-rankings-with-press-council-complaint.

Ganz, Kian. 2011. "Demystifying India's Legal Market." *Livemint*, November 25. Available online at https://www.livemint.com/Opinion/7wgxYotcuLyw2yG2GoHcvL/Demystifying-India8217s-legal-market.html.

Ganz, Kian. 2012. "Fascination with LLMs in India." *Livemint*, January 19. Available online at www.livemint.com/Opinion/.

Ganz, Kian. 2015. "Can Foreign Law Firms Enter Now." *Livemint*, March 3. Available online at www.livemint.com/Politics/Y1W6WftQGES2pGatn2SKaO/Can-foreign-law-fi rms -enter-India-now.html.

Garg, Abhinav. 2017. "Almost Half of All Indian Lawyers Are Fake, Bar Council Claims." *India Times*, January 23.

Garth, Bryant G. 2015. "Notes toward an Understanding of the US Market in Foreign LL.M. Students: From the British Empire and the Inns of Court to the US LL.M." *Indiana Journal of Global Legal Studies* 22: 67.

Garth, Bryant G. 2016. "Brazil and the Field of Socio-Legal Studies: Globalization, the Hegemony of the US, the Place of Law, and Elite Reproduction." *Brazil Journal of Empirical Legal Studies* 3: 12.

Garth, Bryant G. 2020. "Having It Both Ways. The Challenge of Legal Education Innovation and Reform at UCI and Elsewhere: Against the Grain and/or Aspiring to Be Elite." *UC Irvine Law Review* 10: 373.

Garth, Bryant G., and Sterling, Joyce. 2009. "Exploring Inequality in the Corporate Law Firm Apprenticeship: Doing the Time, Finding the Love." *Georgetown Journal of Legal Ethics* 22: 1361.

Geetha, V. 2006. *Theorizing Feminism: Gender*. Calcutta: Stree.

Geetha, V. 2007. *Theorizing Feminism: Patriarchy*. Calcutta: Stree.

Geetha, V. 2017. "Sexual Harassment and Elusive Justice." *EPW Engage* 52, no. 44 (November).

George, Sheba. 2005. *When Women Come First: Gender and Class in Transnational Migration*. Berkeley: University of California Press.

Gerzema, John, and D'Antonio, Michael. 2013. *The Athena Doctrine: How Women (and the Men Who Think Like Them) Will Rule the Future*. Hoboken, NJ: John Wiley & Sons.

Gibson, Donald E., and Lawrence, Barbara S. 2010. "Women's and Men's Career Referents: How Gender Composition and Comparison Level Shape Career Expectations." *Organization Science* 21(6): 1159–1175.

Gingerich, Jonathan, Khanna, Vikramaditya S., and Singh, Aditya. 2017. "The Anatomy of Legal Recruitment in India: Tracing the Tracks of Globalization." In Wilkins et al., *The Indian Legal Profession*, pp. 548–577.

Gingerich, Jonathan, and Robinson, Nicholas. 2017. "Responding to the Market: The Impact of the Rise of Corporate Law Firms on Elite Legal Education in India." In Wilkins et al., *The Indian Legal Profession*.

Glick, Peter, and Fiske, Susan. T. 2001. "An Ambivalent Alliance: Hostile and Benevolent Sexism as Complementary Justifications for Gender Inequality." *American Psychologist* 56(2): 109–118.

Goldin, Claudia Dale, and Rouse, Cecilia Elena. 2000. "Orchestrating Impartiality: The Impact of 'Blind' Auditions on Female Musicians." Princeton, NJ: Industrial Relations Section, Princeton University.

Goldthorpe, John H. 1983. "Women and Class Analysis: In Defence of the Conventional View." *Sociology* 17(4): 465–488.

Gopal Jayal, Niraja. 2013. *Citizenship and Its Discontents: An Indian History*. Cambridge, MA: Harvard University Press.

Gopinath, Gayatri. 1996. "Funny Boys and Girls: Notes on a Queer South Asian Planet." In Russell Leong, *Asian American Sexualities: Dimensions of the Gay and Lesbian Experience*. New York: Routledge.

Gopinath, Gayatri. 2005. *Impossible Desires: Queer Diasporas and South Asian Public Cultures*. Durham, NC: Duke University Press.

Gopinath, Gayatri. 2018. *Unruly Visions: The Aesthetic Practices of Queer Diaspora*. Durham, NC: uke University Press.

Gorman, Elizabeth H. 2005. "Gender Stereotypes, Same-Gender Preferences, and Organizational Variation in the Hiring of Women: Evidence from Law Firms." *American Sociological Review* 70(4): 702–728.

Gorman, Elizabeth H. 2006. "Work Uncertainty and the Promotion of Professional Women: The Case of Law Firm Partnership." *Social Forces* 85(2): 865–890.

Gorman, Elizabeth H., and Kmec, Julie A. 2009. "Hierarchical Rank and Women's Organizational Mobility: Glass Ceilings in Corporate Law Firms." *American Journal of Sociology* 114(5): 1428–1474.

Goswami, Manu. 2004. *Producing India: From Colonial Economy to National Space.* Chicago: University of Chicago Press.

Gothoskar, Sujata. 2000. "Teleworking and Gender." *Economic and Political Weekly* 35(26): 2293–2298.

Greenwald, Maurine Weiner. 1990. *Women, War, and Work: The Impact of World War I On Women Workers in the United States.* Ithaca, NY: Cornell University Press.

Greenwood, Royston, Oliver, Christine, Lawrence, Thomas B., and Meyer, Renate E., eds. 2017. *The Sage Handbook of Organizational Institutionalism.* London: Sage.

Grewal, Inderpal. 2005. *Transnational America: Feminisms, Diasporas, Neoliberalisms.* Durham, NC: Duke University Press.

Grover, Shalini. 2009. "Lived Experiences: Marriage, Notions of Love, and Kinship Support Amongst Poor Women in Delhi. *Contributions to Indian Sociology* 43(1): 1–33.

Grusky, David B., and Ku, Manwai C. 2008. "Gloom, Doom, and Inequality." *Social Stratification: Class, Race, and Gender in Sociological Perspective* 3: 2–28.

Gulati, Mitu, and Wilkins, David B. 1996. "Why Are There So Few Black Lawyers in Corporate Law Firms? An Institutional Analysis." 84 *California Law Review* 493–625.

Gulhati, Kaval. 1990. "Attitudes Toward Women Managers: Comparison of Attitudes of Male and Female Managers in India." *Economic and Political Weekly* 25, no. 7/8 (February): 41–48.

Gupta, Arpita, Khanna, Vikramaditya, and Wilkins, David. 2017. "Overview of Legal Practice in India and the Indian Legal Profession." In Wilkins et al., *The Indian Legal Profession.*

Gupta, Ashok, Koshal, Manjulika, and Koshal, Rajinder. K. 1998. "Women Managers in India: Challenges and Opportunities." *Equal Opportunities International* 17(8): 4–18.

Gupta, Namrata, and Sharma, Arun K. 2003. "Patrifocal Concerns in the Lives of Women in Academic Science: Continuity of Tradition and Emerging Challenges." *Indian Journal of Gender Studies* 10(2): 279–305.

Gupta, Sushma. 2006. *History of Legal Education.* New Delhi: Deep and Deep Publications.

Gustafson, Kaaryn S. 2011. *Cheating Welfare: Public Assistance and the Criminalization of Poverty.* New York: NYU Press.

Hacking, Ian. 1999. *The Social Construction of What?* Cambridge, MA: Harvard University Press.

Hagan, John, and Kay, Fiona. 1995. *Gender in Practice: A Study of Lawyers' Lives.* Oxford: Oxford University Press.

Hakim, Catherine. 2006. "Women, Careers, and Work-Life Preferences." *British Journal of Guidance & Counselling* 34(3): 279–294.

Halberstam, Judith, and Halberstam, Jack. 2011. *The Queer Art of Failure.* Durham, NC: Duke University Press.

Hallett, Tim. 2010. "The Myth Incarnate: Recoupling Processes, Turmoil, and Inhabited Institutions in an Urban Elementary School." *American Sociological Review* 75(1): 52–74.

Halley, Janet. 2008. *Split Decisions: How and Why to Take a Break from Feminism*. Princeton, NJ: Princeton University Press.

Halley, Janet, Kotiswaran, Prabha, Rebouché, Rachel, and Shamir, Hila. 2018. *Governance Feminism: An Introduction*. Minneapolis: University of Minnesota Press.

Halliday, Terence. 2009. "Recursivity and Global Normmaking: A Sociolegal Agenda." *Annual Review of Law and Social Science*, 263–289.

Halliday, Terence, and Carruthers, Bruce G. 2007. "The Recursivity of Law: Global Norm Making and National Lawmaking in the Globalization of Corporate Insolvency Regimes." 112 *American Journal of Sociology* 1135–1202.

Halliday, Terence C., and Shaffer, Gregory, eds. 2015. *Transnational Legal Orders*. Cambridge: Cambridge University Press.

Hannan, Michael, and Freeman, John. 1977. "The Population Ecology of Organizations." 82 *American Journal of Sociology* 929–964.

Hatmaker, Deneen M. 2013. "Engineering Identity: Gender and Professional Identity Negotiation among Women Engineers." *Gender, Work & Organization* 20: 382–396.

Hays, Sharon. 1998. *The Cultural Contradictions of Motherhood*. New Haven, CT and London: Yale University Press.

Headworth, Spencer, Nelson, Robert L., Dinovitzer, Ronit, and Wilkins, David B., eds. 2016. *Diversity in Practice*. Cambridge, UK and New York: Cambridge University Press.

Heinz, John P., and Laumann, Edward O. 1978. "The Legal Profession: Client Interests, Professional Roles, and Social Hierarchies." *Michigan Law Review* 76(7): 1111–1142.

Heinz, John, and Laumann, Edward. 1982. *Chicago Lawyers: The Social Structure of the Bar*. New York: Russell Sage Foundation.

Heinz, John, Nelson, Robert, Sandefur, Rebecca, and Laumann, Edward. 2005. *Urban Lawyers: The New Social Structure of the Bar*. Chicago: University of Chicago Press.

Hertz, Rosanna, and Jonathan B. Imber, eds. 1995. *Studying Elites Using Qualitative Methods*. Vol. 175. London: Sage.

Hindu Editorial. 2016. "The Curious Case of Justice Karnan." February 17. Available online at www.thehindu.com/opinion/editorial/the-curious-case-of-justice-karnan/article8245394.ece.

Hochschild, Arlie Russell. 1979. "Emotion Work, Feeling Rules, and Social Structure." *American Journal of Sociology* 85(3): 551–575.

Hochschild, Arlie Russell. 1997. *The Time Bind: When Work Becomes Home and Home Becomes Work*. New York: Metropolitan Books.

Hochschild, Arlie Russell, and Machung, Anne. 2012. *The Second Shift: Working Families and the Revolution at Home*. New York: Penguin.

Hull, Kathleen E., and Nelson, Robert L. 1998. "Gender Inequality in Law: Problems of Structure and Agency in Recent Studies of Gender in Anglo-American Legal Professions." *Law & Social Inquiry* 23(3): 681–705.

Humberd, Beth, Ladge, Jamie J., and Harrington, Brad. 2015. "The 'New' Dad: Navigating Fathering Identity Within Organizational Contexts." *Journal of Business and Psychology* 30(2): 249–266.

Hunter, Rosemary. 2002. "Talking Up Equality: Women Barristers and the Denial of Discrimination." *Feminist Legal Studies* 10(2): 113–130.

Hurun Global Rich List. 2015. Released by the Hurun Report, available online at http://www.hurun.net/en/ArticleShow.aspx?nid=9607.

Ibarra, Herminia. 1997. "Paving an Alternative Route: Gender Differences in Managerial Networks." *Social Psychology Quarterly* 91–102.

Ibarra, Herminia, Ely, Robin, and Kolb, Deborah. 2013. "Women Rising: The Unseen Barriers." *Harvard Business Review* 91(9): 60–66.

Indian Today Web Desk. 2018. "Remember Justice Karnan? He Has Launched a Party, Will Field Women from All LS Seats Next Year." Available online at https://www.indiatoday .in/india/story/remember-justice-karnan-he-has-launched-a-party-will-field-women -from-all-ls-seats-next-year-1255850-2018-06-09.

Isoke, Zenzele. 2013. "Women, Hip Hop, and Cultural Resistance in Dubai." *Souls* 15(4): 316–337.

Jackson, David. 1998. "Breaking Out of the Binary Trap: Boys' Underachievement, Schooling and Gender Relations." In D. Epstein et al., eds., *Failing Boys? Issues in Gender and Achievement*, pp. 77–95. Buckingham, UK: Open University Press.

Jackson, Michelle V., and Evans, Geoffrey. 2017. "Rebuilding Walls: Market Transition and Social Mobility in the Post-Socialist Societies of Europe." *Sociological Science* 4: 54–79.

Jacobs, Jerry A., and Gerson, Kathleen. 2004. *The Time Divide*. Cambridge, MA: Harvard University Press.

Jain, Chirayu, Jayaraj, Spadika, Muraleedharan, Sanjana, Singh, Harjas, and Galanter, Marc. 2015–2016. "The Elusive Island of Excellence—A Study on Student Demographics, Accessibility and Inclusivity at National Law School 2015–16." *Accessibility and Inclusivity at National Law School* 16.

Jayawardena, Kumari. 2016. *Feminism and Nationalism in the Third World*. London: Verso Books.

Jeyaranjan, J., and Swaminathan, Padmini. 1999. "Resilience of Gender Inequities: Women and Employment in Chennai." *Economic and Political Weekly* 2–11.

Jhabvala, Renana, and Sinha, Shalini. 2002. "Liberalisation and the Woman Worker." *Economic and Political Weekly* 37(21): 2037–2044.

Jodhka, Surinder S. 2012. *Caste*. New Delhi: Oxford University Press.

Jodhka, Surinder S., and Naudet, Jules. 2017. "Introduction. Towards a Sociology of India's Economic Elite: Beyond the Neo-Orientalist and Managerialist Perspectives." *South Asia Multidisciplinary Academic Journal* 15.

Jodhka, Surinder S., and Newman, Katherine. 2007. "In the Name of Globalisation: Meritocracy, Productivity and the Hidden Language of Caste." *Economic and Political Weekly*, 4125–4132.

Jodhka, Surinder S., and Prakash, Aseem. 2016. *The Indian Middle Class*. New Delhi: Oxford University Press.

Johnson, Emily S. 2019. *This Is Our Message: Women's Leadership in the New Christian Right*. Oxford and New York: Oxford University Press.

Johnson, Rachel L., Roter, Debra, Powe, Neil R., and Cooper, Lisa A. 2004. "Patient Race/Ethnicity and Quality of Patient-Physician Communication During Medical Visits." *American Journal of Public Health* 9412(12): 2084–2090.

Johnston, Deirdre D., and Swanson, Debra H. 2006. "Constructing the 'Good Mother': The Experience of Mothering Ideologies by Work Status." *Sex Roles* 54: 509–519.

Joseph, Suad, ed. 1999. *Intimate Selving in Arab Families: Gender, Self, And Identity*. Syracuse, NY: Syracuse University Press.

Judiesch, Michael K., and Lyness, Karen S. 1999. "Left Behind? The Impact of Leaves of Absence on Managers' Career Success." *Academy of Management Journal* 42(6): 641–651.

Kannabiran, Kalpana. 2018. "In the Footprints of Bhanwari Devi: Feminist Cascades and# MeToo in India." Hyderabad: Council for Social Development.

Kannabiran, Kalpana, and Ballakrishnen, Swethaa. 2021. *Gender Regimes and the Politics of Privacy: Feminist (re)Readings of Puttaswamy v. Union on India*. New Delhi: Zubaan.

Kannabiran, Kalpana, and Swaminathan, Padmini, eds. 2017. *Re-presenting Feminist Methodologies: Interdisciplinary Explorations*. New Delhi: Routledge.

Kanter, Rosabeth Moss. 1972. *Commitment and Community: Communes and Utopias in Sociological Perspective*. Cambridge, MA: Harvard University Press.

Kanter, Rosabeth Moss. [1977] 1993. *Men and Women of the Corporation: New Edition*. New York: Basic Books.

Kapur, Ratna. 2012. "Pink Chaddis and Slutwalk Couture: The Postcolonial Politics of Feminism Lite." *Feminist Legal Studies* 20(1): 1–20.

Kapur, Ratna. 2018. *Gender, Alterity and Human Rights: Freedom in a Fishbowl*. London: Edward Elgar.

Karmall, Naazneen. 2012. "Richest Indians: How Indian Entrepreneurs Fared in 2012." *Forbes India*.

Kathuria, Poonam, and Bhaiya, Abha. 2018. *Indian Feminisms: Individual and Collective Journeys*. New Delhi, Delhi: Zubaan.

Kaufmann, Katja, Messner, Matthias, and Solis, Alex. 2013. *Returns to Elite Higher Education in the Marriage Market: Evidence from Chile*. No. 489. IGIER (Innocenzo Gasparini Institute for Economic Research), Bocconi University.

Kay, Fiona M., Alarie, Stacey L., and Adjei, Jones K. 2016. "Undermining Gender Equality: Female Attrition from Private Law Practice." *Law & Society Review* 50: 766–801.

Kay, Fiona M., and Gorman, Elizabeth H. 2008. "Women in the Legal Profession." *Annual Review of Law and Social Science* 4: 299–332.

Kay, Fiona M., and Gorman, Elizabeth H. 2012. "Developmental Practices, Organizational Culture, and Minority Representation in Organizational Leadership: The Case of Partners in Large US Law Firms." *Annals of the American Academy of Political and Social Science* 639(1): 91–113.

Kay, Fiona M., and Hagan, John. 1998. "Raising the Bar: The Gender Stratification of Law-Firm Capital." *American Sociological Review*, 728–743.

Kellogg, Katherine C. 2011. *Challenging Operations: Medical Reform and Resistance in Surgery*. Chicago: University of Chicago Press.

Kesavan, Mukul. 2016. "Before the Change: When Austerity, Simplicity Ruled Middle Class Everyday Life." *Hindustan Times*, July 24.

Khadria, Binod. 2001. "Shifting Paradigms of Globalization: The Twenty-first Century Transition Towards Generics in Skilled Migration from India." *International Migration* 39: 45–71.

Khan, Shamus R. 2012. *Privilege: The Making of an Adolescent Elite at St. Paul's School*. Princeton, NJ and Oxford: Princeton University Press.

Khan, Shamus R. 2013. "The Ease of Mobility." In Thomas Birtchnell and Javier Caletrío, eds., *Elite Mobilities*, pp. 148–160. New York: Routledge.

Khanna, Vikramaditya S. 2017. "The Evolving Global Supply Chain for Legal Services: India's Role as a Critical Link." In Wilkins et al., *The Indian Legal Profession*.

Khorakiwala, Rahela. 2018. "Legal Consciousness as Viewed through the Judicial Iconography of the Madras High Court." *Asian Journal of Law and Society* 5(1): 1–23.

King, Eden B., Botsford, Whitney, Hebl, Michelle R., Kazama, Stephanie, Dawson, Jeremy F., and Perkins, Andrew. 2012. "Benevolent Sexism at Work: Gender Differences in the Distribution of Challenging Developmental Experiences." *Journal of Management* 38(6): 1835–1866.

Klug, Heinz. 2000. *Constituting Democracy: Law, Globalism, and South Africa's Political Reconstruction*. Cambridge and New York: Cambridge University Press.

Kobrynowicz, Diane, and Biernat, Monica. 1997. "Decoding Subjective Evaluations: How Stereotypes Provide Shifting Standards." *Journal of Experimental Social Psychology* 33(6): 579–601.

Kodoth, Praveena, and Eapen, Mridul. 2005. "Looking Beyond Gender Parity: Gender Inequities of Some Dimensions of Well-Being in Kerala." *Economic and Political Weekly* 40(30): 3278–3286.

Korzec, Rebecca. 1997. "Working on the 'Mommy-Track': Motherhood and Women Lawyers." 8 *Hastings Women's Law Journal* 117.

Kram, Kathy E., and Hampton, Marion M. 1998. "When Women Lead: The Visibility-Vulnerability Spiral." *Psychodynamics of Leadership,* 193–218.

Kram, Kathy E., and Hampton, Marion M. 2003. "When Women Lead: The Visibility-Vulnerability Spiral." In Ely et al., eds., *Reader in Gender, Work, and Organization.* Oxford: Blackwell.

Kray, Laura J., Thompson, Leigh, and Galinsky, Adam. 2001. "Battle of the Sexes: Gender Stereotype Confirmation and Reactance in Negotiations." *Journal of Personality and Social Psychology* 80(6): 942–958.

Krishnan, Jayanth K. 2004. "Professor Kingsfield Goes to Delhi: American Academics, the Ford Foundation, and the Development of Legal Education in India." *American Journal of Legal History* 46(4): 447–499.

Krishnan, Jayanth. 2009. "(Un)Wanted Outsiders: The Debate Over Excluding American and British Law Firms from a Thriving Capital Market." Draft Conference Paper on file with author.

Krishnan, Jayanth K. 2010. "Globetrotting Law Firms." *Georgetown Journal of Legal Ethics* 23: 57.

Krishnan, Jayanth. 2013. "Peel-Off Lawyers: Legal Professionals in India's Corporate Law Firm Sector." *Socio-Legal Review* 9: 13–14.

Kumar, A. K. Shiva. 1996. "UNDP's Gender-Related Development Index: A Computation for Indian States." *Economic and Political Weekly* 31(14): 887–895.

Kumar, Neelam. 2001. "Gender and Stratification in Science: An Empirical Study in the Indian Setting." *Indian Journal of Gender Studies* 8(1): 51–67.

Kumar, Neelam, ed. 2012. *Gender and Science: Studies across Cultures.* New Delhi: Cambridge University Press India.

Kumar, Radha. 1997. *The History of Doing: An Illustrated Account of Movements for Women's Rights and Feminism in India 1800–1990.* New Delhi: Zubaan.

Kurien, Prema A. 2003. "To Be or Not to Be South Asian: Contemporary Indian American Politics." *Journal of Asian American Studies* 6(3): 261–288.

Laurison, Daniel, and Friedman, Sam. 2016. "The Class Pay Gap in Higher Professional and Managerial Occupations." *American Sociological Review* 81(4): 668–695.

Lawyers Collective v. Bar Council of India. 2009. Chadbourne, Ashurst, White & Case, and Others.

Le Renard, Amélie. 2014. *A Society of Young Women: Opportunities of Place, Power, and Reform in Saudi Arabia.* Stanford, CA: Stanford University Press.

Legally India. 2012. "US Job Market Remains in Dumps; 92% of Indian LLM Grads Come Home Empty Handed?" January 19. Available online at www.legallyindia.com/analysis /li-mint-us-job-market-remains-indumps-92-of-indian-llm-grads-comehome-empty -handed-20120119-2506.

Legally India. 2013. "RTI Reveals: 1.3 Million Advocates." February 18. Available online at www.legallyindia.com/the-benchand-the-bar/rti-reveals-number-of-lawyers-india -20130218-3448.

Legally India. 2014. "Untangling the Madras HC turmoil: A bar at war, a question of caste, or business as usual?" January 17. Available online at www.legallyindia.com/analysis /madras-hc-turmoil-a-bar-atwar-20140117-4250.

Levanon, Asaf, England, Paula, and Allison, Paul. 2009. "Occupational Feminization and Pay: Assessing Causal Dynamics Using 1950–2000 U.S. Census Data." *Social Forces* 88(2): 865–891.

Levinson, Justin D., and Young, Danielle. 2010. "Implicit Gender Bias in the Legal Profession: An Empirical Study." 18 *Duke Journal of Gender Law & Policy* 1–33 (Fall).

Lewis, Patricia. 2013. "The Search for an Authentic Entrepreneurial Identity: Difference and Professionalism Among Women Business Owners." *Gender, Work & Organization* 20(3): 252–266.

Liu, Sida. 2006. "Client Influence and the Contingency of Professionalism: The Work of Elite Corporate Lawyers in China." *Law & Society Review* 40(4): 751–782.

Liu, Sida. 2008. "Globalization as Boundary-Blurring: International and Local Law Firms in China's Corporate Law Market." *Law & Society Review* 42(4): 771–804.

Liu, Sida, and Halliday, Terrance. 2009. "Recursivity in Legal Change: Lawyers and Reforms of China's Criminal Procedure Law." 34 *Law and Social Inquiry* 911–950.

Liu, Sida, Trubek, David M., and Wilkins, David B. 2016. "Mapping the Ecology of China's Corporate Legal Sector: Globalization and Its Impact on Lawyers and Society." *Asian Journal of Law and Society* 3(2): 273–297.

Loomba, Ania, and Lukose, Ritty A. 2012. *South Asian Feminisms*. Durham, NC: Duke University Press.

Lorde, Audre. 2007[1984]. *Sister Outsider: Essays and Speeches*. Berkeley, CA: Crossing Press.

Lorenz, Edward N. 1995. *The Essence of Chaos*. Seattle: University of Washington Press.

Love, Heather. 2015. "Doing Being Deviant: Deviance Studies, Description, and the Queer Ordinary." *differences* 26(1): 74–95.

Lukose, Ritty. 2009. *Liberalization's Children: Gender, Youth, and Consumer Citizenship in Globalizing India*. Durham, NC: Duke University Press.

Lukose, Ritty. 2018. "Decolonizing Feminism in the #MeToo Era." *Cambridge Journal of Anthropology* 36(2): 34–52.

Lyness, Karen, and Heilman, Madeline. 2006. "When Fit Is Fundamental: Performance Evaluations and Promotions of Upper-Level Female and Male Managers." *Journal of Applied Psychology* 91(4): 777–801.

Macdonald, Cameron Lynne. 2011. *Shadow Mothers: Nannies, Au Pairs, and the Micropolitics of Mothering*. Berkeley: University of California Press.

Macdonald, Keith M. 1995. *The Sociology of the Professions*. London: SAGE Publications.

Mahmood, Saba. 2011. *Politics of Piety: The Islamic Revival and the Feminist Subject*. Princeton, NJ: Princeton University Press.

Makhija, Sonal, and Raha, Swaga. 2012. "Challenges Faced by Indian Women Legal Professionals." Rainmaker India. Available online at www.scribd.com/document/101516872/Challenges-Faced-by-Indian-Women-Legal-Professionals-Executive-Summary.

Mandavia, Megha. 2016. "Heirs of India's Biggest Tycoons Are Charting Their Own Entrepreneurial Path." *Economic Times*. February 4. Available online at http://economictimes.indiatimes.com/articleshow/50842432.cms?utm_source=contentofinterest&utm_mediu m=text&utm_campaign=cppst.

Maqsood, Ammara. 2017. *The New Pakistani Middle Class*. Cambridge, MA: Harvard University Press.

Masood, Ayesha. 2019. "Influence of Marriage on Women's Participation in Medicine: The Case of Doctor Brides of Pakistan." *Sex Roles* 80(1–2): 105–122.

Massad, Joseph A. 2008. *Desiring Arabs*. Chicago: University of Chicago Press.

Massoud, Mark Fathi. 2013. *Law's Fragile State: Colonial, Authoritarian, and Humanitarian Legacies in Sudan*. Cambridge, UK and New York: Cambridge University Press.

Mathur, Nita. 2017. Women's Withdrawal from India's Rural Workforce: Explaining the Trend. *Social Change* 47(1): 125–133.

McAdam, Mario Diani Doug. 2003. *Social Movements and Networks: Relational Approaches to Collective Action*. Oxford: Oxford University Press.

McCammon, Holly J., Campbell, Karen E., Granberg, Ellen M., and Mowery, Christine. 2001. "How Movements Win: Gendered Opportunity Structures and US Women's Suffrage Movements, 1866 to 1919." *American Sociological Review*, 49–70.

McPherson, Miller, Smith-Lovin, Lynn, and Cook, James M. 2001. "Birds of a Feather: Homophily in Social Networks." *Annual Review of Sociology* 27(1): 415–444.

Mehrotra, Santosh, and Jajati, Parida K. 2017. "Why Is the Labour Force Participation of Women Declining in India?" *World Development* 98: 360–380.

Menkel-Meadow, Carrie. 1985. "Portia in a Different Voice: Speculations on a Women's Lawyering Process." *Berkeley Women's Law Journal* 1–39.

Menkel-Meadow, Carrie. 1986. "The Comparative Sociology of Women Lawyers: The 'Feminization' of the Legal Profession." 24 *Osgoode Hall Law Journal* 897.

Menkel-Meadow, Carrie. 1989. "Exploring a Research Agenda of the Feminization of the Legal Profession: Theories of Gender and Social Change." 14 *Law & Social Inquiry* 289–319.

Menon, Nivedita. 2004. *Recovering Subversion: Feminist Politics Beyond the Law*. Champaign: University of Illinois Press.

Menon, Nivedita. 2012. *Seeing Like a Feminist*. London: Penguin.

Menon, N. R. Madhava, and Prakash, Surya. 2009. *Turning Point: Memoirs of Padmashree Professor N. R. Madhava Menon*. Delhi: Universal Law.

Merry, Sally Engle. 2009. *Human Rights and Gender Violence: Translating International Law into Local Justice*. Chicago: University of Chicago Press.

Merry, Sally Engle. 2011. "Measuring the World: Indicators, Human Rights, and Global Governance." *Current Anthropology* 52(S3): 83–95.

Merton, Robert. 1936. "The Unanticipated Consequences of Purposive Social Action." *American Sociological Review* 1(6): 894–904.

Meyer, David S., and Whittier, Nancy. 1994. "Social Movement Spillover." *Social Problems* 41(2): 277–298.

Meyer, John W., and Rowan, Brian. 1977. "Institutionalized Organizations: Formal Structure as Myth and Ceremony." 83 *American Journal of Sociology* 340–363.

Meyer, John W., Scott, W. Richard, and Deal, Terence E. 1983. "Institutional and Technical Sources of Organizational Structure: Exploring the Structure of Education Organizations." In Meyer and Scott, eds., *Organizational Environments: Ritual and Rationality*, pp. 45–67. Beverly Hills, CA: Sage.

Meyerowitz, June. 1994. *Not June Cleaver: Women and Gender in Postwar America, 1945–1960*. Vol. 79. Philadelphia, PA: Temple University Press.

Michelson, Ethan. 2013. "Women in the Legal Profession, 1970–2010: A Study of the Global Supply of Lawyers." *Indiana Journal of Global Legal Studies* 20: 1071–1098.

Milanovik, Branko. 2013. Global Income Inequality in Numbers: In History and Now." *Global Policy* 4, no. 2 (May).

Mirchandani, Kiran. 2004. "Practices of Global Capital: Gaps, Cracks and Ironies in Transnational Call Centres in India." *Global Networks* 4(4): 355–373.

Mishra, Saurabh K. 2015. "Women in Indian Courts of Law: A Study of Women Legal Professionals in the District Court of Lucknow, Uttar Pradesh, India." e-cadernos 24 October journals.openedition.org/eces/1976.

Mishra, Soni. 2016. "I Was Sexually Harassed in the Corridors of the Supreme Court." *The Week*, November 13.

Mitra, Durba. 2020. *Indian Sex Life: Sexuality and the Colonial Origins of Modern Social Thought*. Princeton, NJ: Princeton University Press.

Mobley, Melton G., Jaret, Charles, Marsh, Kristin, and Lim, Yoon Yoon. 1994. "Mentoring, Job Satisfaction, Gender, and the Legal Profession." *Sex Roles* 31: 79–98.

Mohanty, Chandra Talpade. 2003. *Feminism without Borders: Decolonizing Theory, Practicing Solidarity*. Durham, NC: Duke University Press.

Mohanty, Chandra Talpade, Russo, Ann, and Torres, Lourdes. eds. 1991. *Third World Women and the Politics of Feminism*. Vol. 632. Bloomington: Indiana University Press.

Moog, Robert. S. 1998. "Elite-Court Relations in India: An Unsatisfactory Arrangement." *Asian Survey* 38(4): 410–423.

Morrill, Calvin, and Fine, Gary A. 1997. "Ethnographic Contributions to Organizational Sociology." *Sociological Methods and Research* 25(4): 424–451.

Morrison, Charles. 1972. "Munshis and Their Masters: The Organization of an Occupational Relationship in the Indian Legal System." *Journal of Asian Studies* 31(2): 309–328.

Mukherjee, Sanjukta. 2008. "Producing the Knowledge Professional: Gendered Geographies of Alienation in India's New High-Tech Workplace." In Carole Upadhya and Aninhalli R. Vasavi, *In an Outpost of the Global Economy: Work and Workers in India's Information Technology Industry*, pp. 50–75. New Delhi: Routledge.

Mukhija, Nivedita. 2016. "FemTalk #1: Prof. V. Elisabeth on Feminism, NLS, and Armchair Activism." Available online at https://thefeministmarshmallow.wordpress.com/2016/02/26/femtalk1-prof-v-s-elizabeth-on-feminism-nls-and-armchair-activism/.

Mukhopadhyay, Maitrayee. 2004. "Mainstreaming Gender or 'Streaming' Gender Away: Feminists Marooned in the Development Business." *IDS Bulletin* 35: 95–103.

Murphy, Thomas E. 1970. "Female Wage Discrimination: A Study of the Equal Pay Act 1963–1970." *University of Cincinnati Law Review* 39: 615.

Nadeem, Shehzad. 2009. "Macaulay's (Cyber) Children: The Cultural Politics of Outsourcing in India." *Cultural Sociology* 3(1): 102–122.

Nadeem, Shehzad. 2013. *Dead Ringers: How Outsourcing Is Changing the Way Indians Understand Themselves*. Princeton, NJ: Princeton University Press.

Nagar, Richa. 2019. *Hungry Translations: Relearning the World Through Radical Vulnerability*. Champaign: University of Illinois Press.

Nagla, B. K. 2001. "Sociology of Legal Profession: A Study of Women Lawyers in India" 1 *MDU Law Journal* 73–94.

Nanda, Ashish, Wilkins, David B., and Fong, Bryon. 2017. "Mapping India's Corporate Law Firm Sector." In Wilkins et al., *The Indian Legal Profession*, p. 69.

Naqvi, Farah. 2011. "Perspectives of Indian Women Managers in the Public Sector." *Indian Journal of Gender Studies* 18(3): 279–309.

Narayan, Ambar, Van der Weide, Roy, Cojocaru, Alexandru, Lakner, Christoph, Redaelli, Silvia, Mahler, Gerszon, Ramasubbaiah, Rakesh, and Thewissen, Stefan. 2018. *Fair Progress?: Economic Mobility Across Generations Around the World*. Washington, DC: World Bank.

Narrain, Arvind. 2007. "Rethinking Citizenship: A Queer Journey." *Indian Journal of Gender Studies* 14(1): 61–71.

Narrain, Siddharth. 2009. "Crystallising Queer Politics—The Naz Foundation Case and Its Implications for India's Transgender Communities." *NUJS Law Review* 2: 455.

Nath, Deepika. 2000. "Gently Shattering the Glass Ceiling: Experiences of Indian Women Managers." *Women in Management Review* 15(1): 44–52.

Naudet, Jules. 2018. *Stepping into the Elite: Trajectories of Social Achievement in India, France, and the United States*. New Delhi: Oxford University Press.

Naudet, Jules, and Dubost, Claire-Lise. 2017. The Indian Exception: The Densification of the Network of Corporate Interlocks and the Specificities of the Indian Business System (2000–2012). *Socio-Economic Review* 15, no. 2 (April): 405–434.

Nayar, Baldev Raj. 1998. "Political Structure and India's Economic Reforms of 1990s." 71 *Pacific Affairs* 335–358.

Nelson, Maggie. 2015. *The Argonauts*. Minneapolis, MN: Graywolf Press.

Nelson, Robert L. 1988. *Partners with Power: The Social Transformation of the Large Law Firm*. Berkeley: University of California Press.

Nelson, Robert L., Dinovitzer, Ronit, Plickert, Gabriele, Sandefur, Rebecca, and Sterling, Joyce. 2009. "After the JD II: Second Results from a National Study of Legal Careers."

American Bar Foundation and The NALP Foundation for Law Career Research and Education, 1–95.

O'Brien, John. 2017. *Keeping It Halal: The Everyday Lives of Muslim American Teenage Boys*. Princeton, NJ: Princeton University Press.

O'Connor, Lindsey Trimble, and Cech, Erin A. 2018. "Not Just a Mother's Problem: The Consequences of Perceived Workplace Flexibility Bias for All Workers." *Sociological Perspectives* 61(5): 808–829.

Olson, Elizabeth. 2016. "Women Make Up Majority of US Law Students for First Time." *New York Times* B4.

O'Neill, Olivia A., and O'Reilly, Charles. 2011. "Reducing the Backlash Effect: Self-monitoring and Women's Promotions." *Journal of Occupational and Organizational Psychology* 84(4): 825–832.

Ong, Aihwa. 2010. *Spirits of Resistance and Capitalist Discipline: Factory Women in Malaysia*. Albany: SUNY Press.

Ong, Aihwa, and Collier, Stephen, eds. 2005. *Global Assemblages: Technology, Politics and Ethics as Anthropological Problems*. Malden, MA: Blackwell.

Ortner, Sherry B. 2010. "Access: Reflections on Studying Up in Hollywood." *Ethnography* 11(2): 211–233.

Padavic, Irene, Ely, Robin J., and Reid, Erin M. 2019. "Explaining the Persistence of Gender Inequality: The Work–Family Narrative as a Social Defense Against the 24/7 Work Culture." *Administrative Science Quarterly* 65(1): 61–111.

Padgett, John F., and Powell, Walter W. 2012. *The Emergence of Organizations and Markets*. Princeton, NJ: Princeton University Press.

Palmisano, Samuel J. 2006. "The Globally Integrated Enterprise." 85 *Foreign Affairs* 127–136.

Papa, Mihaela, and Wilkins, David B. 2011. "Globalization, Lawyers and India: Toward a Theoretical Synthesis of Globalization Studies and the Sociology of the Legal Profession." *International Journal of the Legal Profession* 18(3): 175–209.

Parsons, Talcott. 1940. "An Analytical Approach to the Theory of Social Stratification." *American Journal of Sociology* 45(6): 841–862.

Patel, Atish. 2015. "India Has World's Third-Largest Number of Billionaires." *Wall Street Journal*, February 4.

Patel, Reena. 2010. *Working the Night Shift: Women in India's Call Center Industry*. Stanford, CA: Stanford University Press.

Patel, Reena, and Parmentier, Mary Jane. 2005. "The Persistence of Traditional Gender Roles in the Information Technology Sector: A Study of Female Engineers in India." *Information Technologies and International Development* 2(3): 29–46.

Paul, John Jeya. 1991. *The Legal Profession in Colonial South India*. Bombay: Oxford University Press.

Paul, Tinku. 2009. *Women Empowerment Through Work Participation*. New Delhi: New Century.

Pearce, Russell, Wald, Eli, and Ballakrishnen, Swethaa S. 2015. "Difference Blindness vs. Bias Awareness: Why Law Firms with the Best of Intentions Have Failed to Create Diverse Partnerships." 83 *Fordham Law Review* 2407–2440.

Pedulla, David S., and Thébaud, Sarah. 2015. "Can We Finish the Revolution? Gender, Work-Family Ideals, and Institutional Constraint." *American Sociological Review* 80(1): 116–139.

Phillips, Damon. 2005. "Organizational Genealogies and the Persistence of Gender Inequality: The Case of Silicon Valley Law Firms." *Administrative Science Quarterly* 50(3): 440–472.

Pierce, Jennifer. 1996. *Gender Trials: Emotional Lives in Contemporary Law Firms*. Berkeley: University of California Press.

Piketty, Thomas, and Saez, Emmanuel. 2003. "Income Inequality in the United States, 1913–1998." *Quarterly Journal of Economics* 118, no. 1 (February): 1–41.

Plickert, Gabriele. 2019. "A Life Course Approach to Workplace Discrimination and Employment: Evidence from a U.S. National Sample of Women and Men Lawyers." In Marta Choroszewicz and Tracey L. Adams, eds., *Gender, Age and Inequality in the Professions: Exploring the Disordering, Disruptive and Chaotic Properties of Communication*. New York: Routledge.

Plickert, Gabriele, and Hagan, John. 2011. "Professional Work and the Timing of Family Formation among Young Lawyers in US and German Cities." 18 *International Journal of the Legal Profession* 237–261.

Ponniah, Ujithra. 2017. "Reproducing Elite Lives: Women in Aggarwal Family Businesses." *South Asia Multidisciplinary Academic Journal* 15.

Portes, Alejandro. 2010. *Economic Sociology: A Systematic Inquiry*. Princeton, NJ: Princeton University Press.

Portes, Alejandro, Fernández-Kelly, Patricia, and Haller, William. 2009. "The Adaptation of the Immigrant Second Generation in America: A Theoretical Overview and Recent Evidence." *Journal of Ethnic and Migration Studies* 35(7): 1077–1104.

Post, Corinne. 2015. "When Is Female Leadership an Advantage? Coordination Requirements, Team Cohesion, and Team Interaction Norms." *Journal of Organizational Behavior* 36(8): 1153–1175.

Postar, Adeen. 2011. "Selective Bibliography Relating to Law Students and Lawyers with Disabilities." 19 *American University of Gender, Social Policy, & the Law* 1237.

Powell, Walter W., and DiMaggio, Paul J., eds. 1991. *The New Institutionalism in Organizational Analysis*. Chicago: University of Chicago Press.

Powell Gary N., Butterfield, Anthony D., and Parent, Jane D. 2002. "Gender and Managerial Stereotypes: Have the Times Changed?" *Journal of Management* 28/2: 177–193.

Prager, Laila. 2018. "At the Margins of History: Women and Heritage in the UAE," presented at Varieties of Emirati Womanhood: Subjectivities, Creativities, and Confines, NYUAD Institute International Workshop, March 28–29.

Prager, Laila. 2020. "Emirati Women Leaders in the Cultural Sector: From 'State Feminism' to Empowerment?" *Hawwa Journal of Women of the Middle East and the Islamic World* 18(1): 51–74.

Prahalad, Krishna C., and Doz, Yves L. 1999. *The Multinational Mission: Balancing Local Demands and Global Vision*. New York: Simon & Schuster.

Pratt, Michael G. 2000. "The Good, the Bad, and the Ambivalent: Managing Identification among Amway Distributors." 45 *Administrative Science Quarterly* 456–493.

Preciado, Paul B. 2019. *An Apartment on Uranus: Chronicles of the Crossing*. South Pasadena, CA: Semiotext(e).

Priyadharshini, Esther. 2003. "Coming Unstuck: Thinking Otherwise about 'Studying Up.'" *Anthropology & Education Quarterly* 34(4): 420–437.

Purdum, Todd S. 2014. *An Idea Whose Time Has Come: Two Presidents, Two Parties, and the Battle for the Civil Rights Act of 1964*. New York: Henry Holt.

Radhakrishnan, Smitha. 2009. "Professional Women, Good Families: Respectable Femininity and the Cultural Politics of a 'New' India." *Qualitative Sociology* 32(2): 195–212.

Radhakrishnan, Smitha. 2011. *Appropriately Indian. Gender and Culture in a New Transnational Class*. Durham, NC: Duke University Press.

Ragins, Belle Rose, Cotton, John L., and Miller, Janice S. 2000. "Marginal Mentoring: The Effects of Type of Mentor, Quality of Relationship, and Program Design on Work and Career Attitudes." *Academy of Management Journal* 43(6): 1177–1194.

Rajkotia, Malavika. 2017. *Intimacy Undone: Marriage, Divorce and Family Law in India*. Delhi: Speaking Tiger.

Raju, Saraswati, and Bagchi, Deipica. eds. 1993. *Women and Work in South Asia: Regional Patterns and Perspectives*. Oxon and New York: Routledge.

Ramarajan, Lakshmi, and Reid, Erin. 2013. "Shattering the Myth of Separate Worlds: Negotiating Nonwork Identities at Work." *Academy of Management Review* 38, no. 4: 621–644.

Ramasubramanian, R. 2015. "Madras High Court: 'Never Before Has It Fallen to Such Low Levels,' Said the CJI." *Scroll India*, September 29.

Ramaswami, Aarti, Dreher, George F., Bretz, Robert, and Wiethoff, Carolyn. 2010. "The Interactive Effects of Gender and Mentoring on Career Attainment: Making the Case for Female Lawyers." *Journal of Career Development* 37(4): 692–716.

Rao, Rahul. 2015. "Echoes of Imperialism in LGBT Activism." *Echoes of Empire: Memory, Identity and Colonial Legacies*, 355–372.

Ray, Raka. 2000a. "Masculinity, Femininity and Servitude: Domestic Workers in Calcutta in the Late Twentieth Century." *Feminist Studies* 26(3).

Ray, Raka. 2000b. *Fields of Protest: Women's Movements in India.* Delhi: Zubaan.

Ray, Raka, and Qayum, Seemin. 2009. *Cultures of Servitude: Modernity, Domesticity, and Class in India.* Stanford, CA: Stanford University Press.

Reichman, Nancy J., and Sterling, Joyce S. 2001. "Recasting the Brass Ring: Deconstructing and Reconstructing Workplace Opportunities for Women Lawyers." *Capital University Law Review* 29: 923.

Reichman, Nancy, and Sterling, Joyce. 2004. "Sticky Floors, Broken Steps, and Concrete Ceilings in Legal Careers." *Texas Journal of Women and the Law* 14: 28–76.

Reichman, Nancy, and Sterling, Joyce. 2013. "Parenthood Status and Compensation in Law Practice." *Indiana Journal of Global Legal Studies* 20(2): 1203–1222.

Reid, Erin. 2015. "Embracing, Passing, Revealing, and the Ideal Worker Image: How People Navigate Expected and Experienced Professional Identities." *Organization Science* 26(4): 997–1017.

Reid, Erin, and Ramarajan, Lakshmi. 2016. "Managing the High Intensity Workplace." *Harvard Business Review* 94(6): 84–90.

Reskin, Barbara. 1988. "Bringing the Men Back In: Sex Differentiation and the Devaluation of Women's Work." *Gender and Society* 2(1): 58–81.

Reskin, Barbara. 1993. "Sex Segregation in the workplace." *Annual Review of Sociology* 19(1): 241–270.

Reskin, Barbara F. 2000. "Getting It Right: Sex and Race Inequality in Work Organizations." *Annual Review of Sociology* 26: 707–709.

Reynoso, Cruz. 2004. "A Survey of Latino Lawyers in Los Angeles County—Their Professional Lives and Opinions." *UC Davis Law Review* 38: 1563.

Rezvani, Selena. 2014. "4 Feminine Traits that You Should Maximize at Work." *Forbes.* May 2.

Rhode, Deborah L. 1991. "The 'No-Problem' Problem: Feminist Challenges and Cultural Change." *Yale Law Journal* 100(6): 1731–1793.

Rhode, Deborah L. 2011. "From Platitudes to Priorities: Diversity and Gender Equity in Law Firms." *Georgetown Journal of Legal Ethics* 24: 1041–2077.

Rhode, Deborah L. 2016. *Women and Leadership.* Oxford: Oxford University Press.

Ridgeway, Cecilia L. 2011. *Framed by Gender: How Gender Inequality Persists in the Modern World.* Oxford and New York: Oxford University Press.

Ridgeway, Cecilia L., and Correll, Shelley. 2004. "Unpacking the Gender System: A Theoretical Perspective on Gender Beliefs and Social Relations." *Gender & Society* 18(4): 510–531.

Risman, Barbara. J. 2004. Gender as a Social Structure: Theory Wrestling with Activism." *Gender & Society* 18(4): 429–450.

Rivera, Lauren A. 2012. "Hiring as Cultural Matching: The Case of Elite Professional Service Firms." *American Sociological Review* 77(6): 999–1022.

Rivera, Lauren A. 2016. *Pedigree: How Elite Students Get Elite Jobs.* Princeton, NJ: Princeton University Press.

Roberts, Laura Morgan, Anthony J. Mayo, and David A. Thomas. 2019. *Race, Work, and Leadership: New Perspectives on the Black Experience*. Cambridge, MA: Harvard Business Press,

Rosalio, Wences. 1970. "Electoral Participation and the Occupational Composition of Cabinets and Parliaments." 75 *American Journal of Sociology* 185.

Rosener, J. 1990. "Ways Women Lead." *Harvard Business Review* 68(6): 119–125.

Roth, Benita. 2004. *Separate Roads to Feminism: Black, Chicana, and White Feminist Movements in America's Second Wave*. Cambridge and New York: Cambridge University Press.

Roy, Srila. 2011. "Politics, Passion and Professionalization in Contemporary Indian Feminism." *Sociology* 45(4): 587–602.

Roy, Srila. 2015. "The Indian Women's Movement: Within and Beyond NGOization." *Journal of South Asian Development* 10(1): 96–117.

Roy, Srila. 2018. "# MeToo Is a Crucial Moment to Revisit the History of Indian Feminism." *EPW Engage* 53(42), October 20.

Rubin, Gayle. 2011. *Deviations: A Gayle Rubin Reader*. Durham, NC: Duke University Press.

Rudman, Laurie, and Glick, Peter. 1999. "Feminized Management and Backlash Toward Agentic Women: The Hidden Costs to Women of a Kinder, Gentler Image of Middle Managers." *Journal of Personality and Social Psychology* 77(5): 1004–1023.

Rudman, Laurie, and Glick, Peter. 2001. "Prescriptive Gender Stereotypes and Backlash Toward Agentic Women." *Journal of Social Issues* 57(4): 743–762.

Rudman, Laurie, and Phelan, Julie. 2008. "Backlash Effects for Disconfirming Gender Stereotypes in Organizations." *Research in Organizational Behavior* 28: 61–79.

Rukmini, S. 2018. "Indian Girls Brush Up Against Reality." *LiveMint*, November 13.

Sahay, Sundeep, Nicholson, Brian, and Krishna, Srinivas. 2000. *Global IT Outsourcing: Software Development Across Borders*. Cambridge: Cambridge University Press.

Said, Edward. 1978. *Orientalism*. London: Routledge & Kegan Paul.

Salzinger, Leslie. 2003. *Genders in Production: Making Workers in Mexico's Global Factories*. Berkeley: University of California Press.

Sameh, Catherine Z. 2019. *Axis of Hope: Iranian Women's Rights: Activism across Borders*. Seattle: University of Washington Press.

Sandefur, Rebecca L. 2001. "Work and Honor in the Law: Prestige and the Division of Lawyers' Labor." *American Sociological Review* 66(3): 382–403.

Sandefur, Rebecca. L. 2007. "Lawyers' Pro Bono Service and American-Style Civil Legal Assistance." *Law & Society Review* 41: 79–112.

Santos, de Sousa Bonaventura. 2016. *Epistemologies of the South: Justice against Epistemicide*. Oxon and New York: Routledge.

Santos, de Sousa Bonaventura, and Rodríguez-Garavito, César A. 2005. Eds. *Law and Globalization from Below: Towards a Cosmopolitan Legality*. New York: Cambridge University Press.

Saradamoni, Kunjulekshmi. 1983. "Changing Land Relations and Women: A Case Study of Palghat District, Kerala." In Vina Mazumdar, ed., *Women and Rural Transformations*, pp. 35–171. New Delhi: Concept Publications.

Sarda, Kanu. 2017. "12 Lakh Lawyers Plague India's Courts." *New Indian Express*, February 5.

Sassen, Saskia. 2000. "Territory and Territoriality in the Global Economy." *International Sociology* 15(2): 372–393.

Scharff, Christina. 2009. "Young Women's Dis-identification with Feminism: Negotiating Heteronormativity, Neoliberalism and Difference." PhD dissertation, London School of Economics and Political Science (LSE).

Schukoske, Jane E. 2009. "Legal Education Reform in India: Dialogue Among Indian Law Teachers." *Jindal Global Law Review* 1(1): 251–279.

Schultz, Ulrike, and Shaw, Gisela, eds. 2003. *Women in the World's Legal Professions*. London: Bloomsbury.

Serano, Julia. 2014. "Empowering Femininity." *Ms. Magazine*, July 28.

Seron, Carroll, and Ferris, Kerry. 1995. "Negotiating Professionalism: The Gendered Social Capital of Flexible Time." *Work and Occupations* 22(1): 22–47.

Seron, Carroll, Silbey, Susan S., Cech, Erin, and Rubineau, Brian. 2016. "Persistence Is Cultural: Professional Socialization and the Reproduction of Sex Segregation." *Work and Occupations* 43(2): 178–214.

Sethi, Raj Mohini. 1987. "Women Lawyers: A Study in Professionalisation." *Journal of the Indian Law* 29(1): 29–47.

Shami, Seteney. 1988. "Studying Your Own: The Complexities of a Shared Culture." In Soraya Altorki and Camillia Fawzi El-Solh, eds., *Arab Women in the Field: Studying Your Own Society*, pp. 115–138. Syracuse, NY: Syracuse University Press.

Sharafi, Mitra J. 2015, November. "South Asian Legal History." *Annual Review of Law and Social Science* 11: 309–336.

Sharma, Rohit, Iyer, Nikhil, Sonkar, Siddharth, Namboothiri, Gatha, Cholera, Mahima, Bhojani, Roma, and Krishna, Shri. 2020. *The NUJS Diversity Report, 2019* (February 13, 2020). The WB National University of Juridical Sciences. Available at SSRN: https://ssrn.com/abstract=3550684.

Sharma, Sheetal. 2002. "Women Lawyers Practicing at Delhi Courts: A Sociological Study." Dissertation, Jawaharlal Nehru University.

Sheikh, Danish, Neziraj, Jeton, Khouri, Amahl, Lagarce, Jean-Luc, Jie, Zhan, Bazeed, Mariam, and Loza, Santiago. 2018. *Global Queer Plays*. London: Oberon Books.

Shrivastava, Prachi. 2014. "Untangling the Madras HC Turmoil: A Bar at War, a Question of Caste, or Business as Usual?" Legally India. Available online at https://www.legallyindia.com/analysis/madras-hc-turmoil-a-bar-at-war-20140117-4250.

Siddique, Aboobacker P. 2005. "Panchayati Raj and Women in Kerala." In Zoya Hasan and Ritu Menon, eds., *The Diversity of Muslim Women's Lives in India*, p. 266. New Brunswick, NJ: Rutgers University Press.

Silbaugh, Katharine. 1996. "Turning Labor into Love: Housework and the Law." *Northwestern University Law Review* 91(1): 1–86.

Silbey, Susan S. 1997. "1996 Presidential Address: 'Let Them Eat Cake': Globalization, Postmodern Colonialism, and the Possibilities of Justice." *Law and Society Review*, 207–235.

Silver, Carole. 2011. "The Variable Value of U.S. Legal Education in the Global Legal Services Market." *Georgetown Journal of Legal Ethics* 24(1): 1–58.

Singh, Aditya. 2017. "Globalization of the Legal Profession and Regulation of Law Practice in India: The 'Foreign Entry' Debate. In Wilkins et al., eds., *The Indian Legal Profession*.

Singh, Satyendra. 2009. "How Market Orientation and Outsourcing Create Capability and Impact Business Performance." *Thunderbird International Business Review* 51: 457–471.

Singh, Yogendra. 2000. *Culture Change in India: Identity and Globalization*. Jaipur: Rawat Publications.

Sircar, Oishik. 2016. "The Fraught Terrain of Law and Feminism: 20 Years of Subversive Sites." 12(1) *Socio-Legal Review* 133–152.

Sircar, Oishik. 2017. "New Queer Politics in the New India: Notes on Failure and Stuckness in a Negative Moment." *Unbound: Harvard Journal of the Legal Left* 11: 1–36.

Smith-Doerr, Laurel. 2004. "Flexibility and Fairness: Effects of the Network Form of Organization on Gender Equity in Life Science Careers." *Sociological Perspectives* 47(1): 25–54.

Snow, David A., and McAdam, Doug. 2000. "Identity Work Processes in the Context of Social Movements: Clarifying the Identity/Movement Nexus." *Self, Identity, and Social Movements* 13: 41–67.

Sommerlad, Hilary. 1994. "The Myth of Feminisation: Women and Cultural Change in the Legal Profession." *International Journal of the Legal Profession* 1(1)31–53.

Sommerlad, Hilary. 2002. "Women Solicitors in a Fractured Profession: Intersections of Gender and Professionalism in England and Wales." *International Journal of the Legal Profession* 9(3): 213–234.

Sommerlad, Hilary. 2011. "Minorities, Merit, and Misrecognition in the Globalized Profession." *Fordham Law Review* 80: 2481.

Sommerlad, Hilary. 2015. "The 'Social Magic' of Merit: Diversity, Equity, and Inclusion in the English and Welsh Legal Profession." 83 *Fordham Law Review* 2325.

Sood, Mamta, and Chadda, Rakesh Kumar. 2010. "Women in Medicine: A Perspective." *Indian Journal of Gender Studies* 17(2): 277–285.

Sorabji, Richard. 2010. *Opening Doors: The Untold Story of Cornelia Sorabji, Reformer, Lawyer and Champion of Women's Rights in India.* London: Bloomsbury.

Spade, Dean, and Willse, Craig. 2015. *Marriage Will Never Set Us Free.* Subversion Press.

Spradley, James P. 1979. *The Ethnographic Interview.* New York: Holt, Rinehart and Winston.

Sreekumar, Sharmila. 2007. "The Land of 'Gender Paradox'? Getting Past the Commonsense of Contemporary Kerala." *Inter-Asia Cultural Studies* 8(1): 34–54.

Srivastava, Utkarsh. 2016. "In Defence of the All India Bar Examination." *The Wire*, March 17.

Staines, Graham, Tavris, Carol, and Jayaratne, Toby E. 1974. "The Queen Bee Syndrome." *Psychology Today* 7(8): 55–60.

Stanford, Heather Bennett. 2009. "Do You Want to Be an Attorney or a Mother: Arguing for a Feminist Solution to the Problem of Double Blinds in Employment and Family Responsibilities Discrimination." *American University Journal of Gender, Social Policy & the Law* 17: 627.

Steele, Claude M. 1997. "A Threat in the Air: How Stereotypes Shape Intellectual Identity and Performance." *American Psychologist* 52(6): 613–34.

Sterling, Joyce S., and Reichman, Nancy. 2012. "Navigating the Gap: Reflections On 20 Years Researching Gender Disparities in the Legal Profession." *Florida International University Law Review* 8: 515.

Sterling, Joyce S., and Reichman, Nancy. 2016. "Overlooked and Undervalued: Women in Private Law Practice." *Annual Review of Law and Social Science* 12, 373–393.

Stewart, Ann. 1995. "Debating Gender Justice in India." 4(2) *Social and Legal Studies* 253–274.

Stinchcombe, Arthur L. 1963. "Some Empirical Consequences of the Davis-Moore Theory of Stratification." *American Sociological Review* 28, no. 5: 805–808.

Sturm, Susan. 2001. "Second Generation Employment Discrimination: A Structural Approach." *Columbia Law Review* 101: 458.

Sturm, Susan. 2006. "The Architecture of Inclusion: Advancing Workplace Equity in Higher Education." *Harvard Journal of Law & Gender* 29: 247.

Subramanian, Ajantha. 2015. "Making Merit: The Indian Institutes of Technology and the Social Life of Caste." *Comparative Studies in Society and History* 57(2): 291–322.

Suchman, Mark C. 1995. "Managing Legitimacy: Strategic and Institutional Approaches." *Academy of Management Review* 20(3): 571–610.

Suchman, Mark C., and Cahill, Mia L. 1996. "The Hired Gun as Facilitator: Lawyers and the Suppression of Business Disputes in Silicon Valley. *Law & Social Inquiry* 21: 679–712.

Swaminathan, Padmini. 2012. *Women and Work.* New Delhi: Orient BlackSwan.

Tambe, Ashwini. 2018. "Reckoning with the Silences of #MeToo." *Feminist Studies* 44(1): 197–203.

Taylor, Marianne G. 1996. "The Development of Children's Beliefs about Social and Biological Aspects of Gender Differences." *Child Development* 67: 1555–1571.

Taylor, Phil, and Bain, Peter. 2005. "'India Calling to the Far Away Towns': The Call Centre Labour Process and Globalization." *Work, Employment and Society* 19(2): 261–282.

Tellis, Ashley. 2012. "Disrupting the Dinner Table: Re-thinking the 'Queer Movement' in Contemporary India." *Jindal Global Law Review* 4(1): 142–156.

Terjesen, Siri, Sealy, Ruth, and Singh, Val. 2009. "Women Directors on Corporate Boards: A Review and Research Agenda." *Corporate Governance: An International Review* 17: 320–337.

Thébaud, Sarah. 2010. "Masculinity, Bargaining, and Breadwinning: Understanding Men's Housework in the Cultural Context of Paid Work." *Gender & Society* 24(3): 330–354.

Thomas, Gillian. 2017. *Because of Sex: One Law, Ten Cases, and Fifty Years That Changed American Women's Lives at Work*. New York: Picador USA.

Thomas, Sonja. 2018. *Privileged Minorities: Syrian Christianity, Gender, and Minority Rights in Postcolonial India*. Seattle: University of Washington Press.

Thornton, Patricia H. 1999. "The Sociology of Entrepreneurship." *Annual Review of Sociology* 25: 19–46.

Thornton, Patricia H. 2004. *Markets from Culture: Institutional Logics and Organizational Decisions in Higher Education Publishing*. Stanford, CA: Stanford University Press.

Tomlinson, Jennifer, Valizade, Danat, Muzio, Daniel, Charlwood, Andy, and Aulakh, Sundeep. 2019. "Privileges and Penalties in the Legal Profession: An Intersectional Analysis of Career Progression." *British Journal of Sociology* 70(3): 1043–1066.

Tomlinson, John. 2012. "Cultural Imperialism." *The Wiley-Blackwell Encyclopedia of Globalization*. Oxford: Blackwell.

Torche, Florencia. 2015. "Analyses of Intergenerational Mobility: An Interdisciplinary Review." *ANNALS of the American Academy of Political and Social Science* 657(1): 37–62.

Trauth, Eileen M. 2002. "Odd Girl Out: An Individual Differences Perspective on Women in the IT Profession." *Information Technology & People* 15(2): 98–118.

Treiman, Donald J., and Hartmann, Heidi I. 1981. *Women, Work, and Wages: Equal Pay for Jobs of Equal Value*. Vol. 2101. Washington, DC: National Academy Press.

Trubek, David M., and Santos, Alvaro, eds. 2006. *The New Law and Economic Development: A Critical Appraisal*. Cambridge: Cambridge University Press.

Tumin, Melvin M. 1953. "Some Principles of Stratification: A Critical Analysis." *American Sociological Review* 18(4): 387–394.

Upadhya, Carol. 2016. *Reengineering India: Work, Capital, and Class in an Offshore Economy*. New Delhi: Oxford University Press.

Utrata, Jennifer. 2015. *Women without Men: Single Mothers and Family Change in the New Russia*. Ithaca, NY: Cornell University Press.

Van den Broek, Diane, Callaghan, George, and Thompson, Paul. 2004. "Teams without Teamwork? Explaining the Call Centre Paradox." *Economic and Industrial Democracy* 25(2): 197–218.

Varottil, Umakanth. 2017. "Due Diligence in Share Acquisitions: Navigating the Insider Trading Regime." *Journal of Business Law* 3: 237–259.

Veblen, Thorstein. [1899]. *The Theory of the Leisure Class: An Economic Study of Institutions*. 1994 reprint, New York: Penguin Books.

Venkatesan, J. 2011. "Former BCI Vice-Chief Gets Bail in Corruption Case." *The Hindu*, April 20.

Vijayakumar, C. 2015. "Judges and Castes: A Counterview." *The Hindu*, March 19.

Vijayakumar, Gowri. 2013. "'I'll Be Like Water': Gender, Class, and Flexible Aspirations at the Edge of India's Knowledge Economy." *Gender & Society* 27(6): 777–798.

Vinze, Medha. D. 1987. *Women Entrepreneurs in India: A Socio-Economic Study of Delhi, 1975–85*. New Delhi: Mittal Publications.

Visweswaran, Kamala. 1997. "Histories of Feminist Ethnography." *Annual Review of Anthropology* 26(1): 591–621.

Vyawahare, Malavika. 2013. "A Conversation With: Bar Council of India Chairman Manan Kumar Mishra." *India Ink*. January 24.

Wald, Eli. 2009. "Glass Ceilings and Dead Ends: Professional Ideologies: Gender Stereotypes, and the Future of Women Lawyers at Large Law Firms." *Fordham Law Review* 78: 2245.

Wallace, Jean E. 2001. "The Benefits of Mentoring for Female Lawyers." *Journal of Vocational Behavior* 58(3): 366–391.

Walsh, Janet. 2012. "Not Worth the Sacrifice? Women's Aspirations and Career Progression in Law Firms." *Gender, Work & Organization* 19: 508–531.

Wayne, Julie H., and Cordeiro, Bryanne L. 2003. "Who Is a Good Organizational Citizen? Social Perception of Male and Female Employees Who Use Family Leave." *Sex Roles* 49: 233–246.

Weatherspoon, Floyd. 2010. "The Status of African American Males in the Legal Profession: A Pipeline of Institutional Roadblocks and Barriers." *Mississippi Law Journal* 80: 259.

Weick, Karl E. 1985. "The Significance of Corporate Culture." In Peter J. Frost, et al., *Organizational Culture*, pp. 381–389. Beverly Hills, CA: Sage.

West, Candace, and Zimmerman, Don H. 1987. "Doing Gender." *Gender & Society* 1(2): 125–151.

Whittington, Kjersten Bunker 2007. "Employment Structures as Opportunity Structures: The Effects of Location on Male and Female Scientific Dissemination." Dissertation Draft. Stanford, CA: Department of Sociology, Stanford University.

Whittington, Kjersten Bunker, and Smith-Doerr, Laurel. 2005. "Gender and Commercial Science: Women's Patenting in the Life Sciences." *Journal of Technology Transfer* 30: 355–370.

Whittington, Kjersten Bunker, and Smith-Doerr, Laurel. 2008. "Women Inventors in Context: Disparities in Patenting across Academia and Industry." *Gender & Society* 22(2): 194–218.

Wilder, Gita Z. 2007. *Women in the Profession: Findings from the First Wave of the After the JD Study*. Washington, DC: NALP Foundation for Law Career Research and Education.

Wilkins, David B. 1998. "Fragmenting Professionalism: Racial Identity and the Ideology of Bleached Out Lawyering." *International Journal of the Legal Profession* 5(2–3): 141–173.

Wilkins, David B. 2009. "Team of Rivals—Toward a New Model of the Corporate Attorney-Client Relationship." *Fordham Law Review* 78: 2067.

Wilkins, David B., and Fong, Bryon. 2017. "Harvard Law School Report on the State of Black Alumni II: 2000–2016." *HLS Center on the Legal Profession Research Paper* 2018-2.

Wilkins, David B., and Gulati, G. Mitu. 1996. "Why Are There So Few Black Lawyers in Corporate Law Firms—An Institutional Analysis." *California Law Review* 84: 493.

Wilkins, David B., Khanna, Vikramaditya S., and Trubek, David M., eds. 2017. *The Indian Legal Profession in the Age of Globalization: The Rise of the Corporate Legal Sector and its Impact on Lawyers and Society*. Cambridge: Cambridge University Press.

Williams, Christine L., Muller, Chandra M., and Kilanski, Kristine. 2012. "Gendered Organizations in the New Economy." *Gender & Society* 26(4): 549–573.

Williams, Joan C. 2000. *Why Work and Family Conflict and What to Do About It*. New York: Oxford University Press.

Williams, Joan C. 2001. "Canaries in the Mine: Work/Family Conflict and the Law." *Fordham Law Review* 70: 2221.

Williams, Joan C. 2014. "Double Jeopardy? An Empirical Study with Implications for the Debates Over Implicit Bias and Intersectionality." *Harvard Journal of Law & Gender* 37: 185.

Williams, Joan C., and Dempsey, Rachel. 2014. *What Works for Women at Work: Four Patterns Working Women Need to Know*. New York: New York University Press.

Williamson, Oliver E. 1991. "Comparative Economic Organization: The Analysis of Discrete Structural Alternatives." *Administrative Science Quarterly*, 269–296.

Witz, Anne. 2013. *Professions and Patriarchy*. New York: Routledge.

Woetzel, Jonathan, Madgavkar, Anu, Sneader, Kevin, Tonby, Oliver, Lin, Diaan-Yi, Lydon, John, Sha Sha, Krishnan, Mekala, Ellingrud, Kweilin, and Gubieski, Michael. 2018. "The Power of Parity: Advancing Women's Equality in Asia Pacific." *McKinsey Report*, May 1.

Wynn, Alison T. 2018. "Misery Has Company: The Shared Emotional Consequences of Everwork Among Women and Men." *Sociological Forum* 33: 712–734.

Wynn, Alison T., and Correll, Shelley J. 2018. "Puncturing the Pipeline: Do Technology Companies Alienate Women in Recruiting Sessions?" *Social Studies of Science* 48(1): 149–164.

Yamunan, Sruthisagar. 2017. "Justice Karnan Is a Standing Momentum to the Failure of the Collegium System, Claims Former Judge." *Scroll India*, March 12.

Yin, Robert K. 2003. *Applications of Case Study Research (Applied Social Research Methods)*. 4th Edition. Thousand Oaks, CA: Sage.

Zaheer, Srilata. 1995. "Overcoming the Liability of Foreignness." *Academy of Management Journal* 38(2): 341–363.

Zahidi, Saadia. 2018. *Fifty Million Rising: The New Generation of Working Women Transforming the Muslim World*. London: Hachette UK.

INDEX

Names in *italic* are pseudonyms of interviewees.

THIS BOOK has been composed in Miller, a Scotch Roman typeface designed by Matthew Carter and first released by Font Bureau in 1997. It resembles Monticello, the typeface developed for The Papers of Thomas Jefferson in the 1940s by C. H. Griffith and P. J. Conkwright and reinterpreted in digital form by Carter in 2003.

Pleasant Jefferson ("P. J.") Conkwright (1905–1986) was Typographer at Princeton University Press from 1939 to 1970. He was an acclaimed book designer and AIGA Medalist.

The ornament used throughout this book was designed by Pierre Simon Fournier (1712–1768) and was a favorite of Conkwright's, used in his design of the *Princeton University Library Chronicle.*